GW00320322

Stephen F. Kelly was born and brought up [illegible] Merseyside. Educated at Ruskin College, Oxford, and the London School of Economics, he was for many years a political correspondent with Tribune. In 1978, he joined Granada Television, working on programmes such as *World in Action* and *What The Papers Say*. Now a freelance writer and television producer, he devotes most of his time to writing about football and labour history. He is a regular contributor to many newspapers and magazines, and is also Fellow in Media at the University of Huddersfield. His latest book is a revised edition of the highly acclaimed *Dalglish*, also published by Headline.

Also by Stephen F. Kelly

Idle Hands, Clenched Fists
You'll Never Walk Alone
Forever Everton
Back Page Football
Back Page United
Victorian Lakeland Photographers
A Game of Two Halves
Liverpool in Europe
Dalglish
The Kop
Graeme Souness: A Soccer Revolutionary

Not Just A Game

The Best Football Writing of the Season

Stephen F. Kelly

HEADLINE

For
Judith, Nicholas and Emma

This selection and the introduction
copyright © 1995 Stephen F. Kelly

Individual pieces copyrighted as shown on page x

The right of Stephen F. Kelly to be identified as the Author of the Work has been asserted by him in accordance with the Copyright, Designs and Patents Act 1988.

First published in paperback in 1995
by HEADLINE BOOK PUBLISHING

10 9 8 7 6 5 4 3 2

All rights reserved. No part of this publication may be reproduced, stored in a retrieval system, or transmitted, in any form or by any means without the prior written permission of the publisher, nor be otherwise circulated in any form of binding or cover other than that in which it is published and without a similar condition being imposed on the subsequent purchaser.

ISBN 0 7472 4983 0

Typeset by
Letterpart Limited, Reigate, Surrey

Printed and bound in Great Britain by
Cox & Wyman Ltd, Reading, Berks

HEADLINE BOOK PUBLISHING
A division of Hodder Headline PLC
338 Euston Road
London NW1 3BH

Contents

CHAPTER THREE

The Players

CHAPTER FOUR

The Managers

CHAPTER FIVE

The Teams

CHAPTER SIX

Games of the Season

CHAPTER SEVEN

The Business of Football

CHAPTER EIGHT

The Press

Acknowledgements

I am first indebted to the many journalists and writers whose contributions you see in these pages and especially to their various newspapers, magazines and publishers for permission to reproduce their work here. This volume is very much their efforts, rather than mine.

Warm thanks are also due to Samantha Clarke who did much of the laborious work of cutting, pasting and photocopying, as well as making many useful suggestions. Her endeavours helped ease the burden of work considerably. I am grateful also to all those colleagues and friends who delivered articles and bundles of back copies of various newspapers at regular intervals. But in particular I would like to mention Anthony Rowe Jones and Hugh Cairns. My thanks also to David Bull for supplying me with cuttings from various fanzines as well as permission to use extracts from his book *The Commons People*.

I am also indebted to my agent John Pawsey for his continuing support and especially to my publishers, Headline, and in particular Ian Marshall, who has always been at the end of a telephone ready to offer advice and support, as well as putting together this nightmare of an administrative production.

Finally, I am, as ever, grateful to my family who, for ten months or more, have had to cope with ever-mounting piles of newspapers in rooms throughout the house. My thanks to Judith, my wife, for her encouragement and help, as well as to Nicholas for unearthing the occasional piece from one of his many soccer magazines and to Emma who can't decide between Peter Rabbit and Jamie Redknapp.

Acknowledgements and thanks are also due to the following authors and publishers for the use of copyright material:

FourFourTwo magazine and editor Paul Simpson for various articles from *FourFourTwo*; Headline Book Publishing for an extract from Stephen F. Kelly's book *Souness: A Soccer Revolutionary*; Little, Brown and Company for an extract from Harry Pearson's book *The Far Corner*; *FHM* magazine and Tim Glynne-Jones for 'The Hardest Team in Britain'; the editor of *Through The Wind And The Rain* and Alan Cookson for the article on *Cracker*; the Daily Telegraph Limited for various articles from the *Daily Telegraph* and the *Sunday Telegraph*; Times Newspapers Limited 1994/95 for various articles from the *Sunday Times*; Headline Book Publishing for an extract from *Cantona My Story* by Eric Cantona; Newspaper Publishing Plc for various articles from the *Independent* and the *Independent on Sunday*; Eamon Dunphy for his article 'Lament for a Lost Game' published in the *Independent on Sunday*; Stephen Brenkley for his article 'Knighton in White Armour' published in the *Independent on Sunday*; Hunter Davies and Sheil Land Associates for permission to reproduce Hunter Davies' article on Jürgen Klinsmann from the *Independent*; Guardian Newspapers Ltd for various articles in the *Guardian* and the *Observer*; Frank Keating for his article in the *Spectator*; David Bull and Southampton Football Club for David Bull's article; David Bull and Juma for Kenneth Clarke and Gordon Brown's articles from *Football and the Commons People*; Associated Newspapers Limited for various pieces from the *Mail On Sunday*; the editor of *The Game* for Glyn Wilmhurst's article; Pete Davies for his article from *FourFourTwo* magazine; Ivan Ponting, Steve Hale and the Bluecoat Press for an extract from their book *The Boot Room*; Simon Inglis for his article 'Hi-tech Huddersfield'; Simon Cheetham and Juma for *Gladys Protheroe, Football Genius*; Gary Lineker and the *Observer* for his article on Ray Wilkins; the editor of *Matchday* for Chris Green's article; Simon and Schuster for an extract from Alex Fynn and Lynton Guest's book *Out of Time*; Verso Books for an extract from Tony Mason's book *Passion of the People, Football in South America*; Headline Book Publishing for an extract from Kevin Baldwin's *This Supporting Life*; Orion Publishing for an extract from Simon Kuper's *Football Against The Enemy*.

Finally, the author and the publishers wish to point out that every effort has been made to trace all copyright holders for permission to include their pieces in this anthology. They apologise to those whose names may have been inadvertently omitted and for any errors that may have occurred in the form of acknowledgement.

Introduction

Some years ago I edited an anthology of football writings titled *A Game of Two Halves*. It sold well, proving that there is a demand for good, honest football writing. Camus, Priestley, Pinter, Orwell and many others found their way into that edition, writers you might never have associated with the game. Its success sparked off the idea of an annual compilation of the season's best football writing. There were some who guessed I might find it difficult to unearth enough pieces to fill a book. On the contrary, an initial trawl netted well over 200 articles worthy of publication, twice as many as appear here.

It may not have been such a glorious year for football but it was certainly a bumper season for journalism. It was a season when soccer's headlines seemed to hit the front pages almost as often as the back pages. Sleaze, scandal, drugs, and court cases. You name it, and it was there splattered across the tabloids and the broadsheets. The headlines might not always have been welcomed by the footballing authorities, but the revelations were far too sensational to be ignored.

Fortunately, it wasn't all sleaze and scandal. There was the World Cup, surely as exhilarating and well staged a sporting spectacle as any we have ever seen. A World Cup that ended in victory for the people's choice and tears for Baggio. There may not have been too much for British supporters to cheer, but we sat glued to our TV sets. And, of course, there was always the Irish, playing their usual brand of carefree soccer. They may have looked casual, but in fact they were just as passionate, just as determined and committed as Italy, Brazil or Argentina.

There was Kenny Dalglish, reaching out to new frontiers with Premiership champions Blackburn Rovers. And there was nostalgia as the wizard of dribble, Sir Stanley Matthews, celebrated his 80th birthday. And, of course, there was sadness with the death of one of soccer's golden boys, Billy Wright, and that legend of Barnsley, Skinner Normanton.

But nobody featured more than Eric Cantona whose one kick too many initially led to a prison sentence, later reduced to community service. At times, it seemed that whatever the publication, Cantona was being profiled. Rain forests must have been destroyed as the finest wordsmiths conjured up new images in an attempt to explain the enigma and the sardines.

Good football writing is not simply a matter of eloquent words; ideas are equally important. Hopefully this volume reflects not just fine words but the more offbeat and quirky sides to our game, from the Barlinnie prison team to an afternoon on the bench alongside the Stockport County manager. And there were thoughtful pieces as well, many of which were needed in this year of sleaze.

Accolades for the year are inevitably spread. *The Sun*, with its scoop on alleged soccer bribes, provided a story, whatever the eventual outcome, that will, as *The Sun* would say, run and run. But it also demonstrated that it is the media, especially the tabloids and investigative television programmes such as *World In Action* and *Panorama*, that have set the pace in uncovering the game's seedier side. And not before time.

Football may be about romance, but romance cannot survive on a diet of lies and mistrust. Eventually, the truth will out. Hopefully football will be the better for this season's revelations. For far too long, many of football's problems have been swept under the carpet by a far too reverential press.

The broadsheets, too, have continued their lonely campaign to provide insights coupled with quality writing, most notably the *Daily Telegraph*, which has set demanding standards with its detailed coverage of sport. The Monday morning sports supplements are a welcome innovation as well.

Over the last year, football has gained a new respectability. No longer the preserve of the working man, it is now the nation's game, as talked about in the dealing rooms of the financial institutions as it is on the shop floor of the car factories, and as likely to attract female support as it does male support. It is a revolution that is being matched by its breadth of reporting, with football as likely to be found in the yuppie magazines as it is in the back pages of the newspapers.

Indeed, one of the outstanding journalistic successes of the season has been the appearance of the glossy football magazine, in particular *FourFourTwo* and *The Game*, which have tapped into the changing market, reaching out to a new audience of supporters. Others have followed suit, though not all have attempted to be as eloquent.

Not that there hasn't always been fine football writing. Writers as diverse as Albert Camus, Arthur Hopcraft, Willis Hall and Harold Pinter have endowed the game with their crafted words over the years. And their efforts have been supplemented by working journalists like John Arlott, Geoffrey Green, Frank Keating, Ian Wooldridge, John Moynihan and, of course, Hugh McIlvanney.

What is remarkable about today's best football writing is that it is not confined to one or two journals, but can be spotted across a broad section of newspapers and magazines. Even the fanzines, with their anarchic style and cynicism, have thrown up cutting analysis and comment, perhaps not always as prosaic but just as important; and, to the average fan who buys fanzines outside the football ground, perhaps more relevant. What a pity that most football programmes have not followed suit and tapped into this changing market; instead, they continue to supply the usual diet of colour action shots and the manager's generally worthless ghost-written comments.

The publishing industry also has latched on to the new market opened up by the phenomenal success of Nick Hornby's *Fever Pitch*. Simon Kuper's *Football Against The Enemy* has this year added a fresh insight into the world's most popular game, while others, such as Gladys Protheroe, have injected humour. Football publishing has suddenly taken on a new lease of life. The ghosted biographies and player diaries are fast becoming a relic of the past.

There is no doubt much that has been missed in this anthology. It would have been impossible to collate all the commendable writing of the season. And, anyhow, this is a subjective, eclectic choice. The criterion for entry in this volume is that the work has been published in the past year. As a consequence, some pieces refer to seasons past, but the reader will find that the bulk refers to the season just gone. Nor is this edition an attempt to display all the fine writing of last season; it is simply a sample that gives a taste of the season just gone. Not all events, nor all crucial games and issues have been covered. It is not a complete record of the year. That would require an anthology of much greater length.

But hopefully the reader can dip in and still come away with a feel for the season while enjoying writing of the highest quality. And, with luck, we shall reappear next season with another bumper edition of the season's writings.

Stephen F. Kelly
Manchester May 1995

Chapter One

The World Cup

Introduction

When FIFA announced that the United States would host the 1994 World Cup finals, the news was greeted with astonishment. How could a nation that had only ever dabbled at the game hope to stage it successfully? There was talk of changing the rules, bigger goals, sin bins and other such gimmicks. The American TV moguls were even said to be demanding regular stoppages to accommodate the advertisers. In a nutshell, the critics, and there were plenty of them in Britain, predicted that it would be a disaster.

Instead, it turned out to be as successful a World Cup as any, full of drama and suspense. The stadiums, massive and comfortable, were packed for every game. The organisation, superb, the television coverage dazzling. Maybe some of the kick-off times were far from ideal and the weather was undoubtedly too hot. Unfortunately, the latter was out of FIFA's control.

Even Maradona turned up, but, after a sensational start when he looked to be back to his best, he failed a drugs test and was on his way home again. Favourites Italy came within a whisker of early elimination, while the East Europeans impressed with a new adventurous blend of football. As ever, the Africans and Brazilians excited us all, but it was surely the Americans who won our hearts.

And, of course, there were the stars. Romario burst on to the scene, Roberto Baggio finally came to life, while Ilie Dumitrescu, Martin Dahlin, Hristo Stoichkov, Alexi Lalas, and many more, delighted us with their natural skills. It turned out to be a World Cup to remember.

Balls, Bubblegum and Bowls
Giles Smith

Eric Wynalda had taken the ball down the left wing and then cut in hard past two defenders. All Roy Wegerle had to do, on the edge of the six-yard box, was push the cross past the exposed goal-keeper. He was still turning away as his team-mates jumped all over him, piling up into an elated pyramid. USA 1 Mexico 0.

In the crowd, a handful of Americans were on their feet, thumping the air. Ninety-one thousand Mexicans weren't so pleased. The horns got louder, the flags flapped angrily, the whistling grew more shrill. This is what the US team call a home fixture.

Posters have gone up in Pasadena, home of the Rose Bowl, where the World Cup final will be played. The picture shows two players jumping for a high ball. The text reads: 'More collisions than rush hour on the 405.' And then, lower down: 'World Cup Soccer: don't miss it for the world.' One small plug for the game America can't bring itself to love.

It's not as if they've never tried. As long ago as 1967, CBS television attempted to sell soccer to America by broadcasting English league games. They enlisted Danny Blanchflower as presenter. When play was soggy and dull (which would have been more often than not), Blanchflower would say so. This did not go down well with CBS, according to James A Michener in his 1976 book *Sports in America*: 'The television people . . . were accustomed to the ultra-sweet blandness of the American broadcaster.' Within a season, Blanchflower and soccer were axed.

Since then, little joy. Somehow the game the rest of the world plays doesn't catch on in the world's biggest nation. Michener again: 'The superiority of [American football], with its violence, its variation in action and its more frequent opportunities for scoring, became evident, and fans could show no interest in the more repetitious, and low-scoring soccer version.'

One of the people charged with selling soccer in 1994 is Hank Steinbrecher, a middle-aged man with a moustache and a smart suit. Before he became executive director and secretary general of the United States Soccer Federation, he worked for the Quaker Oats Company and marketed the sports drink Gatorade. He knows about supply and demand. When he was in the process of appointing the Serbian Bora Milutinovic as national team coach, he is said to have warned him about the press, saying: 'Worse then *hating* you, they simply don't *care* about you.'

Steinbrecher was at the Rose Bowl last weekend, watching the national side play their final warm-up match before the competition proper and claiming all kinds of early, off-the-pitch victories as the press packed round him at half-time. 'People were asking, would football change to accommodate television? In the event, television has changed to accommodate sport – for the first time in history.' In other words, there will be no commercial breaks during live transmission; instead, American audiences can ready themselves for an eight-minute ad slab in the interval.

Maybe the television companies are lulled, but what about the people? Soccer's detractors – many of whom seem to have columns in the leading American newspapers – wave copies of the Harris Poll, which suggests that only 20 per cent of Americans know their country is hosting the World Cup and that less than half of those are considering watching any of it on television.

You can conduct your own unofficial survey on any street. A woman serving in one of Pasadena's sports shops told me she played soccer for seven years in junior high school and high school, but until this year, when it parked on her front yard, she had never heard of the World Cup. Steinbrecher and the soccer lobby fight figures with figures. They drop the stat bomb: 750 million watch the Super Bowl? Well *two billion* worldwide will tune in for the World Cup, so what do you reckon to *that*? This is big talk. It arouses advertisers, endorsement moguls, anyone with something to sell. But it doesn't impress America. As yet, America isn't playing.

Scott Cross wanted to call his little store in the mall 'The World Cup Shop', but this year, if you want to use the words 'World' and 'Cup' in a business context, you must pay administrators $5,000 for the privilege. Cross settled for 'World Soccer Shop' and moved in a couple of weeks ago with his boxes of unendorsed enamel badges ('pins') and unofficial long, thin pennants, American college style. 'We didn't know about scarves,' Cross says, 'until someone from Europe came over and said, "Where's your scarves?" '

For official World Cup souvenirs you must leave the mall and walk down Colorado Avenue to a store so newly arrived it doesn't yet have a name above the door. They're still unpacking the goods, racking the plastic drinks beakers emblazoned with Striker, the official World Cup dog (imagine Snoopy interbred with Goofy and stuck inside a football kit), and piling up the T-shirts made out to all nations, large, garish, extra large, extra garish.

The businessman is from Oklahoma. He gives me his card. It says 'Stoneware by Ray Chehrehgosha' – some other venture, some other time. He says he's rented a store like this in each of the World Cup cities and he's certain he can shift the product because if the Americans don't buy it, the visitors will. But even as he speaks, the Americans are in the store, couples drifting off the street hand in hand, turning the goods over, a little cautiously maybe, in a state of mild bemusement, but, hey, some of this stuff is *cool* . . .

By August, neither of these stores will be here. Scott and Ray have arranged short leases. A week or so after the World Cup final, when the last tourist has dragged himself reluctantly to the airport and the television has gone back to normal, they'll close down, cash up and vanish. Just like soccer, the doubters say.

On Friday at 5.30 in the afternoon, as the sun begins to lose its heat, the US squad go training at the Rose Bowl. Mountains ring the empty stadium. The turf is expensively dense, richly spongey – a Hollywood lawn. As they file out of the locker-room, it's apparent that many of the squad have special hair. Tony Meola, goalkeeper and captain, has his long locks pulled back in a slick, black ponytail, like a 1980s advertising executive. Cobi Jones sports a pop star's sprig of short dreadlocks. And Alexi Lalas, the central defender who scored the second of the goals that embarrassed England, maintains a shoulder-length cascade and a bright red, four-inch goatee.

They play some games of one-touch and try out some set-pieces while Milutinovic (known to all as 'Bora') calls out from the side in a mix of broken English and Spanish. There's talent in this side – the smooth midfielder Thomas Dooley, plucked out of the German Bundesliga; the canny Tab Ramos, who plays in Spain – but their preparation for the finals has got ragged. This year they've only managed to draw with Bolivia and Moldova; they've lost to Iceland and Chile. They need a little spark.

'This is our home ground,' says Alexi Lalas as he leaves the pitch.

'Sure, tomorrow it's going to feel like we're down Mexico way. But I feed off that – the booing and that stuff.' He doesn't sound convincing. 'I know their whole team,' says Cle Kooiman, a defender who plays club football in Mexico, has a reputation for tough stuff and must be aware that the next day's crowd will be breathing heat down his neck. 'They play pure Latin style. We play a European/Latin style. We can break them down.' Dooley, to his evident delight, has found a German film crew to talk to.

Back at the hotel, Lalas meets me in the lobby, his hair stuffed under a baseball cap, and gives me a copy of his new CD, *Woodland*. If you're British, you feel instinctively queasy about footballers meddling with pop music. But Lalas is an American and his CD has a confident swagger. He specialises in fuzz guitar and a growly voice and he sounds like he's having a good time. The second track is called 'Kickin' Balls'. It's a kind of rallying cry:

> *'I used my head like my daddy said*
> *And it got me where I am.*
> *It's not against the law,*
> *Bring anyone at all,*
> *We're all just kickin' balls.'*

On Saturday, the Mexican fans were outside the gates three hours before the start, whistling to be admitted, lowing into long plastic horns, singing 'May'co, May'co, May'co'. Many were Los Angelinos, but some had driven across the border to see their rivals taken apart. An American fan walked by. I asked her if she had seen any others. 'Yeah, three,' she said. 'Well, that's including me.'

During the American national anthem, when even the Mexicans were silent, the team stood with their hands over their hearts and declared their allegiance to the flag. They're an odd amalgam – part-Polish, part-German, part-Colombian, part-Serbian . . . But then, in some respects, you can't get much more American than that.

This was by no means a startling display of football. Mexico looked stiff, the US looked clumsy. But they pushed themselves forward and they scored and they held out while 91,000 bayed and whistled and threw intimidatingly fast Mexican waves round and round the Rose Bowl. It's the kind of courage which wins fans.

Independent on Sunday, 12 June 1994

With no representatives, British hopes were pinned on Ireland and Jack Charlton. They did not disappoint, opening their account with a 1–0 win over favourites Italy, courtesy of a Ray Houghton goal. There was to be much rejoicing, especially on the streets of Dublin.

Our Kid
Bobby Charlton

It does not surprise me that our Jack has been a success as a manager. He was always very enthusiastic, always interested in the tactics of the game. When he was at Leeds United, he worked under a really top-class manager in Don Revie. He learned a lot from that and obviously saw management as something he could do in the future.

What he did learn from Don Revie was how to communicate with and motivate players, how to be meticulous in your planning. All the sort of things Don used to do is what Jack is doing now. To be honest, though, he is managing with fewer assets than Leeds used to have. That says a lot about him, because he has had just fantastic results.

Without question, his greatest strength as a manager is motivation. He has the ability to get the best out of his players so that when they go on the field they know exactly what they are going to do. They are happy in their minds, and the plans have all been laid. He makes them realise they are all good players, and they go out and enjoy it.

It is a happy-go-lucky atmosphere when you go with the Irish team and could not be more different from travelling with England. Every time I go away with England and the press are around, I feel so intense. It comes across as a matter of life or death. But it is not a matter of life or death for the Irish; it is just a good day out.

During the last World Cup in Italy, the BBC set up an interview with our kid and me. Every time I had gone with the BBC to a team hotel before, you needed accreditation to get through all the security to see someone. But when we arrived at the Irish camp before the quarter-final game against the Italians in Rome, there was no security at all.

In fact, we really doubted whether we were at the right place. There were no guards on the doors and there were no guards in the hotel. When we eventually found them, the police and the players and everybody, they were all in the bar singing and laughing and joking. And why not? This was the day after Ireland had qualified for the last eight, and they still had about three days to go to the game.

It would certainly be wrong to imagine Jack and his players do not take their football seriously. In addition to giving each player specific instructions, he works out an overall plan and decides on the route he needs to take to beat the opposition. Sometimes he has to revert to the long ball, which was just common sense for the players he had when he first started. But the longer he has had those players, the more they have started to play football. They do not just hump it upfield any more. They study the opposition and decide what course of action to take.

One of their biggest advantages has been that nobody took Ireland seriously. You mentioned them and people thought, 'Well, that's not a serious football nation.' But everyone who thinks like that catches a cold. People playing against them never really take them seriously enough until it is too late. Mind you, all that could change with the terrific win against Germany in Hanover.

I have a very high regard for what Jack and his players have achieved. I mean, they have completely revolutionised Irish sport. People used to think of it as being Gaelic football and hurling; but you go over there now and all they talk about is football.

It is a complete culture change in sport and it has happened so quickly, too. They were very lucky inasmuch as one of the first times they burst on to the scene, in the finals of the 1988 European Championship, they beat England. When they did that, they were on their way.

They could go a long way in this World Cup because they are bringing in a lot of young players now. After a long, hard season, I am sure Jack would not really be expecting the older hands like Paul McGrath, Tony Cascarino, Ray Houghton and even Andy Townsend to perform better in a tournament like the World Cup than they did four years ago without some injection of youth.

He will be looking a lot to the likes of Roy Keane, Phil Babb, Gary Kelly and Jason McAteer, and so will the older players. The biggest problem, after the sort of gruelling season we have at home, is that it is going to be very hot in the United States. So the youngsters should be able to deal with it better.

But it is an exciting adventure, the World Cup, isn't it? Especially for the Irish, with so many of their fellow-countrymen settled in the United States. So they will feel that bit more comfortable, not quite so far away from home. I think the Americans will be on the side of the Irish and want them to do well.

The first match is crucial. If Ireland do not lose to Italy in New Jersey, I think they could do well. The Italians are like the Irish, of course, in that so many of their people have emigrated to the United States and a lot will be expected of the team.

It is exactly the type of situation Jack loves. It is going to be a very, very high-profile match; and by the time it comes around, nobody will give Ireland much of a chance. But they will perform to their best. They always have done and I do not see why it should be any different this time.

I must be honest, though: Jack is not perfect, you know. Because he is abrasive, he falls out with people left, right and centre. He is abrasive with his players, too, and I have no doubt that is one of the reasons he is successful. There is a lot of respect there, but there is a bit of fear as well.

He has never changed over the years. Even as a kid, he was hot-headed. You could easily light his fuse. I think, because of that, he was intensely competitive when he became a manager. Although we do not really have much contact these days, I have been very proud of his achievements and I am sure there is more to come. It will be interesting to see him in the United States.

Sunday Telegraph, 5 June 1994

A Strange Place to Celebrate
Sarah Edworthy

It was 8pm, an hour before kick-off in the steamy heat of Giants Stadium, New Jersey, and we were shivering in the wind-swept car park of Lamb Doyles pub on the grey hilly outskirts of Dublin.

One taxi driver had dropped us off (with – pure genius – the tale of why it was worth a bet at 25-1 for Ray Houghton to score the first goal); another car was due to take us on to the location of the city's Italian football party. We had no idea where we were going.

'We have to make this arrangement,' explained Maria di Mascio, president of the Club Italiano Dublino and proprietress of Di Mascio's fish and chip shop.

'You'd think we were unpopular! Whenever we've put up signs, locals take them down or turn them in the opposite direction. It's just their mischievous sense of humour.'

At the appointed time, a silver Fiat drew up, the driver leaned across and said in a cheery Irish brogue: 'Hi, I'm Ernesto, Maria's brother, but call me Ernie. I'm the black sheep of the family. The Irishman. The only one that doesn't speak Italian.'

And we were off, winding up tiny mountain roads, to watch Italia v Irlanda in the secluded clubhouse where Dublin's 3,000-strong Italian community – fish and chip shop owners one and all – meet to play football, drink, dance and, once a year, to choose a girl to send home for the Miss Italia competition.

Inside it was Nastro Azzurro beer and Guinness all round. There was no pre-match discussion among these families. They had started chanting 'Ee-tal-ya,' and 'there's only one Berto Baggio,' long before they had managed to find Raiuno, the Italian television station, on the giant screen.

The older generation had dressed up; the young down – painted, draped and adorned in the tricolore's green, white and red.

The noise was worse than rush-hour in Naples when the match kicked off. There was no hope of hearing the Italian commentary – or the Irish commentary from the televisions in the bar (for those with Irish husbands and wives).

And the atmosphere was bruising: car horns blared, rattles crackled, caterers' trays were banged like drums, men stamped on tables and chairs, women waved scarves and led the singing. Toddlers were taught to join in Mexican waves.

It was hysteria for Ee-tal-ya. Their hero, Roberto Baggio, might be a Buddhist but there was nothing calm and meditative about the worshipping of his genius. And then, in the 12th minute, Ray Houghton scored Ireland's goal.

The reaction was extraordinary. Everyone in the room erupted in more cheers, more horns, more clapping and more stamping on chairs. Had they mistaken the orange, white and green of the Irish flag for the green, white and red of Italy? Had they taken to heart Jack Charlton's endearing theory that Ireland's 4–5–1 formation was no different from Italy's 4–3–3? Had they muddled the sides?

Not at all. It was suddenly clear that if you are called Angelo, Lucia, Gino or Rudolfo and were brought up in Dublin speaking both Italian and English (with an Irish lilt), this fixture was a no-lose situation.

Close-ups of Jack Charlton and Baggio both earned thumbs-up signs and applause. Throughout the rest of the match, the allegiance of the masses was simple to follow.

Until Houghton's goal, the leaning was towards Italy. For the rest of the first half they cheered on Ireland's historic lead. Only in the second half was there some resurgence of genetic loyalty towards the mother country.

'We really wanted a draw you see,' admitted Luciano Valentine, 25, a chef at the Aprile takeaway. 'I wanted Italy to win because we have been getting sick all week from customers, but I don't really mind. I was born in Dublin.'

'I'm glad I took my Italian flag off the car,' admitted Maria di Mascio. 'We'll never live this down in the takeaways. A draw would have been lovely. But the Irish deserved to win. Italy didn't play well. I kept saying to Baggio: "Here take my glasses you fool".'

Far from feeling foolish themselves for dressing up extravagantly in Italian colours only to be celebrating a Republic win, the community stalwarts explained it in terms of their history. They had, after all, come from Italy, home of great gastronomy, and resolved to spend their lives selling chips.

'We all come from the same valley outside Rome,' explained Lucia di Mascio. 'The first families to come over after the Second World War found a great affinity with Ireland because it is a Catholic country too.

'The only business we can see was to feed the Irish, who wanted fish and chips, but it was always difficult to find people to work in the evenings so they brought over more people from Monte Cassino. Ireland has given all of us our bread.'

Only one or two saw it differently. The owners of a nearby takeaway called the club to say they would no longer be joining the party. Some Republic fans had smashed their windows to taunts of 'we beat you'. Initial dismay passed when someone reasoned: 'What the hell, it's nothing sinister – only too much beer speaking.'

'Give the Irish the first laugh and we'll have the last one,' said Mario Borza who, having lost a bet on the result, faced the prospect of having his long hair cut short.

Daily Telegraph, 20 June 1994

Maradona: A God Felled by his own Hand

Ian Ridley

'I like to feel I am a leader. I like to feel responsible, more responsible than anyone else. I don't know if it's selfishness or love but when I get on to a field I feel I have a duty to give and suffer more than anyone else. I have learned from football that love is not only very close to passion but also to suffering.'

The words belong to Diego Armando Maradona, spoken at his zenith after he had lifted Argentina to their World Cup win of 1986; at a time when the urchin from the shanty town of Villa Fiorito in the suburbs of Buenos Aires was dragging ragamuffin Napoli towards two Italian championships, their only ones. Now the love is lost, the passion spent. But the suffering goes on.

Dallas has had matters of human tragedy in perspective for 31 years now and Maradona's expulsion from the World Cup for the use of medication containing ephedrine and four other banned compounds that can act to stimulate both nervous system and weight loss is, rather, mere folly.

Those with a passion for watching the game that matches Maradona's passion for playing it, however, will long remember where they were, and those being barbecued in the 100-degree heat of the Texan city will recall the coldness that gripped them when they heard the news. Say it ain't so, Diego.

Anglo-Saxon attitudes towards Maradona have always been ambivalent, embodied in his two goals that beat England in the 1986 World Cup quarter-final. The sleight of hand for the first drew approbation, the sleight of foot for the second admiration.

The problem was glimpsed in that 45 minutes of football. Maradona's gift has also been his curse. His prodigious talent has earned forgiveness too swiftly, enabling the man-child to be indulged. The game's governing body, FIFA, clearly had to act on the evidence of his urine sample, but they did so with the heavy heart that ailed us all.

For though there was a duty to condemn, it was also an affair to sadden. 'Dirty Diego cheats again' does not suffice. As the mind cleared at the end of a confusing day on Thursday that spilled into Friday and more details were revealed, the finger pointed to Maradona's personal doctor and dietician, Daniel Cerrini. He had, it emerged, administered two medicines obtained in Argentina to ease nasal congestion and an allergy.

Ignorance on the part of a man manipulated can never be defence, only mitigation. The case is, however, the latest in a litany of examples of Maradona volunteering for the gallows. The dope was duped. Again. Agents and acolytes, clubs in need of revenue and glamour, the organised-crime bosses of the Camorra of southern Italy, providing him with whores and cocaine, have all sought their slice. Now little, perhaps nothing, is left.

On Saturday night a week ago, Diego Maradona was jabbing the air at Argentina's expert 2–1 victory over Nigeria, in which he had initiated both goals. It topped even his performance in the 4–0 win over Greece, which saw him score and run joyously, even manically, to a television camera.

Then, just as he was about to make for the dressing-rooms of Foxboro Stadium, near Boston, a member of the Green Cross medical staff moved to escort him to the doping test room. His number, the famous 10, had come up.

In line with FIFA regulations, the numbers of two of the 22 squad members – one participating, one a substitute – were drawn by lot at half-time by a 'doping doctor', J M Ferret. One official from each team observed as the numbers were placed in an envelope. Fifteen minutes from the end of the match, the envelope was opened and the numbers examined by the same personnel.

Also routinely, five minutes before the final whistle, the forms requesting the numbers were taken to the Argentine doctor, Ernesto Ugalde, and his Nigerian opposite number, who signed a form confirming receipt. Dr Ugalde had made no mention of Maradona on a separate form provided before the game to detail any medication taken by players. He was later to say he was unaware of it.

Maradona and Sergio Vasquez were the two Argentines required to urinate into separate beakers, the contents of which were then divided into two bottles per player and sealed for delivery to FIFA's laboratory in Los Angeles.

It did not take Maradona long to provide a sample, nothing like the two and a half hours, and seven litres of water, of Sweden's Jonas Thern or the three hours of the Republic of Ireland's Tommy Coyne after other matches. Within half an hour, Maradona was at a press conference, smiling and saying that he was overwhelmed at all the goodwill towards him and that he was fitter than he expected to be at this stage. He had had to lose 13lb before the tournament, his 5ft 6in frame now carrying 11 stones.

His mood was equally relaxed at training in New England on the Monday and again on Tuesday when he sauntered across to a group of journalists, carrying his young daughter Giannina, and said that he had just run 20 kilometres and was looking forward to Thursday's match against Bulgaria as his deliverance day.

On Wednesday, the team flew to Dallas and little looked amiss as Maradona walked the pitch of the Cotton Bowl in the early evening with the team. There were to be no interviews, however, the first sign that something was indeed wrong.

FIFA had received notice of a positive test within 24 hours of the specimen's receipt and were quick to inform the president of the Argentine Football Association, Julio Grondola. He then exercised a right to a second test, on the second bottle, also in LA but conducted by different technicians.

The result was confirmed in the early hours of Thursday morning and Grondola told Maradona, at about the same time that FIFA's hierarchy of president, Joäo Havelange, its secretary-general, Sepp Blatter, and the Scot, David Will, senior vice-president in charge of disciplinary matters, were woken up to have their fears confirmed.

At a chaotic press conference some 10 hours later in the swish Four Seasons Hotel in the Dallas suburb of Las Colinas, after a 10-man FIFA committee had deliberated for an hour, they seemed genuinely disturbed at the outcome, and especially that it had been Maradona involved.

In sombre tones, Blatter announced that the Argentine FA had withdrawn Maradona – thus jumping before they were pushed – and that the punishment was in line with the sending home of Scotland's Willie Johnston for taking a similar substance in Argentina in 1978. As then, when Johnston was subsequently banned from international football, the case would be reviewed after the World Cup.

There was a sharp collective intake of breath as FIFA's medical expert Dr Michel D'Hooghe spoke. He concluded, at odds with the player's account, that Maradona had taken a 'cocktail' of five drugs, which were not to be found simply in over-the-counter medicines. They were ephedrine, norephedrine, pseudoephedrine, norpseudoephedrine and methephedrine and, yes, he said, they could aid weight loss and there was no doubt they could be used to enhance performance.

Blatter was more concerned with human rather than pharmacological theories. 'It is a human, moral problem, not just a doping problem,' he said. Havelange, coming late to the proceedings after flying in from Washington, echoed him: 'I was always praying that the result would be different. I love all these players like they were my children. It saddens us very much because Maradona has been such a great star for soccer but this is for the good of maintaining fair play and justice.'

Back at the team's Sheraton Park hotel in North Dallas, the lobby was crammed with bemused fans. Hector Baez and his sister Diana, rock musicians exiled in LA, had driven through the night for the game against Bulgaria only to be confronted with the news when they checked in at 5.30am.

'There are always problems with Maradona,' Hector said. 'Why? Because people envy him.' Added Diana: 'There's no fan saying anything bad about Diego.'

Maradona remained in his room, granting an interview only to Argentina's Channel 13, with whom he had a contract. 'I did not take drugs,' he said tearfully, 'I would not let down those who love me. I hope the boys can go on to show that Argentina goes on living after Maradona. FIFA beat me over the head and it hurts me deeply. We Argentines live by football.'

Later, 15 minutes after seeing his country beaten 2–0 by Bulgaria, he held court for five minutes in an ante-room of the Sheraton Park lobby for about a dozen Argentine reporters who had missed the game to stay on the Maradona beat.

He reiterated his innocence but added this time, significantly, that he had taken medication only on advice but needed no stimulation to play. He hopes to play again – he claims to have had offers from Napoli and Bolivar of Bolivia. He would be considering his future after rejoining his wife Claudia and daughters Dalma and Giannina in Boston before flying to Buenos Aires. It was a forlorn end to a fateful day.

As insects to flypaper are Argentina to controversy. Just when the world was beginning to applaud them for a surprising adventure to add to traditional canniness against Greece and Nigeria, and to speak of their rehabilitation after the disgrace of Italia '90, examination of their integrity returns.

The world, too, was mostly delighted by Maradona's rejuvenation, after a 16-month ban for cocaine use and rejection by the Newell's Old Boys club. He may not have had the pace which once enabled him to cover 30 metres in 3.8 seconds but that left foot could still seek out any defence's weak spot.

At 17, the nation's prodigy was deemed too young by Cesar Luis Menotti in 1978; now it had seemed he was too old at 33. But he had got himself fit for one last tilt at the windmill – with chemical help, it now appears.

Thursday night's match would have seen him set a World Cup finals record of 22 appearances. But on the team sheet all reference to No 10 had been removed. The announcer seemed insensitive in reading the team list and pausing after 'Diego' before adding 'Simeone'.

In his absence, the Argentine fans did their best to lift the team at the Cotton Bowl with their traditional welcome of streamers and torn-up paper. 'Gracias Diego, Genio,' said one banner. Mostly, though, they were flat, which the team, half-hearted but fully baked in the heat, reflected. Maradona's replacement, Leonardo Rodriguez, wore No 20 but was half the player. The thought occurred that Argentina were playing cutely to lose by one goal and meet Mexico in New York. If so, they cut it too fine, late goals by Nigeria and Bulgaria conspiring to send them to Los Angeles for Romania today.

Perhaps the siege mentality that has served them so well in the past will return. Perhaps Fernando Redondo will assume the mantle his midfield passing skills have promised. Of more concern to them, ultimately, may be the pulled muscle of Claudio Caniggia. Still, this day had drained them.

'Maradona is an essential player in our team so we missed him very much both on and off the field,' said the Argentina coach Alfio Basile at the Cotton Bowl at about the same time as Maradona was preparing to fly away and Simeone and Ariel Ortega were this time taking drug tests; at about the same time as the first of 14 Argentine fans was being arrested following a scuffle.

'It was of great impact for the team. It took our spirit and morale. We all love him very much but we have to go on,' Basile went on. The players, said a FIFA press officer, were too 'shell-shocked to speak'. A day that had begun in clamour was ending in wearied silence.

There is a belief in journalism that you should always follow the best; that they always give you a story. But while the professional in us relished the potency and poignancy in the tale of the fallen idol, the human being in us was left to lament the spiritual cost of it all.

How much of the riches of a man who once earned £2m a year with Napoli and commanded transfer fees totalling £16m remain is not known. One can only hope that Diego Maradona finally receives the right help from the right people before some shanty town of the soul reclaims the urchin.

Independent on Sunday, 3 July 1994

The Colombians were much fancied to do well in the competition, especially after defeating Argentina 5–0 in a World Cup qualifier and having had a run of 19 games without defeat. But when Andrés Escobar put the ball into his own net against the United States, Colombia were on their way home, defeated and humiliated. Sadly, the despair did not end there. A few days later, Andrés Escobar paid for his own goal with his life, murdered outside a restaurant in Medellín.

A Colombian Tragedy
Rob Hughes

The struggle for football's soul and sanity goes on. Yesterday in Medellín, approaching 100,000 shocked citizens filed past the body of Andrés Escobar, the unfortunate player whose own goal against the United States helped to eliminate his country, Colombia, from the World Cup. In the first round of the competition, 91 goals were scored; one was an own goal, and for that, it seems, Escobar was shot 12 times by his assailants outside the El Indio restaurant in Medellín. 'Thanks for the auto-goal' were the last words he is said to have heard.

The morning after, some of us were put on the spot by American broadcasters. What kind of a game is it, what kind of low society, that can produce fanatics who would kill a man because of an accident on the field? We could respond by asking what kind of society is the United States, whose own sporting icon, O.J. Simpson, is charged with two cases of first degree murder. Simpson's preliminary court hearing, relayed live by television, has tens of millions of Americans hypnotised.

The tragedy in Medellín interrupts a game which so many Americans believed to be un-American, yet which in cities such as Orlando has produced street parties of 20,000, turning the area into Mardi Gras. And in Silicon Valley, outside San Francisco, the Brazilians have virtually colonised a sober region with samba.

So there has been a conversion of sorts, behind which lurks virtually a century-old American scepticism to the game which takes sometimes irrational hold on 190 other countries across the globe.

Colombia is a place where life has always seemed more precarious than in many other parts. But its players, very gifted individuals, had arrived at this World Cup pledging their efforts 'to show the world that our country is about more joyful things than drugs and murder'.

Yet Colombia's defeat and humiliation by the United States, which was a brilliant result for conspiracy theorists, left a bitter taste, with huge disappointment that a team of such a high level of skill could perform so poorly. Although the players could be moody and unpredictable, defeat seemed as inconceivable as such a lethargic showing.

One police spokesman in Medellín raised the suggestion that drug traffickers had made huge bets in favour of the team winning the World Cup and that revenge against the unfortunate Escobar was a motive. Later reports contradict that and suggest that it was the heated passion of the argument outside the restaurant that led to murder. Yesterday, the police said they had arrested a man who had confessed to the crime.

One of the startling aspects of this terrible killing is that Escobar, had he not loved his home city, might have been well away from the danger, living the quiet life in Switzerland. He was known for his calm amid the storms of defensive panics and four years ago he transferred to Young Boys, in Bern, where he found a tranquillity tolerable for barely six months. He returned home, home to a country which, according to an Amnesty International letter to *The Times* six weeks ago, loses 3,500 of its citizens a year, victims of political killings and 'disappearances'.

It seems Colombia's players could neither win nor lose. Another Medellín player, Gabriel Gómez, nicknamed Barrabas (a demon) because, at the age of 12, he had an untameable personality and was sent by his father to live rough on the mean streets of Guayaquil, had abruptly quit the Colombian team hours before the game against the United States.

Gómez, who is now under protective police surveillance and has a bodyguard, intimated that his life had been threatened by a fax to the team's hotel; a fax believed to have come from another betting cartel who stood to lose if Colombia fulfilled their potential and won the World Cup.

Remember, this is the side that had the courage, the reliability, and the astounding attacking ability to win 5–0 against Argentina in Buenos Aires last September.

That was a World Cup qualifying encounter. Colombia, a team liberated under the management of Francisco Maturana, a professor of dentistry, had realised their potential over 19 unbeaten games. Maturana had taken over when his predecessor resigned after death threats.

From outside the country, we are scratching the surface of the extremes that exist there. The passions of football, an opiate to people living their lives of near desperation, were celebrated last September by the President, César Gaviria Trujillo, heading 40,000 jubilant supporters when the heroes returned from Buenos Aires. Escobar was at that time fighting an injury which undoubtedly took away the edge of his pace, the calmness of his temperament under pressure. Then, when he turned, stretched and the ball entered his own net off the outside of his boot in the match against the United States, he seems to have brought about a terrible, untimely death. The height of his career, spanning 55 internationals, had been to score one other goal – against England at Wembley in 1988 – during a match that was drawn 1–1.

But what more can we say to Americans, those who ignore the fact that 2.5 million spectators have so far peacefully attended World Cup matches in their country with fewer arrests than at the average baseball, basketball or NFL encounters?

We are outsiders looking in. The case of Simpson, being tried close to Hollywood, exposes the pressures and the surreal aspects of life for a sportsman – guilty or innocent – living in a goldfish bowl. The drugs allegations against Diego Maradona, while not remotely parallel to the charges against America's sporting idol, have been reported as a kind of tragedy.

When such stars are involved, blaming their sport is no more thoughtful than the simplistic sound-bites such as 'Maradona – prima donna' or 'pray for O.J.' that have been produced in the past fortnight. What should be felt far more deeply is the lament for an apparently innocent victim, Andrés Escobar.

The Times, 4 July 1994

Ireland v Holland
Cynthia Bateman

Jack Charlton as always left the field to the applause and cheers of Ireland's faithful fans. He had known in his heart all along that the Republic in going this far had done better than could have been expected. He had warned the Irish people to prepare for disappointment, while keeping his team confident.

For months it had seemed that only the faith of a tiny nation and the indomitable spirit of his men had carried the Republic through the qualifying rounds.

'Reality has at last intruded into our little party,' said a quiet Irishman as Bergkamp punished a slip by Phelan with an 11th-minute goal which whistled into the net in the Florida Citrus Bowl. Jonk extinguished any flickering grand expectations five minutes before half time with Holland's second after a blunder by Ireland's goalkeeper Bonner.

A philosophical Charlton admitted his side had given away the goals. 'But if we had to go out I'm glad it was to the Dutch. We would have liked a goal to show we can score now and again,' he added wryly.

Asked what he had said to the unfortunate Bonner, Charlton said: 'What do you say to a player who knows what he has done wrong? He just sat with his head in his hands in the dressing room. I told him to get out there and play properly in the second half. He knows what he should have done and so does Terry Phelan.'

Dick Advocaat, the Holland coach, said: 'The Irish really went for it in the second half. You have to wait until the final whistle to be sure you have really won against the Irish.'

Ireland had thought that if they were to progress at all they could do it here yesterday, when the sun was blanketed by cooling cloud and against a Holland side that seemed to be a shadow of its old self.

Holland had retreated into deep meditation behind closed doors after only scraping through to qualify, but their coach Dick Advocaat resisted the temptation to change to a 4–4–2 formation from their familiar 4–3–3.

The Republic, as always seems the case, were offered a gift in the opening minutes but looked the horse in the mouth. Sheridan's tapped free-kick giving Staunton a chance from just outside the area which was deflected by Overmars for a corner which also went begging.

This charade out of the way, Holland took charge. Charlton played his two fastest full-backs, Kelly and Phelan, in an attempt to stifle the Dutch speed on the flanks. But both Overmars and Van Vossen, who continually swapped sides in a successful attempt to confuse, had their measure. Kelly matched Van Vossen on pace but at 19 could not match him on technique. Phelan was simply skinned time and again by Overmars.

Babb and McGrath withstood this threat for some time, Babb in particular denying Holland two early opportunities with good clearing headers. But Holland were dominating with the possession play for which they are famous.

Phelan then tried a headed back-pass which lacked pace and fell to Overmars. Babb chased him towards goal but was unable to prevent the cross, and McGrath, vainly trying to get back with Bergkamp, was unable to prevent the Holland striker putting a low strike past Bonner.

It was Bergkamp's 21st goal in 36 international appearances, the Inter Milan striker once again vindicating his selection after a fade in form early in the finals.

Kelly responded with a sprint down the right and a square cross but Coyne was a shade too far forward to meet it, and Sheridan was a touch too far back.

The Dutch came back, the veteran Koeman producing two long-range speculative strikes from 35 yards that were driven hard and low but, thankfully for the Irish, slightly wide. When Jonk chipped a long ball to Bergkamp, whose cross dropped an inch too long for Rijkaard, Ireland were under siege.

Characteristically and to their credit, with the Dutch supporters silencing the Irish who were less in evidence than in previous matches, the Republic fought back, reverting to their old favourite, the long ball.

But international football punishes mistakes and things looked ominous when a sloppy short pass from Keane, trying to reach Townsend a mere five yards away, eventually gave Overmars a shot saved by an alert Bonner.

But Bonner had his head in his hands seconds later. Jonk from 30 yards producing a stinging right-foot drive on target. Bonner managed only to half-stop the ball, which then spun off his gloves and looped over his left shoulder and into the net to give Holland an unassailable lead.

'There's nobody else to blame but me,' said Bonner afterwards. 'I feel so sorry for all the Irish fans. I feel like I've let them down. But you don't go out there intending to make mistakes.'

The second half offered little hope for the Irish until McAteer replaced Staunton just after the hour. Fresh legs brought a fresh outlook and the Republic players at last began to produce the kind of performances of which they are capable. They were through time and again on the Holland defence but could not find the telling final touch.

Charlton played his last card of the tournament with 15 minutes left. Ace or joker? Cascarino was on the bench for the first time having struggled with a calf injury. He had done no running and no acclimatisation training. His legs the Irish did not need. It was his head they were after.

On the break Holland produced a scare, only for their substitute Roy to shoot high. The Republic were straight back on the attack with the Dutch kept at full stretch.

With seconds on the clock, Houghton slipped into the penalty area. McGrath ran through foot-high to take control, catching Rijkaard with his boot. The Irish idol took the ball on and tucked away a left-foot shot, only to be penalised for dangerous play. It would in any case have been too little consolation for a team who believed they could go further, even if the rest of the world did not.

Guardian, 5 July 1994

In the final Brazil met Italy in what many anticipated would be a final to remember. It was billed as Romario against Baggio. In the event it was more a game to forget. There was too much at stake. Defences dominated and after 120 minutes it remained goalless. Only then did the drama begin.

PELÉ'S HEIRS

Joe Lovejoy

More than half of the 24 wannabes will have played already but, for the romantics among us, the World Cup does not start in earnest until the most glamorous team of them all make their entrance in San Francisco tomorrow.

For the spreading-waistline generation, Brazil *are* the World Cup. Germany may have won it more often, but nobody ever won it quite like the peerless Pelé and his coruscating supporting cast.

The great man's heirs take centre stage in Stanford stadium against a maverick Russian side, burdened not only by tradition and the expectations of some 150 million back home, but also by the hopes of just about everyone else. Citizenship and allegiance may vary, but the rational majority recognise that if the greatest show on Earth is to be lifted out of the mundane rut it fell into four years ago, it is football's beach boys who are likeliest to make it sing, over in sunny California.

Everybody's favourite 'other' country have disappointed their admirers for a long time now. It is 24 years since a shimmering team who crystallised all that is best about the sport won the old Jules Rimet Trophy for the third time in four tournaments, earning the right to keep it.

Too long in exile. Carlos Alberto Gomez Parreira is trying hard to convince a sceptical audience that now is the hour. The 51-year-old coach conducts twice-daily press conferences for an insatiable media wearing a fixed, world-weary smile. If he looks as if he has seen it and done it all before, the attitude is excusable. He has.

Parreira is, with Bora Milutinovic of the United States, one of only two men to have led three different countries to the World Cup finals. Visits to Spain in 1982, with Kuwait, and Italia '90, with the

United Arab Emirates, sandwiched his first period as Brazil's chief coach. That ended, after just 12 months, with defeat by Uruguay in the final of the 1987 Copa America.

The latest in a long line of Carlos Albertos (he is resigned to newspapers forever using the wrong picture) admits he is uncomfortable in a seat not so much hot as electrified, and plans to seek alternative employment next season, regardless of the outcome here.

Brazil's prospects of justifying their status as favourites, at Germany's expense, have scarcely been enhanced by the departure of their outstanding centre-half, Ricardo Gomes. The more accomplished of the two Ricardos at the heart of Brazil's defence damaged a thigh during the final warm-up game against El Salvador last Sunday, and has been replaced in the squad by a comparative journeyman in Renaldo.

The loss is a significant one, Ricardo Gomes having been the rock on which Paris St-Germain's French title was founded, but Parreira reacted with little more than a sanguine shrug. He was well blessed with central defenders, he said. He still expected to reach the final, with Germany providing the opposition.

'Technically, I consider our team to be the best in the world right now. We don't have the superstars we had before, but the standard is good. Nearly all of them played in the last World Cup, so they have been through it all before, and know what they face.'

He perceived other advantages. 'The home team are not going to win it this time, and Brazil have a lot of support here. Everybody seems to have a Brazilian cousin, and they've all adopted us as their second choice. We are going to have the people behind us, and the weather will also help. It is hot, and the tempo of the game will not be as quick as it is in Europe. The tempo here will favour teams who play passing, possession football, as we do.'

Watching the Brazilians at work under the palm trees of the Santa Clara university campus, it was easy to be seduced by Parreira's reasons to be cheerful, parts 1, 2 and 3. There had to be reservations, though. Apart from a record of under-achievement, they are in danger of alienating local support if they do not 'wise up', as one columnist beseeched them.

Last Sunday's 4–0 victory over El Salvador at Fresno was marred by a brawl between security men and Brazilian journalists, whose tirade of 'Damn Yankee' abuse did nothing for pan-American relations. Worse, Brazil scored an own goal in the PR game by excluding non-Brazilians from their press briefings.

When tomorrow's whistle goes, it could all be different, of course, with Romario, Bebeto and Rai showing a nation of gridiron philistines what the Beautiful Game is all about. Parreira is sure of it. 'The conditions are right for us to be hot favourites. We have good, mature players, with mental discipline, which has not always been the case in the past. They proved this in qualifying, which was not easy for us.'

His second tenure threatened to be even shorter than the first when a goalless draw with Ecuador was followed by a 2–0 defeat in Bolivia, but Brazil waxed stronger the longer the series went on, scoring five against Venezuela, putting six past Bolivia and clinching qualification with a comfortable 2–0 win at home to Uruguay.

The progressive improvement was easily explained. 'We had 15 players coming from Europe, and only seven based in Brazil. We made a slow start because the players from Europe were out of season, and had gone four, or in some cases six, weeks without training.'

Recalling his best striker had helped. Romario's mind and mouth are as fertile as those mesmeric feet, and he talked himself out of the team when he tried to pick it. Banishment hurt, but there was full remission. Parreira accepted that to do without him for the decisive qualifier would have been to hack off his nose to spite Brazil's favourite face.

Irritating or not, motormouth can play, as he was quick to demonstrate in scoring two goals in the last 20 minutes against the Uruguayans to win the group, ahead of Bolivia. He is fireproof after that and, back to his old ways, he has been telling anyone prepared to listen that Bebeto must be his partner. The alternative, Muller, 'plays well only at club level'. With the World Cup at hand, kid gloves are deemed more appropriate than the big stick, and Parreira will not make an issue of the loose talk this time.

Romario and the mosquito-like Bebeto will be as good a goalscoring partnership as any in the competition, and Brazil look reasonably solid in defence, with Jorginho, still probably the best right-back in the world, the pick of a flat back four likely to feature Ricardo Rocha, formerly of Real Madrid, and Aldair in the middle, with

Branco, of the blockbusting shot, on the left.

If the favourites are to be found wanting it will be in midfield, where there is no Rivelino or Socrates to call the shots these days. The nearest they have is Rai, younger brother of Socrates, but a shaving more than a chip off the old block.

Dropped by Paris St-Germain earlier in the season, his presence here is testimony to a characteristic which is variously described as Parreira's strong suit or Achilles' heel. Unswerving, or blind, loyalty.

The coach remains convinced that if he perseveres, Rai will reward him by filling the playmaking void, but time is short and, as a last resort, the man who can be both idol and idle was dropped for the El Salvador game. Shock and horror back home until Parreira made it plain that this was merely part of the motivation process.

'Rai needed someone to give him a spark,' he said. 'He is a very good player – technically our best. His passing, dribbling and finishing are all of the highest class, but he had stopped burning. I needed to do something to get him playing again.'

The rest of them, it has to be said, are drones, the old Corinthian approach having given way to a modern pragmatism which rendered seat-of-the-pants players like Garrincha and Jairzinho an endangered, if not extinct, species. Scorning wingers in favour of 4–4–2 hardly squares with Parreira's assertion that 'we tried to play the European way, and it didn't work. Now we've gone all the way back to our roots.'

Style, it was reassuring to hear, was still important, but so was success. Parreira believes the two can go hand in hand. 'If we want to win the World Cup again, we have got to play the right way. That means stylish football. But also competitive football. It's no use playing beautifully, then going home after three games.

'We know what we are able to do, and know how we must go about it. The prize is the greatest of all. Not moneywise. We are not trying to win the World Cup for that. My players are already rich men, who are making a good living. What they lack now is a special feeling inside – the feeling of being world champions. There is no substitute for that, and you certainly can't buy it. You have to play from the heart.'

Rousing stuff. History beckons, starting tomorrow.

Sunday Times, 19 June 1994

Justice for Brazil
David Miller

Justice, of the most unsatisfactory kind, was finally done. Brazil, consistently the most attacking team of the fifteenth World Cup finals and of the ultimate match against Italy, became the first to win the trophy on a penalty shoot-out. They thus became the first four-time winners.

There is no more wretched conclusion to a great match than this, but the truth is that Brazil had been dominant throughout much of 120 minutes. Moreover, the luck that had patronised Italy for four weeks stayed with them when a shot by Mauro Silva in the 75th minute, fumbled by Pagliuca in goal, rebounded into play off the post.

In extra time, too, the initiative belonged to Brazil. In the third minute, Bebeto missed from two yards after a cross by Cafu, while in the fourth minute of the second period of extra time Romario, latching on to another cross from Cafu, hooked a shot wide from no more than four yards.

The renowned defensive qualities of Italy enabled them to survive for two hours, their attack blunted by the evident injury to Roberto Baggio. It was ironic that the last kick of the match, Baggio's miss on Italy's fifth penalty kick, giving Brazil a 3–2 advantage, should have decided the destiny of the cup. It was the most ill-judged decision to allow Roberto Baggio to take a penalty, for with a hamstring injury it is not possible to pull the foot back properly for the striking blow.

After receiving the trophy, which is such wine for millions back home, the Brazilian players paraded a memorial banner for Ayrton Senna, as did many in the crowd.

It is said that this Brazilian team is not of the standard of their better, more famous teams of the past. Be that as it may, it was a revelation to see, in a first half in which more than two thirds of the play was conducted in Italian territory, the Italians being surpassed in technique time after time.

In a contest as fascinating as the chess match between England and Brazil in the first round in Guadalajara in 1970, Brazil played some lyrical football, exhibiting the full range of their wonderful skills.

When Cafu, a substitute after only 20 minutes for Jorginho at right back, made the kind of technical error which you see every 30 seconds in the Premiership, the 30,000 or so Brazilian supporters in the stadium sighed in dismay in unison.

From the kick-off, Italy's game plan was clear: to always keep more men goalside of the ball than the opposition. That was often nine or ten men. Never mind, the Brazilians came at them persistently like a cloud of yellow bees. Here were the Italians, whose own skills are of the highest order, being left flat-footed.

There was a moment that took the crowd's breath just on the half-hour when Romario, 30 yards from goal, pulled the ball backwards with his right foot on to his left and in one instant flipped the ball with his left over an oncoming Italian.

Yet half-time came without score and in any such situation the chance must always be that the team under the whip will score on the breakaway. Not that there had been many of these moments for Italy. The nearest they came to scoring was in the eighteenth minute when Aldair slipped making a tackle on Massaro, who ran through to drive a 14-yard shot straight at Taffarel when he might have put the ball either side of him. That was an escape for Brazil but, beyond that, Italy had little to cheer them.

The rest of the time, the crowd sat back, entranced by the weaving patterns of Brazil. After 12 minutes, a cross by Dunga was headed by Romario hard at Pagliuca and five minutes later Romario, dragging three men with him on a waltzing run, slipped the ball left to Bebeto whose shot from wide on the left was turned behind by Maldini.

In the 25th minute, Brazil's best chance of the first half came and went. Mussi fouled Zinho on Brazil's left. Branco's 30-yard drive was fumbled by Pagliuca and, although Mazinho reached the rebounding ball inside the goal area wide of the left-hand post, he fell as he attempted to turn it back to the waiting Romario and Bebeto.

Italy had replaced Mussi after 35 minutes with Apolloni and, within a few minutes of coming on to the field, he was booked for upending Romario as the two Brazilian forwards exchanged a flicker of passes. As Italian players in the defensive wall for Branco's free kick refused to retreat ten yards, Albertini was booked.

Italy opened out more in the second half, although it was still Brazil who were calling the tune. Their frustration showed when

Zinho shot wildly and wide from at least 30 yards.

The evidence of Baggio's injury was apparent when he scooped the ball high over from 16 yards towards the end of normal time with a restricted right-leg action that he would repeat when missing his penalty kick.

Exciting breakaways by Cafu on the right again and again produced danger for Italy in normal and extra time, while the introduction of Viola for the second half of extra time produced a new nightmare for Italy. His powerful dribbling all but floored the wearying Italian defence. However, in the last ten minutes his colleagues, having run their lungs and legs empty for two hours, were on the point of collapse.

The Times, 18 July 1994

Tears for Baggio
David Lacey

In the end the 1994 World Cup went to the right team for the wrong reasons after a final it did not need. To Roberto Baggio fell the last word. He missed his cue.

Brazil won the tournament for the fourth time, and the first time since 1970, when Italy's luck finally vanished over the crossbar in an historic but unwanted penalty shoot-out which followed a goalless and often turgid two hours in the Rose Bowl here yesterday. It was a wretched way to decide one of the better competitions but the more positive team had won.

Brazil had set the pace, provided the majority of attacking movements and wasted what chances there were created. To the extent that they often succeeded in denying possession and space to Romario and Bebeto, Brazil's most likely match-winners, it was an impressive exhibition of containment by Italy. But the World Cup, and this World Cup in particular, deserved better.

This was not 1970, when Brazil had beaten Italy 4–1 in a celebration of the game's finer arts. Yesterday demonstrated modern football's pragmatism honestly enough but the present Brazil side did not have the flair to impose their style on the opposition's tightly organised defence and midfield.

Not until the 75th minute did either team look like breaking the deadlock. Then a 30-yard cross-shot from Mauro Silva slipped through Pagliuca's hands, bounced on to the left-hand post and sprang back to a surprised and grateful Italian goalkeeper. Pagliuca was so relieved he kissed the post.

Pagliuca enjoyed further escapes in extra-time, leaving the final to be decided by the lottery of penalties. Baresi, who had received treatment for cramp only a few minutes earlier, lifted the first over the bar but cheered up when Pagliuca saved from Marcio Santos.

Albertini, Romario, Evani and Branco then brought the shoot-out to 2–2 before Massaro's over-deliberate penalty failed to fool Taffarel. Dunga having put Brazil ahead, it was left to Roberto Baggio to keep Italy alive. His penalty was an action replay of Baresi's, a tired response from a man who had been carrying a hamstring injury for 120 minutes.

In fact fatigue was probably the factor most responsible for denying what had often been an exhilarating tournament a fitting climax. In extra-time some of the Brazilians had trouble raising a jog. The Italians, who had conserved some of their energies for the possibility of another half-hour, still could not find the extra pace to grab a late winner.

Arrigo Sacchi, the Italy manager, broke the mould of his country's traditional caution with Milan but yesterday Italy reverted to type. Probably they lacked the confidence to take on Brazil in an open-ended match and Roberto Baggio, though he played, was clearly hampered.

The decision to recall Baresi, who had not appeared in the Italian defence since damaging a knee against Norway in their second game, was the greater surprise. In fact Baresi looked more and more like his old self the longer the match went on.

Both he and Maldini had outstanding games but their excellence was mirrored by Aldair and Marcio Santos. But Brazil did not have the midfield guile to open up avenues of approach for Romario and Bebeto.

The crosses of Cafu, who replaced Jorginho in the first half, and the dribbling skills of the other substitute Viola caused Italy problems late in the game but the finishing was poor throughout. Massaro wasted Italy's best opportunity early in the game and they had few others. Roberto Baggio had one or two near-misses but injury had taken the snap from his shooting.

If Italy had an edge it was in midfield, where Albertini, Dino Baggio and Donadoni had improved steadily as the tournament progressed. Brazil had Dunga's thrust; they did not have Albertini's guile.

Neither side achieved a serious scoring attempt for nearly a quarter-of-an-hour. Then the 16th minute brought the final to life, albeit briefly. Suddenly Italy gave the ball away in their own half and Romario was dashing at the defence with Bebeto haring through in the inside-left position. Romario's precisely timed pass released Bebeto but his angle was narrow and Maldini stepped across to block the ball as it was driven in towards the near post.

Two minutes later a slip by Aldair offered Italy a rare glimpse of goal. Massaro was through and his shot was true but Taffarel had read the angles well and was out to save.

Apolloni replaced a lame Mussi 11 minutes before half-time. One of Mussi's last acts was to deny Romario a shot, Apolloni's first to get himself booked for fouling the Brazilian before he could reach a return pass from Bebeto.

The second half saw the Italian defence reshuffled but only to restore Benarrivo and Maldini to their normal positions at right- and left-back, while Apollini joined Baresi in the centre.

Italy's luck held into extra-time, only three minutes of which had passed when Pagliuca failed to cut out a dipping cross from Cafu. Bebeto, waiting at the far post, had only to prod the ball into the net, but instead he sliced it square.

Guardian, 18 July 1994

Romario
Rob Hughes

You are held up in Rio de Janeiro traffic. Suddenly, he is all over your bonnet. The windscreen is a blur. Then you see his face – the face of a street urchin who isn't going to go away with his sponge until you pay cruzeiros. To him and his family, this is no street game: it is the bread of life. Many years later, you meet again, only this time Romario de Souza Faria is a millionaire who could buy all the bakeries, indeed all the homes, he likes.

Romario is still tiny, still difficult to shake off, still wilfully imposing himself on others. His street credibility is no longer that of the squeegee boy. He scores goals for a living and for fun, and he already knows that tomorrow he will swoop once, maybe twice, to take the World Cup to Brazil.

A television audience of two billion will stare at him when the World Cup is screened in 180 countries around the world. Those not already familiar with his style may glimpse what makes Romario, child of the *favelas*, the Brazilian shanties, supreme among goal-scorers.

Romario is born and bred a carioca, a son of Rio. He personifies fantasy in sport: he has not outgrown the childlike responses that are key elements to winning in a man's world.

At 28, he has just discovered, temporarily perhaps, how to control his nature for as long as it takes to win a seven-match tournament. The moment Romario began to behave spelt bad news for defenders and the likely end of Brazil's barren World Cup span lasting most of his lifetime.

He came to this World Cup on a par with the Bulgarian, Hristo Stoichkov (his team-mate at Barcelona), and Italy's idol, Roberto Baggio. Romario has managed to stay physically and mentally sound longer than either of them, sustaining belief that where others push themselves to limits in a cruel climate, he draws strength under hothouse conditions.

His warm blood helps. He is a cobra, according to Bobby Robson, the former England manager who gained a fair few of his grey hairs waiting for Romario to come back off the beach while Robson was in charge at the Dutch club, PSV Eindhoven.

'I'm the face of Rio,' Romario said this week. 'I'm the type who likes samba and carnival. I love life. I want to enjoy it. I love the sun and the beach. That's what the carioca is like.'

Romario, who scored his promised 30 goals in his first season for Barcelona to help them to win the Spanish league, likes the company of strikers; elite strikers. Stoichkov, a potential rival since Romario's transfer for $4 million (about £2,650,000) to Barcelona last summer threatened the Bulgarian's place, is to become godfather to Romario's daughter, Monica.

As for Bebeto, the Brazilian with whom Romario shares the attack but refused to sit next to on the plane to the United States, the two are good friends. They told us so. 'We are different people,' Romario said. 'Bebeto stays home, I am a street cat.' They share more than the penalty box, where Bebeto is the brain and Romario the instinct.

A month ago, Romario's father was kidnapped. Soon afterwards Bebeto's pregnant wife was held at machine-gunpoint. The father was released without payment of a $7 million ransom; Mrs Bebeto gave up her car and Rolex watch in time to give birth to a son. Mattheus, named after Lothar Matthäus, the German captain.

You may have seen the harmony with which Romario, Bebeto and company celebrated their cradle-rocking routine for the television cameras. 'If any of you has a wife who is pregnant,' Romario joked with the media, 'put in your requests.'

A far cry this time from the arrogant, ungovernable Romario who once dismissed Bebeto as a *chorao*, a cry-baby. Or from the Romario who reached to criticism from Pelé by saying he would not listen to 'a museum piece'.

And far from the player Carlos Alberto Parreira, Brazil's coach, left out of the 1993 tour of the United States, saying Romario was far from his thoughts. 'I have five goalscorers,' Parreira insisted. 'I can start only two. I cannot destroy the unity of the group by bad behaviour. Nothing happened between me and Romario, but he went to the newspapers; like a rocket coming from the moon, he made a big noise.'

Romario is good at that. He told colleagues at Eindhoven that they were nothing without his goals, they should accept his need to go out at night, to sleep in the day, to laze through training.

'My strength,' he suggested at this World Cup, 'is sometimes people think I'm sleeping.' Never. Every footballer worth his $1 million salary has videoed Romario's goals. Goals like the one he conjured out of thin air for Eindhoven against the world's best libero of the time, Franco Baresi, of AC Milan, in the European Cup two seasons ago.

Romario had characteristically told the Italy captain he would score. Baresi, not unwilling to put a cheeky upstart over the touchline, reacted like a startled rabbit when Romario, his back to the opponent, flicked the ball over Baresi's shoulder. Before the Italian could move, Romario had scampered around him, controlled the ball on his thigh and, sensing rather than seeing the goal, scored with a delicate overhead shot from ten yards.

Trying to get hold of this 5ft 6in dancer is like trying to eat soup off a fork. He slithers and slides beyond grasp. He has scored five and created four of Brazil's 11 goals in six matches. And, short of criticising Parreira for leaving Valdo and Edmundo, his friends but also instinctive ball-players, out of the squad, Romario has employed angelic restraint so far.

The devil crossing the angel in him has cost Romario dear in the past. Before the 1990 World Cup, his leg was broken. In November, Romario had an operation to relieve pain in the left eye, apparently caused by heat. In January, he laid a left hook on Diego Simeone, when the Argentinian was playing for Sevilla.

A hat-trick one week, suspended the next. The life and times of Romario. But watch him closely, see how he goes into the box as Sherlock Holmes did into a room of crime – not sure what he is looking for, but knowing when he finds it.

We all know. It is a goal or three for his country, his team, but chiefly, himself. 'We are there to make them, we are there to miss them,' he mused after heading the only goal of a host of chances against Sweden in the semi-final on Wednesday.

He describes goalscoring as 'just a matter of being well positioned, of placing yourself'. Oh yes? Genius never does explain or express itself adequately.

When asked what his calling is, what his driving force might be, there is no humility. 'Without a doubt we [Roberto Baggio and himself] are the two players who have scored the most decisive goals. Whoever emerges with the trophy will be considered the best player. I hope Baggio plays, but I'm going to make sure this opportunity does not go away.'

Romario is back to the street kid who saw no limits, no barrier. 'You know, Senna has died and Brazil is left with a void. If I can lead Brazil to a fourth World Cup, I will definitely be a possible replacement.' Definitely.

The Times, 16 July 1994

Chapter Two

The People's Game

A Corner that is Forever the North East

Harry Pearson

I support Middlesbrough. When people ask me why, I say: because I'm a glory-seeker.

That isn't the real reason. The real reason is that I was born a few miles outside the town, in a village called Great Ayton. Captain James Cook, the explorer, went to school in Great Ayton. When we were told that by our primary teacher we were very impressed. We went, 'Ah brilliant, Miss. Was the man with the pointy ears with him an' all?'

We didn't really. We had all known about Captain James Cook (1728–1779) since the day we were born. Before, practically. He was the greatest man in the history of Cleveland. He visited Hawaii, landed at Botany Bay and made the first map of New Zealand. It's quite poignant, when you think about it, that the most important figure in my home town's history should be famous for getting as far away from it as was humanly possible.

At primary school we spent a lot of time learning about famous people from the North-East. There were four of them: Captain James Cook (navigator), George Stephenson (railway engineer), Bobby Shafto (went to sea, silver buckles on his knee) and Bobby Charlton (footballer). Of these by far the best was Bobby Charlton, because he was still alive and had a bald head like Mr Barlow who taught 2A in the temporary classroom and because he scored goals for Manchester United and England (the world champions). In fact so impressed was I by Bobby Charlton that I asked my mum for a book about him. This was a new departure for me. You didn't ask for books. Like shoes and jumpers, books were given to you *whether you wanted them or not.* Usually instead of something useful like a Hot Wheels Track.

I saw the Bobby Charlton book advertised in an issue of *Charles Buchan's Football Monthly*. It was the first book I ever felt would enrich my life. I still have it. It's sitting on the desk beside me as I write. *This Game of Soccer* by Bobby Charlton (with thanks to Neil Durden-Smith). On the back of the dust-jacket there is a picture of Charlton in an England shirt, cheeks puffed out, shooting with his left foot. Above it, in pencil, in the wobbly disjointed writing of a small boy I have added the helpful caption 'Bo bby Ch arlt on'. In those days I was always writing captions on pictures in football books. Perhaps this was some early indication that I wanted to be an editor. Or a vandal. Which pretty much amounts to the same thing.

Only joking.

In the main, though, my freelance caption-writing was a desperate bid to boost the status of Middlesbrough FC. In those days the Boro languished in a numbing pool of mediocrity just below the top clubs in Division Two. They never featured in any of the football annuals I was given at Christmas. To rectify this situation I would find a likely black and white picture, one of, say, Peter Thompson of Liverpool giving the ball a 'Did you spill my pint?' stare as he dived forward to nod it goalwards, under the headline: 'The eyes have it! Peter Thompson of Liverpool has his sights fixed as he connects with a spectacular header.' Then I'd take a black felt-tip, colour in the white collar and cuffs of Thompson's Liverpool shirt so that it more closely, at least to my eyes, resembled Boro's solid red top, cross out the words 'Peter Thompson' and 'Liverpool' and write in above them with my felt-tip, 'Arthur Horsfield' and 'Middlesbrough'. It fooled practically nobody. Nevertheless, as a reward for my ceaseless efforts Boro won the Second Division championship five years later, though Jack Charlton rather churlishly took the credit.

On the second page of *This Game of Soccer* there is a picture of the house in Beatrice Terrace, Ashington where Jack Charlton and brother Bobby were born. I had no idea where Ashington was, but I was determined to see Bobby Charlton's house. I asked my mum, 'Where's Ashington?'

'Near Newcastle,' she said. Her lack of precision was a dreadful error. From that moment on whenever our Riley 1.5 crossed the Tees, heading north into County Durham and the general direction of Tyneside, I began scanning the area for anything that resembled the famous building. The Charltons' house was a Victorian mid-terraced brick miner's cottage. There were a lot of Victorian mid-terraced brick miners' cottages in the North-East, and over a period of about eighteen months I must have pointed at all of them.

'There it is!'

'What?'

'Bobby Charlton's house.'

'No it isn't.'

'It looks like it.'

'His house is in Ashington.'

'Isn't this Ashington?'

'No.'

'Where's this?'

'Stockton.'

And so it went on. I spotted lookalike dwellings in Bearpark and Fatfield and Billy Row and Pity Me. Off the A1, and the A19, the A68 and from the train to Seaton Carew.

'There it is!'

'Oh, for Christ's sake . . .'

Only the recently begun urban renewal programme prevented my mum and dad from going mental. Had it not been for the respite provided by the concrete and design concepts of new towns such as Peterlee and Washington, my ceaseless cries of excitement would have driven them mad. Sixties town planning saved my parents' sanity. Sadly, it had the reverse effect on everybody else's.

Then, after a particularly lengthy and fruitless spell of Bobby-Charlton's-house-spotting, I was packed off to my grandparents while my mum and dad recuperated. Undeterred by my failure, and sticking to my task with all the doggedness of Barry Davies pursuing a metaphor, I asked my grandfather, 'Where's Ashington?'

'Northumberland,' he said, and, pulling a pre-war road atlas of Great Britain off the shelf, he sat down in his chair by the fire. I went and perched on the arm, looking over his shoulder, my eyes watering from the astringent mist of Brylcreem, Lanolin and Yardley's that seemed to hover permanently around him; the miasma of manhood.

We often did this. My grandfather didn't own many books, but those he did have were large, well used and full of pictures. He'd turn the pages, point things out and tell stories. Sometimes these tales were relevant to the substance of the picture, often they had only the loosest connection to it. A painting of *HMS Discovery* in a book about Captain Cook might warrant a detailed summary of rigging techniques, or a brief dissertation on the strength of the tea served up on Tees tugboats (you could float a spanner on it); a drawing by Frederick Remington of outlaws crossing the Rio Grande could prompt the tale of Wild Bill Hickcock (shot in the back while gambling), or cousin Gilbert (swam in the Tees with his bowler hat on). My grandfather's anecdotes were tinged with small town egalitarianism, an equality of emphasis. He made no more or less of a drama out of the Battle of Quebec than he did of a right hook that decked an Eston plater in a pub on Redcar seafront.

My grandfather took a pencil from a cup on the mantelpiece which propped up his pools coupon. He opened the road atlas deliberately, flicked through it, pausing for some reason over a street map of Bristol. Eventually he found the North-East. Pressing the book open and using the pencil as a pointer he showed me Ashington. He did not stop there. Soon the pencil was tapping other towns and villages. Every one of them had some footballing significance, a history, a tale attached: Crook (once beat Barcelona), Gateshead (Hughie Gallacher committed suicide there), West Auckland (won the first World Cup), Esh Winning (birthplace of Raich Carter), Cockfield (the wonder village), Durham (sold George Camsell to the Boro), Bishop Auckland (the best amateur team in history), Hazlerigg Colliery (where Len Shackleton worked), South Bank (little Wilfie Mannion).

My grandfather's hand circled the map, stirring up soccer wherever it went.

The Far Corner, 1994

Gladys Protheroe
Simon Cheetham

When, on 16th January 1907, Jenny Simpson gave birth to a tiny baby girl, who could have guessed the influence that infant would have on the greatest game on Earth, the Beautiful Game? The bonny cherub was christened Gladys by her mother and her father, Alf 'Stubby' Simpson, a hard-working, honest professional footballer who had loyally served Burslem Port Vale and Leicester Fosse before ending his playing days as a tough tackling full back at Vicarage Road, Watford.

Alf Simpson never achieved great success in his playing career, although he was respected and trusted by his fellow professionals, and his robust, hard but fair style won him many plaudits from the terraces. Simpson played in the days when the clubs treated their players poorly, paying them a pittance, while the grounds and stadia were overflowing with spectators. But although Simpson was never a wealthy man, he always made certain his wife and new family were provided for. Like many fellow players, Simpson's career was interrupted by the Great War, and after returning to these shores having fought for King and Country in a conflict where he had lost many team-mates, Alf tried to pick up the threads.

The years in the trenches had taken their toll, and it was obvious to everyone at Vicarage Road that Simpson had lost a yard or two, and would not be able to hold his own in the cut and thrust of the Football League. As it happened, Watford's full time groundsman had been mysteriously involved with some kind of Prohibition incident while visiting friends in Chicago, so when Watford manager Harold Bell offered Alf the opportunity to take over the responsibilities of the Vicarage Road pitch, Alf jumped at the chance to stay in the game in some capacity.

Simpson was given a cosy club house close to Vicarage Road, a hut full of garden tools, a wage of £6. 10.6 per week (only a slight drop from his player's salary) and a budget of £50 per year for seed and other essentials, and was more or less left to get on with tending the pitch.

So Gladys' formative years were spent in a football environment. She often accompanied her father as he repaired divots, painted white lines and carried out general maintenance duties, and the bonny child soon became well known to the players and officials of Watford Football Club, even appearing as club mascot in the team photographs for two seasons in the early 1920s.

As Gladys grew up she attended St. Mathilda's Convent, then Watford Girls High School, excelling in English and sport. Her prowess on the football field had been noticed at a very young age, and before her tenth birthday Gladys was drafted into the Hertfordshire Ladies team. Due to injuries and the Great War, Gladys was given her opportunity at right half, and played a major role in the Herts Ladies reaching the semi-finals of the wartime Ladies F.A. Cup. Their Cup-run ended with a 3–1 defeat by Middlesex at Stamford Bridge before an excited crowd of over 75,000. Gladys was the baby of the team, playing against women three and four times her age, but she won respect and praise from all quarters with her deft tackling and intelligent passing. *The Watford Observer* reported that 'The Herts Ladies bowed out of the Cup, just one game from the final, but there is plenty to look forward to. Young Simpson played her little heart out – remember the name, she's one for the future'.

By the end of the Great War, Gladys was a regular in the Herts Ladies team and her performances had caught the eye of England manager Lady Dorothy Palmer-Gray. In May 1918, Gladys was called up for an end-of-season get-together of the national squad that was held at Crystal Palace. Gladys won the first of her 64 England 'Bonnets', as they were then called, in a friendly against Scotland played at Brentford's ground, Griffin Park, a game that ended in a 2–2 draw. Her mother, Jenny Simpson, was obviously delighted with Gladys' progress in football, but was concerned that her daughter's love of the game would hinder her studies. With Alf away fighting for his country, Jenny was worried that perhaps Gladys would neglect her schoolwork through devoting all of her time to the game. But, although Gladys did skip a number of lessons to attend training sessions, she was blessed with a natural common-sense that has served her well right up to the present day. Her grasp of languages, mathematics and science were well above average, and Gladys eventually left school in 1920 with a completed education.

When Alf Simpson returned home from the campaign in Flanders to begin his new career as groundsman, he was amazed to see that his daughter Gladys had blossomed from a small, innocent girl into a wily, gifted wing-half. Alf had been caught in a mustard gas attack while in the trenches, and his health deteriorated rapidly in the post-war years. Eventually it became obvious that many of the physical duties involved with being a groundsman were too much for him to cope with. The answer to the Simpson family problem was simple; with Harold Bell's blessing, Gladys joined her father on the staff at Vicarage Road as Assistant Groundsman. The father and daughter team were featured in the October 1922 edition of the magazine *National Turf & Grass*. The article told of Gladys' enthusiasm, and of how she sometimes joined in training sessions with the professional players. The black and white photograph shows Alf and his daughter sitting together on the club's ride-on lawnmower, the caption reading 'Alf and Gladys Simpson – keeping Vicarage Road in splendid condition'. As the years went by, Alf handed more and more responsibility over to his daughter, and by the late 1920s she was dealing with the complete running of the pitch and ground maintenance as well as captaining Herts Ladies and having won over 25 England Bonnets.

In June 1931 Watford signed a will o' the wisp winger from Charlton Athletic. The player's name was Ernest Protheroe, and his speed and craft at The Valley had earned him the nickname of 'The Whippet'. Protheroe was signed for £500, a tidy amount for Watford in those days, and his arrival at the club caused quite a stir. *The Watford Observer* ran the headline 'The Brewers Sign Nippy Protheroe' on the sports page, adding that the new signing had not been able to gain a regular first team place at Charlton, but it was hoped that he would be able to contribute to Watford's future success. During the summer of 1931 Gladys was involved in the Ladies European Championships in Basle, where she helped England to the bronze medal. The semi-final was a spiteful, niggly affair against Italy, the holders, and England went down 1–0.

Seven players were booked, including Gladys for kicking the ball away at a free kick, and the popular press dubbed the game The Battle of Basle. The Italians went on to beat Spain 3–1 in the final to retain the trophy. On a personal basis it was a successful tournament for Gladys. She was the only England player named in the Swiss press 'Team of the Tournament', and there were rumours that FC Bruges were ready to put a bid in for Gladys, making her the first English professional lady player.

On the first day of training for the 1931/32 season Gladys was hard at work re-seeding the Rookery End goalmouth, and when the Watford squad arrived for the team photograph she and her father helped the photographer erect his tripod. The players looked very smart in their crisply starched shirts, their heavily greased hair slicked down onto their heads. As the players jockeyed for position on the wooden benches, Gladys noticed the shy new signing sitting at the end of the front row. As their gaze met, Gladys noticed how very blue Ernest's eyes were, and somewhere deep inside her, she felt her heart skip a beat.

Ernest Protheroe was a great success at Vicarage Road. The crowd took to his surging runs and inch-perfect crosses, and by Christmas he had inspired Watford to one of their best starts to a season for many years. Although the skilful winger and the hardworking groundswoman had only exchanged the occasional 'Good day' both sensed a mutual attraction, and at the club's Christmas party Ernest plucked up the courage to ask Gladys to dance. Within moments the two young people were chatting away like old friends. Ernest walked Gladys home, and as he saw her to her gate he asked whether she would like to accompany him on a country walk the following Sunday afternoon. Gladys agreed. Soon they began to step out on a regular basis. Everything seemed to be going splendidly for the young couple. Ernest was the club's leading goalscorer; his two goals against Southern United on New Year's Day had put Watford in touch with the leaders and in with a great chance of promotion to Division Two. Gladys' playing career with Watford Ladies was going equally well. Watford 'Gals' as they were known, had reached the semi-finals of the Ladies F.A. Cup, and were tipped by many experts to go all the way.

By now Ernest and Gladys' romance was common knowledge and there were constant references to the 'sporting couple' in the local press. The two young lovers had talked of their future together, the possibility of becoming engaged, perhaps buying a small house in nearby Croxley Green and maybe even starting a family. But their plans of domestic stability were thrown into confusion when, in April 1932, Italian giants Verona contacted Watford to say they were prepared to pay 28 million Lira (£14,000, then a record transfer fee) for Watford's star winger. Apparently, Protheroe's skill had alerted the Italian scouts, and they had secretly attended the Watford v. Brighton game in which Ernest scored twice and made the other goal as the home side romped to a 3–0 win.

Watford were staggered by the offer. The club had teetered on the brink of bankruptcy for years, but suddenly here was the chance to pay off all their debts and still have a small fortune to invest in new talent.

The Watford board met on 24th April 1932 and unanimously decided to accept Verona's offer. In those days, before freedom of contract, the management and players had little or no influence in such matters, so when Ernest arrived for training the next morning there was a note pinned to his peg instructing him to go directly to the manager's office. Fearing he was in for a dressing down, Ernest tapped nervously on the door before being invited in to the room full of cigar-smoking directors drinking large brandy and sodas. The transfer bid was explained to Ernest, and he was introduced to the Verona chairman, Signor Picca, a neatly dressed man in a huge fur coat.

Ernest was offered a signing-on fee of £2,500 and a weekly wage of over £60, nearly five times the amount he was earning at Vicarage Road. Ernest asked for an hour to think over the offer, which Signor Picca reluctantly agreed to.

On leaving the office Ernest ran down to the pitch where Gladys was re-painting the centre circle. He explained the situation to his love, then told her he was confused and worried. If he turned down this opportunity would he ever get such a chance again? Yet, if he accepted – what would become of their relationship? Gladys told him it was a decision that only he could make. Ernest fell silent for a moment, then cleared his throat and dropped down onto one knee. He asked Gladys to be his wife. It did not take Gladys more than a split second to agree to Ernest's proposal. There in the centre-circle they planned their future. Ernest would sign for Verona, fly out to Italy with Signor Picca and find an apartment where the newlyweds could set up home. Then, after Gladys had served her notice at Vicarage Road and attended to all the loose ends, she would fly out to join Ernest. But first, they would be married.

The wedding of Ernest Protheroe and pretty Gladys Simpson was the talk of the football world. Protheroe's massive transfer fee had stunned the Watford supporters, but they realised that a young ambitious sportsman like Ernest had to accept the challenge that awaited him in Italy. Signor Picca was delighted to get his man, and Ernest put pen to paper in front of a host of pressmen from both English and Italian newspapers.

Verona agreed to wait for a fortnight so Ernest and Gladys could be married in Watford, and Ernest's debut was arranged for Verona's last home game of the season against A.C. Milan. On Saturday morning, 16th April 1932, Ernest made Gladys his wife at the cramped church in Croxley Green. The service was attended by the complete Watford squad, as well as their opponents that afternoon, Leyton Orient. The wedding photographs show that Gladys wore a long white silk dress, with a veil covering her pretty face. Embroidered into the veil were the initials 'W.F.C.', while Ernest looked immaculate in a dark suit with a red rose buttonhole.

The Watford Observer carried a special commemorative brochure with their next edition listing all the guests, told of the moving speeches made by Ernest's fellow players and of how proud Gladys' parents were of their beautiful daughter. Before the kick-off of the afternoon's match, Ernest (now of course officially a Verona player, and therefore unable to play for Watford) and his new bride walked around the touchline to thank the supporters for a lovely carriage clock that they had chipped in for. Watford had to win by three clear goals if they were to make it into a promotion spot, but without Protheroe's guile on the wing they were unable to break down the Leyton defence, and the game ended 0–0. The result meant that it would be Fulham who were promoted, and Watford would remain in the Third Division (South) for another year at least. The newlyweds watched the game, then sneaked away just before the final whistle to a secret destination for their wedding night.

As time was so tight, Gladys and Ernest had decided to have a few days in Brighton, then enjoy a proper honeymoon in Italy later in the summer. The four days went by so quickly, and soon it was time for Ernest to fly from Croydon Airport out to his new club. The two young lovers stood and embraced on the tarmac until the captain could wait no longer. Then with tears in his eyes, the skilful little winger walked up the steps to the aeroplane, turned, waved to his wife, and flew out into the unknown. Gladys watched as the plane soared into the spring sky, and dreamed of the day when they would be together again.

Ernest was an instant hit in Verona. The crowd for his debut was over 80,000, and he capped a fine performance by scoring the winner as his new club beat A.C. Milan 2–1. The fanatical Italian press dubbed him 'Il Protho' and Gladys proudly read about his searing pace and the rasping volley that had won him the respect of the knowledgeable fans. Verona had installed a telephone in Ernest's apartment so he could be in constant touch with his new wife, and they would chat for hours every evening, telling each other the events of their day. Gladys was to leave Watford on 5th May, then fly out the next day to join Ernest. She was full of questions: how hot was it? Were the other players friendly? Did Verona play with a flat back four? Was the food tasty? Had he found an apartment for them?

Gladys Protheroe, Football Genius, 1994

The Latin Mentality
Tony Mason

You can change your wife but you can't change your mother or your football club. Or so they say in Buenos Aires. The truth of this (as far as South American football is concerned) was proved in 1985 when a Carioca entrepreneur left $360m in his will to the Bangu club traditionally supported by the poorest of the working class. The entrepreneur's footballing allegiance had not changed with his fortune.

This passionate lifelong loyalty was evident at Argentinian games on the eve of professionalism. Outside the ground children often sold parasols, bricks and boxes for the smaller supporter to stand on, oranges and apples, soft drinks, newspapers, pictures of footballers and sweets. Matches often started late because the field was occupied by newspaper and radio reporters in irrepressible pursuit of the last-minute first-hand quote and hordes of small and not so small, boys (*pibes* in Spanish) who would sometimes knock the ball out of the referee's hands to begin a kickabout of their own.

Once the game began, crowds tended to be noisy when their favourites were attacking, silent and anxious when they were defending. The reception of a goal by the home team astonished visitors like Motherwell's Bobby Ferrier: 'When the only goal of the match was scored, 50,000 people waved their handkerchiefs for a full five minutes. Goals were often greeted by pitch invasions with the scorer kissed and knocked over in the rush to congratulate him, and this in spite of the fences.'

Popular support for the game reached a peak in 1954 when the sale of tickets per match averaged 15,056. This does not include the many club members (River Plate had 72,000 in 1958). For big games grounds would be full many hours before the start. When England visited Buenos Aires in 1953 the River Plate ground opened at 10am and rapidly filled, though kick-off was not until mid-afternoon. This was the period when spectators at River chanted: '*La gente ya no come por ver a Walter Gomez*' ('People are not eating so that they can see Walter Gomez'). Gomez was a Uruguayan forward whose attractions led to family meals being delayed so men could get to matches. Until the 1960s, dances for the young did not begin until 8pm on Sundays so as not to coincide with football.

Many stories have been told to illustrate the passion for football in Brazil. A match was being played in Rio in the national Championship. Many of the audience at a local theatre had brought transistors. 'All stirred so audibly when a goal was scored that the male lead in the play stopped, looked out, and asked, "What's the score?" ' From the 1950s until the 1970s, attendances at matches in Brazil were the highest in the world. Brazilian crowds support their teams with such pandemonium that the action in the stands is often more exciting than that on the pitch. Flags wave, drums are beaten, songs are sung, confetti, powder and rice thrown. Fireworks fill the stadiums with a 'magical cloud-like mist'. By the 1960s every Brazilian fan held a transistor radio to the ear to listen to the match commentary. Samba bands first played at Flamengo matches in the 1940s and were soon imitated by other clubs.

The first organised fan club was probably at Flamengo in 1941. By the end of the 1980s they had 30 in Rio alone. The fan clubs (*torcidas*) are not promoted by the football club. All the organisation is done by the most active fans. Corinthians of Sao Paulo are alleged to have the most famous fans, with over 60 per cent of the population claiming allegiance. By the early 1980s, 11 torcidas were devoted to them, including the first all-female one. One of them is called '*Camisa* 12 [shirt number twelve]' which says something of their aim: to be the team's extra man. The word for supporter in Brazil is *torcedor*. The verb *torcer* means to twist, turn, fold or bend. So a torcedor describes someone continually crossing fingers in the hope that it will help the team to victory. Many Brazilian fans seek supernatural help. On the eve of the game offerings are placed at crossroads to bring good luck to favoured teams and bad luck to the opposition. Many will pray to the saints, an amalgamation of African gods and Christian saints. Players pour water on their boots and wash their feet with herbs prescribed by a *Pai de Santo*, a type of priest practising the rites of *umbanda* or *candomblé*. Immediately before the game hands are joined in a chain and everyone prays for victory. These practices originate with poor blacks, but are now part of the subculture of football in Brazil.

The response to the death of one of Brazil's most famous players, Garrincha, is a telling example of the importance of football to Brazilians. He died after a drinking bout on 16 January 1983 at the age of 49. For five years he had lived in a rented house in Bangu. His body lay in state at the Maracana stadium. Managers, former players and the supporters of Rio clubs held a vigil and the public queued up to file past the corpse. The burial took place on 21 January in Pau Grande, the small textile town about 35 miles from Rio where Garrincha had been born and lived for the first 30 years of his life. At 8.30am the body left the Maracana on a fire engine. Supporters accompanied the cortege. The main road out of Rio, the Avenida Brazil, was crowded with people, many carrying national flags, and traffic stopped while the procession passed. Thousands more made their way to Pau Grande itself and many had to abandon their cars and continue on foot, transistors to their ears as they listened to descriptions of the event. Extra trains had been laid on, and on a line which passed close by the cemetery engine drivers sounded their whistles. Fixed to a tree at the entrance to a nearby factory a notice read: 'Garrincha – You made the whole world smile. Today you make it cry.' The cortege took two hours to travel the 35 miles. Crowds both inside and outside the church were so large the priest decided not to celebrate mass but performed a simple benediction over the body. The coffin was lifted onto the shoulders of Botafogo fans and the national hymn was sung.

The scale of the demonstration surprised everyone. Garrincha was mourned as a hero of Brazilian football. It could also be argued that his death symbolised an era of success for Brazil, both on and off the football field, which had gone.

Footballers in South America could rise to heights which others rarely match. In Argentina, Brazil and Uruguay it did not seem ridiculous to speak of football as art. Here was grace under pressure, with individual ball control of an almost magical kind and passing more like a caress than a kick. But there was another side to the passion for football in South America. If the play was more flamboyant and the crowd more colourful, both could erupt into violence.

In 1945, the President of Botafogo wrote to the British Ambassador in Rio suggesting a visit from a British team. Rio agreed, suggesting such a tour might be extended throughout South America. But embassies elsewhere did not think it a good idea. Santiago thought British professionals would 'indulge on the voyage, get beaten and end up making unsportsmanlike excuses'.

Buenos Aires was even more doubtful. 'Local interest in football has to be seen to be believed; games between the leaders in the championship draw crowds of 80,000 . . . Under their own rules and on their own grounds the Argentine players are first class, and even the best First Division teams from England would have their work cut out. Any football team below tip-top standard would do our football reputation more harm than good. The local rules differ considerably from the English, particularly in regard to charging: an Argentine goalkeeper is untouchable; as soon as he gets the ball into his hands he is entitled to a free-kick. Argentine players and spectators are very excitable and the sight of a 12st Arsenal forward charging an Argentine goalkeeper with the ball into the net might start a battle.' Montevideo was doubtful, Bogotá and La Paz opposed. Even Rio had second thoughts after consulting the 'staff football expert'. Lima was opposed because 'it is our experience that Latins are lousy losers'.

But how justified were these suspicions? Was South American football more prone to violence than its European counterpart? Did football players and spectators find it harder to accept defeat, harder to accept the decisions of the referee?

The game in Brazil remained firmly in the hands and at the feet of the elite well into the 1920s. Teams would enter the field and raise their right arms with closed fists shouting hip hip hurrah, three times, in the fashion of the English Corinthians. It meant spectators were guaranteed an honest match, with both sides playing to win.

In Buenos Aires, elite control had never been quite so complete. In June 1910, on the ground of the Western Railway Club at Caballito, the Second Division match with Bocas Juniors was prematurely ended by a crowd invasion. The Western Railway's linesman was assaulted by one of the Boca players and the referee by another. The Boca captain made no effort to intervene. There were no police on duty, which cost the home club a fine. The Boca players were suspended for a year and the game replayed on a neutral ground. By 1912 the *Buenos Aires Herald* was complaining about 'chronic rowdyism' at grounds and a Racing official allegedly threatened the referee with a gun at half-time during the match against visiting Exeter City in 1914.

In 1924, the year of Uruguay's first Olympic victory, the first fences went up around the pitch to keep spectators from the players in Argentina. Yet games were still interrupted as the Combined Scottish Eleven (who toured in 1923) found when playing a Provincial side in Buenos Aires. When a corner kick was erroneously awarded to the Scots by the referee, several spectators formed a line in front of the ball so it could not be taken. The Scottish player kicked it out for a goal-kick so that the game could continue.

Chelsea saw the darker side of South American football during their six-week adventure in 1929, most infamously during their fourth match against a Capital eleven played on the Boca ground. They were warned by the local English-language press that it was not going to be easy as: 'they would be pitted against . . . men who have played football since they were children (who) have probably better stamina because they eat better and have lived in cleaner air, and they have therefore become faster. Add to that a sufficiency of pluck and a sound knowledge of the intricacies of the game and . . . you have the reasons why Chelsea must not hope to win more than the gate receipts.'

Having finished ninth in the Second Division in 1928/29, Chelsea were hardly one of England's premier teams. But for the match against Capital, all other First Division matches scheduled for that day were postponed. Chelsea lost 3–2, although it ended early in what the *Buenos Aires Herald* called 'disorderly scenes'. Chelsea began with a tackle by Wilson on an Argentine forward. He was injured and an 'unruly element in the crowd' ran on to the pitch. One spectator struck the Chelsea captain in the face. Luis Monti, the Argentine international, then kicked Rodger, the Chelsea centre-half, in the groin. Rodger was removed in pain and there was some fighting on the field. According to Chelsea director Charles Crisp, one Argentinian player kicked through the glass panel of the dressing room. The *Herald* reporter went on to characterise the Argentine football fan: '(He) is the most wonderful winner in the world. When Monti kicked Rodger in the groin a happy shout of acclamation went up. When Rodger fainted and was carried off the field the public cheered. (The Argentine footballer) must learn to lose as well as to win. Any player can win gracefully. But it takes a better man to lose gracefully. Locally, they lose disgracefully.'

Passion of the People, Football in South America, 1995

Scout's Honour
Shaun Campbell

What's the hardest job in football? Marking Alan Shearer? Being Paul Merson's PR man? No. The hardest job in football is scouting. On this subject at least, the scouts of England are unanimous, and they have a point. It takes a special kind of human being to watch up to 10 matches a week, most on grounds you've never heard of between players you will never know of, and in weather you've never dreamt of. Unpaid.

'It's a very hard job for very little money. Always has been,' says Nottingham Forest assistant manager and chief scout Alan Hill. 'The people who do it love the game, and their rewards are finding a young player who makes it to the first team.' Very satisfying I'm sure, but it's not a reward you can feel in your wallet, like that of the callow youth now drawing first team wages, who you spotted at the age of nine when he was scoring goals and picking his nose at regular intervals.

At most top clubs there is a salaried, full-time chief scout and/or a youth development officer. It's customary for the scouting staff to be split into two divisions, with the chief scout and a small team looking after the professionals, and another team dedicated to the youngsters. 'We have 34 scouts, with six concentrating on the senior and the rest on the junior side of things,' says Hill. 'They get their expenses paid and tickets for the games. That's it.'

'They aren't appreciated enough, says Everton's chief scout Brian Greenhalgh. 'They go out in all weathers, watching games week in, week out, and they do it for very little. We reward some of our scouts but not all of them. It depends on ability, experience and knowledge of area. A bonus can, occasionally, be paid. But there's a tendency to think that because they love the game that's enough.'

The typical scout's public profile is as low as a lizard's armpit. Their names are virtually unknown, their tasks rarely discussed. Yet their importance to a club is universally recognised within the game.

One of the first things Alex Ferguson did after his appointment as manager of Manchester United was to re-organise the club's scouting and youth development policies. 'Manchester City were doing better than us. Even Oldham and Crewe were doing better than us. So I called meetings of our scouts and told them I wasn't satisfied with the standard of youngster they were bringing to the club. They were hurt and shocked but it had to be done.' One or two scouts left but the result of Ferguson's work can be seen not just in Ryan Giggs and Lee Sharpe, but in a growing number of young players groomed in the junior ranks – Nicky Butt, Keith Gillespie, David Beckham, Paul Scholes, Gary Neville.

It's an impressive list, and shows clearly that United are building an effective alternative resource to the cash needed for the spiralling transfer market. Liverpool, traditionally big spenders in the transfer market, are now seeing the fruits of a restructured youth policy. One of Anfield's favourite sons, Steve Heighway, was lured back from the USA by Kenny Dalglish to head the scheme. Robbie Fowler and Steve McManaman are two of the graduates.

So scouts may be underpaid and virtually unknown, but they are vital. Who are they? What exactly do they do? And, as Desmond Lynam might say, how do they do it?

They're a mixed breed but they share a fanatical devotion to the game, stamina, and, one suspects, understanding wives. Some, like Steve Kember, chief scout of Crystal Palace, are former pros. Others, like Glyn Williams of Chelsea, are former PE teachers. There are former managers and coaches, and people who have just been close to the game in one way or another for a long time, like John Griffin of Cambridge United.

'I'm not sure if the old picture of the scout wearing a cloth cap and with a fag hanging out of the corner of his mouth, standing on the touchline looking for talent, is true now,' says Leeds United chief scout Geoff Sleight. 'It's a bit more organised on a network basis. You might have certain people feeding information from local football up to non-League, and then to the Third Division. It's a pyramid system, feeding up to the top.'

Scouting is a job of two halves: assessing teams and assessing players. Watching next Saturday's opposition and compiling a report for the manager and coaches is generally performed by the chief scout and the senior team. Sleight says: 'You want to know everything. Who's doing well, what sort of form they're in. You've got to go, because it's something you can't pick up on the telly. You can't see the shape of the play, you can't see who's making what runs off the camera.'

But knowing what you face and how to deal with it is a different matter. As Sleight explains: 'I was at QPR against Wimbledon and Ferdinand was a £10m player that day. I told the gaffer and he said, "Well if he's worth £10m, we've got a problem". We did. He scored two goals against us.'

'We watch the opposition sides home and away, three times in all,' says Forest's Alan Hill. 'It's mainly a report on their formation and set plays. Other clubs go into much more detail with the weaknesses of every player, but by the time you've got that into the heads of your players, it's gone out the other end. Nearly 75 per cent of goals come from set plays, so if you know what corners and free-kicks they take it's obviously an advantage. Every penalty I see I give a report to our goalkeepers.'

Assessing opponents is a key role for the chief scout's team, but it's watching individual players that makes up most of the typical scout's existence. What exactly they're watching for varies. 'If you're looking for someone to play in your first team, obviously you're looking for the finished article,' says Tottenham chief scout John Moncur. 'But at schoolboy level you're looking for potential, natural ability.'

As far as senior players are concerned Sleight looks for 'pace, athleticism, and some intelligence. If I had to narrow it down I would be looking for someone who can control the ball and pass. Personally I do like a bit of pace, or a change of pace, which is a subtle difference. Gazza has a change in pace, but he's not quick. Then I look for skills in specific positions. Rightly or wrongly I don't like small goalkeepers.' It isn't just small keepers that get short shrift from scouts: Kevin Keegan's lack of stature led two clubs to reject him before he was finally discovered by Scunthorpe. Moncur adds: 'Defenders have to be able to head the ball. Midfielders I divide into two; I want someone who is aware and can orchestrate play, but I also like players who can win the ball.'

This is a pretty uncontentious area as far as scouts are concerned. Some stress skill above all else, many point to a quality which goes under various names – commitment, discipline, attitude. John Griffin, now at Cambridge but formerly chief scout at Crystal Palace, remembers the day Ian Wright came to Selhurst Park: 'It was his attitude more than anything else that you saw in him – his absolute will to want to play, forgetting even his skills which everyone knows about now. But it was his attitude that made everyone stand up and say, "Yeah, he'll do".'

'Enthusiasm is a better word,' says Crewe Alexandra manager Dario Gradi, whose 10-year tenancy of the hot seat has seen players such as David Platt, Geoff Thomas, John Pemberton and Rob Jones come through the ranks from the club. 'You can't give people enthusiasm. They've either got it or they haven't. And their enthusiasm is often tested as kids. We've had boys here who've been injured for a year or more. Do they stick with it, keep doing the work they have to do to get better despite getting knocked back by the doctor? Perhaps they grow too quickly, perhaps they don't grow enough. Very few come through smoothly.'

Alan Hill says finding the youngsters is 'the hardest job in football'. Gradi doesn't agree: 'I think it's a great ability to be able to watch non-League players and spot their potential. People like Colin Murphy, Brain Eastwick, Dave Bassett and Bobby Gould are outstanding at that. They've got that ability to see someone and say "he's going to be a good player". I go and watch them and say, "no I don't think he will" and two years later he is.

'But if you're going to watch a kid play, I don't think that's so clever. I think anyone who's got an idea can do that, particularly if they have experience of working with kids. I can do that now. I can't be sure I'm going to get it right, but I can be sure of the ones who aren't going to make it. You can compare them with people you've seen at the same stage. Once you've seen Ray Wilkins at 14 years of age, which I was fortunate enough to see, you know who's going to make it. I've seen captains of England Schoolboys who I knew would never make it. They're strong, well-developed boys, very effective. But the problem with those kids is that they've never had to develop any skills to win. They've got by on their strength, so when everybody else catches up and they've got to produce a trick or two, they don't have it.'

Recognising that young people grow at different rates is an important truth for scouts. 'You can see a kid at 12 years old who looks an outstanding prospect,' says Moncur. 'But two years later he might have grown by 18 inches, and he's become all gangly and uncoordinated. But you must remember what he was like, because the chances are it will come back when his muscle catches up with his bones.'

Scouts have different viewing habits, too. Glyn Williams of Chelsea and Griffin like to pay at the gate and mingle unobtrusively with the crowd, if there is one. 'Glen Hoddle can't get away with that, but no one recognises me,' says Williams. Geoff Sleight reckons the directors' box is the place to be. 'I like to sit next to the chairman. At some places you're so far back you're on another planet, and other times you're so close you can smell and feel the action, but you can't see the shape. So the chairman's seat is the best one, not that you can always get it.'

Moncur likes to watch from the end rather than the side. 'If I'm watching schoolboys I like to go behind the goal. Then you can see the forward coming at you and I think you get a better idea of his movement, what kind of runs he makes and how hard he wants to work. It's the same when I'm looking at a defender, although then I watch from behind the goal he's defending.'

Former professional footballers don't always make the best scouts. Griffin says categorically: 'You'll find most good scouts in this game never made it as pros. That is an absolute definite. I can't put a finger on it.' Moncur says: 'People who have played professionally, or have coached at a high level, are always looking for the finished article, whereas a good scout will always look for potential. I find that scouting at schoolboy level is a completely separate job. The people who have spent a lifetime in the game at playing level are always comparing a youngster to themselves, to what they used to do and how they used to play.'

Everton's Brian Greenhalgh concedes that it's schoolteachers with no playing experience who find most of the kids. 'But somebody who's had a wide range of experience should have a better balanced view than someone whose experience is limited. Good scouts watch a lot of different games at different levels.'

So where do scouts find their protégés? 'If a player's got natural ability he'll find you,' says Moncur. That was true with goalkeeper Chris Woods as Hill recalls. 'His mum and dad wrote letters every day asking for a trial, because he was a farmer's son playing out in the sticks in Lincolnshire, and not many people went out there. His parents just kept writing letters and in the end we decided to bring him over to Forest and take a look at him. He was 12 then and we took him on, but when it came to his final trial match when he was

14, everyone turned him down. But I'd worked with him for two years and I said yes. Eventually BC [Brian Clough] said, "It's on your 'ead, son". So Chris stayed and he played his first match for us, when he was only 18, at Wembley in the League Cup final against Liverpool. It ended nil-nil and he played again in the replay at Old Trafford which we won one-nil. Brian came up then and said, "Thanks very much".'

Writing letters earned Ian Wright his place at Crystal Palace after several clubs had already rejected him. Other players have slipped past the scouting screen. Matthew Le Tissier was pushed forward by a Guernsey schoolteacher. Ryan Giggs' name came to Alex Ferguson's attention through a club steward. The initial tip for Lee Sharpe came from a Manchester journalist who had retired to Torquay.

But scouts are prepared to travel. Geoff Sleight flew to South Africa and Australia to watch Philomen Masinga and Lucas Redebe, and brought them both back to Leeds. Kevin Sharp and Jamie Forrester were recruited from Auxerre in France. 'I've been in Europe several times this season,' he says, and of his regular schedule comments: 'I'm normally at a game on Monday, Tuesday and Wednesday, and obviously always on a Saturday. Sometimes a Sunday, but Sky TV helps a lot. And Friday you're watching TV, daft as it seems. There's snippets from Germany, Italy and Spain, all over the place.'

Griffin, who has to look for cheaper players, finds them in the inner cities. 'I think many of the best players come from the worst areas,' he says. 'It's like the boxers, it's a chance for them to make something out of their lives. You've got to have the ability as well, but the will to want to do something with your life is very important. Some of the kids with ability just don't work hard enough.'

Moncur doesn't entirely agree. 'The best places to find young players are the areas where there are good youth Leagues. East London a few years ago was a great catchment area, but everybody in East London has grown up and left now. So you have to go to the outlying areas like Basildon and Harlow, where there are a lot of young families and a lot of football being played. But I've always found that kids come from all walks of life. You don't get too many from public school, because they don't play football as a rule, but you always get the odd one who wants to play the game.'

The big question remains. How is it that a player of, say Ian Wright's ability, was rejected by so many clubs? What is it that one scout sees in a player, but another doesn't? In short, what makes a good scout?

Everyone agrees on certain basic principles, such as what Moncur calls the 'willingness to get off your arse and get out there'. Alan Hill adds: 'You need a good eye, a good knowledge of the game, and a good approach when you talk to people. The first impression a player and his family get of a football club is often from the scout. It's important they can deal with people well.'

Moncur says there are many reasons why a club doesn't choose a particular player, however good the scout's report. 'We can all make mistakes and let players go. It happens to the best people,' he says. 'You can't take on 20 kids a year, however good they are. And if a player can't get into your first team, then *he* wants to go.

'You can hold him for so long, but that's not being fair on the player or the club. We sold my son [John] to Swindon for £80,000 three years ago, and West Ham bought him for £1m this summer. These things happen. But if a player leaves here and does well, I reckon I've done my job as youth development officer well. I can turn round and say to people that there are lots of players in the League who started their careers at Tottenham, and maybe that's why they're doing well. That's the only way to look at it.'

Griffin concedes he can't define the qualities a scout needs, but tries anyway. 'I just look and I see quality, that's the only way I can put it. People tell me I'm a liar when I say this, but you can see it in five minutes. I went to this game last night and I saw an 18-year-old. I'm not going to say who he is, because this is my job and I'm trying to get him. I could have left within three minutes, because I'd seen what I needed to see. The ball came to him and he was comfortable with it. He was quick, he knew what he wanted and you could just tell from his body language. It's just ability, I can't use any other word.

'But scouts do see it differently from others. I can go to games with football people, who are not scouts, and they would not have seen the players I've been watching for 90 minutes, the player who has been absolutely outstanding. Not seen him at all.

'But then I went to watch Geoff Thomas at Crewe and every time I saw him David Platt was in the side and I never noticed him. To be fair, each time he was played as a striker. I think David Platt's a very ordinary player personally, but his attitude and his will are just brilliant. He just keeps making those runs time and time again, and most people don't see it. They will say "great run when he scored that goal" and not have noticed the other 19 runs he'd made. I think he's limited, but he's still the first person you'd put in your side.'

But it was QPR's Chris Geiler, the 'producer' of 65 players at youth, under-21, B and full international levels, who provided the definite answer to the question of what makes a good scout. 'You can either do it or you can't. It's like maths. I don't know, what a stupid question.'

FourFourTwo, February 1995

Sik as a Parrot
Dr George Sik

Now, here's a story that can't possibly be true. A North London club signed two Argentinian players over a decade ago. On their first day at the club, the manager introduced them to all of their new team-mates, who had gathered in a circle, intrigued by the new arrivals. Pointing very deliberately at the ball, he said 'Ball!' Then, with equal precision, he pointed at the goal and said 'Goal!' Warming to his theme, he began pointing to the ball and goal in turn, saying 'Ball! Goal! Ball! Goal! . . .' When one of the Argentinian players pointed out that he and his colleague actually spoke a little English, the manager replied: 'I wasn't talking to you – I was talking to them!'

Today, we have more foreign players in Britain. But what are the psychological pressures they face, and will some cope better than others?

Any change is stressful – even change for the better. Some people cope better with change than others. Those considered less psychologically 'conservative' (regardless of their politics) cope best. Not that a player should be too laid back about a move abroad. Not getting sufficiently keyed-up can lead to a complacent performance. Studies of the best competitors suggest that there's a winning combination of some anxiety (a bit of adrenalin, the heart pumping) but also optimism and the feeling that it's all doing you good is most effective. Panic or indeed insufficient excitement can be equally ineffective. This might explain Jürgen Klinsmann's successful debut. He'd have to have been a supreme optimist to have signed for Spurs when he did.

Optimism is one aspect of personality which had been found by psychologists to fluctuate very little in life, regardless of the passage of time or the knocks taken along the way. Basically, optimists remain optimists and pessimists remain pessimists, whatever happens. Perhaps that's why certain managers apparently refuse to smile.

Then, of course, there is the language problem. It is little coincidence that the British players and managers who have succeeded abroad have made the effort to learn the local language. Paul Gascoigne has suggested that as his mastery of Italian has increased, so has his peace of mind.

Besides, the basic language of football is pretty universal. Having been born in Prague, I know that certain Czech words would not exist, were it not for the game's popularity. Despite the fact that the words for foot and ball are totally different from their English equivalents, the game is called fotbal and the thing which people are trying to score in is called a gol (though goalposts themselves have a separate word). There is even the term ofsajd, which, despite its unfamiliar spelling, is pronounced exactly the way Tony Adams shouts it. Such universality of football terms helps players changing countries, because in the everyday terms at least, there is less potential for confusion. It's said that certain colonies of Eskimos have several words for white and only one for all other colours put together. This may be a problem for kit designers, but the chances are that even there, footballing terms would be recognisable (if any Eskimo readers could confirm this, I'd be grateful).

Although there are differences between individuals, the need to be accepted is universal. Research shows people are often prepared to say all kinds of things which they can see with their own eyes are untrue, just to fit in with the rest of the group (who, for the purposes of the experiment, have been set up to talk rubbish). People will say one line is shorter than another when it's quite obviously longer out of sheer peer pressure. Set against this, the fact that Jan Molby has a Scouse accent seems a very trivial concession. Nevertheless, players coming to a club from abroad will be keener than ever to settle in. A psychological study carried out at Crystal Palace under Malcolm Allison proved that footballers, for all their professionalism, are more likely to pass the ball to their friends, so a desire to be accepted by other players is unsurprisingly high on a foreign player's set of priorities.

Then there is the rapport with the fans. These days foreign players are often the first to win the approval of the home crowd and have chants invented in their honour. The away fans may be more of a problem. Witness Eric Cantona's tremendous popularity with Manchester United's fans, but the equally strong animosity towards him from many fans of other clubs. Eric has been very much an exception to many rules: he prefers not to speak English; makes little attempt to adapt (having very strong views of his own) and even has interests off the pitch which are far removed from many players. There is no doubting his flair, but some managers appear to have been more prepared to accommodate his style than others. As a role model for foreign players coming here, his example may not be the easiest to follow. Nevertheless, he's now a Spitting Image puppet and they now use 'Ooh aah Cantona!' to advertise language courses.

All in all, there is no reason why players should not succeed abroad. It's worth remembering, though, that the stress of change and the pangs of homesickness can strike without so much as a cross-channel crossing. Joey Beauchamp had difficulty moving from Oxford United to West Ham, and ended up at Swindon. I expect that in that instance, the apples-and-pears language barrier proved to be the major factor.

FourFourTwo, November 1994

Say it Ain't so, Bruce
Ken Jones

Talk of a fix has always been with us. It goes back centuries, perhaps even as far as the Colosseum. The bent match, the bent fight, the bent race. In truth, rare, but fictionally appealing.

To be informed, on a sunny morning in California, of Bruce Grobbelaar's alleged indiscretion, was to be reminded that sport is nothing if the integrity of its performers cannot be relied upon.

Out of scandal grows doubt. Can we trust these people? Can we be sure they are always on the level, above suspicion, honest and upright, beyond temptation? Generally, this is the case, but unfortunately not always.

What usually mitigates against the notion of rigging on a grand scale is the diligence of bookmakers. Try hitting them with a large bet that contradicts all plausible considerations and immediately they run for cover.

Going back some years in time, there was a betting scandal in English football that resulted in prison sentences. It wrecked the careers of some substantial players. Because the Football League maintained a paltry maximum wage of £20 per week, the system was held partly to blame.

When the scandal was at its height I attended a meeting at the Football Association and innocently came across a document carelessly left lying around by officials. It showed that players other than the accused had been under investigation. One or two were of a friendly persuasion and known to me socially. There was no way of using this information but it altered my perception of them.

The curiously inept performance Colombia gave when losing to USA in the World Cup last summer after being installed among the tournament favourites, prompted the suspicion that their resolve was undermined by threats from gamblers in their own country. In choosing not to investigate the matter fully, especially following the murder of the defender, Andrés Escobar, in his homeland, FIFA did the game a considerable disservice. It mattered much more in my mind than Diego Maradona's reliance on stimulants.

Any number of sportsmen are gamblers by nature that it would never cross the minds of the majority to betray the faith that is held in them.

Following the scandal previously referred to, bets on single results were no longer permitted, but it is possible to wager on an exact scoreline. How that can be rigged without involving both sets of players is beyond my comprehension.

Down the years I have come across tales of matches which for the purpose of securing survival in the division were not what they appeared to be. One involved the cooperation of four players, the goalkeeper, and the three most likely scorers. Interestingly, in view of yesterday's allegations, it produced a negative return, an equaliser coming inadvertently, the ball going in off a defender.

Elsewhere in the world there has been reasons to suggest that some players were persuaded not to commit themselves fully.

Evidence of a betting coup once threatened the ruination of football in West Germany before the national team began to assemble an impressive record in the World Cup finals.

Because of his reputation as a compulsive gambler, wagering huge amounts in casinos and on the golf course, Michael Jordan set off tremors of anxiety in the National Basketball Association. An attempt to fix the baseball World Series more than 70 years ago – the Chicago White Sox scandal – is still written about.

In my experience the great majority of footballers could be trusted even when salaries were only a fraction of what they are now.

Consideration of the vast rewards available legitimately makes Grobbelaar's alleged confession all the more puzzling. It makes no sense. It does not speak so much of greed as stupidity.

Blatant disregard for a moral obligation is the worst thing that can happen in sport. Immediately it puts credibility at risk. It betrays the romance of sporting achievement. It is one step from the sewer. When the White Sox scandal exploded, a boy tearfully besieged Shoeless Joe Jackson to deny complicity. 'Say it ain't so' he pleaded. At this range something similar can be asked of Grobbelaar.

Independent, 10 November 1994

Eric Cantona's famous kung-fu kick at Selhurst Park was to produce more headlines and more comment than any other sports story. It may have been provoked but it was reckless. United, the Football Association and the courts dealt harshly with him. He was banned for the season and sentenced to community service. In the end his one kick too many almost certainly cost United the title. But it raised the issue of spectator abuse at football grounds.

My Philosophy
Eric Cantona

'A player who throws his shirt on the ground, even if he has scored three goals in the match, must be sanctioned because that's not what we expect from sport. This doesn't correspond to the idea which I have of football in general and of football at Olympique Marseille in particular.'

These strong words were spoken on 30 January 1989 by, you could well guess, Bernard Tapie. It is true that his way of looking at football is the opposite of mine. Recent events have proved, to those who had any doubts about it, that his noble ideas do accommodate less honourable behaviour, at least in relation to what constitutes in my eyes the *raison d'être* of sport.

In any case, I had discovered, in the course of a friendly match between Olympique Marseille and Torpedo Moscow, in aid of the Armenian Disaster Fund, in Sedan the devastating power a single image can create. I merely had to throw my shirt on the ground that day for my future at Marseille to be put in doubt. Before me, the English player Laurie Cunningham had dared to do the same thing.

Then it had been at the Vélodrome stadium on 14 May 1985, Marseille were playing Lens and needed to win to ensure that they stayed up in the premier division. Early in the game Cunningham was replaced by Eric Di Meco. He was very upset by that and threw his shirt onto the grass. This act was greeted by whistles from the public.

At Sedan, a local but smaller ground than the Vélodrome, the cameras were rolling, but the only image that is transmitted shows a bare-chested player making his way to the dressing rooms.

Each time I see my puppet on the television show that is the French equivalent to *Spitting Image*, it is always that gesture of irritation which comes to the screen the most often. It's funny. I like Picasso, as my character is named (because of my interest in art), and I think that what he does and says in the studio does no harm to anyone. 'Ah! But what about the importance of setting an example for the young people?' you say to me. My reply to that is that I think one should stop treating the heart and soul of youngsters as clay to be modelled in whatever fashion you like. I am not there to educate anyone; I don't see that as my role. They should be able to work things out for themselves.

Children go where they find sincerity and authenticity. In my way of working, of carrying out my career, I don't betray anybody and they know it. I don't consider that it would be better to teach them to deny their own emotions for the benefit of the established order. Is it in teaching people to be submissive that they become adult citizens?

At Sedan, as later at Nîmes, I wanted to tell the public that they were being cheated, because I was being set up as a scapegoat by the management. It was too easy to set me up in the firing line.

Inevitably, the press also joined in with the attack, as can be witnessed for example by the comments of the journalist Denis Chaumier in *L'Equipe*: 'By his gesture, Cantona has practically scuppered himself.' The public was given just one side of the story.

Those remarks were not helpful and my best reply comes in the fact that the ship is still sailing. In reality, this gesture was a natural part of my personality. I take responsibility for it. There are perhaps more beautiful or more ugly personalities. The great feature of someone who wants to please at any price is his capacity for hiding from the public certain things which should be condemned. You need a particular talent only to want to please. I don't have this talent.

What makes it worse for such critics is that I have an enormous fault: I don't attach any importance to what people say about me at my expense. What does me a lot of good comes from within myself, from the conviction that I have played a good match, and not from what others say. It's incredible but there are some players who prefer to read their name mentioned by error as having scored a goal on Saturday afternoon in the league championship rather than having scored a goal without anybody knowing about it.

I shall never renounce the kind of relationship I have with the public, the press and the television. If I hadn't had the strength of character to take responsibility for my mouthing off, in ten years of my career I would have sunk. Nobody would have come to fish me out. I leave it to politicians and to our managers to be sufficiently smooth to disguise all of their emotions. I do not see that I should follow their lead.

Cantona – My Story, 1994

Verbal Punches – the Player's View
Lee Chapman

Eric Cantona's reprehensible actions at Selhurst Park have been universally condemned and rightly so. He has been punished by his beloved club and further action could follow when the Football Association meet to decide his fate.

The pictures were shocking, but what was equally as galling to this seasoned professional was the speed at which an army of sanctimonious over-hysterical so-called experts (fees of course negotiated) jumped on the lynching bandwagon and demanded his head on a plate.

His punishment should, and does, fit the crime, but many of these unsympathetic pundits were once players themselves and nearly all have experienced varying levels of verbal abuse from supporters during their careers. They seemed to conveniently forget just how devastating this vitriol could be and how it could unsettle even the most placid of characters.

Over the years, and particularly in the last 10 days, my conversations with fellow professionals, including those at the very top, have left me in no doubt that nearly all have at one time or another felt like taking retribution against certain fans *à la* Cantona. Their good fortune has been an ability to exercise a degree of self-control, a quality that Eric has been sadly lacking on numerous occasions during his controversial career.

As a goalscoring centre-forward with a high profile off the field I have been an obvious target of those needing to offload their vitriol. Some of the abuse has been of an extremely personal nature and although these attacks have had no basis in fact, I have had to learn to subdue any emotions and create an illusion of indifference. After 17 years' practice I have long since passed the point where I still need to pretend.

The philosophy of 'ignore it, don't let it affect you' was passed on to me by senior colleagues and I in turn have passed it on to those of lesser experience, often at crucial stages of matches when it seemed to be affecting performance.

This attitude has prevailed to such an extent that verbal abuse is deemed to be an intrinsic part of a footballer's life and indeed it may have been acceptable in bygone days when good natured jeering and ridicule were an amusing diversion from the game.

Today that is sadly not the case. Shouting obscenities and more sinister, xenophobic and racist abuse is now the norm at football grounds all around the country. To say that footballers are highly paid and should therefore have to put up with such behaviour is a viewpoint which is morally bankrupt.

That footballers should have to suffer this form of abuse is a sad indictment of the state of our national sport. Many supporters now behave in a manner which would be unacceptable in any other walk of life apart from the environment within a football stadium.

I am not alone in not permitting my children to attend most grounds because of the unacceptable language which is freely used at matches. Football may have tackled the threat from these hooligans hell-bent on physical confrontations but it now faces the potentially more insidious threat from those with warped minds.

The situation has, in my opinion, deteriorated noticeably over recent seasons, a fact I believe is not entirely unrelated to the move towards all-seater stadia. A minority undesirable element present at most grounds normally stood behind the goal. Now those same supporters are becoming increasingly unsegregated and being spread around the stadium.

I hear reports about the reluctance of stewards and police to take any form of action against those spoiling the enjoyment of others. Some stewards view their job as a means of watching the game for free and do not want to get involved in confrontation, while policing policy seems to be one of allowing behaviour within the ground which would not be tolerated outside.

Those fans directly involved in the Cantona incident reflect the situation perfectly. Many of those self-righteous football lovers have told us just how shocked and disgusted they were by the Frenchman's actions. They had gone with the intention of enjoying a decent game of football only for it to be spoiled by his disgusting attack and yet many of these supporters were laughing at the fan who launched the tirade of racist remarks moments before.

Sunday Telegraph, 5 February 1995

The Ireland/England friendly in Dublin turned out to be yet another night of shame as English fans rioted, forcing the referee to abandon the match.

No Surrender
Glenn Moore

It began with chants of 'No surrender to the IRA', and ended with the wail of sirens and bark of police dogs. In between there was a little bit of football but, in the circumstances of what happened at Lansdowne Road last night, that is irrelevant.

Less than 24 hours after the British and Irish governments announced solid progress on the Ulster question, England's football supporters have done inestimable harm to Anglo-Irish relations, in particular, and English football in general.

From the moment supporters began gathering in England the day before the game trouble was on the agenda, with fights at Manchester Airport between Leeds and Manchester United fans. The problems continued in Ireland with running battles – primarily between gangs of English fans – in Dublin on Tuesday night and yesterday afternoon. About 30 known hooligans were reported to have travelled and there was evidence of right-wing extremists being among the 3,000 band of fans.

By the time the match had begun the Irish police – who cancelled all leave – were understandably concerned. It did not take long for their worries to be realised.

Most of the English fans were based in the Upper West tier at the end England were defending. Given the antiquated nature of the seating, the location seemed a risk. But away fans are often put in the upper tier (it is common practice at Millwall, for example) as it reduces the chance of pitch invasions.

However, it also gives supporters an excellent location to propel missiles from and, soon after the Irish scored, bits of metal, then chairs, then whole benches, began hurtling from the stand. Everything happened so quickly. The Irish police appeared to be caught by surprise.

There were plain-clothes officers among the English supporters, but they were hopelessly outnumbered. It took a long time for the riot police to arrive and the stadium's outdated design – long benches and narrow aisles – made it impossible for them to penetrate the mob.

It was a wonder none of the players was hit and, within minutes Dennis Jol, the Dutch referee, had taken the players off. It quickly became clear there were only two possibilities: either the police cleared 2,000-plus fans out of the upper tier, or the match was abandoned. In the circumstances, abandonment was the only possibility.

Jack Charlton, the Irish manager and former English international, went over to appeal for calm but was greeted with chants of Judas and pelted with missiles. Charlton, visibly angry, argued with several supporters and had an altercation with a cameraman. 'Send them home,' he told officials, and had to be physically restrained after he grabbed one fan, apparently Irish, whom he said he had seen throw a bottle back into the crowd.

This was not a small minority. This was a substantial number of fans bent on causing trouble, and it seems astonishing that FA officials can pick out known hooligans in the ground – as they did last night – but are unable to prevent them travelling with England.

As the Irish fans – who were impeccably behaved – filed out of the ground riot police moved in and stood guard on the English and waited. It took more than an hour to clear the area, and 90 minutes before transport arrived at the, fortunately convenient, railway station under the stand.

But it was still not over. As the public address announcer, who was a model of calm and sanity, told the supporters who came by ferry they could board the train for Dun Laoghaire, a scuffle broke out on the lower tier.

It quickly became a full-scale fight between the well-armed police and English fans. I saw one fan, cornered, heavily beaten by several police officers. But there were innocents there. I also saw a supporter attempting to shield his terrified girlfriend as the battle raged around them. Some Valentine's Day treat.

Again, missiles rained down from the upper tier. Eventually, two hours after the abandonment, that train left. Another, bound for the airport and city centre, departed and, after two-and-a-half hours, the stadium was quiet. Sensible people cancelled plans for a night out in the city while England, stunned and distressed, flew back to Luton.

In the match itself they had gone behind in the 27th minute to a well-taken goal from David Kelly, and minutes later David Platt put the ball in the Irish net but the whistle had already gone for offside. The two events may have been the catalyst for the missile-throwing for it broke out at this point but, as Graham Kelly said, it appears there were some elements bent on causing trouble from the very start.

Until these people are incarcerated, or decide to use their energies elsewhere, it seems England cannot risk playing outside the country again.

As Kelly, again, noted, supporters who want to travel and riot will do so even if the FA does not sell tickets. At the other end there will always be touts willing to supply them. Even if the FA bought all spare tickets, and exported a massive police presence, there can be no guarantee of peace.

Neither can the safety of spectators be assured for the European Championship finals. Any repeat of these incidents in England and it could well be that Terry Venables will have been wasting his time because there will be no finals to play in – certainly not in England.

Independent on Sunday, 19 February 1995

Lament for a Lost Game

Eamon Dunphy

After the English hooligans shamed their country at Lansdowne Road last Wednesday evening, anger was not the prevailing emotion. Those among the 46,000 crowd unfamiliar with the nature of English football were in shock, their feelings most eloquently expressed on the face of a small Irish boy whose hurt and bemusement was frozen on a television image transmitted around the world the following day.

Like many another Irish father, Seamus Eager had pulled every string available to get the precious tickets to take his lad James to this game. It seems important to explain – especially to those with power and influence in English football – exactly why James looked forward so much to this occasion. James is seven years old, a Manchester United fan. Of course he is an Irish fan as well, and the prospect of seeing Jack Charlton's Republic of Ireland team must have made him a happy boy as he fell asleep on Tuesday night.

But for small Irish boys, and for many who are older and no longer dreaming, English football is magic and, win or lose, Wednesday was to be a very special night. Shearer, Beardsley, Ince, Le Tissier, Platt and Anderton were coming to our city, to a town that loves English football, its great players and clubs, as if they were our own. Whatever the politicians and other advocates of Irish nationalism told us to the contrary, about cruel England and the imperatives of history, we knew different.

We were acquainted with another England, for we knew about Tom Finney, Stanley Matthews, Bobby Charlton and Bobby Moore. We knew about English grace and decency for we had seen their football teams play: Manchester United, Spurs, Danny Blanchflower's glorious double team, the Liverpool of Dalglish and Keegan.

The combined efforts of the British Paratroop Regiment, the Irish Republican Army and implacable native historians could not persuade us that our devotion to English football was some kind of heresy. We knew something else as well: that when our best footballers went to live and work in England they enjoyed parity of esteem in a fair and pleasant land.

This week's invasion may alter our perspective, crystallising as it has for many of us who are aware of what is good, uniquely so, in the English character, an uneasy feeling that ultimately our affection has been misplaced. We have, in the words of the Irish poet Patrick Kavanagh lamenting a lost love:

Loved not as I should
a creature made of clay
When the angel woos
the clay he'll lose
his wings at the dawn of day

In James Eager's face, we saw that look of love betrayed.

Sadly, more experienced observers of Wednesday's ugly theatre were not surprised by the scenes we witnessed. For two decades at least we have known that behind the glamorous façade, English soccer is rotten to the core, providing a fertile environment for spivs, racists, and violent fantasists, administered in the main by the type of person John Betjeman identified as:

That man with double chin
who'll always cheat and always win
who washes his repulsive skin
in women's tears

Too many of the gentlemen who define the values that obtain in James Eager's beloved illusion conform to that description. Last Wednesday, as the fans streamed sadly from the stadium, leaving behind the scum, caged yet in command of our game, a pall of despair descended on Lansdowne Road as the inquest began. English journalists wandered around, muttering abjectly of their shame.

These men are veterans, not fond of platitudes, nor given to idle expressions of regret. Their despair was genuine, poignantly so.

They wondered aloud what had become of their game, even more profoundly what has happened to their country. When Graham Kelly, the Football Association's Chief Executive, appeared to proffer the official line, nobody was inclined towards rigorous interrogation. The problem is bigger than this decent football fan.

Listening to Kelly field questions – all of them echoes of so many other nights of shame – I recalled some lines from 'Slough', the Betjeman poem quoted above:

But spare the bald young clerks who add
the profits of the stinking cad
It's not their fault that they are mad,
they've tasted Hell.
It's not their fault they do not know
the birdsong from the radio
It's not their fault they often go to Maidenhead
And talk of sports and makes of cars
In various bogus Tudor bars
And daren't look up and see the stars
But belch instead.
Come friendly bombs and fall on Slough
It isn't fit for humans now.

For Slough, read English football, which is no longer the game of Tom Finney or Bobby Charlton or indeed Alan Shearer, the greatest of contemporary players. The single most potent symbol of English soccer today is Eric Cantona whose malevolent spirit haunted many souls in Dublin last Wednesday night. What an inspiration Cantona must be for those young men, alienated to the point of derangement, who vented their fascist rage on the innocents around them.

Cantona is not, of course, alone in his disgrace. But his case is the most instructive as to the nature of English football today. His club, Manchester United, have stood by him. Bobby Charlton is, ironically, a director. Still. After the incident at Selhurst Park last month, the Bic Razor company filmed a new commercial featuring this irredeemable blackguard. Before his most recent offence, the sportswear company Nike distributed an advertising video on which Cantona boasts about spitting at fans and kicking opponents. Banished from France, Eric Cantona has in England become a cult hero, marketing thuggish behaviour with impunity.

When he assaulted an ITN reporter last week Cantona was pardoned by Alex Ferguson and the President of the Football Association, Sir Bert Millichip, who argued that the incident was 'unrelated to football'. In which case football must be unrelated to life. The truth is that Sir Bert and other apologists for Cantona are unrelated to reality. And will remain so detached, the events in Dublin last week notwithstanding.

Urging reality on the clerks who administer English football has long been futile. They feel themselves to be, and are, largely, helpless as the waves of violence, racism and corruption, the prevailing values of contemporary English society, engulf their sport. This nation has lost its identity, dark forces have been unleashed, most visibly on Saturday afternoons when the masses come out to play.

English football's crime is not to be the source of evil frustration rather to offer a home to those who rage and hate, those who wish to be known as Thatcher's Children, the greedy, ostentatious, new merchant class, unloved, unlovable, uncouth, claiming the best seats in the house.

Yes, it is true, as Graham Kelly argued last week, that football cannot be held responsible for the endemic yobbishness of England post-Thatcher. That is not, alas, the indictment. What one can see, what is so clear, and sadly unacknowledged when men like Kelly try to rationalise their troubles, is that, far from declaring loutishness repugnant to the game, English football is, in the case of Cantona, indulging the basest elements in society.

In this regard, the book of evidence is thick. John Fashanu, a footballer with a propensity for violence, is a hero in this game. Intelligent, articulate, persuasive, imitated, Fashanu is another menacing omen of our time. The BBC clearly disagree, employing Fashanu as your friendly game show host. Vinnie Jones is another role model for the men who prematurely ended last week's game. Paul Ince was wearing an England shirt in Dublin, pending further investigation of the Cantona affair. Dennis Wise was selected for the game but withdrew after being found guilty of criminal assault on a London taxi-driver. One singles out these footballers reluctantly to illustrate the tolerance within the game for behaviour unbecoming the hero. Cantona and the others named here have prospered despite their sins. An idea of what is acceptable, worse, celebrated, is abroad. As we saw on Wednesday the signals transmitted from within the game have been received by those who follow English football.

And, thus, in ever growing numbers, people who are disturbed, by racist grievance, or violent fetish, populate the great stadiums of England, the hitherto sacred cathedrals of popular culture, giving blasphemous expression to the poison in the darker recesses of England's soul.

When Manchester United play Liverpool, two malicious mobs congregate. At one end, the Liverpool crowd chant vicious doggerel about the bodies of the Busby Babes being scraped off the ice on that Munich runway after the tragic crash of February 1958. The response from Manchester's finest reminds the enemy of the Hillsborough tragedy in 1989 when 91 Liverpool fans perished on a day we can never forget. This disgusting theatre, throbbing with hate, exposes a truth about England we are loath to reflect upon.

There are other revealing images associated now with the game that once, long ago, was known for Bobby Charlton: the corrupt yet unconvicted managers; the brazen spivs called agents; the banal conspirators in this story, the hacks of print journalism and television commentary who bray about the 'good things in the game' when turning blind eyes to the decadence evidently infesting the sport of Association Football. Where once we raged against the dying of the light, we are now resigned, bewildered like young James, consoled, as he cannot be, for having known Charlton, Best, and Bobby Moore. We wooed English angels. He must make do with English clay.

Come, friendly bombs, and fall on Slough
It isn't fit for humans now
There isn't grass to graze a cow
Swarm over, Death!

Independent on Sunday, 19 February 1995

AN ASIAN DREAM
Guy Hodgson

In a pub a few hundred yards from Ewood Park, the view among locals was almost unanimous. 'Get rid of the Pakis and Blackburn would starve,' a fat, red-faced man said, to the accompaniment of chuckles from his cronies. So that was it then, Asia's contribution to east Lancashire – curry houses and the corner shop.

No one mentioned football, and why should they? No Asian player has made it in any significant way in British professional football, and not a single boy with Indian, Pakistani or Sri Lankan roots is on the books of the Premiership leaders, Blackburn Rovers. The consensus in the smoky bar was simple and brutal: 'Pakis can't play.'

Yet, on the town's playing fields of Pleasington, and on the all-weather pitch at Brookhouse, it was obvious they could. Asian boys did not suffer by comparison to their white contemporaries; they stood out with their quick feet and balance. If anything, it was the few Afro-Caribbean youths who looked clumsy, grasping at proficiency in unfamiliar surroundings.

The picture, however, was wholly misleading. There are around 1,900 professionals in England today and 300 of them are black. The England team is packed with black players, but not one Asian.

'Attitudes are not helpful,' Ibrahim Kala, who ran a predominantly Asian Under-15 team in Greater Manchester, admitted. 'We'd be playing matches and I'd be the only person on the sideline supporting the players. The opposition would have dozens of mums and dads shouting, while we'd have no one.

'Asian kids live football round here – you see them playing in all weathers, and the law of averages says some of them should make the grade. I accept they have to make an effort to go beyond their communities to get spotted, but club scouts should be prepared to come to us too.

'I've seen examples where the best player on a team has been ignored because he is Asian, while the second best – who is white – is given a trial. There needs to be positive discrimination to break down barriers, most of which are in the mind.'

Clubs need to break the vicious cycle of no players now equalling no players ever, and Blackburn Rovers more so than most. Already, 15 per cent of the town's 140,000 population is of Asian extraction, and the demographic trend is upwards. The estimate is that within 20 years one in three inhabitants will belong to an ethnic minority, which provides a simple rule of mathematics: either the club attracts black spectators to Ewood Park, or they will never be able to compete in crowd terms with Manchester United and their ilk.

'In the long term, Blackburn Rovers have to attract Asian players and spectators,' John Tummon, a co-ordinator in the north west for the Commission for Racial Equality's 'Kick Racism Out Of Football' campaign, said. 'They won't pull their weight financially, even with Jack Walker's money, and won't fulfil their potential if they don't. The same applies to clubs like Leicester and Bradford.'

Blackburn's awareness of this problem has led them to target much of their community programme in this direction, and they have been rewarded with more Asian faces in their crowd. That, according to the club's community officer, Peter Devine, is encouraging, but he concedes that the day when Ewood Park rings to the sound of young Asian voices remains in the distance.

'There are no Asians playing even at a good standard of non-League football, never mind at professional level,' Devine said. 'They tend to play among themselves, in their own leagues, so they're never put in the shop window. The only way they are ever going to make it is by progressing through a higher standard of football.'

Devine has written to every Asian club in the area stressing the point, and much emphasis has been placed on coaching schemes in areas of Blackburn that are predominantly non-white. 'There are a lot of talented players technically,' he said, 'particularly on Astroturf pitches, but they don't seem to progress from there.

'I can't condone racial taunts for one second, and I can understand why Asian players would not want to risk being the target of them, but I'm afraid things aren't going to change. Asians are going to have to combat that just like black players have done.'

Devine agrees that an Indian or Pakistani player will have an effect far beyond his talent. 'We'd attract thousands of Asian supporters,' Devine said. 'Players too. It just needs one.'

Independent, 10 February 1995

Blue Racists
David Bull

So, have you done it? Have you signed up for the new North American Soccer League?

I was amused to learn, last month, that there's now a freephone number in the USA, which you can ring if you fancy your chances in this league. If you get through, then your skills on a touchphone come into play. If your talents lie in backroom work, you press '3'. If you want to coach, you press '2'. And if you reckon you can make it as a player, then it's number '1' for you.

I ask you! Whatever happened to scouting? But, then, it's hard to imagine an unassuming American (need this sentence continue?) standing on a windswept touchline, admiring a youth – a youth who's then pursued to his parents' home where, over cucumber sandwiches and a cup of tea, a visitor from *The Manager* (put out the red carpet) is promised.

Ah! Romance! But what does modern America know about romance if it isn't full of more heaving and heavy breathing than your average Wimbledon game?

And what do they know about honouring promises? The World Cup, we were constantly reminded in July, was awarded to this soccer-free zone (*football-free* if we might be allowed to use our language literally) on condition that it get a professional league in place.

If that promise is being somewhat slowly followed through, many of us have had to eat our words about allowing the World Cup finals to go there. And, despite the Great British absence, our game has done rather well in recruiting stars of the tournament.

I am *so* looking forward to seeing Daniel Amokachi today. In fact, I can't remember when I last looked forward to watching Everton, a team that I equate with negative play. I wouldn't mind that they consistently beat Saints – *honest!* – if they ever came remotely close to entertaining me.

The other negative aspect of Everton, of course, has been the *Everton Are White* anthem of some of its fans – although there are those who would blame the Goodison Park Board for having maintained the most 'Lily White' teamsheets in the English game.

All credit to Mike Walker, then, for his determined attack on that shameful tradition. *Black* was the only colour he would contemplate, it seemed, for a partner for Paul Rideout. First, it was Martin Dahlin, Sweden's World Cup striker. Then Chris Armstrong, the Crystal Palace forward who glided across the Dell turf in such superior style when Palace were last here two seasons ago. And finally, there was Daniel Amokachi, one of the Nigerians who had thrilled us in the World Cup, only to be cheated by the rule-defying referee who allowed Maldini to stay on.

Football fans everywhere will be wishing Amokachi well and hoping that he can cope with the inevitable tag of being Everton's 'token' black. It's heartening, then, to know that he has become so accepted at Goodison that he's already been nicknamed 'Amataxi'. Why? Because he's big and black and carries a lot of passengers.

If that sounds like good fanzine humour, remember that the Everton fanzine, *When Skies Are Grey*, has taken on the Goodison racists and their Graham Ennis was a key player in the production of the Football Supporters Association leaflet, *United Colours of Football*, that was being distributed at the start of this season.

In other words, there are many Everton fans who want to dissociate themselves from those offensive loudmouths in their midst, whose racist comments on Frankie Bennett and Ken Monkou made the news when Everton were here for the start of last season.

Just as I'd want to distance myself – literally, if I could – from the foul-mouthed season-ticket holder in Row 11 of the Lower East Stand who tested my tolerance with his references to Forest's Bryan Roy. The absence of Ipswich's Chris Kiwomya spared us a repeat performance last Saturday, but I shall not be silent if Daniel Amokachi falls foul of his tongue today.

Indeed, if having to sit near offensive people is one of the prices we pay for all-seater stadia with lots of season tickets, one of the great advantages is that we can identify them by their seat number and report them.

They must shut up or get out if football is to be united in colours not only on the field but on the terraces.

The Southampton Football Club programme, October 1994

An episode of Granada Television's Cracker *written by Liverpool writer Jimmy McGovern concerned the Hillsborough disaster. At the same time, the former Nottingham Forest manager Brian Clough also wrote disparagingly about Liverpool fans at Hillsborough. Inevitably, both people brought a storm of protests from many in Liverpool and prompted this piece in a Liverpool fanzine.*

Cracker and Crackers
Alan Cookson

I once wrote a Hillsborough article for TTW&R. Steve rejected it on the grounds that the subject was all that the Liverpool fanzines seemed to be talking about at that time. I had to agree that it was such a well worn path that it was in danger of becoming a trench. However, it has been back on the agenda lately for all the wrong reasons. Jimmy McGovern's script for a three-part *Cracker* was bound to be controversial. The fact that McGovern is from this area only made it more so. The story suggested that an individual who survived Hillsborough had, on the death of his father, suddenly turned psychotic and murders policemen, *Sun* journalists and a number of other people. I approached the programme with an open mind and I was prepared to accept it might have something to say on the pain and heartache that many still have to live with on a daily basis.

Indeed, *Cracker* almost redeemed itself in the last episode when the killer was given his five minutes in the cell with Fitz to explain himself. What McGovern seemed to be trying to say was 'Hey, you might have forgotten about it but this tragedy wrecked, *and continues to wreck*, a lot of lives'. Perhaps we are angry because we'd already known that and didn't need reminding. However, the piece failed ultimately because it just felt like a sordid exploitation of that tragedy. He could have written about a fictional disaster and made the point just as well. He could still have used all of the same discrete parallels; the guilty cop, the 'anything for a story' tabloid hack and most viewers would have got the point. Instead, the tragedy was blatantly exploited to create primetime TV. Its intentions may have been honourable but ultimately it wasn't worth it Mr McGovern, because you hurt too many people by abusing the disaster in this way.

Then we have Brian Clough's characteristically clumsy attempt to give his own perspective on Hillsborough. I am particularly angered by what this dickhead has written because in issue 19 I went out on a limb and wished him well in his retirement. So; you're a bitter old man, you think everyone's forgotten you, got a book to write, most controversial thing that happened in the whole of your career, what are you going to do to make sure you sell lots of books? You got it in one. Should we be surprised? Who cares about the truth? Me, actually. The fact that one of the country's top Law Lords looked at this and never uttered a word of criticism about the fans is overruled by the far more knowledgeable Clough. He was there, you see.

Sadly, there are people out there who will accept what Clough says as gospel. That is why this glory exploitation is unforgivable. I tried to understand what Clough was trying to say. Was there a chance that the fans really did contribute to the tragedy? Yes, perhaps it was our fault; just as in the same way those people who bought tickets for that fateful Pan Am flight were to blame for their own demise over Lockerbie; just as those oil workers were to blame for the Piper Alpha platform turning into a fireball. It's easy if you take away the real guilty parties. Just shut them out and then all you are left with is the only people you can blame – the victims. They should have set off earlier, or stayed at home altogether eh Cloughie?

Bollocks. All of the people in the three disasters mentioned above died because somebody didn't do their jobs properly. The consequences were tragic, but let's examine Clough's logic in a little more depth. After all, a crowd of people can be a dangerous thing. It has no collective thinking, just the instinct of a herd. This is exactly why it is necessary to have crowd control wherever many people gather; concerts, sporting events, they even have a degree of crowd control at Henley and Cowes (er, so I'm told). The point is ANY crowd is a potential menace if they are allowed to get out of control. Just like a juggernaut. Not through malice or any bad intent whatsoever, but because of what they are. If the driver of a juggernaut falls asleep at the wheel, who are you going to prosecute? The driver or the juggernaut?

Ultimately, we dignify Clough's ramblings by even bothering to get steamed up about them. He should just be ignored. If only the press would take no notice. The publicity they are giving him is all he wanted anyway. If he had a valid contribution to make, he should have made it to the Taylor Inquiry five years ago. Hillsborough won't go away. It happened and many people are still coming to terms with it. It is right that we do remember it with respect and all the dignity we can muster. If other people would leave the matter alone, so would we. It isn't easy when people like Clough and McGovern insist on feeding off it like vultures.

Through the Wind and the Rain, Winter 1994

The Taylor Report, following the Hillsborough disaster, recommended the building of all-seater grounds. As the season kicked off, many fans found themselves in new surrounds, sitting in plush, double-decker stands, a far cry from the cold, damp terraces of the past.

More Safe and Comfortable
Chris Lightbown

Some of the Wolves fans walking into Molineux for last weekend's home match found themselves gasping in amazement. It was not just the sight of four glistening new stands but the presence of well-presented stewards, the babble of happy voices from a youth club underneath the stands and the sight of scores of disabled people effortlessly integrated into the crowd.

Such gasps will soon spread far beyond Molineux. Gone are Liverpool's Kop, Manchester United's Stretford End and Aston Villa's Holte End. In their wake are gleaming all-seat stands offering unparalled levels of comfort and safety. The cause of these changes is the Taylor Report – drafted from the inquiry following the Hillsborough disaster – which demanded that English football's decrepit stadiums be converted into safe, comfortable grounds. The first report deadline, affecting the Premier and First Divisions, fell yesterday, and at the start of the 1994–95 season, every indication seemed to be that football has come remarkably close to fulfilling Taylor's vision.

At least £400m has been spent on transforming stadiums, with no less than 528,000 seats being installed in the top two divisions. Four clubs have moved to new grounds and as many as 25 may follow. Hooliganism has not gone, but like the danger and squalor which characterised English football grounds for a century, it has been pushed to the margins of a sport whose public face increasingly belongs to happy families.

More remarkable still is that football has not only come close to fulfilling the letter but also much of the spirit of the Taylor Report, a spirit which lay in a hidden agenda which few have ever understood.

Most people will never forget the horror they felt as the death toll from Hillsborough climbed throughout the night of April 15, 1989. First two, then seven, 11, 25, 40 and eventually 96 people, had been crushed to death. The sense of national outrage fuelled the government's request that the then Lord Justice Taylor examine the causes and make recommendations. It was a rare moment of unity between government and public, but very few understood the way Taylor went on to interpret his brief.

When his final report was issued in January 1990, attention focused on just one of Taylor's 78 recommendations – that League clubs should convert their stadiums to all-seat at a rate dictated by a ferociously tight timetable.

Shock obliterated any understanding of the rest of Taylor's report, let alone its hidden agenda. But this was spelt out in the opening words. 'It is a depressing and chastening fact,' Taylor wrote, 'that mine is the ninth official report covering crowd safety and control at football grounds.' In other words, football was incapable of putting its own house in order, and as the rest of Taylor's opening chapter made clear, he saw his task as recommending mandatory enforcement of whatever it took to stop another disaster.

Ostensibly, Taylor's solution was seats. But as the final words of the opening chapter said, football required 'a totally new approach . . . both in bricks and mortar and in human relationships'. Seats were only part of Taylor's agenda.

Taylor believed spectators' welfare would never be paramount while they remained an anonymous mass of terrace fodder. But by forcing clubs to install seats, he might make them find out who their fans were and give them value in return for the higher price seats would command. Safety, comfort, commercial realism and contact between clubs and fans could all be triggered by the installation of seats: that was Taylor's hidden agenda and that is what has happened.

At Leeds, the secretary, Nigel Pleasants, spoke with pride about Elland Road becoming a 40,000 all-seat stadium with a shopping mall and giant video screen, and said it had brought about a shift in the expectations of fans and club.

'For decades, success equalled where you were in the League and the Taylor Report wasn't going to promote a club if they improved their stadium. But Taylor forced us to re-evaluate and now we are seeing the benefits of what he envisaged.' Benefits which, according to Pleasants, include a more civilised atmosphere, far better relationships between club and fans, and should the team's form slump, a far greater chance that fans will keep coming to Elland Road because of such changes.

At Norwich, the chairman, Robert Chase, not only pointed out that his was the first Premier League club to go all-seat, but that Norwich have gone for quality – among other features, the stands are heated and ventilated – and have adopted a character committing the club to maintaining the highest possible standards of off-field service to the fans.

'Taylor triggered something that was inevitable,' Chase said, 'but it still took Taylor to make it happen. By forcing clubs to go all-seater, he made them raise standards across the board so that fans would be prepared to pay for seats. Now many of us are going beyond the standards he set out because once people get a taste of how things should be, their expectations naturally rise.'

Notts County's chief executive, Neal Hook, oversaw the most dramatic turnaround any ground has seen when County rebuilt three sides of the ground in 17 weeks, installing 13,000 seats. He said: 'We would never have built all these stands if Taylor hadn't made us. But now we're glad we did because by sorting out the ground for the next 20 years, we can concentrate on the team.'

And Taylor prompted County, among others, into the realm of commercial reality, as the mushy-peas saga illustrates. When County asked their fans what refreshments they wanted in the rebuilt stadium, mushy peas topped the list. But their caterers refused to provide them, believing mushy peas to be non-profit-making, whereupon County sacked their caterers, produced their own food and kept all the profits, which doubled.

Such consumer surveys and follow-up may be standard practice in the outside world but in football terms they are revolutionary and mean some clubs are approaching the point Arsenal's vice-chairman, David Dein, predicted shortly after Taylor delivered his report. Dein said: 'Making serious money off the pitch will subsidise the buying of players and at that point our top clubs can operate like the Barcelonas and Milans.'

Dein's own club, whose commercial income outstripped gate receipts for the first time last season, are a classic example of that process but Newcastle are an even more dramatic one. Ten days ago, Newcastle thanked the fans who had bought £500 bonds, because the £2.5m profit had enabled the club to buy Philippe Albert.

In fact, the profit from the sale of bonds also enabled Newcastle to build an 11,000-seat stand at the Gallowgate end of their ground and subsidise its prices. Seating St James's Park led to Newcastle's annual turnover soaring from £5m to £16m in three years, every seat in the ground being turned into a season ticket and Newcastle being able to bid for any player their manager wants.

But the Taylor effect may prove to be even more pronounced at clubs with less regional kudos than Newcastle. Middlesbrough are a good example of a club whose destiny may be irrevocably altered for the better by Taylor. The club plans to move to a £16m ground close to the A19 next year and while Middlesbrough has always been a mini-regional club whose natural catchment area is not just Middlesbrough but Teesside, it could not assert its status until forced to move from Middlesbrough to a location with transport links to the wider locality.

Most intriguing of all may be Chelsea, whose slump was sparked by an ill-conceived stand development in the 1970s. One senior figure involved in stadium development said: 'Chelsea may be catapulted to the very top of the pack because everything in its redevelopment is geared to raising money, regardless of what happens at the gate. Out of necessity, Ken Bates had to think in Taylor terms before the report and has a deep understanding of what is going on.'

Some lower-division clubs have found themselves in a similar position. Although the government eventually exempted Second and Third Division clubs from having to go all-seat, many have done so anyway. Northampton's secretary, Barry Collins, said that while his club's move to a state-of-the-art stadium on the edge of town would have happened without Taylor, Northampton made it an all-seater 'because otherwise we would be telling our fans that we are not trying to get into the First Division'.

The Taylor revolution does not stop there. Stewards are replacing police in grounds to the extent that a club as big as Sunderland had six police-free matches last season. This season Aston Villa expect to save £7,000 a match on policing, with Taylor's seats again placing the accent on quality. As Robert Chase said: 'The days of clubs using fans as stewards are over. We tell our stewards to see themselves as airline stewards, showing people to their seats while being fully trained for an emergency.'

Meanwhile, fans will soon be able to buy tickets for any Premier or First Division match by ringing one of two phone lines for the

Leagues. Premier League officials are preparing criteria for their clubs, based, they say 'on the levels of quality Taylor inspired'. The revolution rolls on.

It must never be forgotten, though, that it was an enforced revolution; that 96 people being crushed to death was not enough to make football clean up its act. Only Taylor's insistence that his all-seat timetable be given the force of law made the difference.

Even then, it took the creation of a supervisory agency, the Football Licensing Authority, to ensure clubs complied with Taylor. One of the FLA's nine inspectors said: 'The first reaction from clubs was that Taylor would go away just as every report on football safety had gone away. Then they panicked when they realised we wouldn't hesitate to close them down if we had to.'

Since then, gentle diplomacy by FLA inspectors, albeit with the threat of closure in the background, has been sufficient to push most clubs down Taylor's path. That much of the financing has come from another outside agency that insists on high quality, the Football Trust, has helped push clubs away from merely bolting seats to terraces, the initial reaction of many.

Some fans undoubtedly have been priced out of the game and more will be. Many clubs run schemes allowing children into the ground for £1 or free in order to capture the next generation. But few have shown the consideration of Notts County, who have allocated a block of tickets to unemployed people and employ a worker to find ways of ensuring that low-paid people are not squeezed out.

None the less, the fears of a torrent of yuppies supplanting traditional fans who cannot afford seats has, by and large, not been realised and the most likely explanation for attendances increasing for the eighth consecutive season is that disillusioned fans are returning. Whether fans should continue to foot such a high proportion of the Taylor bill, or more money could be squeezed out of television, as Alex Fynn has insisted, is a moot point.

The certainty, in the words of Simon Inglis, expert on stadiums and member of the FLA, is that 'our generation is paying the price of years of neglect and clubs are getting squeezed between paying for Taylor and paying their players. But that very pressure is making them come up with imaginative ways of raising revenue that, so far, tend to work for fans' benefit'.

The final reaction of most clubs has been that Taylor pushed them into common-sense that was unlikely to break out unless decreed.

Once the dust settles, the likelihood is that English football will be left with stadiums ranging from the adequate to the magnificent with more nearer the latter than the former. Since the Taylor effect has been to make the superclubs even more profitable, it is inevitable that they will soon start chattering about breakaways, and the lack of anyone of national stature understanding what the whole process has been about suggests that the small-minded squabbling may pick up where it left off.

But against that, so many club people have genuinely seen Taylor's light – as opposed to seeing it simply as a marketing opportunity – that it is possible some of them may provide football's next generation of national leadership.

We shall see. In the meantime, let us be thankful for what we have got – a crop of stadiums that are less likely to be venues of death than their predecessors were.

For such small mercies, let us be grateful.

Sunday Times, 21 August 1994

One of the most important revolutions of recent years has been not just the new all-seater grounds but the numbers of women who are now watching and playing the game. Thankfully football is no longer a 'man's game'.

A Man's Game
Jody Brett-Kelly

Sarah, a personnel manager, and her older sister, Jane, a lawyer, are spending a total of £3,000 to watch the World Cup live in the United States.

Sue, sister No 3, will be coming straight home from work every night to watch the games on television. She will also be taping them so she can re-hash the games with her sisters when they get home.

Sarah's colleagues think she's mad to spend her savings and most of her holidays sitting in a sweaty crowd: 'I'm going over for the same reason any man goes over: it's the best soccer in the world.'

Monica Hartland, 55, the gregarious deputy chairman of the

National Federation of Football Supporters' Clubs is also off to the US even though she hasn't got tickets to any of the games and may have to watch them on TV sitting in a bar outside the stadium.

Her scientist husband will not be watching with her: he's off to a convention. 'I wouldn't dream of going with someone who is merely interested, it has to be someone fanatical,' she says.

They are part of a huge new sweep of women passionate about football. Around 35 per cent of the 3.6 million World Cup tickets sold have been to women, US promoters said this week.

Around 11 to 12m viewers could be watching each game in the first round on ITV and past viewer numbers suggest more women may be plonked in front of their TVs than men, despite the absence of Ryan Giggs' rear view.

Around 25 million viewers watched the England v West Germany game during the last World Cup and ITV says 48 per cent of its audience were women compared to 41 per cent men, the remainder being children.

On BBC it was almost even, with 46 per cent men and 43 per cent women. TV executives seem to have responded to this increasing female interest in the sport with the emergence of a new breed of female-friendly TV soccer pundits, notably the ex-Liverpool and Scotland player, that handsome Alan Hansen.

But men who dismiss female fans as just 'chicks watching out for the bits' or 'girlies tut-tutting over how South Korea's kit does nothing for them', should take a bit more notice.

These women are not just lured by the game's new glamorous image and pin-up players, though many admit they cannot be bothered with discussions about how many goals were scored from indirect free-kicks in the last 10 World Cups. They do, however, know all about the pace and poise of the tournament's best players.

Accountant Anne Guerin, 33, a Chelsea and Ireland fan since she was 14 years old, says: 'I'm attracted to the game because of its intensity and I can hold my own in most discussions, but I never lose sleep over it and I know some men do. They're desperate about it, it's kind of a tribal thing. I guess that's the difference between men and women.'

The game's popularity with women is well entrenched in the US, where around 40 per cent of the country's 16m soccer players are female and soccer is the second most popular sport for both boys and girls after basketball.

A world championship for the United States men's football team may be as likely as finding your chilli dog covered with gravy but the US women's team won the FIFA Women's World Championship title as recently as 1991.

A World Cup press officer based in New York was rather indignant when I asked if they were putting on anything to attract more women spectators. 'The game,' she answered, adding that fans attending the matches would be 'passionate fans, male or female'.

In the United Kingdom increases in the number of women interested in the game have been rapid, though it was not until 1990 that the Schools Football Association was allowed to 'actively encourage' football for girls.

Over the last five years the number of women who paid to watch at least one game has risen by 25 per cent to 1.041 million in 1994 according to the British Market Research Bureau with a 10 per cent rise since last year. The biggest increases were in women aged 25 to 34.

Research by the Centre for Football Research at Leicester University shows this season one in eight people at Premier League games were women. That figure goes up to one in five for smaller clubs such as Oldham.

More women are playing soccer as well: 460 women's teams are now registered with the Football Association – most having signed up over the last five prolific years – compared to just 44 teams in 1969.

The surge in interest has been largely due to the fall in hooliganism; the new all-seater stadia, some of which have vegetarian restaurants; the skills and style shown in the 1990 World Cup in Italy; and the charisma of Premier League players, many of whom are now treated as if they were rock stars.

It is true that women love the new glamour of the sport – but so do men. Some of my male friends spent a whole morning discussing whether you could call Ruud Gullit's hair-do 'a ponytail' or whether it was that his dreadlocks were interwoven.

The game itself has become more feminine according to John Williams, a senior researcher at the Centre for Football Research: 'When people started to see Italian football they realised the game was not about brute strength and force and muddy fields.

'The Italians were more graceful, more athletic and brought more feminine qualities to the game. British football regarded theorising and analysing the game as feminine: they are now realising commitment, courage and loyalty are not enough.'

Women have also lent the game a sort of fashion credence. Once, only big fat boys would wear football shirts out in public, if only to hold in their bellies. Now 1970s Adidas football shirts are *de rigueur* for football watching and clubbing.

Daily Telegraph, 18 June 1994

Scottish football, once the pride of Europe, plumbed new depths during the 1994/95 season. With the exception of Rangers, the Scottish League and the Scottish national side were third rate and in desperate need of new ideas.

A Scottish Lament
John Arlidge

Question: which European nation failed to qualify for the 1994 World Cup, saw its leading club sides knocked out of this year's European competitions in the first round and has no players in the leading continental teams? If you are thinking of Albania, Greece or Portugal, look a little closer to home. The answer is Scotland.

As Aston Villa, Newcastle, Manchester United, Arsenal and Chelsea play second-round European ties this week, the talk north of the border is of football in crisis. Fans, managers and players – stuck on the European sidelines for the first time in 35 seasons – say that defeats last month for Rangers, Dundee United and Aberdeen by teams from Greece, Slovakia and Latvia confirm that the Scottish game has slumped to an all-time low.

The sense of gloom has prompted a re-examination of the sport among senior managers and Scottish Football Association officials. They are frustrated that 27 years after the triumphant days of Scottish football, when Celtic became the first British side to win the European Cup, teams now appear to be unable to overcome the weakest continental opponents.

Craig Brown, the national team manager, said: 'Scotland has an impressive footballing history. We have produced two of the game's great managers – Sir Matt Busby and Bill Shankly – and we qualified for five World Cups in a row from 1974 to 1990. But in recent years standards have fallen sharply.

'We are no longer producing superstars – the Kenny Dalglishes, Graeme Sounesses, Gordon Strachans and Steve Nicols of the future. If you tried to put a value on our Premier Division players today, you would see that the best are worth around £2m, compared with £5m for Ryan Giggs and £3m for many other players in the English and European leagues. Looked at in those terms we are poor relations and that is frustrating.'

Managers who have tasted success in Europe agree, but they say that talk of a crisis is premature. They point to Rangers' successful run in the European Champions' League two years ago when the Ibrox side came within 90 minutes of the final, and say one bad season does not spell disaster. Willie Miller, captain of the 1983 European Cup-Winners' Cup victors, Aberdeen, and now their manager, said: 'Two years ago we were shouting from the rooftops how good our game was. It does not go from that stage to this in such a short time. Yes, this year has been unfortunate. But our club sides will be back in Europe next season.'

Miller was one of 10 Premier Division managers questioned in a recent newspaper investigation into the state of Scottish football. Asked why the national game was in decline, some blamed the overwhelming dominance of Rangers, who have topped the Premier Division for the last six seasons. Others highlighted an influx of foreign players which, they said, had stifled home-grown talent. Most agreed, however, that if Scottish sides are to compete successfully in Europe in coming years, coaches and players need to transform the traditional Scottish style of play.

Tommy Burns, Celtic's new manager, explained. 'Our club sides tend to be dour, fast, rugged and competitive. Players have great team spirit but they lack ingenuity. If we are going to compete with sides in the great footballing nations we will have to increase our skills level and slow the pace of the game a bit. We have to overhaul our footballing culture.'

Managers and coaches could encourage new ways of playing among existing professionals but, Burns said, increased public investment was needed to create environments in which youngsters could develop their technique. 'We in Scotland have failed to invest in football,' he explained. 'Unlike England, we don't have a national soccer school, nor any indoor pitches where young players can practise their skills during the winter months when many outdoor training grounds are unfit for play.

'Other European countries, in particular the Scandinavian nations which used to be something of a footballing joke, have not been so short-sighted. They have poured millions of pounds into the game in recent years developing just such facilities. And look at the results. In the past two years, Denmark have won the European Championship, Sweden came third in the World Cup and Norway, unlike Scotland, qualified for USA 94.'

SFA officials are pinning their hopes for the future on new investment and a youth development programme which, they say, will create a new skills base. The association has published coaching guidelines to encourage seven-a-side games for children under 12, with smaller pitches and goals, in an effort to foster more patient, skilful play. At the same time, 22 recently appointed community development officers are working to promote the 'new football' in schools and colleges.

'Kids today have a huge choice of leisure activities,' Ross Mathie, development officer at the SFA said. 'We have to invest in football to ensure that it can compete with other sports and rival attractions like computers and videos. That means setting up attractive indoor training centres which can be used all year round. There, we can teach them the skills they will need to become tomorrow's professionals – the people who will guarantee Scotland a place at the highest level of European and international competition in the next century. We cannot afford to fail.'

Independent, 20 October 1994

Changing the Rules
Steve Coppell

My decision to try and return to football management has caused quite a stir in those closest to me. How can a reasonably sane young man, having endured the slings and arrows of outrageous fortune for nine years as a manager, actually want to go back to that existence?

My career move might seem even more inexplicable given that I have been in a position during my sabbatical to represent the group of people with the most experience in the game – the managers – in various footballing forums. In doing so, I have been able to ensure that managers have a significant influence on the future direction of the game.

The degree of puzzlement has been amplified by the current hysteria that surrounds football, both on and off the pitch. Because of my involvement in the Premier League inquiry into the game's finances, it would be wrong to air my views here on off-the-field matters. However, the apparent 'refereeing crisis' is something that has occupied my thinking for a good part of this season.

On behalf of the LMA, I have been actively trying to improve communication between referees, managers, players and supporters. At the beginning of the season, the new FIFA mandatory guidelines – including the instruction to referees always to show yellow cards for certain offences – did not cause any major tremors in the game.

The World Cup had shown the positive effect the changes could have, and the pre-season meetings here between referees, managers and players ensured that everyone knew exactly what was going to happen. There was a willingness by all parties to support the new initiative.

The football at the beginning of the season, and to a large extent now, was the brightest and most fluent I had seen in English football. Everyone was congratulating each other, and the most important people in football – the spectators – appeared to be the biggest winners.

Then the secondary effects began to come through. Referees, constantly reminding us that they are only human, had genuine mistakes highlighted, replayed and dissected by the television pundits, whose attitude changed from complimentary to highly critical overnight.

Players, and more especially managers, who had tried to conform to the new spirit despite the apparent injustices, have slowly returned to old ways. Now refereeing decisions are regularly being called into question because players and managers know that an offence can result in a red card and suspension.

The effect of the large number of yellow and red cards is growing all the time. More and more players are being suspended for reaching 21, 31 and 41 disciplinary points, with some even verging on 51. Key players are missing large chunks of the season, and many believe it is not the players' fault.

Most importantly, it is the paying customers who are missing out. We have all seen that it is not much fun watching 11 play against nine. When you buy a season ticket at the beginning of a season, you do not want to find one of your team's best players forced to sit out four games at a vital time of the year.

In a game as physically competitive as football, indiscipline will always be with us. What we therefore need to look at is the way that transgressions are punished.

The biggest criticism made of referees has always been an alleged lack of consistency. I believe that referees this season have been more consistent than ever before. However, more consistency brings robotic performances, with referees unable to use common sense. It means that if a player kicks the ball away in a meaningless show of petulance, then he must be cautioned.

I have been told of one non-League defender who, coming to the end of a long career without ever being booked, found himself being cautioned for a poorly timed tackle. When he complained to the referee about his proud record being destroyed, he was promptly sent off for dissent.

Consistency means that the offence is being punished with no consideration of the personalities involved, the stage of the game, or the often understandable emotions involved.

At this stage of the season, when relegation and its consequences are a real threat, many managers have reacted loudly. With the press quite happy to encourage this, many managers have put their tongues into overdrive, and quite a few have to answer Football Association charges as a consequence.

More and more clubs will be sending videos to the FA, hoping that referees will review their decisions and perhaps change a sending-off to a caution. There will also be a growing chorus of appeals for a fourth official to use current television wizardry to assist the referee. In short, the pressure for decision-making perfection has produced more controversy to fill the back pages.

FIFA has been inventive and innovative in its rule adjustments over the past couple of seasons. Many people now feel that two new proposals would eliminate a number of problems in the game.

The first concerns dissent and kicking the ball away. These offences have led to a succession of yellow and red cards this season.

Where these offences have been committed after the award of a free-kick, I believe a more appropriate punishment would be to move the free-kick 10 metres closer to the offender's goal. This would reduce such transgressions to a minimum and make for a better spectacle, as rugby found after introducing a similar rule.

The second change would deal with what has been the main area of controversy this season – the large number of sending-offs after fouls which have denied goal-scoring opportunities, whether inside or outside the penalty area. Surely the ideal punishment for this should not be a red card, but to give the attacking team back their goal-scoring opportunity.

This could be done by awarding a penalty, even if the offence is committed outside the box. For example, under this rule Neil Ruddock would not have been sent off in Liverpool's FA Cup game against Burnley last week, but Burnley would have been awarded a penalty. There would still be huge arguments, of course, but at least with 22 players on the pitch there would be a better contest for the full 90 minutes.

To be fair to the FA, I know for a fact that they have tried to propose the immediate 10-metre punishment to FIFA, which has a very complicated procedure for changing the rules. However, because of lack of support, the proposal was not accepted.

It would seem that FIFA only like rule changes proposed from within, and initiated by the prospect of financial gain from World Cup television income. Perhaps we should hope for every World Cup to be held in the United States.

Independent, 13 February 1995

Chapter Three

The Players

Self-destruct Cantona
Jim White

Wednesday night was one of the most depressing of my life. I sat at Selhurst Park and watched the player who had given me more pleasure than any self-destruct. Around me the United fans shared the same emotions: shame, disappointment, sorrow. We always knew in the back of our mind that we had the most volatile player in United's history on a short-term tenancy rather than freehold, and we sensed, as he slugged it out with some wobbly jowelled south London xenophobe, that the tenancy was over. We felt bereaved: as in all bereavements the sorrow was not for the person who has gone but for ourselves, those left behind to face life without him.

None of us, however, were surprised. The very genetic characteristics that make Cantona a genius as a footballer are those which make it almost certain he will implode.

When, in November 1992, he arrived at an Old Trafford which had not seen the championship trophy for 26 years, there was a long tradition behind him of purchased forwards who had been destroyed by the expectations of the place. So stomach-wrenching was the nervous anticipation of the task ahead for Alan Brazil, for instance, that he threw up before each of his games for United. Cantona felt no nerves on arrival. Why should he? He had an unswerving conviction in his own ability. Immediately he played with an audacity which was breathtaking: his first pass as a United player was an outrageous defence-splitter. He won us over with that touch, changed overnight from being a one-eyebrowed Leeds git into a demigod.

Over the next two years Cantona became the King. With no fear of the consequences of his actions, he would try things other players would not contemplate, whether for fear of ridicule, for fear of failure, or for fear of the manager's fury. And when those things came off, he added a dimension to the team that had not existed before: a Double-winning dimension.

But the man who did not worry about messing up a back flick equally did not concern himself with what might happen – sending-off, suspension, fines – should he exact revenge on an opponent with a stud. He just did it.

This is the conflict within Cantona: the temperament that allowed him to succeed as a player is fundamentally unsuited to a sport which requires its practitioners to abide by the rules. One minute he was inspiring his team-mates with a goal, the next he was jeopardising their efforts with a kick. Alex Ferguson, the best man-manager in British football, knew this about Cantona: the one came with the other. You could not legislate for someone who did not think before he acted, so you swallowed hard and got the best out of him while you could. Two and a half years of Cantona was more than anyone else has managed.

Thus it was no surprise to those of us who loved him that, three days after we thought he had won us the championship with a wonder goal against Blackburn, he would do his best to lose it by removing himself from the competition. After near-misses with the crowds at Swindon, Leeds and Southampton, he finally stepped through the invisible curtain which separates fan from player. When confronted by an ugly, foul-mouthed yob yelling abuse three feet from our chins, most of us would like to lash out. But we don't.

All sorts of filters and checks come into play: we worry he might hit us back; we worry we might get arrested; were we professional footballers we might worry that our boot sponsors would disown us should we use their product in that way. So we would walk away. Cantona has no checks: he simply acts. There is a nobility, a purity, a heroism about someone who behaves so absolutely.

Of course the filters which control us are the cement which binds society: some might call them the mechanisms of civilisation. If we went around administering the drop-kick that prats richly deserve, chaos would ensue. Nevertheless some of the comments about

Cantona have been ludicrous. Roy Hattersley, on *Newsnight*, said his assault was the worst thing that has ever happened in a British football ground: you can be sure the families of the 93 Hillsborough victims would not agree. We have to have rules and Cantona has to be punished for transgressing them: a rest of the season ban, and a charge of actual bodily harm seem appropriate to me.

And until, should it happen, the day he reappears again in a red (or black or blue and white with bits on) shirt, we have to take comfort in the gag circulating in Newcastle at the moment. It was lucky it wasn't Andy Cole who launched a drop-kick at that fan, the Geordies reckon. Because he would have missed.

Independent, 28 January 1995

Alan Shearer
Glyn Wilmshurst

Sardines and trawlers don't regularly feature in Alan Shearer's press interviews. For the Blackburn striker, quotations from French philosophers à la Eric Cantona are out. Shrieking rows with journalists are definitely out. And two-footed kung-fu kicks at supporters are unimaginable. In fact a greater contrast between two brilliantly talented footballers would be difficult to find.

Where Cantona, last season's PFA Player of the Year, is hot-headed and unpredictable, Shearer, the 1995 players' choice, is cool, hard but, dare we say it – wholesome. He comes across as one of the most genuine of the Premiership's star players.

Shearer's phenomenal scoring record at Blackburn – more than 30 goals for the second consecutive season – has driven the Lancashire club towards the Championship title. It has also offered a much-needed boost to the game's credibility. In a season of shock and scandal, Shearer's success has been a massive relief.

The respect from his peers was clear when the 24-year-old picked up the PFA trophy at the glitzy ceremony at a Park Lane hotel. For all the dramas of drugs, bungs and riots, the best player in the country typified all the virtues of a half-imagined yesteryear – modest, tough and fair.

He has already banged in 31 league goals this season for a club which, despite resentment from other fans about the size of Jack Walker's wallet, is a reminder of a previous era, when Blackburn won three FA Cup finals in a row. With his baggy shorts, broad shoulders and unflashy style, Shearer himself could have stepped out of a long-gone era before drugs and bungs.

The Blackburn centre-forward stepped up to accept the players' top award on the day Crystal Palace fan Paul Nixon was killed at the FA Cup clash against Manchester United. Football needed leadership and Shearer was up to the challenge.

'When I looked round and saw so many good young players, lads like Robbie Fowler, and I thought that if we have problems, and to be fair it is obvious that we have – we also have the means to solve them,' he said.

'We have to see what we do as a privilege. I've learned that anything can be achieved by a little bit of hard work. I look at the list of previous winners, names like Kenny Dalglish, and I get tremendous pride from being placed alongside such a man.'

'Shearer is what it is all about,' said Robbie Fowler after picking up the PFA Young Player of the Year Award. 'The game can't be too bad if it can produce someone like him.'

Even Blackburn boss Kenny Dalglish, never known to dish out praise without good reason, took the opportunity to publicly applaud his star man. Dalglish said: 'You look at all a player's qualities when you see him play – and then you meet him and you look for other things, other strengths. You hope for something extra, something special and when I met Alan Shearer, when I saw his Mum and Dad, I realised I had found it. He has done so much for his club and his game. I'm not sure people realise quite how much character it took for him to come back from his injury. He could have disappeared but he fought back to where he is today, at the top. If the future of football was in Alan's hands we wouldn't have a thing to worry about.'

In temperament he is cool and unflappable. Press criticism of Blackburn's play doesn't rile him. The pressure to score, to keep Blackburn at the top of the Premiership, sits lightly on his shoulders. 'If you can't handle being top of the league then you don't deserve to be there,' he says. 'The top is the place to be and we are thoroughly enjoying it. It's great to be in this position after tasting life at the bottom with Southampton. Of course there's a lot of pressure but it is pressure we are enjoying. I'd sooner be at the top than the bottom. There's a lot more pressure at the bottom when you're fighting for your Premiership status.'

And Blackburn's playing style – what about all those jibes about 'machines'? 'We can play in more than one way,' he says. 'We can play attractive football but the lads are also very hard-working as well.'

Gordon Strachan picked up a special Merit award at the PFA ceremony, then pitched in with his own explanation of Shearer's rapid rise to stardom. The secret? Kenny Dalglish.

'He has grown tremendously at Blackburn but then when you look at his boss Kenny Dalglish it's not so much of a surprise,' says Strachan. 'What qualities Shearer has, and they are great, it has to be a bonus working with Dalglish. He was one of the greatest players, yet the most striking thing about him was his humility. It has rubbed off on Shearer.'

Shearer may not have the skills to match that of Dalglish in his prime. What he does have is the power, directness and sheer strength of the classic English number nine. The £3.3 million transfer from Southampton in July 1992 was a landmark for both player and club.

For Blackburn, who had out-fought Manchester United for the Geordie's signature, it was proof that they were willing to compete with the big boys – and win. Even the financially mighty United were not prepared to match the cash put up by Jack Walker.

For Shearer it was the chance to prove he could be a great goalscorer. He told *The Game*: 'I've always scored goals. But many people looking at my record for Southampton (a goal every three and a half games) would not say I was a prolific scorer. Things have gone well for me at Blackburn but what I have achieved is down to the team. The players' award is a tremendous honour but without my team-mates I would not be there. Right now I just want to keep on enjoying my football. One day I may be interested in a move to Italy but at the moment I am very happy at Blackburn with Kenny Dalglish.'

It has been an amazing three years at Ewood Park. Shearer's goals immediately made the difference between a good team and a brilliant team. When he picked up a serious knee injury during his first season – having already netted 22 goals in 23 games – Blackburn's form dipped dramatically. But with Shearer largely injury-free this season, Blackburn have maintained a remarkable consistency. 'Last season we also played very well but we were beaten to the title by a better side,' he says. 'But we still have to remember we haven't won anything yet.'

Most Premiership champions would expect a few troughs on the path to glory but Blackburn's have been reserved to the cups. That exit at the hands of Swedish part-timers Trelleborgs was a massive blow at the time. But looking back it may have been a blessing in disguise, allowing Blackburn to focus on the Premiership.

'I'm not so sure,' he says. 'It has helped us to focus on the Premiership. But at the same time we'd still prefer to be in Europe, we'd still like to be in the cups.'

So where now for Shearer? If there are areas of his game that concern him, he's not going to advertise them. 'There's no such thing as a perfect player. There are always little things that you can improve on. But weaknesses? I don't talk about the weaknesses.'

Then there's England. Next season could be Alan Shearer's arrival on the international stage. He is already valued at three times the amount Kenny Dalglish paid for him. But if he performs for Blackburn in Europe and England at Euro '96, that figure could spiral still further.

England needs a successor to Gary Lineker. And for all the talk about the almost unnatural depth of English talent in attack, neither Shearer, Cole, Collymore or Fowler have yet had the chance to absolutely prove they will be world class strikers.

Shearer is the heir apparent. Comparisons with Gary Lineker are inevitable. Both score goals for fun. Both are cool and reflective. Both began their careers looking like professionals under the spotlight, giving little away to pushy pressmen. Neither would celebrate a goal by ripping off their shirts and hurtling towards the fans, or doing an impression of Elvis.

'I celebrate the traditional way, perhaps punching the air is the most you will get out of me,' he says. 'You won't find Alan Shearer doing hand stands, head flips or laps of honour.'

Shearer, it appears, will also be asked to perform the same role that so often frustrated Lineker for England – the lone striker. Shearer says the differences in playing styles between England and Blackburn, where he can feed off Chris Sutton, are not as great as many people think.

'It's different. But it's not so much harder playing the lone role.

When you've got players like Peter Beardsley and David Platt coming up in support you will not be isolated,' he says. For now his international record reads – played 14, scored 5. Lineker scored 48 goals for his country. The race is on.

The Game, May 1995

The arrival of German international Jürgen Klinsmann at Tottenham Hotspur was like a breath of fresh air in the English game. At first they said he was a 'diver' and that he would never be able to adapt. But by the end of the season the press had voted him Player of the Year.

JÜRGEN KLINSMANN
Hunter Davies

If Jürgen Klinsmann didn't exist, no one would make him up. A footballer who speaks four languages fluently? You must be joking. One of the world's best-known players, yet he has no agent and doesn't charge for interviews? Pull the other. Drives a 1967 Beetle and gives money to Greenpeace? Give over. Has no laddish tendencies, is pleasant to everyone, and is so nice he makes Gary Lineker look two-faced? Wash your mouth out. So what is he, then? Some sort of saint?

Perhaps the most surprising thing is that three months ago he chose Tottenham. Fresh from the World Cup with Germany, where he scored five goals, he could have gone anywhere. No need to go into Spurs' present problems. Let's just say they haven't exactly got mega pulling power.

They were amazed in Germany that one of their stars should end up in England, of all places, a country which didn't even make the World Cup. They were amazed in England that a blond German should opt for a club with a strong Jewish tradition. Rival fans turned up to jeer at his first match, wearing scuba diving masks and humming the *Dambusters* theme. (Very complicated, this joke, but it refers to his perceived habit of 'diving', ie feigning death when tackled.) That has now stopped, thanks to his own good-humoured responses, such as asking at his first press conference where the nearest diving school was, and thanks to his continued good form, scoring goals galore, entertaining crowds all over the country and practically doubling Spurs' shares and shirt sales. He's this season's hero, admired by small boys everywhere and their mums, a perfect example of the fair-playing, good-living sportsman England once gave to the world; now we have to import them. He even talks about the other 'chaps' in the team, which is not due to some dated language manual but was probably picked up from his manager, Ossie Ardiles, another of nature's Englishmen, this time from Argentina.

A rainy day at Spurs' Mill Hill training ground. Girls and boys bunking off, hoping for autographs. Old men with dogs, getting a free show. Sponsors waiting with contracts. Youth players waiting for life to move on and make them famous. TV people from several nations, waiting for Jürgen. First to grab him was Ian St John and an ITV crew, working on a series for young boys about football skills. 'You probably speak better English than me, ha ha,' said The Saint in his broad Scottish. The director couldn't get over the fact that Jürgen wasn't asking for one penny, yet he'd agreed to a half-hour interview, passing on his wisdom on how to head the ball, turn, trap, volley and shoot. Jürgen got the idea at once, giving his replies in perfect sentences and clear English, apart from some 'v's coming out as 'w's so that volley sounded like wally. 'It is fun, hitting wallies.' How true.

He gave a long answer to one question about boyhood heroes. Did he have any? Yes, but he changed them every day, giving his nicest smile. Which ones exactly? they said, hoping for a neat list. He then started musing philosophically on heroes, about how bad it is to follow people slavishly, how you can abdicate your own responsibilities, look what happens in politics. I bet they don't use any of that.

He is aged 30, even thinner off the pitch than on, nice public school hair, a winning smile but a rather pasty complexion. He comes from Stuttgart where his father has a little bakery business – mum on the front counter, dad in the back, baking away. He has three brothers, one of whom was a good runner, but there are no professional footballers in the family.

At eight or nine he realised he had football gifts – at least, people told him he had, before he himself was aware of it. He left middle school at 16 when a local club, Stuttgart Kickers, then in the second division, offered him professional forms. Any regrets? 'I suppose I could have stayed on and gone to university. A lot of my friends did. I missed out on student life but I have had other experiences they have not had. I did continue at college for two years after I became a footballer, and got a diploma in baking. It was an insurance policy and to please my father.'

At 18, he went to Florida, playing for Stuttgart, and liked it so much he went back on holiday, travelling round on his own. He had several other vacations, touring the States and across Southern Africa. That was really how he learnt his English, forcing himself into situations where he had to speak it.

We'll skip his German football career, his 65 caps, Player of the Year in 1988, World Cup winner in 1990, and jump to Internazionale, of Milan, his first foreign team. 'The money was one attraction. In 1989, they offered me three times what I was getting in Germany. It meant I could be financially secure for life. The other reason was the challenge to learn a new language and understand another mentality.'

He doesn't think he is particularly gifted as a linguist. The club provided a tutor, then it was just a matter of application, sitting down and studying. Most Germans who go abroad do learn the language, he says. Unlike most Brits? He wouldn't comment on that. Such a diplomat.

The Italian mentality was a bit of a shock. 'I am used as a German to being organised, always arriving on time, but in Italy I had to become very tolerant. Something goes wrong in my kitchen, so I ring a workman, who says he'll come at three tomorrow, but he never does and I get very upset, not understanding what is going on. In the end, Italy taught me to be tolerant of other people. That was good for me.'

Other culture shocks in Italy included drinking, or the lack of it. 'In Germany, if you have a few beers then say no thanks, I've had enough, they will make fun of you. In Italy, that never happens. They are very sensible about alcohol. In a crowd of 90,000 at the San Siro stadium, you won't find one drunk.'

He found the Italians very creative, very sociable, very friendly. 'I like being able to go into a cafe, have an espresso, and talk easily to complete strangers.' And the football? 'Oh, I never had problems playing football. It was the best in Europe, when I was there, while the German league had not been as good. Now I think it has balanced out. The standard of football in Germany, Italy, Spain, France and England is much the same.'

In 1992, he moved on to Monaco. The culture shock was not too great as half the locals spoke Italian, but none the less he settled down to learn French from scratch, enrolling at a language school. 'What was totally different about living in Monaco was that their main thing in life is not football, unlike Italy or Britain. Monaco get low gates and most people are more interested in international business than in football. That made life very interesting, observing a different mentality.'

His success in last year's World Cup attracted offers from all over the world, especially when it emerged he was not going back to Monaco. 'My contract there was for two years. I could have stayed longer, but I wanted to move. That's the sort of person I am. I am a traveller. I like new experiences.'

He had arranged his own contract with Monaco, giving himself an escape clause. 'Why do I need an agent? All I need is the services of a good lawyer and a good tax adviser. These people are a help, if you work in different countries as I do.'

Genoa were very keen, but he'd had his Italian experience. Atlético Madrid was very tempting, as he had never played or lived in Spain, but in the end he plumped for Spurs. A famous club, yes, one which he had enjoyed watching on TV as a boy in the Seventies, but then he had also liked watching Manchester United and Liverpool. There were other British clubs interested, but what seems to have played a vital part was the thought of living in London, a city he had only visited once, playing for Germany at Wembley. 'I know nothing about the English lifestyle so I said to myself, let's go there.'

About the first thing he did, on arrival in July, was take an open-top tourist bus ride round the sights. He still can't get over the cosmopolitan nature of London, the different faces and races, the different cultures and communities. 'I drive round on my days off and find that each little area has its own character.' Most London-based players live well out, on mock-Georgian new estates. Jürgen has taken a flat in inner London, not far from Regent's Park. He is not married but lives with an American girl, so it is said. 'I never talk about my private life.'

The club provided him with the latest, smartest BMW, which

rather embarrassed him at first, thinking he was being given special treatment. But it turned out to be a sponsorship deal, available to all the first team. However, he hardly uses it and is thinking of giving it back, now that he's brought over his old but beloved VW Beetle from France. He bought it second hand, 10 years ago. It looked strange in the first team car park, amid the glitter. But then so does he, dressed in his faded jeans and floppy windcheater jacket, compared with the flash suits that most star players wear. He usually looks as if he is off backpacking, rather than to Tramp.

Why didn't he charge for that TV interview? They expected it, and will no doubt promote it using his name. 'I agree to very few things, but when I do, and they are no trouble to me, I never ask for money. If it is a bother, such as last night, when I had to go to a TV studio across London to do a German broadcast, then I will ask them to make a contribution to charity. Last night I said pay a cancer organisation. No, I don't know how much. I leave it to them, but I don't think I get taken for a ride. I know what the rate should be.'

Why not keep the money? 'The answer is simple. I have enough.' He gives generously to Greenpeace and various environmental causes, but says he is a passive not an active supporter. In Germany they confused his Greenpeace interest with the Green Party, which he is not a member of. 'I have political opinions but not a political party.' Oh, more diplomacy. Perhaps he'll become some sort of sporting ambassador when the time comes to retire from football.

He has agreed to two years at Spurs, after which he has no idea what he'll do – but he'll be moving on, somewhere. How about America? 'I am watching their new league with interest, and it seems logical they will succeed this time. The problem for me in the future is not to decide what to do but where to do it. I have not chosen the country yet where I want to live. At the moment, it is between Germany and Italy. But we will see.'

In the meantime, he is improving his English. Not with lessons this time, as this is the first foreign country where he has arrived with a basic knowledge, but by listening. 'Every day I learn a new word.' Not rude ones, I hope. You know how footballers talk. 'No, today I learnt "goose pimples".' Could be very handy, in the wintry months ahead.

Independent, 25 October 1994

Ryan Giggs
Giles Smith

If you play out on the wing, you can hear what the crowd is saying. So, on Saturday afternoons at Old Trafford, Ryan Giggs must have heard these harsh, intolerant voices, thick with frustration. 'Giggs!' they shout. 'Giggs! You *poof*!'

Up in the stands, Giggs' girlfriend hears what's going on, too. She is Dani Behr, a television presenter, and some of the abuse is directed her way. 'Stop screwing Giggsy,' someone shouted at her the last time she was there. 'Cos you're screwing up his game.'

'Giggs at full throttle [is] the most thrilling sight in English football,' wrote Hugh McIlvanney, but that was a year ago. Since when Giggs has begun to look like some kind of victim; of the ragged impatience of football fans, certainly, but also of his own fame and even, to some extent, of the system at the club which produced him.

Ryan Giggs of Manchester United is 21 today and if you're thinking of getting him a present, what he would probably like more than anything is his form back. Nearly everyone agreed, at least for a while: he was the best since Best. It was a lot to do with his balance, the way Giggs could spin and switch and stay on his feet. And it had to do with his pace as well, the way he would push the ball past defenders, lean forward and set off after it – the Giggs run.

All this and good looking, too. United fans pinned his picture to their walls and assembled their personal memory reels of Giggs moments: like his goal against QPR last season. He received the ball on the halfway line and by the time he had finished running there were six QPR players lying on their backs. And also one member of his own side, for good measure.

But then it went wrong. Playing for Wales last season, he took a knock on his ankle, the first injury of his career. It was nothing serious, but it has returned to bug him. He lost form for a patch, then partially regained it as the season ended. This year, though, when not injured or sat on the bench, he has played poorly, passed wildly, has even disappeared from games, which used to seem unthinkable. And his worry seems to have fed on itself. Anxiety seems to possess him when the ball is at his feet.

Off the field is another matter. The day after Manchester United lost 4–0 in Barcelona, Giggs was back in Manchester attending a promotional event for his *Soccer Skills* series, now on Channel 4. The irony of Giggs appearing weekly on national television and telling kids how to cross the ball is not lost on United fans. It's another demonstration of the widening gap they perceive between the on-field achievement and the media package.

The fans see Giggs' face on the front of stylish magazines – *GQ*, *FHM* – and wonder about his priorities, their admiration curdling into ridicule. In the current number of *Red Issue*, an independent Manchester United fanzine, the back page is given over to a 'Spot the Spot' competition. They've taken a photograph of Giggs and brushed out the birthmark on his forehead. 'Using your skill and judgement,' the rubric says, 'place an X where you think the melanoma should be.'

The opportunity to exploit to the maximum a brief commercial life, as footballers will, is relatively new to Giggs. Alex Ferguson, United's manager, kept him away from the media until he was 19. Much was made of this cocooning though in fact this is the general rule at Manchester United and was not devised specifically for Giggs. But his release into the public eye has coincided cruelly with his loss of form.

To show youthful talent in a Manchester United shirt is to court an extraordinary weight of expectation. No football supporters are more tenaciously nostalgic for a golden age – the 1960s of Georgie Best, Denis Law and Bobby Charlton. The attention is a kind of optimism, but it is ready to sour in an instant, when the passes stop connecting, when the goals cease to come. When Best shone against Benfica in 1966, the opposing fans called him 'El Beatle' in dazzled admiration. After Barcelona this year, *Red Issue* christened Giggs, in derision, 'El Take That'.

In the case of Giggs, the familiar build-up-to-knock-down narrative takes a sick twist. Fêted as the new Best, he must now be seen to go the way of Best. In the tabloids and among the fans, the stories bubble and hiss; that Giggs is in the Hacienda club on a Friday night before the match; that he's hit the bottle; that he's girl crazy; that he's in with the team's bad boys, ladding it up. These are stories without substance. Yes, you will see Giggs occasionally at the ritzy Home Club in Manchester, along with other United players and, on a good night, Mick Hucknall. But Giggs also goes home to his mum's for lunch. People close to the team say he is as seriously committed to his football as ever he was.

Manchester United have made no secret of the fact that their central ambitions lie in Europe. They realise that football may come to be played out between the top dogs in a jet-set Euro-league. They intend to have the clout and the cash when the time comes. And the commercial exploitation of Giggs is part of that plan.

'The anti-Giggs faction,' says Richard Kurt, the author of *United We Stood*, 'would say that Giggs should be doing extra training, not poncing around in bookshops.' Kurt is referring to the recently published autobiography, *Ryan Giggs: My Story*, for which the author has already done three separate book-signing appearances in Manchester. This is not the product of some outside deal struck by Giggs: the book is a Manchester United publication, one item in an official merchandise operation which handled £10m last year, 30 per cent of company turnover. (Opening this Saturday at Old Trafford: the new 'Man U Megastore'. It looks like a Sainsbury's.)

As such, *My Story* is an insight into how the club thinks Giggs is best marketed, how he can be made to do his bit for Manchester United plc. Most of the book is pictures and some of the pictures show Giggs in a football kit, playing football. But also there are studio shots of him perching on large white cubes in adventurous knitwear with his black curls teased and gelled. Up to a point, Giggs carries this male model business off: not at a high fashion level, maybe, but some of the images look like pictures you might see hanging in the hairdresser's.

But then there are the oddly lascivious child-shots, Giggs all wet-lipped and doe-eyed, which put you in mind of Macauley Culkin. And then there are the soft porn poses – Giggs topless with his hands behind his neck, his torso cutely angled, glistening with sweat, or more likely sprayed-on water. This is a photo session that even Best at his most saturnalian might have blanched at. And in one of these shots in particular, arms crossed high up on his chest, wearing an unsteady smile, Giggs looks vulnerable, uneasy, like he doesn't belong here, a footballer without a shirt on.

These photographs are taken pre-September 1994, when Giggs still had curls to tease. After this season's Charity Shield match, television replayed numerous times an action sequence in which Giggs could be seen at the periphery, wiping his fringe from his eyes. His team-mates ribbed him mercilessly, so Giggs went off and got himself a tight crop, a kind of snubby, bullet-headed number, not unattractive but plainly functional. Except that when you're Ryan Giggs, you can't visit the barber without consulting your agent or checking in with your endorsement people. And this, Giggs had omitted to do.

At Reebok, the sportswear manufacturers whose product Giggs endorses, anxious executives convened in emergency session. They were paying £100,000 a year for a player with fancy hair, not for a skin-head. From their point of view, this wasn't a haircut, it was asset stripping. Thus is the Samson myth fittingly rewritten for our times: the lithe and capable hero has his locks shorn and his sponsors promptly come over all weak.

Giggs is caught between how Manchester United plc and Reebok see him and how the press does, and perhaps the remarkable thing is how sane he has stayed; or that he has stayed sane at all. Giggs' trial for United took place a month after his 13th birthday. He joined the club at 14, went into the first team at 17.

He seems to owe a kind of calm to his mother, Lynne. In one recent questionnaire he declared she was 'the greatest love of his life'. Unlike Best, Giggs was born in Manchester and is therefore living in his home town, which to some degree must root and normalise him. He has friends from school still about him. They protect him from outsiders and from himself.

Those who deal regularly with him speak of his willingness to look people in the eye, maintaining that he is bright and pleasant and self-possessed, that he is well-placed to deal with the problem at hand, which is recovering his own belief.

With a player like Giggs, this cannot be a simple question of putting in the hours of training, upping his effort levels. His play is, to some degree, about effortlessness. Languid is part of the deal. How do you *try* to be Ryan Giggs? How can you *try* to be inspired? He may just have to wait.

But who would write *anyone* off at 21? Certainly not the younger Giggs fans. Here at least Giggs finds an unquestioningly loyal constituency. When the Queen visited Dartmouth recently and the public failed to turn out, some local schoolchildren were interviewed on the radio about their reluctance to show up and wave flags. Evidently the Royals weren't really their thing. Had it been Ryan Giggs, they said, it would have been different.

Independent, 29 November 1994

Like Ryan Giggs, Peter Marinello was another tagged 'the next George Best'. In 1970 he joined Arsenal from Hibernian. Great things were expected, but it all ended in tears.

Marinello's Lesson
Robert Philip

Ten o'clock on a bleak November morning and Blue Star FC prepare themselves for another game in the local Sunday amateur league; bootlaces tied, hangovers cursed, latest female conquests compared, they kick off with an excited rush.

On the touchline, a lone figure shrouded in the misty drizzle listens to the familiar sounds of sporting battle, allowing his thoughts to wander to a private place these young gallants he coaches can never know. What was it his wife had asked him that morning? 'How long does it take to get there?' – meaning this exposed playing field on the outskirts of Bournemouth. 'Oh, about 25 minutes,' he had replied. 'Or 25 friggin' years,' he thought to himself, 'if you go via Arsenal, Portsmouth, Fulham, Phoenix . . .'

For one brief, shining moment, Peter Marinello was the most celebrated footballer in the land. When he joined Arsenal as a 19-year-old on New Year's Day, 1970, his £100,000 transfer from Hibernian was reported on the nine o'clock news. A normally constrained Highbury director crowed: 'We have signed the nearest thing in soccer to The Beatles.'

Within days of his arrival in London, Marinello had duly made a guest appearance on Top of the Pops, introducing Pan's People . . . was given a weekly column in the *Daily Express* . . . had signed a contract to model the clothes of Italian fashion designer Nino Cerutti . . . been booked to appear on 20ft-high advertising bill-boards encouraging the nation to Drinka Pinta Milka Day . . . and marked his debut for Arsenal at Old Trafford by beating three Manchester United defenders in a mazy, Matthews-esque dribble to score a wonder goal. Oh, how the fans on the North Bank adored their Scottish George Best.

A quarter of a century has passed but Marinello will cheerfully turn out on the wing even yet in an emergency, for at the age of 44 the wondrous skills are still there . . . unlike the money, the fame, the sports car, the houses, the fickle friendships and the many business partnerships. Largely forgotten by the sport he once graced – though he remains a cult hero to former boxing champ Gary Mason, the Big Breakfast's Chris Evans and his other cronies on the Arsenal Celebrities & Veterans XI – he is reduced to living on welfare.

Marinello was back in the news last week when, years after the failure of his two pubs and Tenerife disco, he was finally declared bankrupt. Thus today, which happens to be the 21st birthday of the Welsh George Best (a.k.a. Ryan Giggs), he will report to his nearest Job Centre seeking work.

Yet his is not a maudlin tale; despite some newspaper reports suggesting he has become a bitter recluse, raging against the coaches who systematically suffocated his delicate football skills and the business advisers who became rich at his expense, there is nary a trace of self-pity detectable. Giggs's youth, his much-appreciated talent, his fame, even his financial security, reveal no deep-seated resentment in Marinello.

'Oh, I desperately wish things had worked out better for me and my family these past years,' says Marinello with the merest tinge of regret in a voice which has lost little of its original east Scotland brogue. 'But I had a brilliant time while it lasted. Arsenal were great to me and London was like Disneyland to an Edinburgh teenager back in the Seventies.'

As with George Best 200 miles to the north, Marinello's life became a dizzying blur of starlets, nightclubs and financial schemes. 'That's where Ryan Giggs has to be a wee bit careful. I was too easily led, as was Bestie. But I think Alex Ferguson has been very clever in the way he's handled him. From what I gather, Ryan is pretty level-headed and the credit for that must go to Fergie. He's still only a young lad, so his form is bound to dip at times. But Ryan definitely has the ability to become the greatest player of his generation.'

Exactly the destiny laid before Marinello by many wise old owls all those years ago. Jock Stein, for instance, who allowed him to train with the Hibernian first team at the age of 13, Bob Shankly (brother of Bill), whose only tactical advice was 'go oot and run rings roon' them', and Bertie Mee, who was persuaded to part with a fortune after seeing Marinello run rings roon' Glasgow

Rangers at Ibrox, scoring twice in a 3–1 victory which proved a personal triumph.

It was never to be. Having signed a daring free spirit, Mee and his assistant Don Howe quickly discovered they had no idea what to do with him. The Arsenal supporters loved this young touchline god who was as beautiful as Narcissus, as swift as Mercury, and who would drift past full-backs as though carried by the breeze, but Mee and Howe detected an Achilles' heel. Expressions such as work-rate, tackling back and auxiliary midfielder were all Greek to the young Scot with the Italian name.

In three years Marinello made but 35 fleeting appearances in Arsenal red. 'Perhaps I went to the wrong club. Maybe if I'd gone to Spurs, who also wanted to sign me, I'd have been allowed more freedom. I was a bit of a rebel. Bertie Mee and Don Howe would bombard me with tactics in the dressing room, but as soon as I went out on the pitch I did my own thing. I'd beat the same full-back three times just for the hell of it. Did the crowd no' love that? And as I saw it, my job was to entertain them.'

In 1970–71, Arsenal achieved the League and FA Cup double with the workaholic George Armstrong in the No 7 shirt; from August through to May, Marinello was permitted to parade his sumptuous skills on a mere three occasions, all as a substitute. 'I remember before the start of one season Don Howe got me, Eddie Kelly and Charlie George – one of the best three players I ever saw – to start training five weeks before everyone else. "We're going to build a new Arsenal round you," he told us. What happened? First game of the season at Leicester and none of us were picked.'

Marinello was not without his admirers, however, and early in 1972 Arsenal and Juventus reached agreement for his transfer. 'My grandfathers had come to Scotland from Florence and Naples, so in some ways it would have been like going home,' he explained. 'The Italians had a ban on foreign transfers at the time, but Juventus were sure it would be lifted at the end of the season. It was agreed I would stay at Highbury until that April.

'Who said I was born unlucky? The ban wasn't lifted and the deal was off. How much would it have been worth to me? They were talking in telephone numbers, those long international ones with about 14 bloody figures.'

Instead of Juventus, Marinello was eventually transferred . . . to Portsmouth . . . then Motherwell . . . Fulham (for whom he made a mesmerising debut on Boxing Day 1978 which is still talked of in hushed tones down Craven Cottage way) . . . Phoenix Inferno, of the North American Soccer League . . . Hearts . . . Partick Thistle . . . Meadowbank . . . and Blue Star. 'Actually, I think I'll jot down the numbers of all the clubs I've played for as they appear on the pools coupon and have a go at the national lottery. Winning that would solve a few of life's problems,' he said.

Any other regrets? 'Christ, millions of them. Ryan Giggs could retire now, on his 21st birthday, and never have to work again. I wish I'd never listened to everyone who wanted to take my money and make me super-rich. People say I was never as dedicated as Ryan Giggs. That's rubbish. They talk as though I went out and got pissed every Friday night. I never once had a drink after Tuesdays. It may have looked as though I wasn't trying out there at times but, believe me, I was. I'm still trying to this day with Blue Star.

'The trouble with players like me – and Ryan Giggs and George Best for that matter – is we're never so-so. We're either brilliant or sheer crap. We deal in millimetres, flicking the ball away from some great hulking full-back's foot, timing the cross to perfection. We're like bullfighters who love our art so much we never want to go for the kill. And that can be bloody dangerous.

'How do I honestly compare? Well, there's no one to compare with Best, is there? He's up there with Maradona, Cruyff and the rest of them. I was probably better than [Lee] Sharpe, and maybe as fast as Giggs. Whether I might have been as good a player as him is for others to say. I'll tell you this, Kanchelskis and Sharpe might be more effective than Giggs at this moment, but they're nowhere near as talented.'

Next weekend, while Giggs prepares to face Norwich, Marinello will be preparing Blue Star for their game at Hove. 'Of course it's frustrating coaching players not as gifted as yourself,' he said. 'But I've got one young lad here who's as naturally talented as Giggs. It'll be the same old story. I'll curse and swear at them like Mee and Howe used to wi' me, then take them all for a pint. Actually these days, they take me for a pint . . .'

Daily Telegraph, 28 November 1994

Gazza
Pete Davies

Who is Paul Gascoigne, and what was that Gazza monster that got grafted onto him? Promise often goes unfulfilled, but rarely can it have been so very nearly fulfilled before imploding. And seldom has so much money been made out of so much hype and hope along the way. When that twist and spin left two Dutchmen clutching air in a Sardinian penalty area, when that free-kick fell onto Platt's volley in Bologna, when that other free-kick burst the Arsenal net at Wembley, didn't we all say that a player like this was the one-in-a-generation model, an immaculate conception born with a ball where the rest of us have a heart?

Bobby Robson knew him, maybe better than anyone. Before Italia '90 he told me: 'He's daft in his attitude. He's got to learn about the game, how to play it properly – he's still a kid playing backstreet football. Lot of talent, lot of freshness, there's unbelievable things he'll do – but I'm talking about playing Argentina or Brazil, about being in the last eight in the world. You have to be utterly reliable.' And then, with his own special brand of endearingly circuitous logic, Robson tipped him to be one of the players of the tournament, while suggesting he hadn't made his mind up whether he'd even take him.

When he did, of course, it wasn't the skill alone that won so many fans. It was the way the skill was so seamlessly an expression of character, a mix of fearlessness and cheek, as if your favourite naughty kid had been let loose in the toy shop. But the trouble with naughty kids is that when you give them toys they tend to break them and then attitudes begin to change. So with gruesome inevitability, Gascoigne the Clown Prince became Gazza the Brawling Brat, until finally he appeared as a nervy, wounded creature seeking redemption on the Danny Baker show with heart-tugging confessions of insomnia.

Behind that grim public trajectory was Paul Gascoigne ever a knowable character? Even apart from his obvious genius, the question is worth asking because it was Gazza's tears that changed the image of English football.

It's been fashionable, especially since USA '94, to write of Italia '90 as a bad tournament, but no one in England thought so at the time, not as the extraordinary march to that high-octane semi-final unfolded. And when it was over, we found that Gazza's tears had watered the gasping plant. The exploits of the team in which he starred so brilliantly began the rehabilitation of the English game. We got back into Europe. We got Sky TV applying liberal doses of economic compost to keep the flower blooming until today when, cor blimey and Lord love us, even foreign players want to play here.

So football has become funky again. And then it was announced that the man who'd started it all was the subject of a forthcoming 'authorised' biography penned by his agent and ghost. Enough of all this New Lad malarkey, I thought, this is Gazza we are talking here, the drunken grotesque, the cursing, farting, belching, woman-beating bulimic out of 2-D tabloid heaven. Surely this creature's authorised biography could only be the whinge of all whinges?

Under the cover of sweet reason, behind the veil of some half-decent writing, *Ha'way the Lad* is a slimy piece of work. Written by Mel Stein, it seeks to excuse all, to blame all others, to polish up Gazza the product (of which Gazza the player is only a part) for the next sale, and to let us know that Mel Stein himself is just a wonderful guy, as honest as the Irish game is long.

That Gascoigne likes a drink is hardly news, but to have his manager acknowledging it on as many occasions as he does with nary a reprimand in sight must leave any reader with half a brain wondering, well just how much does he drink then? One instance of this reckless indiscretion is the information airily handed over that, at the Is Molas Hotel in Sardinia during Italia '90, Gascoigne 'even bribed the waiters to serve him bottles of fizzy water topped off with a generous amount of wine'. It's tempting to have a titter at the antics of Gazza the Cheeky Chappie, the Larkabout Lad, but hang on, wasn't that the World Cup he was busy drinking at there?

When *All Played Out* appeared after the tournament, I was much accused of indiscretion myself but, writing the book with Gazza on the front pages every day as I did so, one of the things I kept to myself was my own evidence of his private 'refuelling' that summer. Yet here we have his own manager telling it: his own manager who, in a nasty aside, attacks George Best for having 'climbed unsteadily onto the bandwagon' by slagging off his client.

For the football fan it is, at the end of the day, just all desperately sad. Was Gascoigne, this wonderful player, ever a salvageable character? Myself, I think (sadly) probably not. His own manager, confronted with the hard core evidence of the 1991 FA Cup final, speaks of 'demonic instability'.

In the final, Gazza went 'one better' than the semi-final against Arsenal. Venables recalls: 'He used up so much energy in the dressing rooms he knocked himself out. He was nervous, excited. He was wound up and got the players going.' In the final, he was like an overwound clock.

Ian Hamilton, in his slight but rewarding book *Gazza Italia*, analyses whether the player is suffering from some form of Tourette's Syndrome, displaying 'an excess of nervous energy, and a great production of strange motions and notions: ticks, jerks, mannerisms, grimaces, noises, curses, involuntary imitations and compulsions of all sorts, with an odd elfin humour, and a tendency to antic and outlandish kinds of play.'

Certainly, in 1990, there was evidence enough watching Paul Gascoigne to suggest this was no regular sort of fellow. In calm moments he could be sensitive, thoughtful, in his own way almost articulate and, although Stein pushes his better qualities into hagiographic overdrive, he did seem to have a generous and caring side to him.

After Steve McMahon had come on for England against Ireland in the opening game in Cagliari, and within a few minutes gifted Kevin Sheedy the equaliser with his first touch, it was Gascoigne who was around him the next day when McMahon's soul was black: it was Gazza offering some instinctive sort of cheer, some keep-your-pecker-up company.

But then it was also Gazza, a few beers later, driving a golf cart up and down steep banks outside the bar at dangerously lunatic speeds. It was Gazza gawping down his shorts to see if his wedding tackle had a tan. It was Gazza in Bologna playing tennis in the sun until he dropped, right on the eve of the team's game against Belgium. It was Gazza of whose ceaseless, fizzing, manic pranksterism Terry Butcher said quietly: 'He's a good laugh, you get used to him. Mind you, Woodsy's going to twat him one of these days.'

It was Gazza who, seeing Spurs holding a press conference at Chase Lodge (a small house on the club's training ground), leant out of the window and threw a bucket of water over the multitude. Not once, not twice, but four times. And the same Gazza, an hour later, came round to the press officer and, in his best 'Am-I-forgiven' voice said: 'Are you still talking to me?'

And it was Gazza who, fed piece by piece to the cheque book wolves in those crazy, slavering months afterwards, began literally to be a thing of pieces, a man-boy falling to media bits. Stein said then: 'Gazza's in the Beatles league' – and boy, didn't he milk it? The attempt to create a monopoly in the 'Gazza market' led his advisers to try to ban an unauthorised biography of this footballing Beatle. This attempt created legal history when Justice Harman asked Gascoigne's counsel: 'Do you think Mr Gascoigne is more famous than the Duke of Wellington in 1815?' To which Silverleaf replied: 'I have to say I think it's possible.'

Amid the naff books and records, the endorsements and appearances, in October 1990 Gazza 'went berserk' when the *Star* spotted him in a nightclub with a 'leggy lovely'; the same month in another club, he was allegedly getting whipped (not for the last time) by a stripper. In November he called George Best 'a jealous, drunken fat man', and a 'scum bastard'. (Best replied in kind: 'He wears a number 10 jersey. I thought it was his position but it turns out to be his IQ' . . . 'The only thing Gazza and I have in common is we're both white'). In December there was a fracas involving curses, cameras, and autograph books, while in the *Star* you could 'Buy a pair of Gazza's undies.' In the New Year the bookings totted up, along with the mawkish grousing that he wished 'someone else could be me for a week'. (No thanks, pal, not for all the lire in Lazio). And then came that tackle at Wembley, the recovery, the brawls, the transfer, the belch, the fart, and the Jane Nottage book: *Paul Gascoigne, the Inside Story*.

This spectacular piece of gutter-trawling was ill-written, meretricious, and cruelly entertaining; with the bulimia business, and the detailed depiction of domestic turbulence. But looking back, where else was the Gazza trajectory ever headed but this?

Even when Gazza signed for Lazio in 1992, his old boss Terry Venables was already filled with foreboding. 'I'm pleased for him,' he said, 'but it's like watching your mother-in-law drive off a cliff in your new car.'

You cannot court the media – demanding sums of money for interviews that Stein himself describes as 'outrageous' – without making a monster out of the boy. When Stein says of that Cup final tackle that it was an instance of 'demonic instability', he then claims that the instability in question was 'fuelled by the media'. Fair enough, but who fuelled them?

Likeable Lout Makes Millions, Gets Sorely Confused – should we weep for this? Gascoigne himself sheds tears on a regular basis, but I'd reckon a little sad shake of the head would probably do for the rest of us. I'd reckon most of us probably did that a long while ago, too; we don't need *Ha'way The Lad* to stir any last residual sympathy now.

Because the hard fact is that Paul Gascoigne makes more money in a week than many people do in a year. He makes that money, moreover, for doing the one thing he loves above all else. It's certainly true that at the top of his profession he's been unluckier than most, that he's been subjected to more unceasing pressure than most, and that he's less constitutionally capable than most of coping with it.

But, I'd have to say that our sympathy is almost all played out. Why, indeed, should we feel any sympathy for poor little rich people like Gazza or Di who, made by the media, then run to the people who made them to moan that they're being destroyed?

In one laughable moment, as the SS Gazzamania leaves port for these bleak and stormy waters, Stein serves up two abundantly revealing sentences: 'Perhaps the biggest tribute of all to Paul's marketability was Kevin McKenzie, ebullient editor of the *Sun*, insisting on a personal breakfast meeting with Stein and Lazarus. Kelvin was direct and to the point and ate no babies at the table.' No, Mel, he didn't. He waited until he'd had his 'personal breakfast meeting' and then he went away and he ate your client.

And the client, occasionally, seems to have realised this. When topless pictures of his (then) girlfriend, Sheryl Kyle, appeared in the British tabloids Gazza sneered: 'You expect that from the English. Who are they? What do they do? They're nothing. They get paid for writing crap, following people around and getting pissed up. That's all.' And when the 'news bastards' (as Gazza called them, distinguishing them from the sporting press) had all done, the best player of his generation had been hacked almost to death, reduced, finally, to a mess of broken bones and twisted spirit.

If Gascoigne is as unhappy as the tabloid spin-doctors insist, only he (if anyone) can know the source of that sadness. But

Lawrie McMenemy, after one of Gazza's worst performances for England under Graham Taylor, said: 'His unhappiness comes from the frustration of a person with such great natural ability who is wondering why he is unable to produce it as much as he would like.'

Gascoigne played the way he did because it was born in him. His talent wasn't susceptible to the squad drill approach of the English game. That was why the fans loved him so much. As he told the press: 'I just want to be mesel.' All any fan can hope now is that this 27-year-old-man-child can be 'mesel' again on the pitch, for Lazio (or whoever he plays for) and, ultimately, for England.

Since he certainly has the drive and the guts to recover, fans should not give up hope of seeing him play something like his old self again. Whether he can, and for how long he can, who knows? You fear that, as time goes by, his ability to perform will depend more on that refuelling – and later, when time's gone by and the playing days are done, what then? Best ask George, probably. Your heart hopes it's not too late, your head tells you it might well be.

FourFourTwo, March 1995

Unerring Aim – Ian Rush
Frank Keating

Last week, 25,000 Liverpool football supporters paid over a quarter of a million pounds to pay tribute at a testimonial match to the club's goal-scorer of 14 years, Ian Rush. In his 600 matches for the Anfield club the bony, foxy-faced North Walian has potted 330 goals. If he continues his unerring aim, it will not be too long till Rush has in his sights, in the all-time netfinders' hall of fame, George Camsell, who scored 348, Steve Bloomer (352), and Jimmy Greaves (356). But with his next birthday his 34th, Rush is unlikely to overtake the two on the topmost plinth, Dixie Dean, 379, or Arthur Rowley, 434.

I saw Rowley once in the early 1950s, playing for Fulham. My Uncle Vincent took me, and with all the other boys I was passed down like a stretcher-case over the heads of the throng to the touchline riverbank corner at Craven Cottage. Rowley biffed and barged and snorted around the penalty area in the white shirt. When he wasn't snorting he just grinned. He scored a couple – and soon after waddled off to Leicester City, and then down to the Severn of Shrewsbury Town, where he riddled the rigging for hatfuls more.

Dean might have been the Rowley type, but Greaves and by all accounts Bloomer were not hurly-burly bullocks. I saw a lot of Greaves, right through his prime and beyond. What a player – all the old clichés well up and overflow – the baggy-trousered philanthropist who could make as well as take, the artful dodger, the penalty-area pickpocket. His England mate Johnny Haynes used to say, 'Jim would shoot about two seconds before I'd even *thought* about it.'

Was that like Bloomer? One of the game's eminent historians, Ivan Sharpe, played with Bloomer, and wrote, 'Steve scored with *sudden* shooting. His great haul came principally with first-time shots. His was instantaneous marksmanship, aimed at beating the goalkeeper's *eye*.'

Bloomer was Derby County, and Camsell Middlesbrough. The latter was said to hover, inches onside, and then use his speed to burst onto long through-passes from Jack Carr, who said, 'I'd just hit the pass, then sit on my "hunkers" and watch George score.'

The quality of Rush is that he has a bit of every style. In other words, he has the lot. In his time, his long stride, like Camsell's apparently, would leave defenders as rooted as trees. And, like Greaves, his close-quarter work is as delicate as it is terminal: an instinct for minute angles as well as one for killing. And of them all, only Dean was, by repute, probably the better header.

Rush is a delightfully approachable millionaire, self-effacing, with no 'side' at all. His junior club was Chester, but apart from one lucrative if bewildered year with the Italian club Juventus he has been dyed-red Anfield through and through. The Italian supporters were devoted to him, but he could not settle to the food or the language. On his fast return to Liverpool, he cheerfully admitted that as soon as he had arrived at Juventus, 'I knew the writing was on the wall,' adding nicely, 'Not that I could read it, mind you.' He said at least he had learned the Italian to tell waiters how he liked his steaks cooked. 'I just said "*Bravo*" – you know, "well done".'

Bravo: you bet.

Spectator, 24 December 1994

Steve McManaman
Joe Lovejoy

Outside, amid Anfield's tight terraces, there was disbelief, inside, the players were, as usual, at one with the community. 'Grob-smacked.' Bruce Grobbelaar accused of match fixing – say it ain't so.

Liverpool responded the only way they knew how. They went out and overpowered Chelsea 3–1 to climb to third place in the Premier League. For a couple of hours, at least, the scandal was forgotten. Instead, the talk was of a splendidly resurgent team, and what half of them might do for England, given the chance.

Robbie Fowler, who is not in the squad for Nigeria's visit on Wednesday, scored twice, Neil Ruddock, who is, contributed the third. John Barnes had again looked every reduced inch an international midfield player, and Rob Jones was enterprise personified at right-back.

Last, and anything but least, there was Steve McManaman, the Everton supporter made good on the other side of the park. With the whiff of corruption in the air, 'Macca' was like a breath of the fresh stuff, according to the Liverpool manager, Roy Evans.

Ruddock is in line for his international debut on Wednesday, and there will be a few drinking to that, but the most popular selection with the red half of Merseyside would see McManaman, the genuine Scouse article, given the chance Matthew Le Tissier failed to take against Romania last month.

Much taken with the coltish stringbean's form, Terry Venables is pondering playing him in the roving winger's role Darren Anderton had made his own before losing his place through injury.

McManaman, more than Barnes, is Liverpool's ringmaster these days, taking the ball from the back four and dictating the direction, speed and pattern of play. No mean burden, this, for a 22-year-old, but he insists he is thriving on the extra responsibility, and results would seem to bear him out.

For the moment, at least, any manager in the League would pick him ahead of the more celebrated Ryan Giggs. A vote between McManaman and Le Tissier would be closer, but Venables, for one, seems to prefer the Liverpool tyro's greater adaptability and Duracell work-rate.

Unlike The Dell's adored Saint, McManaman will play anywhere – right wing, left wing or all across the line – without complaint, and is prepared to go and hustle for the ball, rather than have others get it for him.

Against Chelsea he did it all: fetching, carrying, crossing and shooting. All a compelling performance lacked was a goal, and there can be no real complaints with his return of six in 13 League games. Last season he managed just two in 30 appearances, and if that had much to do with the nadir of the Souness regime, the improvement also reflects the consistency which, in good players, comes with maturity.

For all his autocratic faults, Souness was always prepared to give youth its head, and McManaman was tossed in and invited to sink or swim at 19. He swam. Scoring in his second game, away to Manchester City in August 1991, he went on to play 32 games in the League that first season. No forward played more.

It was not easy, coming into a team in decline. With the senior players resistant to his clenched-fist methods, Souness turned increasingly to the more pliable, impressionable younger ones. The dressing-room split along ageist lines, accelerating the downward spiral. Souness said: 'We're asking boys to do men's jobs, and they are doing better than the men.'

McManaman's even temperament served him well in the dark days when disharmony laid a proud club lower than they had been at any time since Shankly arrived on his messianic mission.

So laid-back they say the dentist treats him without a chair, McManaman ploughed his own furrow, ignoring what he calls the 'ag' (aggravation). Kevin Keegan, who keeps in touch with his old club and still visits their Melwood training ground, is greatly impressed. 'Steve doesn't let things affect him, and that's important if you're going to become a top-class player.'

Ian Rush nods in agreement. 'If anyone I've seen was destined to play for England, it was Steve,' he says. 'I could see it from the first time he played for Liverpool.'

McManaman blushes. 'I think I'm a pretty level-headed lad, and I don't think about the praise or the criticism. Both can be embarrassing, and I try not to read it. Even when nice things are written about me, I just get stick from the rest of the lads, so I tend to avoid the subject.'

He is going to have to cope with the embarrassment. Venables came away from Liverpool's 3–2 win against Aston Villa five weeks ago singing his praises, and promptly drafted him into the senior squad for the Romania game four days later. Including him from the outset this time, the England coach said: 'I've seen him quite a lot this season, and he has always done well. He has played on the left, in the hole behind Fowler and Rush and on the right. He plays all three positions, often in the same game.'

That was certainly the way of it last Wednesday, when McManaman started on the right, from where he initiated the move that led to Fowler's second goal, but caused most damage in the inside-left channel. 'This season I've been told to use my initiative and move into areas where I think I can create most danger,' he says. 'I can use my own judgement, and I like that freedom.'

Evans, whose carrot is proving more effective than the Souness stick, is only too willing to accommodate his gifted mophead. 'The lad has been a breath of fresh air,' he enthuses. 'If you have one or two of your own in the team – local lads like Robbie [Fowler] and "Macca" – it is a good feeling. For the fans, especially. They see the kid from round the corner, or the guy who lives next door, has made the big time and they love that. As long as the player doesn't act big-time, of course.

'Macca is still one of them at heart, and they know it. As a player, too, he deserves a pat on the back. I've given him the licence to go anywhere on the field, within reason. We were looking for somebody to start us off when we bring the ball out of defence, and he's quite good at that.

'He's capable of getting all over the field because he's got a great engine. He can get across, as well as up and down, the pitch.'

Evans and Venables both ascribe the likely lad's vaulting progress to the same quality – consistency. 'For all young players,' Venables says, 'that is the hardest thing to achieve. Often they start well when they first come into the side, have a bit of a lull after their first season, and then come again. Sometimes, within a year, you can't believe how much someone has improved. That's often because he's catching on quicker than the others.'

Evans puts it another way: 'I think he has been guilty over the last couple of years of being careless or casual. We've got to keep on his case all the time to focus him on being more positive.

'Confidence is a wonderful thing, and it has definitely helped him.

If you're confident enough to think that you're going to score if you get in the right position, then you will score. Rob Jones gets there, but doesn't think he will, so he doesn't. Macca now thinks he'll score every time, or at least make one for someone else.

'If he gets in on Wednesday, I don't think he'll let England down. In our system, he's smashing. I don't know how Terry is going to play on Wednesday, and I don't want to try to pick his team, or influence him in any way because I think he does a great job, but I think that in the right system, with a reasonably free role, he can cause any team problems.'

A beguiling thought. England, too, could do with a breath of fresh air after that stifling draw with the Romanians.

Sunday Times, 13 November 1994

Duncan Ferguson
Simon O'Hagan

The word the Scots use to describe Duncan Ferguson is 'gallus', meaning arrogant, swashbuckling, happy-go-lucky. That's on one of his good days. Unfortunately, Ferguson has his bad days too, when the face he presents to the world is darker, uglier, and more troubled. As he sets about rebuilding his career, with Everton and in Athens today with Scotland, his biggest challenge lies in quelling the battle between these two sides to his nature.

Not since Charlie Nicholas brought his designer skills to Highbury 11 years ago has the arrival of a Scottish forward in English football created such a sense of anticipation as Ferguson's did at Goodison Park last month. Ferguson comes with a reputation, but, unlike Nicholas, there appears to be nothing fickle about the talent upon which it is founded.

Ask almost anybody in Scottish football how good Ferguson is and you have to jump out of the way to avoid the rush of superlatives. Put more simply, as his fellow-international and former Dundee United team-mate Billy McKinlay does: 'He's got everything.' It is his range of abilities that is most impressive about Ferguson, particularly since his build – 6ft 3in and 13-and-a-half stone – suggests a player who is very good at one thing, but one thing only.

Craig Brown, the Scotland manager, says Ferguson is 'as aggressive a header of the ball as you will find', and given his physical attributes, so he should be. But as Brown adds, 'he's far more skilful on the ground than you would imagine – a player who makes as many goals as he scores. He's got vision.' But perhaps what really explains why nearly £8m has been spent on Ferguson in two transfers is that at 22 – 23 in nine days' time – he has the potential to be even better.

The corollary of that is that all too often potential goes unfulfilled. The element of risk in Joe Royle's £4.3m purchase of Ferguson from Rangers, completed last week, is greater than might be expected when such large sums are involved. But this has less to do with how far Ferguson, already an explosive centre-forward, can develop, than the wildness of his behaviour away from football.

In the numerous run-ins he has had with the law, Ferguson comes across merely as the latest in a line of sportsmen who have had difficulty keeping a grip on their lives in the face of success that has come suddenly and soon. Little in Ferguson's upbringing in Stirling prepared him for what would follow when, having been spotted by Dundee United at the age of 12, he made his first-team debut as a big, raw 18-year-old in 1990 and immediately established himself as a pivotal member of the side.

Under the formidable managership of Jim McLean, United were at that time one of the best footballing sides in Scotland. So it says a lot for Ferguson that, as Maurice Malpas, the United and Scotland defender, remembers, the team adapted to accommodate him. 'He was naturally cut out for the role of target man, but when he joined United that wasn't the way we played,' Malpas said. 'But it was foolish not to use Duncan's assets, and so we tried to get the ball forward a bit more quickly.' Ferguson, left-footed, 'had pace, a great touch, and was good in the air', Malpas remembers. Put those three together and a defender's always going to have problems.

The player Ferguson reminded McLean of was Andy Gray, whose career path, which also featured Dundee United, Everton and Scotland, Ferguson seems to be following. But there was a difference. 'Andy was more determined to prove himself every time he played,' McLean says. 'He didn't get carried away by the publicity. Unfortunately Duncan didn't show the same attitude.'

Once removed from the protective embrace of Tannadice Park, a combination of drink and ill-chosen company put Ferguson in situations he should have turned his back on but couldn't. 'As a big lad he got himself a bit of a reputation,' Malpas said. 'He was the type of person who would respond to provocation.' McLean said Ferguson's problem was that he was unable to distinguish between his real friends and those he had to be wary of. Ferguson, or 'Duncan Disorderly' as he became known, was discovering something that Paul Gascoigne or Ian Botham, men who had similar experiences, could have warned him about – that it's hard to be a star and remain one of the lads at the same time. Someone in the pub will always want to take you on.

A more benign and docile Ferguson – the one who kept pigeons for a hobby – was what Dundee United saw. According to McKinlay, he didn't forget the youth team-mates he had left behind; flush with his first-team pay, he would buy them all lunch at McDonald's. 'There was never any problem between Duncan and the other players,' Malpas said.

Ferguson won his first two caps during a tour to the United States and Canada that was part of Scotland's warm-up for the 1992 European Championship finals. He hardly got a chance in Sweden, but his fourth international appearance, in a friendly against Germany at Hampden in March last year, was one that people in Scotland still talk about.

The Scots lost 1–0, but Ferguson's performance confirmed that he had the confidence to trouble the best defences. Pat Nevin, the Scotland winger, remembers that Ferguson gave Thomas Buchwald 'a roasting' that night, in part because Buchwald had clattered him early on. This, Nevin says, wound Ferguson up sufficiently to get the best out of him, but not too much to provoke an indiscretion. 'The bigger the stage, the better for Duncan,' Malpas says.

By the end of the 1992–93 season, quite a myth had begun to build up around Ferguson. His strike rate – 28 goals in 77 matches for Dundee United – was relatively modest, but there was so much more to his game that Jim McLean was able to persuade Rangers to pay £3.5m for him, a record for a transfer between two Scottish clubs.

The move, however, coincided with two of the lowest points in Ferguson's career. In September last year he was convicted of an assault charge and put on a year's probation. Then in April this year he was involved in a head-butting incident with a Raith Rovers player, John McStay, as a result of which Ferguson will be appearing in court next month. A 12-match ban originally imposed on him by the Scottish Football Association has been suspended pending the outcome of the hearing.

Whatever that is, the consensus is that Ferguson's move to Everton under the steady hand of Joe Royle is the best thing that could have happened to him. His career had stalled in Glasgow, where the suffocating atmosphere of the city's football scene was not what he needed. In an English League where there seem to be any number of other outstanding strikers, Ferguson has the chance to regroup. But a lot depends on how he is handled. 'You've got to be quite firm with him,' Malpas says. 'You can't let him get too blasé or step out of line. But occasionally he needs an arm round his shoulders. If he gets the feeling he's not wanted, he'll play havoc.'

Can Ferguson control the demon inside him? 'It's not a question of whether he can control it,' Malpas says. 'He must control it. I still think he'll find that difficult.' Jim McLean says: 'He's got to show some maturity. He has the potential to be incredibly successful, but he knows there are pitfalls on the way. He's got everything he needs ability-wise. The rest is up to him.'

Being responsible for Ferguson is a bit like having a wayward teenage son. You love him dearly – and there is something endearing about this awkward, gangling young man with the big smile – but you dread the knock on the door in the small hours.

For Craig Brown there really was an anxious wait last week while Ferguson travelled up to Scotland, his arrival at the team's hotel just outside Glasgow delayed by transfer paperwork at Everton. Eventually, Ferguson turned up, to be chaperoned through his press conference by Brown.

'Have you any worries about your temperament for such a big game?' Ferguson was asked. 'I don't know what you mean by that question,' came the smouldering reply. 'I've only been sent off once since I was nine.'

At which point another analogy sprang to mind – that of the wild animal in captivity. A splendid sight, but you wonder whether this was quite what nature intended.

Independent on Sunday, 18 December 1994

When Exeter's Eamonn Dolan discovered he had cancer it seemed his career was over. But Dolan has other plans.

EAMONN DOLAN'S HEARTACHE
Henry Winter

Charing Cross Hospital, west London, yesterday lunchtime. Eamonn Dolan, formerly of West Ham United, Birmingham City and Republic of Ireland Under-21s, leaves smiling after his regular check-up. Another month, another confirmation that the Exeter City striker has recovered from cancer and can start rebuilding a career that once promised so much.

Three days before, a testimonial against the Hammers attracted more than 3,000 to Exeter, who retain his registration. It was meant to be a farewell game, but Dolan played, and played well, lasting 60 minutes against Premiership opposition. It was his first match in 18 months.

A prognosis of testicular cancer, followed by the horrors of chemotherapy, looked to have ended his career at 26. But Dolan treated the testimonial as the first stage of his comeback. On Monday, a popular player who was once part of the Republic's future plans starts pushing for a place in Exeter's reserves.

'The doctors told me playing football professionally again would be an impossibility, but it's now looking a definite possibility,' said Dolan.

Eloquent and thoughtful, the Dagenham-born Dolan tells of a life suddenly far removed from the glamorous veneer of the professional game. His story begins in April 1993.

'I was lying in bed and I felt this shape in one of my testicles,' Dolan recalled. 'I told my wife and she said: "If you're worried about it get it checked out". I didn't. I thought I was fit and it was in an embarrassing region. I thought it might go away. One day soon after, I was in the dressing-room after a match against Port Vale. The doctor came in and said "any problems?" to the players. I said "no". But then as I was walking into the showers, I bumped into his bag by accident. I said "oh, would you mind having a look at this?". I was sent to another doctor the next day. But for that incident I would be dead by now.'

Two weeks after being diagnosed as having cancer, Dolan suffered renewed trauma. His mother died after a long struggle with a carcinoma. 'In some crazy way it helped me. We had spent a year nursing her, so I was prepared for what was happening to me. But it was a surreal time. I could not believe my mother was dead and yet I had cancer as well. I thought, I'm a footballer, fit and healthy, so why have I got cancer?'

Consultants insisted there was no obvious hereditary link. Dolan has his own theory. 'My cancer may have come from some periods of stress. I had a lot of injury problems. Two shoulder operations and an Achilles' tendon problem that went horrifically wrong. There was a hole in my ankle and you could look in and see the Achilles'. The timing of these was bad: just after I had joined Birmingham and Exeter. The trauma of joining a new club, trying to find somewhere to stay, feeling alone, and then getting new injuries was a horrendous situation. It was one of those things that definitely led to the cancer taking hold.'

Whatever the cause, the solution was clear – remove the testicle and endure five months of on-off chemotherapy under the highly respected Professor Newlands at Charing Cross Hospital. Dolan read up on what his body was about to undergo.

'Chemotherapy is just a very sophisticated poison that kills the cancer cells. I had platinum-based chemotherapy. For testicular cancer, particularly a terratoma like mine, platinum is very effective but very toxic and very harsh. It's an odd feeling when you know something that is going to save your life makes you feel so rotten.

'At first, I felt fine and thought my fitness was going to carry me through this. It hit me suddenly. I felt sick, I became lethargic, getting out of bed was a struggle, all my taste buds went, my hearing and eyes were affected, and I got mouth ulcers. My hair fell out. With some people it grows back differently: curly or straighter. With one patient it grew back another colour. I was in a terrible state after chemotherapy, because they pumped me full of steroids and I became very bloated. I was up to 16½ stone when my normal playing weight is 12½. All my fitness had eroded.'

While Newlands and his staff became firm friends of Dolan, he found it difficult to get to know his fellow-patients in the cancer ward. They were all on differing schedules.

'But there was one guy in the next bed called Bill, about 70 years old, who was a bit down at first,' Dolan related. 'Towards the end of that session of treatment we were getting on great. Before I left I said: "Well, Bill. I hope we coincide next time". The first thing I asked when I returned was "How's Bill? When is he coming in?". A nurse looked at me and said: "Sorry Eamonn, but he's died."

'That really struck me. I had never had any doubt that I would get better. And I felt lucky, because I had so much support from the people in my life, family and friends. My wife Erica was in every day. A couple of players came in and the Exeter physio. The people who didn't have that support were those who did badly.'

Many acquaintances laid low. 'Cancer is synonymous with death, isn't it? A lot of people were surprised to see me back. Their reaction is "Eamonn, you look fantastic, I can't believe it".'

The surprises continued this week. Six months after concluding chemotherapy, a good performance against West Ham convinced Dolan his immediate future lay in playing, rather than managing. The dug-out can wait.

Officially he has retired. 'I got £5,000 from the PFA and a smaller sum from Exeter's insurance,' Dolan said. 'If another club does sign me up, hopefully they will pay back that £5,000 like a signing-on fee. With transfer prices these days, £5,000 is value for money if I play well.'

Exeter could keep him but a break might suit both parties. Other clubs' reactions will be interesting. Despite his obvious talent and determination, he expects many rebuffs because of his medical record.

'I will be stigmatised,' Dolan said, mindful that many will associate cancer with Mel Rees, the Sheffield United goalkeeper who died from a different form to Dolan's. 'I will just say to them: "Despite the fact that I've had cancer, I'm fit to play football".' He deserves the chance.

Daily Telegraph, 10 September 1994

CHRIS WADDLE
Joe Lovejoy

The wizard of the dribble shuffled inside like a latter-day Matthews, eluding his full-back before curling a delicious late dipper over the goalkeeper and in via the crossbar. Poor West Ham are unlikely to see it as such, but Chris Waddle's goal at Upton Park was the highlight of a football week destined to be remembered for all the wrong reasons.

At 34, there is life in the old boy yet, as his bête noire is about to discover. After Sheffield Wednesday had won at Gillingham in the third round of the FA Cup, the players whiled away the journey home mulling over who they would like to draw next. In Waddle's case, the discussion was brief. He wanted Wolverhampton Wanderers.

Bert Millichip and his numbered balls having obliged, no one is approaching tomorrow's meeting of two famous old clubs with greater relish. The reasons are obvious. In charge at Molineux these days is one Graham Taylor who, during his ill-starred managership of the England team, truncated Waddle's international career.

Two years ago, when Waddle's mesmeric form took Wednesday to two Cup finals, and made him Footballer of the Year, Taylor helped to dig his own grave by consistently ignoring the best player in the country in favour of his blue-eyed boy, John Barnes.

Given a fair crack of the whip, Waddle might have won a hundred caps. Instead, overlooked for more than three years, he accepts he is unlikely to add to his 62 appearances, made between 1985 and 1991. A rare talent has been short-changed, and it hurts. He would take special pleasure in scoring tomorrow.

The sense of unfulfilment extends beyond the international stage. He has never won the League in England, nor been on the winning side in any Cup final, and while one ambition has now been abandoned, he is not yet ready to give up the other.

'I lost in the European Cup final with Marseille, on penalties, we lost the French Cup to Monaco in the last 10 seconds, and I've lost in three finals here, with Tottenham and Wednesday.' Jinxed? 'I don't think so. You always believe your time will come.'

That belief was reinforced by an uncanny prediction when the fourth round fed Wednesday to the Wolves: 'I'd watched Newcastle play Blackburn on the telly, and when it came to the draw I turned to my missus and said, "If we get Wolves, we'll win the Cup". I wanted them, and I just had this feeling we'd get them.'

He expects a hard, gruelling game – and a win: 'They will bring a lot of support because it's a massive game for them. They'll come with a strong, physical team who will run all day, but we've got to look at it from the point of view that we're a Premier League side and they're not. We've got home advantage and we're in good form at the moment, unbeaten in eight games, so we've got to believe that we'll score goals.'

A decent Cup run is not beyond them, but Waddle had been hoping for rather more back in the summer of '92, when, on his return from France, he chose Wednesday, because of their attractive playing style, in preference to the then champions, Leeds United. That first season back had gone like a dream, strong League form faltering only late on, when progress to Wembley in both the FA and League Cups proved the most lucrative of distractions.

Getting there was to be the high point. To their mortification, Wednesday lost both finals, steamrollered twice by Arsenal's mean machine, and a team as easy on the eye as any in the country broke up.

'Basically,' Waddle said, 'everybody left. Viv Anderson and Danny Wilson went to Barnsley; John Harkes to Derby; Paul Warhurst wasn't the same player once Blackburn were interested and he had to go; Roland Nilsson packed up and went home to Sweden; Peter Shirtliff went to Wolves; Nigel Worthington's contract ran out and he went to Leeds, and Carlton Palmer was sold to Leeds as well. Eighteen months on, of the team likely to play on Monday, there's only me, John Sheridan and Mark Bright left from the Cup finals.'

So many departures had a debilitating effect, on both form and morale: 'I had 11 months out with Achilles' tendon trouble, and when I came back I noticed a big difference between the old team and this one.

'The players who left had been around. We had a team of experienced internationals. Now, apart from John Sheridan, we haven't got anyone in an international team. We're a young side, inexperienced and a bit naive.

'Take the other night, against West Ham. They had two men sent off, but we didn't know how to grasp the game and pass the ball around to make the advantage count. Two years ago, that Cup side would have annihilated West Ham.'

Standards had slipped: 'I don't think this team are going to be as good as the old one, at least not for another two years, and in two years' time I'll be 36. I can feel the frustration sometimes on the park. We used to really fizz it around. These days, we don't pass and move so well. Before, we had good shape and good balance. That team didn't fear anybody; we knew we could go out and get a result against anyone.'

That confidence was eroded by the lengthy absence which deprived Wednesday of their playmaker, and Waddle of the chance to resurrect his international career.

On taking over as England's coach, Terry Venables had named him as one of the players he was looking forward to working with. Twelve months on, it has yet to happen, and time is hardly Waddle's ally.

He said: 'When Terry took over he rang for a chat and asked how I was. Had I been fit, I think I'd have got in, but the Achilles' wasn't right. Players like Anderton and McManaman have come in and done well, and when Barnes got back and people said it was a retrograde step, I thought, do you really need that?'

The answer, of course, is in the affirmative. Too long in exile internationally, he would jump at the chance of a last hurrah.

England's next opponents, the Republic of Ireland, loom large on his cv. He made his debut against them at Wembley a decade ago, and the match in Dublin in November 1990 fractured a relationship with Taylor which had been fragile from the outset.

Waddle was needed that day to organise the midfield in the absence of Paul Gascoigne, mysteriously dropped. When he withdrew, injured, Taylor harboured dark suspicions.

'I think he thought I was messing him about, but I was genuinely injured. I couldn't play for Marseille the following weekend. If that was his reason for ignoring me afterwards, it was a poor excuse.'

Reason, or excuse, exclude him he did, Waddle suffering more than anyone from the changes in personnel, and style, which followed Taylor's installation.

'I was 29, going on 30 – at my peak – and I knew I could do what was required, but I wasn't given a run in the side. Graham Taylor kept me on for a few squads, but I don't think he really wanted to play me.'

Unsurprisingly, he sympathises with Matthew Le Tissier, a kindred spirit who, he feels, merits a run under the present regime.

The hard-done-by mood soon passes. Waddle is playing, and playing well again, for which he gives grateful thanks. Three months ago, at his lowest ebb, he thought it was all over, and was contemplating an alternative career, in coaching or as a media analyst: 'If somebody had offered me a job in October, I'd probably have taken it, because I thought my Achilles' wasn't going to come right.'

It did come right, of course, but only after a long, lonely period of rehabilitation that Waddle calls Groundhog Day: 'The annoying thing was having people say, "You're 34, you're not going to be what you were". Bollocks, I thought. I can be, and I will be. Being 34 is not an illness, you know.'

Convalescence had few compensations, but one was the opportunity to indulge his interest in the tactical side of the game: 'I was sent to Old Trafford to check on United before we played them here. I had to write a report on how we could beat them.' Waddle's master plan? 'I said Paul Ince and Roy Keane, who were playing in midfield, were the key. They suck the opposing midfield players in, creating the space to get the ball round the corner to Mark Hughes, so let Ince and Keane go. Keep our central midfield players in position in front of Hughes. I said drop off and be patient. We looked like the away side, but their only outlet on the day was Keith Gillespie, playing it over the top.'

The result? Wednesday 1 United 0. After that little triumph, turning over the Turnip should be small potatoes.

Sunday Times, 29 January 1995

Merson the Role Model
Henry Winter

In a society where drug habits can be picked up at school break, Paul Merson could have become just another statistic. The Arsenal and England striker, currently beginning rehabilitation after admitting using cocaine, was fortunate that the football family took a sympathetic view of a wayward son.

By eschewing sanctions like long-term suspension or a punitive fine, the Football Association and Professional Footballers' Association have treated Merson leniently. While Merson, whom the police still want to talk to, endeavours to clean up his body and life, the FA and PFA return to ensuring a national disease does not poison the national game.

The Mersons of the future are at risk from drugs at an increasingly early age. Half of Britain's schoolchildren dabble with illegal substances before reaching 16. 'Cannabis is seen quite frequently in certain primary schools among 10 or 11-year-olds,' said Inspector Paul Wotton, of Scotland Yard's Youth Affairs Branch, confirming the problem's inexorable spread.

The man charged with combating the encroachment into football is Alan Hodson, the FA's assistant director of coaching and education (medical education). It was Hodson's random drug-testing programme, introduced this season to detect recreational narcotics as well as performance-enhancers, that helped encourage Merson to run to the *Daily Mirror*.

'Police tell us that kids start experimenting with drugs from 13–14,' said Hodson, who can (with parental permission) test nine-year-olds upwards. 'So I've got from nine, 10, 11 and 12 to frighten them to death.'

Education, through pamphlets and videos, is Hodson's main pre-emptive tactic. The anti-drugs pitch is aimed at the 15,000 pupils (aged nine to 16) at England's 145 centres of excellence, to the 1,500 YT boys, to players, parents, teachers, coaches, and anyone who can 'police' potential drug victims. By now, every adult involved in developing young footballers should – in theory – be able to recognise amphetamines and crack cocaine, spot symptoms of drug or solvent abuse and understand street slang for drugs. Along with the elite testing, the annual cost to the FA of Hodson's campaign is £135,000.

The PFA are equally concerned. Players' union officials spent yesterday putting the finishing touches to a video, containing anti-drug messages from the likes of Alan Shearer and Merson's manager, George Graham.

Focused on footballers it may see wider service. 'We would be delighted to let any school have it,' said Gordon Taylor, the PFA's chief executive.

Such measures, by FA and PFA, stem from stories heard on the grapevine last season. Proliferating rumours about a handful of drug-dabbling professionals and youth-teamers, added to the sinister presence of pushers outside Lancaster Gate to order all club doctors to hold pre-season briefings and, mostly publicly, to introduce random testing.

The crusade involves long-term planning. 'On the Friday after the Merson story came out, four players were tested at Arsenal's training ground,' said Hodson. 'Of course it would appear to the public that we were reacting to it. But I can tell you, as I run this show, that the draw of Arsenal came out on August 25.'

All tests have proved negative. 'But it should come as no surprise if we found some youth players having a problem because of the social drugs problem we've got in this country,' added Hodson. 'I get anonymous phone calls every week asking me to test players. These are from fans and cranks. If the PFA or clubs are worried about a player, they can ask me to give him a confidential test for his benefit. God knows, we maybe could have helped Paul Merson earlier if the club had known and written to me. No club has asked yet. Social drugs are the nation's problem – we'll soon find out if football is being infiltrated.'

The message from supporters is encouraging. While on the rise nationally, drug taking among fans has fallen out of fashion since the house-party and rave boom of five years ago.

'At that time it did become quite *en vogue* for people to take drugs while they were watching matches,' said Tim Crabbe, of the Football Supporters' Association. 'There was certainly a lot of marijuana smoking and quite a few people, in the late 1980s, taking Ecstasy while at a match.'

The centres were Liverpool and Manchester. Some United fans still recall fondly the 1991 European Cup-Winners' Cup final in Rotterdam, not simply for the dramatic defeat of Barcelona, but for the opportunity to immerse themselves, however briefly, in Holland's liberal drug scene.

The inference is clear: the interest of young men in drugs and football will occasionally overlap. 'I have seen people arrested or thrown out of grounds for smoking dope,' added Crabbe. 'But that's always going to happen when you get a large crowd of predominantly young males.'

This group, overwhelmingly working-class, has been hit by the post-Taylor Report hike in ticket prices, another factor which has prevented a fully fledged invasion of the terraces by junkies.

Andy Mitten, of Old Trafford fanzine *United We Stand*, said: 'It costs a lot of money to follow United home and away, as the lads do, and they would be the sort of people affected by the drug culture. If, say, United are playing in London you can't afford to go clubbing when you get home.'

Mitten, a regular at northern and southern nightclubs, where people like Merson would gain access to drugs, notes a divide. The southern drug scene uses more cocaine than up north. 'If you go into a club here in Manchester people are taking Ecstasy or Speed,' added Mitten. 'There is more money in London – it's expensive, cocaine.'

While damaging to the game's image, the Merson case has bequeathed potential positives. Merson, when cleaned up, could prove a high-profile messenger to schools on the perils of drugs.

Inspector Wotton believes that Merson will automatically feature in classroom debates. 'They will be able to discuss how drugs affected his health, his career, his family and his self-esteem.'

Wotton added that a proposed government strategy, at Green Paper stage, allows the use of former addicts to bang the authorities' drum. Merson has agreed to this, and will work with the FA and PFA after completing his rehabilitation.

If Merson's fall and rise prevents one youngster becoming another statistic, the FA's mercy will have been fully justified.

Daily Telegraph, 3 December 1994

Lake's Battle of the Wounded Knee

Phil Shaw

Two practice pitches, 200 miles apart. At Bisham Abbey, in leafy Buckinghamshire, the England squad prepare to meet Uruguay at Wembley. On a green oasis amid the urban decay of Moss Side, the trainee professionals of Manchester City train for their next Lancashire League encounter.

Paul Lake is with one group – City's teenage hopefuls – yet he might so easily have been with the other. Lake thought his youth team days were over when he made Bobby Robson's provisional pool of 30 for the 1990 World Cup finals. Today, still only 26, he is fighting his way back from the injuries that have left him with one of the most battle-scarred knees this side of the OJ Simpson trial.

Walking around with the ligaments of two dead Americans makes Lake fairly unusual, but then he always did stand out. Promised to City from the age of 10, and an associate schoolboy there as long ago as John Bond's reign, he went on to wear nine different numbers during their 1988–89 promotion campaign. Whether at full-back or in central defence, centre or wide midfield, striker or sweeper, he showed a rare blend of power and poise.

It took him into the same Under-21 side as Ince, Batty, Bull and Merson, and the B team with Seaman, Adams and Le Tissier. One pundit was moved to suggest that 'this must be what watching Duncan Edwards was like'. The new England manager, Graham Taylor, was there the night his world, or rather his right knee, fell apart against Aston Villa five years ago.

However, the origins of this saga of despair and dedication go back further still. 'I played too much between 11 and 16, which was stupid,' Lake said. 'I was turning out for City, the school, Tameside Boys and Manchester County. Sometimes 10 games a week. That's storing up a lot of stress, but the better you get the more pressure there is. I sailed through those years, always wanting to get stuck in in the middle of the park. I think I've paid the price for that in later years.'

Instalments started in earnest that September evening when Villa visited Maine Road. Tony Cascarino mis-controlled the ball and Lake went to play it. 'My foot went down, I went to go with the ball and the foot stayed where it was and twisted,' he recalled. 'The whole knee just went.'

He was operated on in December and back in training by April '91, only for the knee to go again 'partially'. Lake battled back and felt ready to return when, a year after the original injury, it went 'completely'. Fast forward to August '92 and week one of the Premier League: 'I'd come back again and got a few goals in the pre-season games in Italy. Then in the second League match, at Middlesbrough, I twisted like I did the first time and knew straight away it was serious. The coach ride home was the longest I've ever known.'

In a sense, Lake's journey was just beginning. At the rehabilitation unit at Lilleshall, in Shropshire, he heard that Rangers' Ian Durrant had been to Los Angeles for surgery to rebuild a similarly shattered knee from donor tendons.

Peter Reid, City's manager at the time, arranged for him to attend the same clinic two and a half years ago. 'I've a lot to thank Reidy for – he wouldn't have let me pack up even if I'd tried,' he said. 'He didn't ask Peter Swales (then chairman) if I could go: he told him. I got new medial and cruciate ligaments, which gave me a fighting chance.'

Lake eventually began running, swimming and cycling six days a week. City's physio, Eamonn Salmon, worked patiently with him. He also received 'incredible help' from Robbie Brightwell and his wife, the former Anne Packer – Olympians both and parents of City's Ian and David Brightwell – who volunteered their time.

The reward came last month when Lake finally reappeared in City's B team on a park pitch at Blackburn. He came off at half-time – 'I wanted to take it steadily' – but has since completed three games. If the reaction after the next one is nothing more than the customary slight soreness and swelling, there could be a comeback in the reserves next week.

'It's been weird playing with the kids. Even the shirt doesn't fit. The sleeves come three-quarters of the way down my arms. But there are some seriously good players who'll definitely make the first team. They're so enthusiastic, they bring the best out of me. It's a case of so far so good, but my first match in the "rezzies" will be the big test.'

When Lake last graced the seniors, City had been champions more recently than United: Swales looked bomb-proof, while Brian Horton, the eighth manager he has served, was with Oxford; even Eric Cantona was still loved in Leeds. Two and a half years, clearly, is an eternity in football, so is he deluding himself by trying to pick up where he left off?

'I really believe I can do it. If I get more games under my belt and do a normal pre-season, I'll be back to my old self.'

Lake hopes to play centre-half until his confidence returns fully, because there is less chance of 'getting hit from the side' if you are facing the game. In terms of watching City, which he has done since he was four, facing the game is harder. 'I get jealous,' he admitted, though self-pity is an emotion he has learned to suppress.

Likewise guilt. Before he first crumpled to the turf he had signed a five-year contract. 'I gave City my loyalty so I felt it was right that they honoured it.' Now, if Lake comes anywhere near fulfilling his early potential, they will have a 'new' £5m player.

'It may sound corny, but I love the game. It's all I know. I also love the club. I went out before the last home match and the reception I got made the hairs on my neck stand up. So I must keep going – I don't want to become one of those guys who say: "If only I'd done so and so".'

Should he break down again, medical advice might be to abandon full-time football rather than risk disability. What then? 'I've got no negative thoughts whatsoever, but I'd want to stay in football. Perhaps play for Stalybridge Celtic, or be a physio,' he said, beaming defiantly. 'I'm an expert on knees.'

Independent, 29 March 1995

Instead of following in the footsteps of fellow Trinidadians Brian Lara and Sonny Ramadhin and becoming a cricketer, Shaka Hislop instead chose a career in English football. At six foot six inches, Reading's goalkeeper is the tallest in the league.

Shaka Hislop
John Davies

Neil Shaka Hislop aims to do what Lord Constantine, Sonny Ramadhin and Brian Lara have done by putting his home island of Trinidad & Tobago on the world's sporting map.

Of course there is a difference. The ennobled Constantine, the pint-sized sorcerer of spin Ramadhin and the world's record-breaking batsman Lara all earned their fame as West Indies Test cricketers.

While the six foot six inch Hislop – who is known by his African-derived second name of 'Shaka' – is carving out a career as a professional footballer with Reading.

A career that only took off 30 months ago when Reading boss Mark McGhee handed the eager 23-year-old Caribbean the number one jersey before a 3–0 Division Two defeat against West Bromwich Albion at the Hawthorns.

Shaka had only arrived in the UK a few weeks earlier from America where he had spent five years at Howard University studying for his degree in mechanical engineering.

'I had always wanted to give professional football a shot,' explains the thoughtful Trinidadian. 'I played college soccer in the States and back home as a kid in Trinidad.

'Of course I am always asked the obvious question about cricket. I did play the game a bit as a lad in Trinidad, but that ended when I went to the USA to complete my education at the age of 18 because cricket is not generally played out there. Even at six foot six inches, I was perhaps not tall enough to have a crack at top-class basketball where the stars are often six foot eight inches upwards! So soccer was the obvious answer. But if I did manage to get into professional soccer, I did not want my career to be one-dimensional so I completed my studies first and qualified as a mechanical engineer.'

Shaka came to England in 1992 looking for a job in engineering but at the same time keeping an eye out for a League club that was prepared to take him on as a novice goalkeeper.

Mark McGhee and his assistant Colin Lee took one look at the enthusiastic West Indian in a practice match, saw his potential and gave him a short-term contract.

Shaka takes up the story of that initial breakthrough at West Brom two years ago. 'I got the opportunity because of an injury to Reading's first-choice keeper Steve Francis,' he recalls, 'I think I must have done reasonably well because I made a further 11 League appearances that season, even though it was hard to displace Francis.'

So it was a very happy Neil Shaka Hislop who flew home to spend the summer of 1993 with his family in Trinidad. He thought he would be spending the next season improving his game and learning enough about soccer and its tactics to establish himself sometime in the future as a regular League footballer.

But he did not know that his lucky star seemed to be guiding him across the Atlantic as he jetted back from Trinidad to join up with Reading for pre-season training.

'When I arrived back at Elm Park, Mark McGhee told me that he had sold Steve Francis to Huddersfield Town,' recalls Hislop.

'Mark said that he had thought long and hard about the situation and had decided to hand me the number one jersey on a permanent basis, adding that it was up to me to grab the opportunity.'

The rest, as they say, is history. But nevertheless a glorious chapter in the 124-year history of Reading Football Club. The Royals triumphantly lifted the Division Two title with Shaka ever-present in a side that only conceded 44 goals in a 46-game

League schedule. The towering Trinidadian kept an impressive 16 clean sheets for a side acclaimed for its passing and attacking skills.

But the Premiership outfits were watching events at Elm Park closely. While they monitored McGhee's phenomenal progress in management, they could not also help noting the remarkable transition that Shaka Hislop had made from novice to arguably the most promising young goalkeeper in the lower divisions.

They noted his staggering mobility and agility for such a big man and, in deference to the old soccer premise that all things being equal a good big'un is always better than a good little'un, began to make enquiries about Shaka, who is the tallest experienced keeper in the 92 Premiership and Endsleigh League clubs.

The only two keepers with League experience to come near to reaching Shaka's rarefied altitude are Coventry veteran Steve Ogrizovic – and what a good 'un he's been – and Ipswich's Canadian-born Craig Forrest. Both head the six foot five inch mark in their bare feet. Coming up on the rails is West Ham's 22-year-old Las Vegas-born Ian Feuer, who hasn't played in the League yet but nudges the clouds at six foot seven inches.

Shaka unstintingly gives credit to Mark McGhee and Colin Lee for launching his career, teaching him to play the game properly and instilling the discipline required of a professional footballer. He admits to being shattered, along with all his Reading team-mates, when McGhee and Lee were head-hunted by Leicester City and moved to Filbert Street just before Christmas.

'From day one I was instilled with Mark and Colin's philosophy about the game,' he says. 'They always insisted on us playing passing football and building up our moves from the back. Even when we were going through a lean spell they stressed that the reason why we were having a bad time was because as a team we were straying from the ideals they had laid down.

'They never abandoned their game plan. It was a system that I respected greatly. So I have been taught from the outset to play the game properly. Of course it was a terrible shock when Mark and Colin left. We guessed it would happen sometime but we hoped it would be later rather than sooner. Mark and Colin had lulled us into a false sense of security. When things were going wrong with the team they could tell us how to put it right and we relied on that.

'Now Mick Gooding and Jimmy Quinn have been given the job as co-managers and fortunately they are two men who we respect because of their tremendous records as players. We all wish them well and know it is up to us to pull out that little bit extra to help them.'

Hislop also pays tribute to former England and Chelsea goalkeeper Peter Bonetti. 'Peter is our specialist goalkeeping coach and comes down to our training ground near Pangbourne every Wednesday to put me through my paces,' he says. 'I must admit he's almost become like an Agony Aunt to me. He has added new dimensions to my game.'

Dimensions that, he might have added, are enticing Premier League scouts to chart his progress in every game. 'As a professional footballer I want to play Premier League,' he admits. 'Of course I have been told that some of the big clubs have been watching me. I just put all the conjecture behind me and try to get on with my game. If the offer to play in the top echelon does come along one day, then perhaps it could be the stepping stone to an England cap.'

The day may not be too far away when England fields the tallest goalkeeper in world football, with the Wembley fans chanting songs of glory to a calypso beat.

Matchday, March 1995

Ally McCoist
Olivia Blair

Once you've met Ally McCoist, you'd forgive him if he was a day late. No wonder Billy Connolly, the Scottish comedian who wrote the introduction to McCoist's autobiography, says: 'He is handsome, he is rich, he is funny and he is happy. He is a very popular person, even with me, and although I count him among my friends, my envy knows no bounds.' The ultimate testimony to McCoist's popularity is that he is one of just a handful of Rangers players who are liked by Celtic fans, just as his hero, Kenny Dalglish, was one of the few Celtic players to be welcome at Ibrox.

McCoist is in Rangers uniform: blue blazer, black trousers, club tie and whiteshirt. The club is one of the few to insist players wear jacket and tie when they turn up for training. He is 5ft 10in but looks smaller.

We sit in the Rangers' dugout, looking out on the scene of so many of McCoist's triumphs. He has been Rangers' top hitman for so long now there is a sense of something missing when his name isn't on the scoresheet. His best season was in 1992/93 when he scored 49 goals in all competitions, retaining the European Golden Boot which he had won the season before, when his 39 goals helped Rangers to their fourth successive Championship. The past two seasons, however, have not been quite so super for the man they call SuperAlly. He recovered well enough from the broken leg he suffered in Scotland's disastrous World Cup qualifier against Portugal to score seven goals in 21 games last season. This season a calf muscle frustratingly kept him out until early December.

During his absence, the emergence of Charlie Miller, the player dubbed 'the new darling of Ibrox', posed a threat to McCoist's status as the Rangers hero. Even Stuart McCall was quoted in the *Daily Record* as saying: 'Charlie can take Ally's place both on and off the field.' But manager Walter Smith is keen to stress that Miller, who is a goalscoring midfielder, is no replacement for McCoist, who Smith believes 'will break every goalscoring record at this club'.

And that is why McCoist is not ready to relinquish his mantle. He has one aim in mind before he retires: 'Ever since I was a boy and used to stand over in that corner of the stand (the corner adjacent to the Broomloan Road end where the away fans now sit) I have wanted to be the Rangers goalscorer. Whoever he was at the time, I wanted to be that player. And now, I want to finish as Rangers' all-time top goalscorer and beat Bob McPhail's record of 229 League goals for Rangers. That's all I want. Then I can end my days happily.' He is nine goals from McPhail's record. Jimmy Smith's record of 383 goals in all competitive games looks impregnable but McCoist, currently on 299, is promising to break it.

'You know, I'm a Glasgow boy and this is my home. Day after day I look around here and think to myself "Where else could you play in front of the same atmosphere as we do here, in front of 46,000 each week?" I wake up every morning and think I'm the luckiest man alive. There's nowhere else for me.' He could never, he stresses, emulate his former striking partner Mo Johnstone (who in 1989 became the first Catholic player to sign for Rangers, having previously played for Celtic) and cross the great divide to play at Parkhead: 'My family's Rangers through and through; I couldn't do that to them.'

True to form, McCoist was late in arriving at Ibrox. In fact, he turned the club down twice before eventually arriving in 1983 after three seasons in Perth with St Johnstone and two wearing years on Wearside playing for Sunderland. When he did arrive, he was by no means the finished article. 'I'd do silly things. Bad tackles would annoy me and destroy my concentration. Worst of all, I'd let missed chances worry me – and that would inevitably lead to more missed chances. I know now that you have to put mistakes like that out of your mind and concentrate 100 per cent on what's happening now, not what might have been three minutes ago. A little of that knowledge might have spared me – and the Rangers fans – some bad times back in the early 1980s.'

McCoist found the net just nine times in his first season, and couldn't even get on the scoresheet when Rangers put eight past Valetta of Malta. 'I wasn't accepted at all by the Rangers punters,' he remembers. 'They were against me totally. Anything I did just wasn't good enough.' The hat-trick he scored against Celtic in the 1984 League Cup final helped, but it wasn't enough. 'It took me a lot longer to settle at Ibrox than I expected,' he admits. 'About two years I reckon, and I was nearly on my way in the middle of that.'

His second year at Rangers, when McCoist was almost sent back to Sunderland, was even worse. During a Scottish Cup defeat by Dundee, the fans at the Copland Road end started singing 'Ally, Ally get to fuck, Ally, get to fuck' as McCoist missed chance after chance. 'I can't tell you how it feels to have a whole stand rising in unison against you. I can still feel physically sick when I recall it.'

When he arrived at the club, one of the current first team players gave him the 'best piece of advice I've ever received: be thick skinned. I obviously didn't heed that in my first two years here.' He chuckles. 'But the same people who stood on the terraces and abused me, now sit there chanting my name.'

Not everyone chants his name, however. Certainly not his many critics south of the border who claim McCoist could not have scored as many goals anywhere but the Scottish League, currently considered one of the weakest in Europe. Even when he won the Golden Boot two years running, outscoring Ian Wright (in 1991–92) and the rest of Europe's hotshots, cynics said the honour had more to do with the inadequacy of Scottish defences than his own gifts as a striker.

'What do I have to do to please the man? McCoist had asked when Graeme Souness failed to give him credit for his goals in 1990. He may as well have asked that of the rest of the world.

He remembers scoring in a cup tie at Ayr, a tap-in from close-range: 'This punter came up to me in a pub afterwards and said: "You got your money easy today, they can't come any simpler than that." I just laughed. He hadn't got a clue about what had gone on in the five seconds before that put me in the position for the tap-in.' Those who consider McCoist to be the supreme goal-poacher, the king of the toe-pokes and tap-ins, the picker-up of other people's pieces, are missing the bigger picture. McCoist is the archetypal penalty-box predator (few of his goals are long-range efforts from outside the box) but his scrapbook of goals includes its fair share of spectacular strikes. David Lacey once called Mark Hughes 'a scorer of great goals, not a great goalscorer'. McCoist is both.

It's hard to pick a favourite from the 299 goals he's scored in 481 appearances for the gers. But McCoist does have a favourite. And it's a tap-in. It's the goal he scored in Rangers' 2–1 win against Leeds in the so-called Battle of Britain at Ibrox in the European Champions' Cup in 1992. 'I saw the corner come over and realised Dave McPherson had every chance of getting a header in on goal. So before the ball even reached Dave, I ran straight at the keeper, jinked to avoid my marker, and when the header was blocked by Lukic I was there to knock the rebound home. The next day most of the papers described it along the lines of: ". . . and McCoist had a simple job to score from close range . . ." Possibly true, but I like to think the hard work was done getting me into the position that made the act of scoring look simple.'

Although McCoist has called himself 'officially the worst header of the ball in Britain', it was his brilliant headed goal in the away leg against Leeds that finished off the English champions and took Rangers through to the next stage of the Champions' League. The goal was set up for him by his striking partner at Ibrox, Mark Hateley, the man whose arrival at the club under Souness threatened McCoist's career four years ago. McCoist has had many different striking partners including 'about 15' at Ibrox (among them Robert Fleck, Mo Johnstone, Kevin Drinkell and Iain Ferguson), but it's alongside 'Big Mark' that the goals have really flowed.

'I had a great spell with Flecky, as well as with wee Mo,' McCoist recalls, 'but it'd be hard to beat my record with Big Mark.' That record is a phenomenal 158 League goals over four seasons, more than 39 goals between them each season. And Hateley acknowledges 'Coisty's' part in that record: 'He would be on my list of all-time greats with Rossi and Lineker and all the others. Let's not have any criticism about him scoring goals in a lesser league. Besides, scoring goals is difficult in any league at any level. The goals against Leeds must have shut up a few big-mouths who like to take a pop at us with all the insults about the standards in Scotland.'

Hateley returned to Rangers from Monaco a far better player than when he went out there. Would McCoist have benefited from a European experience? 'I do look at clubs abroad and wonder if I could have made it there, but it's too late for me now. There are still challenges here for me. No one can tell me winning trophies again and again isn't a challenge. And I've scored goals all my life; I don't believe I have anything to prove to anyone.'

There is one glaring weakness in McCoist's credentials. His 15 goals in 46 internationals compares pretty miserably to Gary Lineker's 48 goals in 80 games for England. Like Kenny Dalglish, McCoist has been criticised for not producing the goods when he's donned the dark blue shirt of Scotland.

Former Scotland coach Andy Roxburgh springs to McCoist's defence: 'You have to remember Rangers are dominating every game, so McCoist is getting lots of opportunities. Balls are coming into the box all the time and he is on the end of them. Scotland are a middle-of-the-road side and so he's not getting the chances. It's our fault, not his.'

McCoist's former captain at Rangers, the ex-Ipswich and England captain Terry Butcher, says McCoist is a better striker than Lineker. 'People say he's only playing in the Scottish League and it's easy to score goals there. But they forget you are under intense pressure the whole time because so much is expected each week. Other teams come to Ibrox and it's their Cup final.' Butcher has gone as far as to name his son Alistair Ian Butcher: 'He's named after McCoist and Durrant, which means he's a cert to be a crackpot.'

Certainly McCoist enjoys looking on the bright side of life. Graeme Souness mistook his flippancy for disrespect, which shows how little he understood the bubbly striker. 'His wit is as sharp as his penalty-box reactions,' said Leeds captain and Scotland team-mate Gary McAllister after that European clash. 'His impact in the dressing room is extraordinary. I've never spoken to anyone who dislikes him.'

Except perhaps French defender Luc Sonor, who tried to get the better of McCoist during a Scotland v France World Cup tie in March 1989. 'You bad player,' said the Frenchman to McCoist. 'Me bad player, but me 2–0 up,' came the reply. In 1990 when McCoist was voted the world's fifth best-looking sportsman, he said: 'I was thrilled until I learned that Ivan Lendl had finished above me.'

There are only two things that would definitely wipe the smile off Ally McCoist's face: a rumour that Souness is returning to Ibrox and the thought of stopping playing. In February 1993 he said: 'When I finally stop playing, Allison (his wife) and I might just disappear for a year. I don't know where, but after 13 years in the public eye, it would be good to merge into the background somewhere. I'll buy a motorbike and we'll do Route 66. Then we might arrive at some resort in the Rockies and learn to ski.' But he admits that 'I just can't think about it, don't think about it. It terrifies me. I just can't imagine what it'd be like without all this,' and for the umpteenth time, he looks almost lovingly around the stadium.

He talks about having a family, about how he would hate it to be difficult for his son to grow up in McCoist's boots: 'I would like to bring him to Ibrox and show him it all, but I wouldn't force it on him.' Five weeks after this interview took place, McCoist announced he was going to become a father.

One incident above all others sums up McCoist. He returned from injury after a month of being written off in the press to score the winner against Aberdeen in the League at Ibrox. It was his 299th League goal. According to the *Rangers News*, as McCoist reeled away, both arms aloft, Walter Smith turned to his chairman David Murray and said: 'I was just going to pull him off.'

When McCoist finally pulls himself off the pitch for good how would he really like to be remembered? 'Aye well,' he says, 'perhaps in ten or 20 years people might look back and say "that McCoist scored some number of goals".'

FourFourTwo, February 1995

In February Sir Stanley Matthews celebrated his 80th birthday, an event that did not go unrecorded. One of the first to wish him Happy Birthday was his former Blackpool team-mate Jimmy Armfield.

Sir Stanley Matthews

Jimmy Armfield

There have been many, probably too many, footballers who have been tagged 'great' in my time, but there is only one Stanley Matthews.

Even today, on his 80th birthday, the name still conjures up something magical to me and I suppose that when I look back on my career with Blackpool and England I still feel that one of my greatest honours was to play behind the great Stan for six seasons.

Other football legends such as Pelé, Finney, Di Stefano and Charlton readily bring magical memories back as well, but with Matthews there was a sort of mystique that made him different.

He was to our football what Fred Perry was to tennis, Len Hutton to cricket and Henry Cotton to golf. Self-taught, they were the people's champions – there was an aura about them that presented professionalism and clean living and because of it Englishmen everywhere loved them.

Of course life was simpler in those days. Television had not taken every move on the pitch into living rooms throughout the land and footballers, top class or second rate, had to play for the same wage.

It seems incredible looking back to the mid-1950s when, as a teenager, I prised a way into the Blackpool team and within a couple of years was on the same salary as the great Stanley Matthews. Frankly I was 'all promise', while Matthews was recognised as the greatest footballer the world had ever seen.

There was one slight difference in pay. Stan got £20 a week throughout the year, while I was offered £20 during the football season but only £18 during the summer.

In a moment of rashness I decided to inquire of Blackpool's tough manager, Joe Smith, why this was so. 'Why is it that Stan gets £20 all year while I, as a first-team player, get £2 less out of season?'

'Because he is a better player than you,' I was told.

After a moment's hesitation I dared: 'Not in summer he's not.'

Smith's reply is not for publication. I should have known better than to try to take Joe on anyway, and secondly even to consider myself in the same breath as the maestro.

Blackpool were a top-class team in those days, the tangerine shirts were world famous and fans everywhere knew the names of Mortensen, Johnstone and, of course, Matthews.

Stan today may be the King of the Potteries, but few will dispute that he earned his real fame with Blackpool, where for 14 years he was just as important to the town as the Tower or the Illuminations.

The war brought Matthews to Blackpool for the first time. He was stationed there in the RAF and guested for the Seasiders in a wartime team including Jack Dodds, Ronnie Dix and Eddie Burbanks. His love affair with Blackpool had begun.

When the war ended Matthews returned to Stoke but never quite picked up the momentum of his career. Transfer speculation ended when he signed for Blackpool in 1947 for £11,500 and a bottle of whisky. Joe Smith always said that was what it cost him to persuade the Stoke board to release Stan for what was even then a lightweight fee.

Thus began the second stage of his career, which had been threatened by six years of war when he should have been at his best. Yet, with Blackpool, he went on a dazzling run that stretched to the early 60s.

In 1948 he was the first winner of the Player of the Year trophy as he helped Blackpool to their first FA Cup final, which they lost 4–2 to Manchester United. It was my first visit to Wembley: I stood on the Kop, on a biscuit tin in which my father had brought the sandwiches for the day, little realising that eight years later I would be playing in the same team as Matthews.

In '51 Blackpool were back at Wembley again, but a Newcastle team inspired by Jackie Milburn had too much for them and won 2–0. At 38, Matthews's last chance of Cup glory looked to have gone, although he never believed that. Everybody wanted Stanley to win the coveted medal before he hung up his boots, and when the team reached the final again in Coronation Year the press had labelled it the Matthews final long before a ball had been kicked. The pressure on Stan must have been enormous.

Everybody in the country, except the townsfolk of Bolton, wanted Blackpool to win. There had to be special deliveries by the Post Office to Bloomfield Road because of the weight of mail wishing Stan success.

By then I was a Blackpool reserve and watched agonisingly as the

Wanderers went 3–1 up in the second half in a game that was, frankly, littered with errors. Stanley Mortensen rescued Blackpool with the only ever hat-trick in a Wembley FA Cup final, but the enduring memory will be of the final 30 minutes, when Matthews created havoc down the left side of Bolton's defence.

He laid on the winner for Bill Perry at a time when 10-man Bolton were beaten. In fact they would probably have been over-run in extra time if the scores had remained level at 90 minutes.

In that last half hour Matthews was in for the kill and, make no mistake, he had a ruthless streak. Once he got on top of an opponent he showed no mercy. He could taunt defenders almost like a matador with a bull. I've seen him toe-poke the ball forward a foot or so and invite his marker to come and get it. Few did.

He was totally confident. It was all down to his fanatical drive for a physical fitness level that was superior to other footballers. This dedication came to him via his father Jack, a barber, and a former middleweight boxer with over 350 fights who was also a fitness fanatic.

Even today Stan still works out. He has never lost that will to train on his own, and that is probably what made him a cut above the rest.

In Blackpool he went down to the beach at eight o'clock every morning, where he did light jogging, exercises and, just as important to him, deep breathing. He came to the ground and trained with the rest of us as well. His fitness level was never in doubt, even when he passed 40.

He didn't smoke or drink and he experimented with health foods long before any other athlete had even considered them. Carrot juice was on the Matthews menu, although I can also recall when he would purposely go on a fast and start to build up for his next game with salads and light meals.

Stan took great pains so as not to disappoint his public. Wherever we played we knew that Stan would be the focus of attention. We knew, as well, that there were critical eyes on him – many waiting and eager to write him off.

He disappointed the cynics, as he wasn't like other footballers who start to worry about the future when they pass 30. Stan was like the batsman who reaches 100 and then stuns the bowler by taking a fresh guard. Incredibly, even after retiring, he told me he thought he'd gone out too soon.

Many accused him of being a loner, but that was down to his

lifestyle more than his character. Very few opted to go down the health-kick road.

He was a great man to have in the dressing-room, he lifted everybody with his presence. He was full of humility, there was never any edge on him as he realised that the next match was always the one on which he would be judged – it was something I never forgot.

In 1961 he left us to return to Stoke for £3,000 and, at 46, I just hoped he was doing the right thing. I should have known better.

He was an instant success, he put 30,000 on the Victoria Ground gate and within two years had taken Stoke to promotion, playing in 36 out of their 42 League matches.

One of my saddest moments came when I had to drop out of his testimonial match as I had flu. Great names turned up and I wanted desperately to play, mainly to say thanks for what Stan had done for my career and for football in general.

You know, we used to joke in the dressing-room at Blackpool that if you get under any pressure just give the ball to Stan. Anything could happen then . . . I doubt there will be another like him.

Daily Telegraph, 1 February 1995

Another reaching a birthday milestone was the former England centre forward Tommy Lawton, 75 in October. John Moynihan paid him a visit.

Tommy Lawton
John Moynihan

Tommy Lawton, the great England centre forward, created so many vivid memories of devastating goals scored with his head and feet that it would be difficult to choose one to toast today, his 75th birthday. But if we must pick one, let us choose the winning goal he headed in the final minutes against Scotland in 1939 at Hampden Park. It came from a cross by Stanley Matthews and Bill Shankly used to growl about the sound the ball made hissing in the net.

'I almost turned a somersault in mid-air after that one,' Lawton recalled. 'But Stan's cross was so accurate – the lace seemed to come straight onto my forehead.' Sheer modesty – Lawton's header was stunning all the same.

There is no need to look far for the credentials which made this Lancastrian field marshal in soccer's hall of fame so formidable on the pitch. Lawton's playing career began with Burnley, in the Second Division, four days after his 17th birthday. It required only 30 seconds for him to score the first goal of a hat-trick against Tottenham. He played First Division football for Everton, Chelsea and Arsenal before retiring in 1955. He made 23 full international appearances for England before and after the war, scoring 22 goals.

Now living in a private nursing home outside Nottingham, Lawton retains a keen interest in the game and has strong opinions about the players of today. 'I think it's a great pity Le Tissier hasn't figured more in internationals,' Lawton said. 'He's got so many gifts and he's far more spontaneous than other players in his approach to the game. He doesn't have to look at the bench every minute to find out what to do. That's the difference between our game and the modern one.'

Le Tissier's cheeky qualities share a similarity with Lawton's flair for the unexpected. He would deceive goalkeepers with shots taken almost lazily with the outside of the right foot on their weaker left sides and many were sent the wrong way by the deceptive powers of his headwork from 'hanging' positions.

Despite an arthritic hip, Lawton remains actively involved with the game he still feels passionately about, writing a weekly column for the *Nottingham Evening Post*.

He believes the FA Carling Premiership is 'rich in striking talent'. He enjoyed Alan Shearer's viperish display against a disappointing United States, capped by a typical headed goal he 'would have been proud to score'. He believes Andy Cole has immense talent – 'so quick, so lethal, but he's lucky to have such an inspirational manager in Kevin Keegan, and Peter Beardsley playing alongside him. Beardsley's a revelation – over 30, yet playing like a youngster.'

Memories crowd round Lawton. When he turned up at Brentford for a testimonial at the age of 65, he looked fit enough to play, still sporting that familiar centre parting. Lawton had joined the club in 1952, after helping Notts County to win the Third Division South championship in 1950, scoring 31 goals. His presence had increased the gates from 9,000 to 35,000, breaking two ground records, but

Lawton's pay was £12 per week in the season, with a possible £2 extra for a win, and £10 out of it.

The maximum wage was still in operation, so Lawton did not make a fortune. 'Hard times' followed after Lawton left the game, his family and old playing colleagues such as Joe Mercer helping him through.

Lawton had been dropped prematurely by Walter Winterbottom one game after playing for an England side captained by his old friend, Frank Swift, in one of their greatest post-war victories, in Turin in 1948. England won 4–0 against Italy, Lawton scoring, but it was Stan Mortensen's angled goal in that match which he recalls as 'the greatest goal I've ever seen'.

For the huge crowds at Stamford Bridge after the war, Lawton was unmistakable – the No 9, Brylcreemed head, his shoulders stooped, his legs stretching, often on frozen turf. When Moscow Dynamo played their historic match there 49 years ago, Lawton and the Chelsea team were presented with bouquets before the match. 'We felt like film stars at a premiere.' Lawton scored in a 3–3 draw, the Dynamo goalkeeper, Tiger Khomich, calling him 'a prima donna – but an excellent header of the ball'.

To many older supporters, like Joe Latham, a retired Merseyside seaman, Lawton remains the best of all time, and that includes Dixie Dean. 'Poor old Everton need him now, don't they? Happy birthday, Tommy – maestro.'

The Times, 6 October 1994

The sudden death of the former England and Wolverhampton Wanderers captain Billy Wright brought back memories of the 1950s and a golden era in English football when Wright was the inspiration behind his country and club.

Death of a Hero: Billy Wright
Ken Jones

Even people who never miss an opportunity to boast that they are utterly uninformed about athletic activity were aware that Billy Wright preserved the flavour of a time in sport that is long gone.

As captain of Wolverhampton Wanderers and in 90 of 105 appearances for England, his international career spanning 13 years, Wright represented values probably beyond the comprehension of a generation that perceives the urge to succeed in sport as the urge to make a million.

Although proud to be a professional, there was always something essentially Corinthian about the conscientious purpose that enabled Wright to complete his career as a ruggedly efficient defender without ever incurring a referee's wrath. The game was all to Wright and remained so until his death, at 70, on Saturday.

If not the most naturally gifted of footballers, and short for the outstanding central defender he became after he inspired conversion from wing half, Wright possessed qualities that even today's managers and coaches would drool over.

Compact, with powerful legs, Wright's principal asset was the speed with which he made interceptions and launched tackles. Not many defenders of that era made their decisions and went in for the ball with his speed and certainty. Walter Winterbottom, who managed England throughout Wright's career, once said of him, 'In the pure qualities of defence, in interception, in recovering at lightning speed when beaten, in firm and indomitable tackling, he has been an important player: one of the best defenders England has ever had, and always, always excellent in the air.'

I think it is important to stress these things about Wright because in tributes there has been a sentimental tendency to dwell more on his modest appreciation of the good things that happened to him after first being rejected by Wolves than his contribution to the most turbulent period in the history of English football.

Wright would joke that the clip of film most frequently requested by the Arsenal players he managed is that which shows Ferenc Puskas making him look foolish before scoring one of the six goals that Hungary ran up at Wembley in November 1953 to finally shatter the arrogant myth of English invincibility.

Worse was to come, a 7–1 defeat in Budapest six months later, and with it the decision that would extend Wright's international career to record proportions. Without a quality centre-half since the defection of Neil Franklin to Bogotá, leading to an inevitable suspension from international football, Winterbottom turned to his captain. 'The Hungarians were the best team I have ever come across and their superiority filled us with gloom,' Wright recalled.

'We couldn't live with them and with the 1954 World Cup in Switzerland coming up, Walter had to rebuild his defence. When he asked me about moving to centre-half I wasn't entirely sure, but I had implicit faith in his judgement.'

There can be no reservations about Wright's worth as a centre-half. It was stubbornly in his nature never to give up and a more precisely defined role that made fewer demands upon imagination suited him perfectly. Certainly the switch suited Wolves and their stern manager, Stan Cullis, who like Wright was chosen to captain England in his early twenties and in preference to men of much greater experience. They didn't always see eye to eye but are inextricably linked with the most successful period in Wolves' history.

None of the game's domestic honours eluded Wright and but for the awful fate that befell Manchester United in 1958 there might have been even greater glory. 'Until the death of so many outstanding young players I felt England would be match for any of the World Cup finalists in Sweden,' he said one night in the sweet long ago. 'Duncan Edwards, Roger Byrne, Tommy Taylor, Eddie Colman, my goodness what a team we could have put out.'

In common with any number of famous players, Wright was uncomfortable in management although Don Howe, a contemporary in the England team who joined him at Highbury as a player, feels that given more time he would have made a success of it.

Arsenal's decision not to renew the three-year contract Wright signed in 1963 hurt him more than he was prepared to admit. 'I didn't take to the job easily,' he said, 'but things were beginning to move and at least I can say that I left them with a lot of outstanding young players.'

It was the one great disappointment in Wright's career. The rest, including a happy marriage to the singer Joy Beverley and advancement in television, was more than he could have imagined.

The importance of being earnest and loyal and fair was strong within Billy Wright. There were failings too, but as Winterbottom said, 'The destructive criticisms of which most of us are guilty from time to time never come from Billy. This is not because he can't think along these lines, or because he prefers the peaceful, uncontroversial life. He simply feels that he does not have the right to make these criticisms.'

I wonder what today's crop of players would have made of him.

Independent, 5 September 1994

The former Barnsley half-back Skinner Normanton might almost have been forgotten were it not for Michael Parkinson keeping his name alive. Sadly Normanton died in April 1995. Michael Parkinson paid tribute to him.

Skinner Normanton
Michael Parkinson

Skinner Normanton died peacefully the other day aged 68. Between 1947 and 1953 he played 134 times for Barnsley and ended his career with a brief spell at Halifax. He retired to his garden where he grew sunflowers and turned out occasionally for the local team when they were a man short.

Sydney Albert Normanton was a local legend when he played at Barnsley. He was the hard man of the side, the minder for ball-playing colleagues of delicate disposition. There wasn't much of him but every ounce counted. He was destructive in the tackle, as unrelenting as a heat-seeking missile in pursuit of the enemy.

If I close my eyes I see two images. The first is a still photograph with Skinner posed in the manner of the day, arms folded and one foot on a leather football. His hair was short and wavy, parted near the middle and rigid with Brylcreem, and his legs were as sturdy as pit props with bulging shinpads and bulbous toecaps that glowed with dubbin and menace.

My second memory is more like a black and white film of the time with Skinner taking a penalty in a cup tie and running from the halfway line before toe-ending the sodden football which became a blur as it passed the motionless goalkeeper, crashed into the underside of the crossbar and rebounded on to the back of the goalkeeper's head and into the net.

The goalkeeper was poleaxed and took several minutes to recover and it wasn't until much later that the iron crossbar stopped quivering from the impact of the shot. For a while it hummed like a male voice choir.

He was a local celebrity. Mothers would tell their children to stop mucking about or they would send for Skinner. He gained a wider audience many years after he retired when I first wrote about him in another paper.

I don't know what it was about the article that captured the imagination. I think it might have been the name. If you wanted to invent a local football hero of the time, someone who worked in the pits during the week and spent Saturday afternoons kicking lumps off the opposition you'd invent a man called something like Skinner Normanton.

Whatever the reason his fame extended far beyond his beloved Oakwell. There used to be a Skinner Normanton Appreciation Society in Kuala Lumpur, and I have been asked about him during all my travels throughout the world. There was something in the name that was irresistible to Brits living abroad, particularly when they were feeling homesick for Saturday afternoons and kick-off time.

Many people believed him to be a mythical character like The Great Wilson of the *Wizard*. I remember Yorkshire Television producing him as a surprise guest on a programme I was doing in Leeds. They brought him into the studio and announced him in triumphant fashion as if they had found Lord Lucan or were about to produce the Loch Ness monster on the end of a lead.

He was smaller than I remembered and was wearing a blue shirt with a nipped in waist. The hair was as immaculate as ever and he looked like he was going to church. I had never seen him in his Sunday best. When he spoke his voice was soft, the manner modest even shy.

It was difficult to convince people that this gentle and diffident man had one time put the fear of God up any member of the human race who didn't wear a Barnsley shirt. Well, that's not strictly true. Sometimes even his own team-mates were victims of Skinner's fierce competitive spirit.

He was once sent off by the manager in a practice game and Danny Blanchflower, who played a season or two with Skinner, rejoiced in the story of his first encounter with the great man.

We bought Danny from Glentoran. At that time Barnsley had a successful side and the new player worried about fitting into what he imagined to be a much more sophisticated set-up than he had been used to in Ireland. Come the first practice game and Danny was picked against Skinner.

He told me: 'I saw this guy coming towards me with the ball and I was looking for him to do something really skilful. I thought that perhaps he might beat me on the inside, or might have a body swerve, or would he just nutmeg me. I was thinking all these possibilities but he just kept coming. The next thing I knew I'm flat on my back and Skinner's footprints are on the front of my shirt.'

There wasn't room for both of them at Oakwell and for a while Skinner fretted in the reserves while Blanchflower began a journey that ended in the Pantheon. Skinner settled for something less but there will be many who didn't know him, nor ever saw him play, who will mourn him.

He played at a time when the game drank deep from its tap roots and although there were many more skilful and talented than he there was no one who better represented what you were up against if you took on a collier from Barnsley.

I was thinking that they ought to name the new stand at Barnsley after him. The Skinner Normanton stand would be a constant reminder that no matter how much we merchandise the modern game we must always remember what it is we are really selling.

Nowadays they talk of image. There was a time, when Skinner was a lad, when it had a soul.

Daily Telegraph, 1 May 1995

Chapter Four

The Managers

Introduction

Last season 13 Premiership managers lost their jobs, making it surely the worst season on record. The line between success and the sack seems to become more blurred with each season. What qualities are needed for the job is anyone's guess; even more puzzling is why anyone should wish to become a manager.

Who'd be a Manager

Glenn Moore

Are you sitting comfortably? If the answer is yes, you are probably not a Premier League manager. Three sackings and a resignation in 11 days will have had all but a handful of bosses glancing nervously over their shoulder. Behind them could be a disgruntled chairman armed and dangerous with a P45.

The bloodletting has been so hectic even Jesus Gil, Atlético Madrid's notorious hire 'em and fire 'em chairman, would feel a bit squeamish. Many managers might be tempted to agree with Brian Clough, who said he was better off out of it, pottering in the garden and seeing his grandchildren.

Job security and football management have long been unrelated concepts. When John Giles resigned as player-manager of West

Bromwich Albion almost 20 years ago his parting comment was that 'the only certainty in management was the sack'. More recently John Barnwell, now the manager of Northampton, noted that 'if you are a manager you don't have fitted carpets.'

But it seems to be getting worse. The prospect of four clubs being relegated from the Premier League at the end of the season is clearly concentrating the minds of some chairmen.

What is particularly frightening for those on the merry-go-round is the speed with which a manager's stock can fall. Ron Atkinson, dismissed on Thursday by Aston Villa, was hailed as a tactical genius six months ago after his team defeated Manchester United in the Coca-Cola Cup final. Even last month he was a hero after Villa knocked Internazionale, the holders, out of the UEFA Cup.

There were similarities with the case of Mike Walker, who was sacked by Everton on Tuesday. A year ago he was feted for taking Norwich City into Europe and defeating Bayern Munich. Everton, having identified Walker as the man to revive their fortunes, wanted him so badly they incurred a hefty fine and tarnished image by recruiting him in controversial circumstances. Yet by this week he had become a liability.

His story mirrors that of Ossie Ardiles, lured from West Bromwich to Tottenham and sacked 16 months later. The man who could replace him, Gerry Francis, is so highly rated that he also figured in speculation about the jobs at Everton and Villa. Yet Francis considers he has been effectively pushed out by his own club, Queen's Park Rangers.

So who will be next? Of the 22 Premiership managers only three – George Graham, Alex Ferguson and Howard Wilkinson – were appointed before the summer of 1991. All three are Championship winners. In the Football League prospects are even grimmer. Just five of its 70 managers have been in place since the start of 1990 (John King at Tranmere, Dave Bassett at Sheffield United, Dario Gradi at Crewe, Danny Bergara at Stockport and Brian Flynn at Wrexham).

At the bottom, financial pressures lead to managers answering the switchboard or painting the stand. At the top, the telephone never stops and every move is scrutinised by the media, every loss magnified. And in between dealing with press, public and chairman, the manager has to oversee coaching, contracts and transfers.

Gerry Francis, quoted last year in Denis Campbell and Andrew

Sheilds' book *Soccer City*, said management 'can be seven-day-a-week hell. It just does not stop, your life is not your own.

'The pressure is immense. I saw Jock Stein [who died of a heart attack during a match when he was manager of Scotland] the day before he died and that will always be a vivid picture in my mind. He looked very stressed. I can understand why Kenny Dalglish left management for a year because it is not just the stresses on you, it is the stresses on your whole family and friends. You are never at home. Your family get it worse because the first people you take the stress out on are the people you love most.'

Yet it is no surprise that so many former players want to take it up, says Steve Coppell, the former Crystal Palace manager and chief executive of the League Managers' Association.

'For many it is all they know,' he said, 'and there is a certain joy to be involved in football. The raw materials are wonderful.

'You go in and make a few calls and deal with some paperwork and then, for a couple of hours every morning, you are in the fresh air having fun with a group of young people who sometimes exasperate you but often motivate you. Then, following an afternoon in the office, you watch football in the evening.'

It sounds tempting, doesn't it? Especially if you work in an office or factory, or cannot find work at all. But, Coppell adds, it has its drawbacks.

'Initially the biggest shock for many ex-players is the workload. From going home at one in the afternoon you are getting back at one in the morning after chasing players at a match somewhere.

'The press are more intrusive and, even if seven or eight players all play badly together, it is always the manager that is to blame.

'From talking to other managers, what comes across most is that it is a lonely occupation. The manager is under pressure from all sides. People you hope are loyal and support you make comments to the press which are couched in threatening terms. You go to functions and supporters come up and, either jokingly or seriously, put you under more pressure. It is an isolated job.'

Liam Brady, now managing Brighton after an unsuccessful spell in charge of Celtic, said: 'It is becoming like Italy, especially the media interest with even the quality broadsheets getting involved. The recent sackings are ridiculous. It takes time to build a side, to get players to do what you want. You have to give the manager a fair crack. If a chairman keeps chopping and changing he might obtain success, but if you look at the successful clubs most have had stability.'

Brady believes that most of the recent sackings have been decided by individual chairmen, not boards. Certainly it would appear that the rise of the high-profile chairman has exacerbated managers' problems: the desire for success – and reflected glory – is greater and the chance of boardroom support is smaller.

When the axe comes it is sometimes unexpected, but there are usually clues. Terry Venables knew he was on the way out at Barcelona when the crowds at the Nou Camp began to wave handkerchiefs, a traditional sign of displeasure. Ron Atkinson, given the reputation of 'Deadly Doug' Ellis, might have guessed his number was up after the chairman publicly expressed his dissatisfaction at recent results.

Other chairmen stop returning their manager's calls, the secretary fails to meet his eye. One manager said it got to the stage where even the groundsman stopped coming to ask whether he wanted the pitch watered.

Brady, who resigned at Celtic, said: 'It got a bit like that. The people who are there to help you are no longer there. I was not dismissed, but I was aware that I had very few friends.'

But, a few months later, he was back in a hot seat. On Thursday Atkinson, within hours of being sacked, was offering his services to any interested party. Coppell admits he would like to return to management – when it suits him to do so.

So why, despite all the aggravation, do they do it? Simple really: like you, like me, they would rather be out there playing and management is the nearest thing to it.

Independent, 12 November 1994

KENNY DALGLISH
Paul Simpson

'I don't even know who Kenny Dalglish is,' exclaims a woman outside Wembley stadium. Her husband laughs: 'You are about to improve your football education.' They are caught in a knot of about 80 people who have collected just below the Twin Towers in the hope that they might see, touch or talk to their idol. But when he finally appears, his sheer physical presence quietens them. He doesn't sign any autographs. Not because he doesn't want to but because the crowd are too timid to ask. He slides through them, silently, a suit bag slung over his shoulder. He isn't flanked by flunkies, but by one overweight guard. Dalglish keeps walking purposefully through the crowd until he sees a man in a wheelchair. Then he turns around, squeezes the man's shoulder with his hand, smiles for the camera and stands up. 'Cheers pal,' he says, squeezing the man on the shoulder for the last time.

The crowd play 'Follow-my-leader' as he strides down the steps and into the car park where the Blackburn coach is waiting. He looks so tanned, he might have just finished a round at his favourite golf course. During matches, he can still look as if, in that memorable phrase he used at Liverpool, his head might explode. But here he looks completely at ease even though Rovers lost 2–0 to United in the Charity Shield (never his favourite team to lose to), had four players booked and had so many illnesses the press had dubbed the club 'Hepatitis Rovers'. At the coach, he hands his suit bag to the driver and turns around to sign autographs. Each signing is accompanied by a nod and a 'Cheers pal'. He poses with his arm around a fan's shoulder and then turns to find his seat but he doesn't get off that lightly. The fan's brother wants his picture taken too. Patiently, Dalglish turns, clasps the fan's shoulder and summons up one last smile, which even looks vaguely sincere. Then with a shake of the hand and a last 'Cheers pal' he climbs onto the half-empty coach.

Saturday 10 September. The players' tunnel Ewood Park, Blackburn. Rovers have shaken off hepatitis and a long list of other ailments to beat Everton 3–0 and stay second in the Premier League. The press are waiting for Dalglish to emerge from the inner sanctum of the dressing rooms. He's not renowned for punctuality so they talk among themselves ('Was that a penalty?' 'Who brought him down?'). There, behind them, almost unnoticed, stands the solitary slim figure of Dalglish. He is wearing the Rovers' regulation suit (blue/black jacket and trousers, white shirt and blue patterned tie) and is waiting, hands in pockets, for the ordeal to begin. The press start at a disadvantage: they know he will punish a daft question just as surely as Shearer punishes a defensive error. One of his friends in the media says: 'He said to me once he just gets bored answering questions about how he feels when the team's won 2–0' (hence his frequent advice to reporters: 'Write what you saw'). The journalists know the whole ritual bores Dalglish so they cover up their unease with false joviality and ask the kind of question he must have been asked a thousand times: 'You must be happy, Kenny, winning 3–0 . . .'

It's hard to say whether Kenny's happy or not. He looks down at the floor, glances at the massed ranks of mini tape recorders and begins to talk in a very soft mumble which is almost calculated to evade the eavesdropping tape recorders. 'This is bloody useless,' says one reporter in despair, trying to shove his tape a few feet closer to the great man. Dalglish is about to deliver his patented post-match press conference interview which runs something like this: 'It was a good team performance. It's good we kept a clean sheet. As long as we can keep it tight at the back, with our forwards we always feel we can nick a goal or two.' If he's feeling talkative, he might flesh this out with a few remarks like 'I was really pleased with the way the fans got behind the lads', 'The lads gave everything they had' or 'The lads make every new player who comes (and there've been a few) feel very welcome.'

Today, he delivers the shortened version. When it's over, the voice just trails off, he looks at the floor and waits for the next question. Like the great movie stars, Dalglish has (either by instinct or design) discovered the art of standing completely still. When he talks, his most flamboyant physical gesture is to rock back on his heels ever so slightly. The tan is a little less obvious now, worn away by the Ewood Park wind. He looks like a cross between Robert Redford and Stephen Hendry.

The next question, about Shearer, has him talking about the team. 'The lads up front deserve credit but it's a team performance . . .' This is not because he has anything against Shearer, it's just that he's been reared on the belief (at Liverpool and Celtic) that no individual is bigger than the team. That applies to Shearer as much as it once did to a player called Kenny Dalglish.

The irony is that, as his old captain Billy McNeil says, 'You can just imagine he loves having Shearer there.' Shearer is the one player at Blackburn, possibly even in the England team, who has the technical ability which marked out the young Dalglish. But as a manager he suppresses all that, talking up the team, expounding an 'All for one and one for all' philosophy which he could have borrowed from the Three Musketeers.

The press conference is almost over. Dalglish makes a joke about 'youth policy' which has the journalists laughing with all the reckless abandon of a PR man laughing when his client makes a joke. Then there's a round of 'Thank you Kenny's' and he walks back towards the dressing room.

Sunday 18 September, Stamford Bridge. 'Don't commit yourself'. Dalglish, in a tan suit which looks several sizes too big for him, is shouting at Rovers' Robbie Slater. This is a slight change of tack: most of the time he's been shouting at Shearer. 'Al! Al! Al!' The chant is semi-continuous interrupted by the odd shout of 'Mark Spacker!' [Nigel Spackman]. Usually, when he knows the game is being televised, he turns his face into a mask but today, after the midweek shock against Trelleborgs, he can't be restrained. When Sutton scores, Dalglish walks onto the pitch, his arms stretched above his head. If the mood takes him, he can be one of the best celebrators of a goal in British football. When Shearer scored his second against Manchester United at Ewood Park last season, his manager's grin would have left a Cheshire Cat feeling like a manic depressive.

Dalglish is, ultimately, a mysterious figure. The Ewood Park crowd chant 'Dalgleesh' and he invariably acknowledges the tribute with a wave. 'He can do no wrong,' says Paul Loftus, editor of the Blackburn fanzine *Loadsamoney*. But his status is remote, God-like. When he first arrived at Ewood Park, the team used to train on a public playing field. 'We used to be lucky to get one man and his dog turning up,' said Tony Parkes, Blackburn's assistant coach. 'When Kenny arrived, 400 people turned up. They didn't believe he'd come to Blackburn. Now they are fascinated by him.' They're not the only ones: Dalglish continues to fascinate the press and even some old colleagues. Asked what motivates Dalglish, Steve Heighway, who worked with him at Anfield, replies: 'He's a fairly complex person. It's not easy to tell what he's thinking and he doesn't confide in many people. I don't know enough about his background or his personal life to say whether he was ambitious to get on.' Liverpool's chief scout Ron Yeats has no doubt what drives his old boss: 'Winning.' His analysis echoes Don Revie's famous observation that 'I have come to the conclusion that Kenny Dalglish has been put on this earth by God to be a winner at everything. I honestly believe he has been blessed.' At golf, where he has a handicap of ten, he is, according to an opponent, a gangster. One of his old Liverpool team-mates agrees. 'He never wanted to lose anything. Not even a game of darts in a pub.'

Being a good loser is not a habit that Dalglish has ever wanted to acquire. That's why he's often been accused of whinging after a defeat (his performance after a defeat at Luton prompted the joke: 'What's the difference between a jumbo jet and Kenny Dalglish? The jumbo stops whining over Luton') Losing was, is and will always be a personal insult for a man whose career has known such extremes of triumph and anguish.

The list of triumphs is immense: five Scottish championship medals, five Scottish Cup medals, five Football League championship medals (as a player), three European Cup winners medals, four League Cup winners medals, three League titles (as a manager) and two FA Cup wins (as a manager), including the 1985/86 double in his first season as manager, two footballer of the year awards, three manager of the year awards and one MBE.

It is an impressive haul for the son of a diesel engineer born a stone's throw from the Glasgow Celtic ground. But public success has been marred by public tragedy: his reign as manager of Liverpool was marred by two tragedies, Heysel and Hillsborough, which left 134 people dead. It was Hillsborough, finally, that caused him to question the value of the sport which has dominated his adult life. Suddenly, winning wasn't everything. He said: 'The FA Cup isn't worth it. Nothing is worth one death, let alone 100.' With that he took his leaving of Liverpool and retired for seven months to Lancashire's golf coast. When he returned to manage Blackburn Rovers, he joked that his wife, Marina, wanted him out of the house. The truth is he was hardly ever in the house. He spent most of the day on the golf course, a few hundred yards from the family home in Southport. And then 'Uncle Jack' (as he used to call Jack Walker) lured him back, not with money, but with the chance to build a winning team. 'You couldn't see Kenny managing a team that didn't have a chance to win the League,' says Yeats. 'If he did, he wouldn't enjoy it.' He didn't, as some have said, come back to prove himself. As he once told a reporter: 'I don't have to prove myself to nobody.'

Some say that, being such a great player himself, he finds it hard to accept the limitations of other players. 'I think he gets frustrated when players without his technical ability can't do what he could do,' says a coach. It's a charge that Dalglish has always denied. In an unusually frank interview with the *Financial Times* in 1989, he said:

'We're all different and I can't expect people to be the same as me. I respect people for what they are or what they do or achieve. You can't succeed by trying to make everyone clones of the manager. I do what I think is right and I just hope that I make more good decisions than bad ones.' His method for motivating players is pretty simple. 'I don't set them any targets. I just tell them to go out and do their best and if they do their best, they should win matches,' he said in the 1993/94 club video.

But what of Dalglish the tactician? At Liverpool, he is said to have changed his tactics more often than any of his predecessors but Hansen, for one, doesn't agree. 'He just played to his strengths and to the other side's weaknesses.' The style of play of his teams has changed with the players but its roots are in the passing game played by Celtic and Liverpool. At Blackburn, Trevor Brooking says: 'He likes to use the width of the pitch. It's not a long ball game but Liverpool had a bit more variation in their midfield play.' Dalglish doesn't like football played in the air. One of his players says: 'He likes constructive play. He always likes us to look to play the ball forward before we play it square or behind.'

His teams are always determined but, latterly, not invincible. Last season's victory over United at Ewood Park was a good example of the best of Dalglish and Rovers. 'It's very easy to see what Manchester United do but it's very hard to stop them doing it,' says a coach. 'But that day, Blackburn did a very professional job.' It wasn't pretty (especially in the first half) but it was effective.

He still gets involved in coaching at Blackburn. 'Ray [Harford, the assistant manager] will start talking,' says a player, 'and suddenly you'll hear this Scottish accent from the back and everyone will look around thinking "What did he say?" '

At 43, he is not above training by example. 'He loves to win those five-a-side matches,' says a player. 'If he's quiet, you know he probably didn't have a great game, but if he's scored a couple of goals, he'll be cracking jokes.'

The press has been waiting for him to quit ever since he left Liverpool but he seems a different man now. The depth of the trauma he endured at Anfield after Hillsborough will never be known but by the time he left, a rash had broken out all over his body, match days were doing his head in and his face had sallowed with the strain. Yeats, who worked in the next office to him, says: 'You could see the pressure getting to him. But when he came into the office to tell me and Steve Heighway I was devastated. It was the only time I've seen Kenny cry.'

He once said: 'I may leave Liverpool but Liverpool will never leave me.' He was wrong: his legend will never leave Liverpool, just as it has never left Celtic; in Govan (where he was born) he is still regarded with the reverence normally reserved for a god.

But it is at Blackburn where this compulsive winner now practises his trade. To friends and colleagues, his unwillingness to explain himself, to let his teams do the talking is laudable, even funny. 'I couldn't point a finger and say that a particular thing was relevant to this, that or the other,' he told an interviewer once. He doesn't want his life explained.

His laconic advice to a biographer would probably be: 'Write what you saw'. A poet, Alan Bold, did just that once. In a poem named after its hero he wrote: 'Subtle, supple, cunning, quick, Dalglish, sheer football magic', which sums up this elusive man as well as anybody ever has.

FourFourTwo, November 1994

Kevin Keegan
Amy Lawrence

'How can I tell my youngsters this is the best club in the world when the bath is not clean and the toilets are dirty?' asked Kevin Keegan on his first day in charge at Newcastle United.

4 February 1992. Newcastle are second from bottom in the Second Division, in financial crisis, and relegation could kill the club. Keegan has never managed a club before. And the toilets are dirty. Keegan wants to prove to his youngsters that playing for Newcastle means playing for 'the best club in the world'. Some task.

His first lesson to the players was taught with a mop not a football. This diligent spring-cleaning gave the baths a shine, but its main aim was to stamp Keegan's authority on the club. It wouldn't be a great surprise if he'd ordered the trophy cabinet to be given a polish while they were at it.

Keegan had famously ridiculed the very idea of a career in management when he finished playing, telling the press in 1985: 'If anybody ever hears that Kevin Keegan is coming back to football full-time, they can laugh as much as I will. It will never happen. That is certain'. Nobody laughed when Keegan returned from his eight-year siesta to manage Newcastle, they just hoped he could save the club from relegation to the Third Division. But the football fraternity did question the wisdom of appointing someone with absolutely no management experience and no contact with the game for the best part of a decade.

Keegan tackled the job the only way he knew how – like Mr Motivator on steroids. 'I feel like I've come home,' he smiled on his first day back at St James' Park. Almost 30,000 fans flocked to the next game at home to Bristol City, to welcome the reborn hero. Keegan had inspired the Geordie faithful, and the Geordie faithful inspired him. The match finished 3–0 to Newcastle and Keegan had embarked on his latest, greatest, adventure.

So why did he turn his back on a life of golf, gee-gees and glorious Spanish sunshine? The man of many perms told *FourFourTwo*: 'I suddenly decided, one beautiful sunny day, I don't want to be doing this all the time, I just stopped enjoying the break and I said to Jean when I got home, "I'm not going to play golf anymore. I want to do something." ' That he wandered into the St James' Park hot-seat is no great surprise. His playing days show he always had a taste for the unexpected, responding brilliantly to raised eyebrows. His transfer from Scunthorpe to Liverpool was about the only logical move in his career.

Inevitably, the 'Anfield way' has shaped Keegan as a manager. Shankly was his mentor. Keegan cites meeting the great man as 'the highlight of my life'. Shankly appears to have been almost as impressed by Keegan: 'Kevin is like a weasel after rats,' he said. 'Always biting and snapping at your legs. He's a perfect size. A fully fledged middleweight, the greatest fighter of them all.'

Comparisons between Liverpool of the 1970s and Newcastle of the 1990s are often made; the well-structured bootroom, the inspirational boss, the fluid and supremely effective football and the air of invincibility that surrounds the club. Shankly's influence on Liverpool left a huge impression on Keegan: 'Liverpool was a myth and Bill Shankly built that myth. Because of the players we had and the characters in the side, people thought "let's watch Liverpool" because they were doing something different.'

In 1991, during his Spanish sabbatical, Keegan visited Anfield to see the Reds take on QPR. Liverpool lost 1–3 and the former king of the Kop was not impressed. He told the *Sun*: 'That team wasn't the Liverpool I know. At times, there was no commitment, no confidence, no passion, no shape and no spark.' Take away the negatives and you have an accurate description of what drives Keegan's Newcastle: confidence, commitment, passion, shape and spark.

Don Revie was another from whom Keegan learned a great deal. As an England player, Kev's perceptions of his much-maligned manager are telling. In his book *Against the World*, Keegan said: 'If I ever became a manager I would be more like Revie than any of the other managers I have known. His team-talks were sensational. Most people thought of him as a tactician . . . but I saw him as a motivator. Sometimes he, and we, would be almost crying. He motivated me. He made me feel I belonged in an England team.'

As a manager, some suggest Keegan isn't a natural tactician, but he compensates by calling on the kind of drive which had, as a player, led Shankly to compare him to a fully fledged middleweight champion and led Uwe Seeler, the captain of the 1970 West German side, to compare him to a little Volkswagen. Newcastle chairman Sir John Hall says: 'There isn't a side anywhere in the UK that wouldn't want Kevin Keegan as manager of their club after what he's done on the park. And all this from a man who had been out of the game for eight years. He'd been playing golf in Marbella. He had his own businesses. He was very independent. Everybody said to me: "John, why have you done this? Why pick someone outside the game?" It was a big gamble for him and ourselves. It's now proven – Kevin was the only person who could have taken control of the playing side of the club and turned it around.'

In the eyes of his chairman he can do no wrong. In the eyes of his players he can do no wrong. In the eyes of his fans, he's God. So what is it that makes Kevin Keegan so brilliant? The talented team he has assembled off the pitch is at the heart of his success. Newcastle's unsung heroes are Terry McDermott, Arthur Cox and Derek Fazackerley. When Keegan took the job, Sir John insisted he had the best support staff: 'It's a team effort. It was my suggestion Kevin got some help. He brought this team in with him because he knows them and they work well together. Their help enables Kevin to have thinking time, which is so important. Football managers and chairmen don't normally get thinking time. We can sit down and think about the future.'

Terry McDermott is Keegan's right-hand man. They have been pals for 20 years and McDermott enthuses that they have never had a cross word in all that time. He feels lucky to be riding on the Geordie bandwagon, but Keegan is also lucky to have someone on board he trusts implicitly. McDermott has vast experience of the game and a large helping of traditional Scouse banter (a bonus in any dressing room). 'I take some of the workload off him,' says McDermott. 'It's a hell of a job for one person. We try and take any problems away from the players. Being a footballer is a pressure job. Kevin will never shut his door to any player. We're forever talking to them. They come into the office and have a cocoa or a bar of chocolate. You'll always find the players in here.' Unlike most Premiership managers, Keegan doesn't have his own office. He prefers to share it with his management team (and any players with a fetish for Milky Ways).

Newcastle realise how many people are desperate to share in their success. St James' Park is a stadium to be proud of, but can't accommodate the numbers of adoring fans (and some of the fans can't afford tickets whatever the capacity). So the club decided to open their training sessions to the general public. Although this might occasionally hamper the work achieved during training sessions (would Keegan give his defence a rollicking in front of 4000 besotted onlookers?) Keegan speaks passionately about it: 'When the hell can they see their heroes? I tell Coley, "These are the ones who will buy your Reebok boots". The lads accept it fully. For the younger ones it's the norm.' For away games, United beam live pictures back to three Newcastle cinemas to satisfy the fans unable to travel with the Toon Army.

Barry Venison, one of several Newcastle players born in the North East, says: 'The hardcore 10,000 who came when we were struggling are unbelievable. They've got to be admired for supporting the team through thick and thin . . . and there was an awful lot of thin and not much thick. If you're not proud to play for them you might as well hang your boots up and go away. Just get that pipe out and go to bed.' Venners admits he gets carried away by the enthusiasm that is sweeping the city. 'The passion of the fans is infectious. I get wound up about games with them. Sometimes I even have to cut myself off because I'm getting too worked up.'

Newcastle's potential is enormous. Keegan, Sir John and the players frequently refer to the 'snowball effect' to describe the rapid growth of the club since 1992, a crucial year in the Magpies' history. Not only did it signal Keegan's return, it was also the year when Sir John took full control of the club. McMenemy says their partnership is 'a dream ticket for Tyneside' and former Newcastle boss Jim Smith cannot overstate the importance of their relationship: 'Kevin has had to change things and buy players. It must be easier talking to one boss rather than a load.' Smith should know. During his spell in charge at St James' Park, he was hampered by an unsettled board and a financial crisis. Sir John says of his arrangement with Keegan: 'There's sympathy and understanding between us. We have a common purpose. That is Newcastle United and the Geordie nation.'

The snowball is fast becoming an avalanche. Sir John's vision for the future should send shock waves throughout European football. He plans to extend the commercial side (the club's turnover has grown from £5m to £24m in two years), the media side (Hall wants to be involved in a weekly newspaper, a radio station and City TV) and a 325-acre soccer academy. 'I want to have a structure and a long-term future. I want to network the whole of the North East, so that in a sense, no Geordie ever has to leave the area again. My eventual dream is to have 11 Geordies playing for Newcastle United and 11 in the reserves. I want to consistently be one of the top three in the UK and one of the top ten in Europe. The only cups I'm concerned with are the Premier League and the European Champions' League. When you've got those, you're somebody.'

Keegan is instrumental in translating this dream into reality. (Sir John persuaded him to sign a ten-year deal, which McDermott believes is 'the best thing the chairman has ever done'.) On the one hand, the two work closely together in plotting the future, and on the other, the success of Keegan's team has provided the foundations to rebuild the club financially.

Keegan's players thrive on bold team spirit, natural ability and composure. It is a prerequisite that all his players are comfortable on the ball, think quickly, and are supremely fit. The tactics are simple. 'Get the ball, pass it to a black and white shirt, and move. That's what to do,' says McDermott. 'It's unfortunate that you get some trainers trying to complicate things with over-elaborate tactics and Christmas tree formations. The art of being a good manager is knowing a good player.' Barry Venison, Scott Sellars, Robert Lee, Ruel Fox, John Beresford and Andy Cole. Not a bad list of players judged by Keegan to be worthy of the famous black and white shirt. They were all good players at their previous clubs, but under the guidance of Keegan and friends they have developed into world beaters. 'I think I'm a good judge of a player,' says Keegan. His discerning eye appears to be instinctive. He recently went to watch a player in Scotland. Within 30 seconds of kick-off, Keegan knew he didn't like the look of him and left. 'As soon as he ran out I saw he was the wrong shape. I've got this thing about the shape of footballers.'

Good judgement is one thing. Persuading quality players to join a struggling club is another. This is obviously not a problem now, but when he became manager of a team in the relegation zone of the Second Division, he desperately needed to boost the squad with talent. Beresford was linked with a host of top-flight clubs and Venison had a pocket full of medals from Liverpool. Venison explains what swayed him: 'The boss was honest with me. He talked to me about potential. He was confident about buying some new players, and felt we could go on to win the Championship. He was true to his word. He got who he wanted and we won the title. Kevin Keegan is the main reason I signed – because he's never been associated with losing.'

The philosophy is straightforward. Keegan's priority is to ensure his players are happy, confident and enjoying their football. His backroom team see to that. Mick Channon, former Southampton and England team-mate, is not surprised by the spirit of Keegan's boys: 'He could never get enough of football. He just loves the game and that has rubbed off on his players.'

One training procedure that has been mysteriously rejected concerns a yellow vest with the words 'I'm a donkey' printed on it. At the end of each week, the squad would vote for the worst trainer, and the winner earned the dubious reward of having to wear the fetching yellow vest. 'It disappeared after the Gaffer won it three times on the trot. Rumour has it he took it away and burned it!' admitted one of the players.

Team spirit gives a football club soul and Newcastle's team spirit is so strong Venison likens it to 'Robin Hood's merry men'. In addition to the obvious teamwork on the field, the lads are close off it. They are together when they go out for meals, drink and chat after matches, go and watch the reserves, and just hang out at their second home – the local health club. 'The atmosphere is mega,' says

Venison. 'We'll all be in a big group, and if you come in it might look a bit insular, but we just have such a good time among ourselves. The dressing room spirit is the hub of any club and within the four walls of ours there is a great togetherness.' McDermott agrees: 'It's a fun club to be at. We wind the players up and they wind us up. They are forever giving us stick.'

There might be a lighthearted atmosphere, but in the words of Venison, Newcastle 'is not a Christmas club'. Management want success, and are ready to be ruthless to get it. The players make a few wisecracks, but they respect what Keegan and McDermott achieved as players. Cox once said that Keegan was a very bad loser and his players know that. At half-time during Newcastle's visit to Aston Villa in October, Keegan reminded his players that their performance wasn't worthy of the famous black and white. In the second half, they came out and won 2–0.

Keegan's methods of motivation are sometimes intuitive and sometimes well planned. Witness the performance of Ruel Fox at Antwerp in the UEFA Cup. Keegan wanted Peter Beardsley back in the side after his cheekbone injury but, to protect him, wanted to give him a less demanding role. He said: 'When Peter's playing in a central position he's here, there and everywhere chasing the ball like a man possessed. I wanted him to play for the whole season so I asked him to play on the right. But I told Ruel Fox (who had been playing in Beardsley's position) "Peter's coming back and wants to play up front, but you've done so well there that I'm not willing to put him back in his best position". Well, Foxy, he's a small lad and he suddenly grew bigger. It wasn't a mickey take. It was an encouragement for Ruel to prove himself.'

Nobody at Newcastle talks about pressure. They prefer to use the word expectation. When Keegan arrived, the first thing he said was that he wanted promotion. He was horrified when someone told him that in saying so he was piling too much pressure on the players. 'This is Newcastle United,' he said. 'What's wrong with saying we want to get out of the Second Division?'

There is no formal hierarchy at St James' Park. Keegan and McDermott both train, joining in the five-a-sides and the physical work. McDermott says they are just 'frustrated footballers' now. When it comes to the drudge inherent in the day-to-day running of a professional football club, King Kev does his share. For away games, he's up at dawn hoiking kit into the away dressing rooms and inspecting facilities in the same way that, two and a half years ago, he inspected the toilets and baths at St James' Park.

McDermott describes the relationship between Keegan and Newcastle as a love affair. Keegan told *FourFourTwo*: 'I knew the supporters very well. My father was a Geordie and my grandfather was in the Stanley Pit disaster of 1909. The call of it was too much. I thought "I don't really fancy management but if I'm going to have a go, this is the club".'

He came to Newcastle seeking a challenge. It was the same spirit which had led him to train and train again to overcome his inadequacies as a player, prompted his move to Hamburg (and led him to learn German well enough to conduct press interviews without an interpreter), took him to Southampton, then to Newcastle and finally back to Newcastle as a manager. At the time of writing, Newcastle are top of the Premier League. And, frighteningly, Keegan is still enthusiastic; still fighting and still learning.

Additional research by Patrick Barclay *and* Francis Collings

FourFourTwo, December 1994

Arsenal's Greedy Gaffer

Tom Watt

I arrived at Highbury at about the same time as George Graham. Over the past couple of months, it has occurred to me to work out exactly how much money I've ploughed into an irrational devotion to The Institution N5 since those famously dismal days of the mid-Sixties. Unlike Sir John Quinton, the Premier League chairman, however, I've no background in bookkeeping.

If I'd had any talent or physical courage whatsoever I'd have loved to have played football for a living. Instead, I've had to settle for a career in the theatre; pretending fictions in the face of the blatantly obvious. (Understandably, perhaps, I feel well-equipped for a late career-change into football management.) I couldn't, therefore, have picked a more suitable club to waste my life supporting.

For as long as I can remember – the extraordinary Liam Brady apart – Arsenal have never offered their fans, far less anybody else, the finer points of the Beautiful Game. But if you wanted drama there was no other team to touch the Gunners from Bobby Gould's pre-Gazza tears at the League Cup final in 1969 when we were beaten by Swindon to the impossible triumph – Stephen Morrow head-to-head with Gianfranco Zola – against Parma in Copenhagen last May.

Still packing them in after a three-month sell-out run at the Marble Halls is The Madness Of King George. The bung saga has taken on the epic and ironic qualities of great theatre in large part because of the club and the manager involved. In three months, Arsenal have seen 60 years of life on the moral high ground slip away, like so much dodgy landfill, because, it would seem, of the very human greed of a man who had enjoyed almost divine status, in Highbury's boardroom at least.

Graham's movie-star aura may be at the root of the problem. He rode into town in the summer of 1986 like a Clint Eastwood, revitalising a club that had slackened on and off the pitch. Since then, he's had a go at them all: Clark Gable, John Wayne, Al Pacino, Henry Fonda and Anthony Perkins.

Even now, most Arsenal fans would admit to wishing that George could be right and the rest of the world could be wrong. After eight-and-a-half years hooked on George, The Movie, it's a painful business coming to terms with George, The Facts.

Uniquely among contemporary managers, Graham had a job for life at Highbury. Instantly and memorably successful, he wore his love of the club and their history very obviously on his sleeve. Unlike the new breed of managers – Robson, Hoddle, Wilkins, Keegan – however, George wasn't into football management for love alone. As a member of Arsenal's Double side in 1971, a dream that Graham the player did so much to help realise, he earned around £12,000. Coming to the end of a playing career now, George would never have had to work again. An awareness of that fact may have contributed to his willingness to drive a hard bargain with his playing staff's salaries while taking the soft moral option himself when the opportunity for personal enrichment was afforded him by a dumpy Norwegian in funny glasses.

It's Michael Douglas in *Wall Street*; greed's an intoxicating vice, particularly if you're so far ahead of the game that you feel unaccountable, even to yourself. As always, football didn't have the foggiest; the FA are about as much use as Mr Magoo when there's a crisis on the way. (Indeed, the authorities' unwillingness to recognise – and therefore control – the activities of agents over the past decade has helped to bring things to such a head.) Just as it took 96 deaths and a Lord Chief Justice to put the game's houses in order, it took the Inland Revenue to uncover what Graham, and doubtless many others, have been doing with supporters' hard-earned cash.

It's pretty generally agreed that George Graham is the villain of this piece, although I must admit to seeing it, too, as a personal tragedy, in the truest sense of the term, for a man whose sin has cost him the destiny he was plainly born to. It seems, though, that everybody from Graham Kelly to the Swindon chairman Roy Hardman would like to cast themselves as the morally outraged victims here, all in the great name of football, of course.

Let's get one thing straight. It's our money – Arsenal fans' money – that found its way into the gaffer's back pocket. They are our illusions about a great institution that have been shown to be just that. All the rest is self-righteousness and flannel. It's clear that, in the current legal climate, the football authorities would struggle to push through a change of underwear never mind the full-scale revolution Mr Kelly hinted at last Thursday. The real power today, of course, is invested in Premiership boardrooms.

Arsenal waited until George Graham had been publicly and independently shown to be guilty and then sacked him. For George and for the club itself there could be no more thorough punishment. For us, I think, it's the end titles on this one, though Arsenal Football Club will never be the same again. For the rest of football, it remains to be seen if there's the courage or the will to keep the cameras rolling.

Observer, 26 February 1995

Royle's Baptism of Fire
Guy Hodgson

The logic of employing football managers would perplex anyone, but even the father of the philosophy, Aristotle, would be hard pushed to explain the punctuality of Joe Royle's arrival at Everton last week.

True, Royle has long since been identified as a young manager on the up, and hardly anyone would dispute he deserves a chance with a big club. But it fits with the game's perverse nature that he should get the job he has long coveted just when his career was taking a down turn.

Timing, in sport as in politics, is everything. How else can you explain why Royle, 45, should be overlooked by Everton when his reputation and the team he managed, Oldham Athletic, were in the ascendant and then be accepted when the club had been relegated from the Premiership and were hovering just above the First Division relegation positions?

Goodison tugged at his ties of loyalty with Oldham twice before. In 1990 he says he waited by the phone for three days for a call to summon him to Everton only to discover his friend and mentor, Howard Kendall, was returning. And in January he hoped again only to see his opportunity disappear, seemingly for good, when Mike Walker was chosen on the back of spectacular progress by Norwich.

Ten months later, however, with Everton bottom of the table, they beckoned in adversity and Royle had succeeded in relative failure where he had lost in success. The new man at the Goodison helm, long since immune from surprise, put it down to pre-ordainment. 'Even when it seemed my chance had gone I still believed I was destined to be manager of Everton,' he said.

Peter Johnson, the club chairman, who had still been the owner of Tranmere and not at Goodison when Walker had been appointed, explained: 'We wanted to return to basics, Everton basics. And no one is more Evertonian than Joe.'

As to the timing, he added: 'We had to leave the manager the chance to escape from relegation and with two thirds of the season to go he has that chance. Four clubs go down this season and I know how difficult it is to get out of the First Division. I certainly don't want to see Everton down there.'

Royle's first instruction to his players was to enjoy themselves. 'Everyone had long faces when I arrived, I want to see smiles' – although his normal ear-to-ear grin has been sorely strained by the demands on his time since his appointment.

At one point this week, in reply to the 101st enquiry into which players he was likely to buy, he replied that as he had not had time to fit in five minutes with the chairman yet it was difficult to answer. The fact that his first match in charge is against Liverpool on

Monday has not helped divert attention.

'It's just taken so long to come,' he said with the weariness of a man who has been at the wrong end of 10 days' anticipation. 'It looked like it would be a benefit in having the extra time to work with the players but with international calls and injuries we've not been able to do as much as I'd liked. It's dragged on a bit and the sooner we get to the game the better.'

As to what had surprised him since his arrival, he replied: 'The size of the place is immense. Although I knew Everton I wasn't quite prepared for how big it is. Just meeting the media is an experience in itself, if we had one reporter at Oldham it constituted a press conference. After the first few days of feeling dizzy I'm getting into it. I'd like to get home a bit more and get some sleep but I'm enjoying it.'

Dialogue with the supporters has scarcely helped clear his head either as their solutions to a season that has yielded only nine goals and one win in 14 Premiership matches have ranged from the detailed (playing their Nigerian World Cup player, Daniel Amokachi, deeper than as an out-and-out striker) to the wider criticism (the minor problem that the goalkeeper, defence, midfield and attack are all hopeless).

'I intend to give the players a chance to prove themselves and show they have what it takes to do well for Everton,' Royle commented before hinting at the stick that will follow if the carrot does not work. 'Having said that, fairly speedy decisions have to be made. We've at least four places to climb before we get any pleasure out of the game.

'I do have one or two ideas about players who would improve the squad but it would be unfair to reveal them at the moment. I'm seeing the chairman later today [Friday] and we'll see what we come up with in that direction. I've read in some places we're buying so and so but at the moment we're nowhere near to signing anybody. When we do, people won't just be discarded for the sake of it. There are a lot of talented players at Everton Football Club. There won't be a fire sale here.'

The change of personnel at the top has had the overwhelming backing of the supporters who appreciate Royle's commitment to Everton goes beyond the normal platitudes of managers searching to say the right things. 'Joe would fight for any club, but would die for this one,' might have been corny but the fans have taken Johnson's appreciation of Royle Blue as gospel.

The new manager is seen as one of their own, indeed even when he was guiding Oldham to two FA Cup semi-finals, a League Cup final and three years in the Premiership, Royle insisted his heart lay at Goodison. He was 14 when he first commanded the attention of the club, who sent a scout around to his house after just one appearance for Liverpool Boys, and the attraction has been mutual since.

Royle was given a rousing welcome by both Everton and Liverpool supporters when he appeared at the first match of his command, a reserve game at Anfield last Saturday that was won 4–0, and the reception he is likely to receive at Goodison on Monday will bear comparison with the triumphant marches into ancient Rome of victorious generals.

Two stories from his Everton days – 102 goals in 229 League appearances and a championship in 1970 – perhaps sum up his character. He was known as 'Cadbury' by his team-mates, who latched on to manager Harry Catterick's desire to see more devil emerge from a large and what should have been an intimidating frame. The nickname referred to his alleged soft centre and would be dropped in at moments when the embarrassment would be greatest.

Royle did not react as expected to that, nor to repeated roughings-up in training by team-mates under instruction from Catterick. He smiled at the bluntness of the tactics and retaliated by making his colleagues incredulous and envious with a stream of Jaguar cars he would turn up in for training.

The cars were the product of his sideline, a used car business he ran in the afternoons, which spoke a lot for his acumen at a time when footballers tended to live for the day rather than the future. It also showed the Royle way: you can make your point without raising the roof.

'I'm not someone who throws tea-cups round the dressing room,' he said. 'I've had my ups and downs with players, of course, but I prefer the quiet word in private to the bawling out in public. I'm not a ratty sort of person.'

Royle's playing ended with a crippled knee and back injuries that still force him to lean forward. But if it was an unfortunate way to end a career that also brought him six caps, the ending could hardly have been more appropriate, a match for Norwich against Everton at Goodison.

He left to a standing ovation and returned last week to another one. His time has come.

Independent, 19 November 1994

Graeme Souness
Stephen F. Kelly

There is an aura about Graeme Souness. He is imposing. When he strides into a room, heads turn. You are in the presence of the distinguished, the fortunate. People pay attention, waiters scurry, tongues wag. Even journalists freeze at asking embarrassing questions while friends are careful not to overstep their mark. Souness carries an authority about him like others carry a wallet; some might call it arrogance.

You can love him or hate him but he rarely inspires mere indifference. Ask a few ex-First Division forwards and they will talk about his vindictiveness; ask those who have served under him and they will complain about his ruthlessness; ask David Murray of Rangers and he will tell you about Souness' revolutionary zeal. But on Merseyside you would be hard put to find anyone who could say much that is complimentary about their one-time adopted son. Liverpudlians can be the warmest of people, but they can be equally vitriolic or scathing; cynical when it comes to southerners, Conservatives or anyone just that bit too flash. As far as they were concerned, Graeme Souness slotted into at least one of those categories. The feeling was pretty much mutual. It was hardly surprising when he once confessed to a journalist that he didn't like scousers, they were always whingeing. And yet Graeme Souness is a hard man to pin down. He does not fit comfortably into any slot. The trouble with Souness is that he is also likeable.

He's a handsome man with a gaunt sad face, a punch-drunk nose, a rough old Scottish smile and Tuscan blue eyes that talk as much as his lips. He doesn't look like a football manager. He's suntanned, fit, with no sign of the statutory limp of most ex-professionals. He likes to keep in shape, enjoys a daily massage and usually sports a designer suntan and a pair of Raybans. With his straight back, he cuts a dashing figure in his Italian suit. He is immaculate, never sloppily dressed. There is a touch of the Godfather, a young Michael, seizing his unexpected opportunity to take over the dynasty. Maybe not quite as ruthless and ambitious as young Michael, but he could easily be the new Padrone, the Ibrox and Anfield Godfather without the Mafia connections.

It's not hard to see why the Italians worshipped him so much. He looks at ease in the sun and warmth of Italy where style and a touch of arrogance are the rule rather than the exception. One journalist remembers spotting him stepping out of a car outside Sampdoria's elegant stadium. 'The crowd raced over to see him, pushing and shoving just to get a glimpse. He looked so classy; smart car, jacket over his shoulders, a woman on each arm, the sun beating down on him. The kids loved him. He was at home.' That same journalist spotted him a few years later in a record store in Glasgow. 'He had two minders diplomatically standing a short distance away, watching carefully as he flicked through the record racks. Outside it was grey and drizzling. I felt sorry for him.'

Souness is no ordinary manager. He would never have served his apprenticeship in the lower divisions. Not for him the Darlingtons, the Doncasters or the Dumbartons of this world. Souness was always destined to arrive and remain at the top. You would never spot him slopping out the showers, humping the kit around or mucking in as most managers do at less fashionable clubs. Nor could you ever imagine him kow-towing to some trumped-up, self-elected club chairman. Souness is his own man. That's what you pay for. Never a reformist, never a yes man, always a revolutionary.

As manager, he was a stark contrast to his Anfield predecessor. Dalglish was the austere professional, fun if you knew him, but a man of few words, privately complicated, even insecure, but not really one of the lads in search of a good night out. Souness was the more fun-loving, wickedly brash, the more worldly, the more publicly complicated, the man who liked a glamorous dame on his arm, a good suntan and a stylish Armani suit. Dalglish was the man who liked to remain off stage, the actor manager; Souness a man who liked to be centre stage, the star attraction.

Archie Gemmill once labelled him 'a chocolate soldier', then waspishly added that 'if Souness was made of chocolate he'd eat himself'. It summed up his arrogance perfectly. Even Souness admits that there was more than an element of truth in the description. 'Archie was 90 per cent right,' he says. 'Maybe I was a bit vain and thought the world revolved around me, but it was my way of motivating myself.' As ever, Souness could rationalise his behaviour.

In another age he might have been a screen idol, a swashbuckling hero, clashing foils on some stone spiral staircase, before diving headlong into the castle moat and sweeping a glamorous maiden off to his hideaway. A Clark Gable, an Errol Flynn, a matinee star of the two and sixpences. But in the nineties Souness found his screen part in the boardrooms of soccer's fiefdoms. He slotted into the majestic mahogany background of Ibrox as if he had always been destined for the role. And the slumbering giant of a club was suddenly and dramatically awakened. In 1986 Souness and Rangers were meant for each other. In 1991 it seemed also that Souness and Liverpool might have been made for each other. But it was not to turn out that way.

At Ibrox he signed the club's first batch of Englishmen, spending like there was no tomorrow; then he recruited Rangers' first black player. As if that wasn't enough he then challenged a hundred years of sectarianism by escorting the first ever Catholic through the doors. Jaws dropped, eyebrows were raised, Scotland was agog. But Souness never flinched. 'I don't give a monkey's,' he insisted. 'Are they good enough? That's all that matters.' It was fighting talk. It didn't endear him to the King Billy traditionalists of the terraces. But there was no doubting that it was not before time. Souness was perhaps the only man with the ambition and courage to have done it. It was a social revolution that had every tongue in Scotland chattering, from the factory floors to the university seminar rooms. Even today, years later, and long after Souness deserted them, they will readily admit that Souness changed the face of Scottish football, ending the years of insularity.

But the revolution that Souness engineered at Ibrox could not be repeated at Anfield. It never needed it. Where drastic measures were desperately called for in Scotland, only the merest of tinkering was necessary in England. Souness failed to comprehend that and with it his costly soccer revolution collapsed. It was reformism that was needed at Anfield, not revolution. If you want a revolution by all means call for Graeme Souness, but if you want something else, Souness isn't your man.

He is a man increasingly more at home in soccer's boardrooms than dressing rooms. He is an achiever, a man with a wider perspective than most managers, a man who knows how to manage money, a man with a vision of what football should be about. Souness would never be content simply with training, selection and transfers. His horizons have been stretched by Italy and a lucrative spell on the board at Ibrox where his influence was able to extend well beyond the football field. He is comfortable with wealthy industrialists like David Murray where profits, style and ambition are paramount. He is the first of a new breed of super manager, involved from the boardroom to the dressing room. Rich as well. His wife claims he told her he is worth £8 million. But if all that makes him sound flamboyant and unapproachable, it would be conveying a wrong impression. There is much more to him. Above all, he is also a charmer. He can be hospitable, welcoming half-strangers into his company, lavishing his friendship upon them. His cold stare soon gives way to a warm smile. Journalists, players, managers, even referees, will all testify to his generosity.

Brian Hall, the former Liverpool midfielder and now Community Officer with the club is fond of reminding people how generous Souness could be to those less fortunate, particularly children. He tells a particularly revealing tale.

We once had a letter from a woman whose child had cystic fibrosis and was very ill. The little boy was a fanatical Liverpool supporter but had never been to the club. We decided to help out. We hired a helicopter and brought the lad up to Melwood, our training ground. Graeme organised it all. The helicopter landed at Melwood one morning, on the pitch, and in the middle of training. Now that might not sound very much but at Liverpool it is sacrilege even to think of putting a helicopter on the training pitch or to even interrupt training. But Graeme did it. And as the lad came off the helicopter Souness had organised a guard of honour for him, all the players were lined up to applaud him off. The youngster spent the day with the team, visiting Anfield as well, with Souness even returning to Anfield to have a further chat with the boy. A month later the young lad died. It was just one of many examples when Souness would put himself out to help people.

It was a different picture from the confrontational, hard-tackling demon that was often painted in the papers.

Souness may be a paradox but he is undeniably a winner, ever the optimist. Few could rival his competitive edge, his burning desire to win. It was an instinct that drove him to success on the football field and a glittering array of honours. It also brought him success in football management as Rangers captured three Scottish championships. But it also heralded its disasters. His marriage failed, he was forced to endure major heart surgery and his reign at Anfield ended in disappointment and humiliation. His ex-wife Danielle says it was always football first with him. 'It was his temperament which was to blame because he would never accept defeat.' There was something of a man occasionally walking a thin tightrope between madness and sanity in him. Others simply claim that he paid the price for his own arrogance and commitment.

The swashbuckling hero of our film is a man of many parts but he is essentially a man of change: fearless, visionary, strident, committed. He knows what he wants. He arrived at Rangers and at Liverpool preaching revolution. In Scotland never was change more essential. At Anfield it was to be a different story. And when he left it was to face a dark void. Since he was a teenager Souness had always known where he was going. From Spurs to Middlesbrough, to Anfield, to Sampdoria, to Glasgow and then back to Liverpool. His destiny had been mapped out. But suddenly as he walked out of Anfield he was no longer a man in demand.

Graeme Souness: A Soccer Revolutionary, 1994

Ray Wilkins
Gary Lineker

The thought of playing Manchester United at Old Trafford in their present mood would be enough to send most managers into nervous, twitchy, cup-smashing mode. Not so Ray Wilkins of Queens Park Rangers, who is looking forward to returning to his former club in the FA Cup this afternoon with a mixture of relish and relaxation.

When we talked in his office last week, Wilkins was the epitome of calmness when he said the game would be 'a nice bit of recreation'. He was confident enough to avoid all managers' clichés and speak with a refreshing honesty in summing up his team's chances. 'We always play well against Manchester United, whether it's here or at Old Trafford, but the bloody thing is, we always lose.'

The key to survival against the Cup holders is whether Wilkins can instil in his players the same lack of anxiety that he himself feels. With Ray it comes naturally and although he may look like Jack Nicholson and sound like Michael Caine, his laid-back persona is certainly no act.

Wilkins is well aware of the importance of his players not being overawed by the occasion and is positive they won't be. 'We'll go there and enjoy it, we'll be put under the cosh, we've no illusions about what's going to happen, but once we get the ball we must be composed.'

What he's talking about is retaining possession and if QPR are to have any chance of reaching the semi-finals they will have to refrain from giving the ball away too easily and too often. If anyone can teach his players the art of possession then it is Ray Wilkins, one of the finest passers of his generation.

During my career there were only three players who I really enjoyed watching train. One was Glenn Hoddle for his extraordinary ability to do practically anything with a football; he could land a perfectly weighted ball at your feet despite facing the opposite direction. Another was Paul Gascoigne, who would try the most audacious things. The other was Wilkins, with whom I spent a few years in the England squad.

I used to marvel at the way he made time for himself with his instant control and then delivered 40 or 50 yard passes with unnerving accuracy time and time again. He was so precise with either foot. I used to watch him, trying to work out if he was left or right-footed (I knew there was something I forgot to ask him). There was also his great enthusiasm and enjoyment for training that was so infectious, even for those of us who didn't tackle the more mundane aspects of the job quite as vigorously as others. Ray told me one of his players had recently asked him in a slightly irritated manner why he was never miserable.

It would be a mistake, though, to confuse his obvious love of the game with a lack of competitiveness. It would be immensely difficult to achieve what he has in the game without tremendous determination and a real desire to be successful.

On the field he has had his moments. In one of his last games for England, during the 1986 World Cup in Mexico, he threw the ball at the referee and, even though it wasn't Steve Backley-like in its ferocity, he was ordered off.

The last time I played against Ray we had, believe it or not, a stormy exchange of words over whether or not I'd made the most of what can only be described as a blatant push. As if I would ever try to influence a refereeing decision.

Wilkins thinks his style of management will be a 'placid' one. 'I believe that ranting and raving stuff goes in one ear and out the other, if you talk to people they'll listen.' He consistently mentioned the name of the equally mild Nils Liedholm, his coach when he was at Milan. He admits that his own training sessions will be influenced by the way the Swede controlled things at the San Siro. 'He used to do at least half an hour every day on technique, and that's something I want to do especially when the weather and ground conditions improve.'

Good technique is vital for his players if they are going to play the game the way Wilkins would like them to. 'When you give the ball away abroad, you just can't get it back, we've been saying it for years with the England team, that we give the ball away too much. I'm not too concerned where our lads pass the ball, sometimes you have to go backwards to go forward, as long as we retain it. When we have the chance to be positive then let's be positive.'

If you're thinking, 'Well, Ray Wilkins would say that, he always passed the ball sideways' you have fallen victim to the common fallacy, inspired by Ron Atkinson's crab analogy. It's nonsense to suggest Wilkins lacked penetration in his game, but once the label was attached to him people tended to notice only his square passes and not the forward ones.

What Wilkins was displaying with his lateral thinking was patience and an understanding of the importance of possession. When the opportunity arose to play the ball forward he was an incisive as anybody. In fact, he is one of the few players in this country who, at his peak, would improve the present Manchester United team.

So how much is Wilkins looking forward to his return for the first time as a manager to the club where he enjoyed so much success, particularly in the FA Cup? 'Oh, I'll love it, it's always great to go back to old clubs, especially when you've left with a nice feeling. But if I'm honest, I wish our ball had come out of the bag first when they made the draw.' He accepts they are the underdogs but knows they have more than just an outsider's chance. 'At some stage in a cup run you have to have a monster result, whoever you play for. This might just be our monster result.'

If his players are half as eager and relaxed as their manager this afternoon they could supply the biggest upset of this year's competition by overcoming the 1994 Double winners. That would leave them one step away from a Wembley appearance and the possibility of Wilkins leading his team out in his first season in charge. I said 'I bet you'd fancy that wouldn't you?' 'Cor I should Cocoa,' he replied. Whatever happened to taking one game at a time?

Observer, 12 March 1995

The Rioch Clan
Louise Taylor

Mobile telephone in one hand, cigar in the other, player agents have been increasingly cast as football's wide boys, but such stereotypes are under challenge from the pin-striped Rioch brothers.

Aiming to confound widespread cynicism, this family firm aspires to imbue the business with a measure of much-needed integrity. At the end of a sleaze-strewn season when Rune Hauge's transfer-market practices played a central part in George Graham's downfall at Arsenal, and Eric Hall delighted in living up to the Arthur Daley image, the credibility of agents has never been lower.

At first glance the Riochs appear unlikely paragons. After all. Bolton are managed by Bruce Rioch, whose brother Ian runs IMR Pro-Sport Management Ltd, the company responsible for looking after the interests of five of the team's best players, including Jason McAteer and Alan Stubbs.

Another brother, Neil, an ex-player, is an IMR employee, too, while the fourth brother, Jim, is poised to join the St Albans-based business, which was also hired to organise the First Division club's commercial arrangements before the League Cup final against Liverpool. This apparent conflict of interests appears compounded by Ian Rioch's additional brief as Bruce's financial adviser.

Yet nobody at Burnden bats an eye, IMR having persuaded the Bolton board that it represents a role model any agent should aspire to. Conservatively dressed in suit and immaculately knotted tie, Ian Rioch looks very much the senior insurance manager he once was. His conversion is peppered with words like responsibility and, yes, integrity, IMR's philosophy being firmly based on that of the Mark McCormack organisation.

'When he took Arnold Palmer on in the 1960s, McCormack became the first sporting agent. I've read and re-read every book he has ever written,' Ian said. Throughout a varied career as a fireman, national publishing sales manager and insurance executive, Rioch, 53, harboured a dream of emulating his idol.

Eighteen months ago he finally made it reality and today IMR has 35 footballers on its books. Back in early 1994, however, its sole clients were Stubbs and McAteer.

At a meeting with Bolton's board, Ian Rioch reassured the chairman, Gordon Hargreaves, that there were no conflicting interests. 'With both Bruce and I working in football it is inevitable that at various times I will be looking after players he is managing.'

Thus far the arrangement has worked in Bolton's favour, the family influence helping persuade young stars they are better off at Burnden Park – other agents might well have convinced them to agitate for moves after Bolton rebuffed Liverpool's multi-million-pound offer for the duo earlier this season.

But what if Bruce leaves for a bigger club and wants to buy McAteer? Ian Rioch is confident that, come what may, the 'excellent' relationship with Gordon Hargreaves can endure. 'We want to establish a professional reputation with chairmen and managers. Touting already contracted players to other clubs is totally out of order.'

Des McBain, Bolton's chief executive, sits in on all negotiations and says that while the board were initially 'not sure' about the Rioch set-up they quickly became 'much more comfortable' with the brothers' role.

'Ian and Neil are not easy meat for the manager to deal with though,' McBain said. 'There is no question of Bruce having it easy with them. We are satisfied because their players have been kept happy here and that is good for Bolton. Agents are a fact of modern football life and IMR are thoroughly professional. We have no problems with them. Unlike some, they handle business in the right way.'

Ian, however, respects those operating at the ducking-and-diving end of the market. 'I think Eric Hall does a very good job for his clients. He makes them a lot of money. Others do too.'

They also generate a mercenary spirit, and Rioch acknowledges that money lust has led to bungs and backhanders. 'The trouble is that the greed factor just tends to take people over. A lot of people in football become obsessed by money, and sometimes clubs lose sight of the supporters. Personally, I don't think it would be a bad thing if transfer fees were abolished but I do believe that all the recent sleaze allegations served as a huge warning, and abuses of the transfer system have stopped. IMR certainly has not encountered any.'

Yet the brothers are not immune from the 'what's in it for me' creed. Before the League Cup final they organised a routine players 'pool', generating extra income from media and commercial spin-offs to be distributed among the squad.

The press were asked to make voluntary contributions for player interviews, with 80% going to the team and 20% to a children's hospital. In practice this was privatisation of information, the tabloids paying handsomely for 'exclusives'. Why, though, should highly salaried professionals be further remunerated for what should be just another part of the job? Greed, it seems, is still good when it comes to fixing the inevitable pre-Cup final pools – and agents actively encourage it.

Another recurring criticism is the way they tend to be 'percentage men', taking perhaps 20% of their clients' earnings in individual deals ranging from signing-on fees to boot contracts. Why, sceptics wonder, cannot agents follow the example of solicitors and set tariffs?

'We take a percentage of signing-on fees, loyalty payments and commercial contracts,' Ian Rioch said. 'But I suspect players would be paying us a lot more if we charged by the hour.'

Anxious to ensure players do not feel tricked into signing away their rights, IMR sends every draft contract and potential client to check the small print with his solicitor before signing. Parental involvement is also welcomed.

The latter comes as no surprise, 'family' playing a big part in the Rioch *raison d'être*, the clan meeting up for weekly meals and holidaying together.

This old-fashioned, almost anachronistic mutual support system – which has seen Ian 'living and breathing' Bruce's biggest footballing dramas – stems from their parents.

Definitely not for wimps, an upbringing by a regimental sergeant major involved plenty of male-bonding. Anything but subservient, Mrs Rioch assumed an active role, Ian recalling the afternoon when, watching Aston Villa, they sat next to a supporter who vociferously criticised two players – Bruce and Neil. 'As we filed out, my mother grabbed him and had him up against a wall giving him a piece of her mind.'

Inherited aggression has been channelled into McCormack-style entrepreneurship but the hard edge is softened by a childhood punctuated by traditional courtesies. Manners, the Riochs believe, maketh the man.

Later the benefits of this fiercely loyal, rather puritan, background were to be allied to modern American management theory. 'We've all been influenced by Americans, by their positive approach to life and marketing,' Ian said. 'It has affected all our lives.'

To the point where their extraordinary marriage of free-market modernity and straight-laced 'standards' might just have a bearing on the changing shape of English football.

Sunday Times, 23 April 1995

The Headmaster of Stenhousemuir
Glenn Gibbons

If Terry Christie maintains his present course, there is a distinct possibility that he will accumulate more awards than Walt Disney.

The Edinburgh headmaster, who doubles as part-time messiah with Stenhousemuir in the Scottish Second Division, has now collected a third consecutive Bell's manager-of-the-month trophy.

Christie won the overall title for February, having already received the divisional honours for December and January, and he would virtually assure a fourth by leading Stenhousemuir to victory over Hibernian in the Scottish Cup quarter-finals at Ochilview Park on Saturday.

Given a track record that prompted Craig Brown, the Scotland manager, to dub Christie 'the best manager in the country', it is not difficult to imagine that Alex Miller, in charge at Hibs, will do most of the worrying this week.

Victories over St Johnstone and Aberdeen in Stenhousemuir's last two ties are the most eye-catching milestones in a career containing more substantial achievements with clubs which, in the order of football life-forms, have the status of amoeba.

After the works team Ferranti Thistle joined the Scottish Football League and became Meadowbank, it was Christie who eventually saw them miss promotion to the Premier Division by a single place.

Assistant manager to Willie McFarlane in 1978, Christie landed the top job in 1980. During his 12-year managership Meadowbank, perennially poor and battling against the disadvantages of playing at a stadium dominated by athletics, spent eight seasons in the First Division.

He left in a swirl of acrimony in 1992 after the club's takeover by Bill Hunter, whose ambitions embraced moving to Livingston and basically effecting a reincarnation.

'I was a director as well as manager of the club,' Christie said, 'and, when Bill Hunter wanted on the board, I was opposed to it. I knew we had to move somewhere else to play because Meadowbank was no use, but the ambition of the new people seemed to me to outstrip reality. I thought Thistle had done very well in a playing sense. Apart from the league performances through the years we reached the League Cup semi-final against Rangers in 1984.

'But, as with all of these little institutions, there is a limit to the dream. Anyway I resigned as a director and at one point had to take out an interim interdict to prevent Hunter from sacking me. But my demise at Meadowbank was basically because of politicking as a director rather than my work as manager.'

Christie has taken Stenhousemuir out of Scotland's lowest league for the first time in their 111-year history and they are now favourites for promotion to the First Division. They surrendered the leadership last weekend but only after their match against Queen of the South was postponed.

As a headmaster for the last 13 years – and a deputy head for the eight years before that – the mathematics teacher is convinced his managerial skills stem from his experience in education. Once head of one of Edinburgh's biggest comprehensives, Ainsley Park, now closed, he is presently in charge of the even larger Musselburgh Grammar.

His football teaching began in 1970 when he graduated with a full certificate from the English coaching school at Durham, where Howard Wilkinson was a fellow pupil.

'In truth coaching certificates don't mean that much,' Christie admitted. 'It's like passing your driving test. The real driving only starts afterwards. In the business of managing football clubs I am largely self-taught.

'I've always had very clear ideas of how I want my teams to play and it's been a question of retaining what works and discarding what doesn't. I don't believe in shouting and bawling. I get excited during a match but in preparing and dealing with players it's very much a matter of doing things quietly.'

Gordon Russell's transfer from East Stirlingshire last week for £10,000 was a record fee for Stenhousemuir, an indication of the constraints under which Christie has to operate. 'We managed it because of the wee cup run,' he said.

Yet the Warriors from the small Stirlingshire village near Falkirk still need to beat Hibs to equal the record of the 1903 team, which reached the Scottish Cup semi-finals and a home tie with Rangers.

Then, as now, there was the temptation to play the game away from Ochilview. Rangers offered a half-share of an Ibrox gate, with a guaranteed £100 minimum. The lure was resisted and 7,560 fans – many standing on layers of turf, upturned buckets and piles of wooden planks – paid £250 to witness Rangers' 4–1 victory.

Only 3,520 will have access to the ground this Saturday and those wearing the green and white of Hibs are entitled to that pang of apprehension traditionally associated with the long wait outside the headmaster's study.

Guardian, 7 March 1995

Making the Gradi
Chris Green

Let's talk tactics. In the opinion of one of the English game's most respected managers – Crewe boss Dario Gradi – it's something we do all too rarely.

'Football is a skilful sport,' he insists. 'Yet we constantly shy away from discussing its technical merits. When you go to a game there are many different skills on display – far more than most sports. I love playing snooker, which involves a high level of technique. I wish I could get the balls to do what I want, but at least no one is challenging you when you're taking a shot! In many other sports – like basketball for instance, where you don't need the wide range of skills soccer demands – technique is endlessly discussed.'

Soccer's current tactical chat is dominated by two opposing paradigms. The ruination of the modern-day game is often blamed on the dreaded long-ball game – elbows-in-the-face football, supposedly espoused by FA coach Charles Hughes on the playing fields of Lilleshall. In the opposite corner stand the past masters, football-as-art theorists. The poetic passing purism preached by Glenn Hoddle, Ossie Ardiles and co.

'It's not as simple – or as black and white – as that,' reasons Gradi. 'Most of the things written about Charlie Hughes are either incorrect or misunderstood. He doesn't advocate sending the ball skywards at every given opportunity There's a lot to be said for his approach of getting the ball quickly into the opposition's final third and keeping it there – because, quite logically, while you've got the ball in that area you've got a bigger percentage chance of creating goalscoring situations.

'So it's not a negative tactic, it's a positive one – and it doesn't mean you can't get the ball there by passing it along the ground. The so-called passing game is based on a patient build-up from the back. But it usually stays there too long so it's often unproductive. Far from being easy on the eye, it can be very dull to watch.

'I'm supposed to be closer to that tactical side of the game – people say my teams play so-called "good football" – but I'm not an advocate of either model in an extreme way. Most managers and coaches fall somewhere in between.'

Gradi's views are respected throughout the game. Unlike most managers or coaches – who played professionally and stayed in the game – he's a PE teacher who drifted into football, becoming a coach at Chelsea in 1970, later Derby, then manager at Wimbledon.

For the last 11 years, he's been boss at Crewe, where his coaching skills have unearthed a steady stream of talent which Alexandra have lucratively sold on, thus keeping the club afloat. David Platt, Geoff Thomas and Rob Jones all became England players after spells under the Gresty Road guru. So what does Gradi do that others don't?

'I think there's a severe lack of brains in football,' he smiles. 'We seem to leave all sense of reason behind in the changing rooms.

'When I was at college, the athletes used to laugh at the footballers because they didn't warm up, or warm down properly, or train in a way that was geared to getting the best out of themselves. Despite being the sport the public care about the most, we're very slow in taking on board developments in other areas of physical fitness.

'No two players are the same. When I had Geoff Thomas here, I had to work with him on his fitness because he hadn't been playing full-time football. You have to encourage players to work on and improve their strengths, but also get them to develop the things they're not so good at so they become all-round better players. You have to adopt and adapt training methods by listening to what is happening elsewhere.'

Despite Dario's obvious influence, Crewe are still a small club – albeit one that's currently enjoying Second Division status for the second time under his control. While the top teams can afford to bring in specialist trainers or even sports psychologists, lower-division clubs have less financial room to manoeuvre. Gradi, unlike many sceptics in his profession, doesn't believe they'll necessarily be forced to go part-time in order to survive.

'It depends on the club. At Crewe, our crowds are on the increase, because we've had a little bit of success and they like the way we play. We've worked hard to improve our financial situation and although we'll never be a wealthy club – there isn't a Sam Hammam on the horizon, for instance – finance isn't a pressing problem.

'Those clubs who can't cope, whether it's because not enough people watch them or because they haven't got other areas of the club in order, will be replaced by progressive-thinking clubs like Wycombe Wanderers. Being able to coach and produce your own players is an obvious advantage for any club at any level.'

Matchday, March 1995

Andy King
Phil Shaw

To hear Andy King reflect on his playing days is like being a priest in a confessional. 'I've not been a perfect professional,' the man who now manages Mansfield Town admits. 'I haven't lived a perfect life.'

King, whose Third Division stragglers defend a 1–0 lead at home to Leeds United in the Coca-Cola Cup tonight, was an associate member of the maverick band which included Tony Currie, Charlie George, Alan Hudson and Frank Worthington. He earned just two England Under-21 caps, though the fact that Ray Wilkins and Glenn Hoddle were his midfield partners says as much for his talents as about how, comparatively speaking, he squandered them.

On re-signing King for Everton, the club he still describes as 'my spiritual home', Howard Kendall hailed him as a 'technically superb player and finisher'. King, alas, was by then obsessed with the finishing technique of his four-legged friends.

'Certain things happened I'd like to have changed,' he said. 'For instance, I wish I'd never seen a racehorse. But footballers get into that because they have afternoons to themselves. That's why I preach to the kids now that they should take up a second trade. Gambling is a great thorn in football's side. It has ruined better players than me and certainly took a toll on my life.'

Now 38 and still turning out for the reserves, King also looks back on two failed marriages and eight changes of club. At Mansfield he demands loyalty and discipline; a case, possibly, of goal-poacher turned gamekeeper. 'I think being able to show where I went wrong makes me better qualified to deal with players. But it's like when your Mum and Dad tried to tell you things – do they listen? When I'm telling the lads to stay out of a betting shop, I have to pinch myself.'

It would be misleading to portray King as being consumed by regret. The exuberance which characterised him as a player is still striking, though of course it takes more than the gift of the gab to make a manager. King played under some of the biggest names – Venables, Docherty, Bingham, Kendall – yet offers a typically unpredictable view of who influenced him most.

'While you absorb ideas, obviously, the person I respected most was Colin Harvey, who now works with me here. But the best preparation I had for this job was being commercial manager of Luton. As a player you know nothing: you travel, play and go home. In that job, I learned how to budget, how to balance incomings and outgoings, and be accountable to a board.'

Luton, his home-town club, helped launch King's return to active service. 'I did a Yosser Hughes and rang David Pleat, saying "gissa job",' he recalled. 'He didn't really have anything for me, but the general manager asked if I could sell. I said if I could park my car at a football club every day, I'd do anything.'

When Mansfield dispensed with their 18th post-war manager last November, King accepted the poisoned chalice. It was the Kenilworth Road connection again; the chairman, Keith Haslam, is the son of Harry, the late Luton manager.

He inherited a team in the lower half of the basement section, squeezed between the catchment areas of the Sheffield clubs and Nottingham Forest. He also found a town with only one surviving pit, a collapsed hosiery industry, no railway station, no jobs, and, some argue, no future. King is 'acutely aware' of the problems, and only hopes to be there long enough to help dispel the gloom.

'I'm in love with football all over again,' he says, surveying Field Mill's unlovely environs, 'though the biggest problem about being in love is losing it. It's inevitable it'll happen to me sooner or later. People say it takes a sacking to make a good manager, but I'd like to think there was a second job in the wind before I found out if that's true.'

This may sound unduly fatalistic, but King saw what befell Steve Wicks, a former QPR colleague, who was dismissed by Scarborough after two pre-season friendlies. 'I'm convinced I was under pressure if we'd lost heavily at Leeds. I was starting to feel it.'

Instead, Simon Ireland's goal ensured that Mansfield triumphed where Manchester United failed 10 days earlier. King had a game plan, involving midfielder Paul Holland as one of five at the back, which his players implemented so well that they could have won more emphatically. 'Holland and Ireland,' he mused. 'Probably as close as I'll ever get to Europe. But seriously, Leeds didn't take us lightly, which made it all the better for me. We actually deserved to win, but from my experience they'll be confident of turning it round. In case we lose 8–0, I'm taking the credit now.'

For a fortnight he has indeed been King of the Stags. However, the task of reviving Mansfield will go on long after Leeds leave town. 'We've come on leaps and bounds, but as a manager I realise the only proof of that will be the League table.

'I've certainly altered our style so that we now reflect my football principles: pass and move. I don't believe that the way that Preston play, for example, can ever be good for the game. What I would say is that if John Beck gets success from it, that's what matters. He may stay in management longer than me. So I don't knock it – I just couldn't do it myself.'

In other respects, King is truly a changed man, as evinced by his recollection of the journey back from a recent defeat at Carlisle. 'I was mulling it over, reliving every kick, and I could hear the players playing cards and laughing. It's not that they don't care, but they soon forget, whereas for a manager it's a seven-day punishment.'

The beautiful pain is relieved by the practical joking which goes on at every club. Before Leeds, King's training-ground moniker was DH. 'As in dickhead,' he explained. Suddenly he became TG – 'tactical genius' – but he is placing no bets as to which title he will hold tomorrow.

Independent, 4 October 1994

Coaching the Coaches
Glenn Moore

A wintry day in South London: it has been raining for three hours and it is freezing. The sports field is deserted except for 15 sodden footballers and an apparently demented grey-haired old fellow who keeps leaping from side-to-side shouting 'you have got to keep the clock ticking'.

This is Arthur Hammond, coach to the starmakers. He's pushing 60, a welder by trade and a football coach by desire. We are apprentice coaches taking the Football Association's Preliminary Badge. This will entitle us to work at the many Schools of Excellence that are sprouting at professional clubs, to make a few bob teaching American kids in the States, and generally be a bit flash about our supposed football knowledge.

It will also make us part of a nebulous body of (primarily) men who are frequently blamed for British players' lack of technique and whose standard and practice are under attack at present.

While the FA is looking at overhauling the coaching structure, it is the Professional Footballers' Association that is setting the pace, having already produced a deeply researched and broad-based critique of current practice and future development.

The report, 'A Kick in the Right Direction', is highly critical of the FA coaching department's educational standards and emphasis. It believes the current coaching awards, the Preliminary and Full Badge, are inadequate. It is a view the FA is slowly coming to agree with and, this week, its coaching department met the PFA officials who had implicitly criticised them in the report.

It was a potentially tense meeting. The FA's coaching 'Godfather', Charles Hughes, is not given to publicity or enthusiastic about criticism, having received a barrel-load of it after the failure of his disciple, Graham Taylor, as England manager.

In the event it was described as 'conciliatory' and, though neither side are willing to go into details, further meetings are planned and the likely consequence is greater professional involvement.

The present courses are overseen by Hughes, the FA's long-serving Director of Coaching. He is widely regarded as the high priest of long-ball football and the popular belief is that coaches are taught direct play to the exclusion of all else.

That suspicion is strengthened when you buy the course books, *The Winning Formula* and *Soccer Skills and Tactics*, which are written by Hughes. The latter is obsessed with statistics. Did you know that 79 per cent of goals are preceded by moves of four passes or fewer; that long forward passes are an element of 27 per cent of goals; and 64 per cent of goals are scored through headers? No? You probably would not care either, except that these statistics helped persuade the last England manager to adopt some of his most criticised policies.

So, armed with a pair of boots, enough figures to pass the maths GCSE, and some trepidation, I went to the NatWest sports ground in Norbury to learn to be a coach. Courses vary, but are at least 26 hours and cost between £40 and £80. This one, through the Surrey FA, cost £55 and consisted of six successive six-hour Sunday sessions and a few hours' weekly written homework.

A reasonable level of fitness and technical proficiency are required. On alternate Sundays the students are taught techniques and then demonstrate how they would coach them. Assessment is in five parts: the three practical coaching demonstrations, a written paper on coaching theory and an examination on the Laws of the Game. All five parts must be passed.

My colleagues were a disparate group ranging from 18 to late thirties in age and from accountant and hairdresser to student and journalist in occupation. All were male. Some were there with a view to making a career from coaching, others to improve their own game, the game of the team they manage or simply to make sense of the game they write about.

On the first session we concentrated on basic skills; turning, trapping, heading, passing. The sort of things you should have been taught at school but were not because all the kids ever wanted to do was play, not learn.

They still do, which was why Arthur was constantly encouraging us to make it fun, to enjoy it, to pump some life into what we were doing. When you have 20 10-year-olds to control, it is a sight easier if they want to do what they are told. Being well organised also helps you to retain their concentration and considerable emphasis was placed on that aspect.

As the weeks went by we graduated to small-sided games. Six against six (not everybody survived the course) with the play frozen – a bit like the players – and defenders and forwards guided to where they should be. A similar process, using video, has enabled Gerry Francis to tighten the Tottenham defence.

We soon realised that when teaching a technique, the person you do not use in your demonstration is the guy who can do it properly. Only if he is doing it wrong can you demonstrate how you would step in and teach him the right way.

Some of it – shooting, volleying, watching someone else demonstrating diving headers on a muddy day – was a lot of fun. Attempting to provide accurate crosses in a swirling wind as a student tried to coach goalkeeping techniques was less so.

Encouragingly there was no mention of statistics at all and, though there was a slight emphasis on moving the ball forward quickly, there was no overt espousal of direct play.

Last year more than 5,000 took the course. Just over a quarter passed. Success enables you to move on, via a preparatory course, to the Advanced course for the Full Badge. This costs £540 and involves a two-week residential stay, usually at Lilleshall. Last year 163 people took this, including 29 in a special course for prison officers. The rest were divided between professionals, who sit one course, and the general public, who do another.

Before the criticism, the praise. If you have ever wondered about taking one of these courses, do so. Even if you never coach a team in your life, you will watch it and play it with a far greater appreciation of both the nuances and the broader picture. It is a considerable commitment (especially in winter) but it is well worth it.

But they are not adequate preparation for coaching the élite players of tomorrow. I passed but do not feel capable of teaching a dozen 15-year-olds, who are probably better players already, how to master the Matthews Move (after Sir Stanley). In time, with further coaching experience, I would – but that is unfair to the first few groups I would deal with.

The course also makes no mention of nutrition, physiology – very important when dealing with players with developing bodies – sports medicine and injuries, warm-ups and warm-downs. The PFA would like to see all these included on a 12-hour course similar to those on the continent. They would also like to see the next stage, the Advanced course, made much more extensive. Successful attendance would be compulsory for professional club managers, as it is in countries like Germany.

At present, for holders of the Preliminary Badge, there is no compulsion to continue learning. Various associations, like the Surrey Football Coaches Association, and the FA, do provide courses but you do not have to do them to retain your qualification.

This, like much else, is likely to change. It will cost money, not least in raising the wages of coaches, but the game, as a whole, is not short of cash. It is short of talented young players and coaches.

Independent, 18 March 1995

Tony Woodcock
Glenn Moore

'Woodcock, pay attention at the back.' Well, it was not quite like that in manager's college, but, Tony Woodcock said, it *was* a bit like going back to school.

Woodcock, once of Nottingham Forest, Arsenal and England, is a graduate of the German football association's coaching course. The course, widely regarded as one of the best in the world, is certain to be a big influence on the English equivalent.

'It is very intensive,' Woodcock said. 'It is six months, working Monday to Friday from 8am to 6pm. You deal with everything to do with football. It's theory and practice, methods of teaching, psychology, normal medicine, orthopaedic medicine. At the end of it you have a week of exams, three to four hours each one. Footballers are not used to exams. You leave school, spend 15–20 years in the game then suddenly you have to deal with all these questions. It is tough but you cannot do anything without one.'

Even to get on the course Woodcock needed a B licence (awarded automatically to internationals, this entitles the holder to coach children), an A licence (a six-week course), and to have done a year's work experience.

The course is residential, based at Cologne University. Handy for Woodcock, who played for Cologne and still lives in the city, not so easy for most of his fellow students who had to move to the city for six months.

'You learn about every type of football,' he said. 'The direct style is one of those discussed. You see how it is done in other countries. You are not told there is a right way and a wrong way to play, just shown the various ways. You are also taught about diet and how the body works; and how professional sport works, how clubs are run, even how the DFB [German FA] is run. It is hard work.' Indeed, one German international failed the course Woodcock was on.

Woodcock admits he is surprised how many British players go straight into management from playing. 'I'm not saying they cannot do a good job, but it would not be possible here. You have to learn the trade first.'

After work experience at Schalke 04 and a lower division club in Cologne – where he worked both as a general manager, then as coach, and who he guided to promotion – Woodcock took and passed the course.

He then went to coach VfB Leipzig, once known as Lokomotiv Leipzig. Before reunification they were the Stasi (secret police) club and were powerful, reaching the European Cup Winners' Cup final in 1987.

Like most East German clubs, they have since struggled and had fallen into the Second Division when Woodcock took over this season. It was something of a culture shock on both sides.

'There were players who had been there 30 years, since they were small children, and it was very hard to motivate them. They did not know anything else and they lacked ambition. In the old East Germany everyone's life was mapped out. The mentality was "I have a nice life, easy money, good job, I do not need someone coming in and wanting more from me". There was not the desire to better themselves.'

The culture clash did not work and, Woodcock, unable to reverse attitudes or results, was released mid-season. He remains under contract to Leipzig until the end of the campaign and cannot go elsewhere. In the meantime he is working for German television – his German, at times, seems more automatic than his English.

Offers have come in, and he is considering the possibility of moving back to England. One intriguing thought arises – if Arsenal really want a former Gunner in the chair, there is no one better qualified.

Independent, 11 May 1995

Stockport County manager Danny Bergara invited FourFourTwo *magazine to join him on the bench. By the end of the season he had fallen out with his chairman and parted company with the club.*

On the Bench with Danny Bergara

Olivia Blair

'Sure you can come on the bench with me,' Stockport manager Danny Bergara had said when I asked him earlier in the week. 'If you don't mind the language, of course.' Never mind the language, you'd have thought that the only word in the Stockport vocabulary was 'Francis', because it's the only word I hear outside the ground. The club were then poised to sell their 6ft 7in striker Kevin Francis to Birmingham or Wimbledon or anyone, and the event, or rather the non-event, was the talk of the town. Bergara tells me later that he's been at the club until 10.30pm on three consecutive nights, trying to set up a deal.

Inside Edgeley Park, 'the big man' is nowhere to be seen as we follow the teams out. Bergara is sitting snugly in the dugout next to his assistant John Sainty and first team coach David Jones. I sit on a seat at the end next to the three subs, relegating physio Roger Wylde to the ground. 'He didn't promise to lay off the swearing, did he?' Wylde asks, and as Bergara lights up his first cigarette, adds that I am lucky to be sitting upwind of the smoke.

One of the girls sitting behind me offers substitute goalkeeper John Keely some sweets. 'I bought them for you,' she pleads. Wylde is complaining about the cold. The skies are darkening, and the wind is blowing strongly towards the Railway End.

Bergara is animated from the first minute, gesticulating wildly in his characteristic dark glasses and baseball cap. 'Toddy, look after him.' He wolf whistles ('that's his speciality,' says Wylde, nudging me) at his left-back Lee Todd, and points frantically at the Cambridge number ten Carlo Corazzin. Keely asks me if I am writing an essay as I scribble frantically, trying to pick up what Bergara is shouting. It's easier to understand John Sainty: 'Don't walk away, you divvy.' It's Todd again. 'Are you going to pick him up or not?' The girls behind me decide that Sainty sounds 'like a bull elephant'.

Bergara's on his second fag by now, and smashes the bench when a header that looks as if it is going in, doesn't. 'Where's Toddy,' he's shouting. Roger Wylde asks Sainty if their number two is the same lad who once had a trial with Stockport. 'No,' comes the reply, 'and if you've got any more boring questions keep them to yourself.'

Meanwhile, Bergara is furious with his right-back Sean Connelly who has just passed the ball when in a glorious shooting position. 'Sean didn't shoot? Tell him to fucking shoot.' 'Yeah, bloody have a kick,' adds Sainty, as Bergara's voice rises to a crescendo next to him. 'Get in there, in there . . . Oooohhhh!' Another chance goes wide, and the first strains of 'Danny Bergara's blue and white army' echo round the ground. 'That's the ball, you can do it, you can do it,' Bergara shouts excitedly. They can't. 'Oh la la la la,' are the last words I hear from Sainty as the first half ends goalless.

'He won't want to speak to you unless they win,' the kit man John Bishop had told me at half-time. After 53 minutes the prospect of a post-match audience with Danny Bergara begins to look more promising. Jim Gannon opens the scoring, only for Cambridge to hit back 14 minutes later. Bergara is going mad. 'I want Chalky right-wing and Toddy left-wing. Can't you see if Chalky goes to the left he blocks Toddy?' This is directed at Sainty.

The crowd applaud sarcastically as Alun Armstrong replaces Jeff Eckhardt ('that's a nine, not a six,' Sainty says to Wylde, handing him the board). Bergara by now is beside himself with frustration as his side stream forward but seem unable to score. He leaps up: 'It's our luck, it's our luck, we're going to score . . . Is it fuck.' Chris Beaumont plays a lovely back-heel to Martin Chalk whose return pass doesn't match it. 'You're joking Chalky,' he says with disgust.

Two minutes into injury time, Jim Gannon scores again, and as the final whistle sounds, Bergara jumps up, arms raised. 'Finished, we win,' he shouts, and rushes down the tunnel. 'That's the only time I enjoy it,' he tells me later over a whisky in his office. 'When we're 2–1 up and the whistle goes. You can see me shouting out there and waving my arms; it's because they don't do what I tell them. But I know if I was out there I wouldn't do any better. I once asked Bobby Charlton why we'd got to Wembley five times in the last three years and lost every time. He said we didn't have enough leaders on the pitch. What can you do?'

But hang on Danny, didn't you just win? 'Yes, yes, we won OK. But it's hard. Last season we had two players who scored over 60 goals between them (Francis and Andy Preece, now at Palace) and neither are playing now, but we still win. But it won't always be like that. We were crying out for someone to stick the chances away.'

FourFourTwo, February 1995

Chapter Five

The Teams

Blackburn Rovers
Jim White

There is an episode in Nick Hornby's *Fever Pitch* when, just after he has bought his flat near Highbury, he fantasises about what things will be like now he lives in such proximity to the focus of his life. He daydreams that he will be able, at five to three on a Saturday afternoon, to open his door and see his neighbours all doing the same, stepping out of their houses to join the short procession to worship at the red and white shrine.

What he discovers instead, among those who live around him, is total indifference to the institution on their doorstep. On match days, the trains arrive from the Home Counties, the buses pour in from the Thames Valley, most of the crowd come whence Hornby came. The London Borough of Islington, meanwhile remains, by and large, unmoved by the goings-on in its heart.

The sight of match day in Blackburn, then, would lift Nick Hornby's spirit. Last Thursday, walking to Ewood Park for the game, you could see, in every other house along the Bolton Road which abuts the ground, people putting on their scarves and hats and Asics-logo track coats and getting ready to walk the few yards to their seat. They came out of the doors of the terraced houses and greeted the people already strolling down the road ('all right, Tony. Three points tonight and it's ours'). As the surge of people closed in on the ground, it was swelled by hundreds of others pouring down over the moor from the estate at the top of the hill rising up above Ewood.

It looked as if the whole town was turning out to watch the Rovers. Which is not far from the truth. Blackburn has a population of 130,000; last Thursday there were more than 28,000 people at the match. In a recent survey, it was discovered that 96 per cent of Rovers season ticket holders live within five miles of the club's headquarters. Which suggests that, roughly, one in five of the local populace turned up to see their team play. Not bad, considering the opposition was Crystal Palace.

'Oh aye, this town's come alive since Kenny arrived,' said Dave Howarth, a season ticket holder, a man in his forties weighed down by Rovers merchandise, as he made his way into the ground. 'I tell you how much it's got us going, women worry about the results. My mother, my wife want to come to the match, that's how much.'

It was not always like this in Blackburn. It is not that long ago that Rovers were something of a joke within the town: a symbol of decline and lack of achievement, a metaphor for a community which had long since seen better days, a place which had run out of luck. Year after year in the Eighties, Rovers would push for promotion from the then Second Division and fall in the final furlong. 'The annual fight against promotion,' their rivals from across the moors in Burnley sniggeringly termed it.

'Supporters genuinely believed we were doing our utmost to stay down,' said Terry Gennoe, who played for the club throughout the years of frustration. 'I remember a bloke came up to me after one time we'd blown it again and said, "You lot have been told to blow it because the club knows it couldn't survive in the top flight." Of course it wasn't true. We were flogging our guts out on the park. But there was this feeling in the town Rovers would never make it.'

It was not just the team that appeared determinedly Second Division. The ground, too, was a source of self-deprecating joviality in the town: in 1989 it was used as a back-cloth for a Hovis advertisement set in the 1930s, that's how comic it was. And when one of the grandstands started to keel over into the river running behind it, it seemed that someone was trying to tell them something.

Bill Fox, the then chairman, approached the council for help in rebuilding it. Cash-strapped and rate-capped, the officials, although sympathetic, could not stump up the necessary. Fortunately one of the directors said he was willing to supply the building materials to construct it gratis from his local steel stock-holding business. His name was Jack Walker.

Four years after Jack Walker made a substantial portion of the £365m he accrued from selling his business available to Blackburn Rovers, the club are closing in on their first title since 1914. On the pitch they are so lavishly endowed that, against Crystal Palace, they could bring in David Batty and Kevin Gallacher – with a combined value of £5m – to cover for the suspended regulars, Tim Sherwood and Colin Hendry. And the ground, so recently collapsing, is now magnificent. Completely rebuilt, it is a muscular, modernist, appropriately steely structure, in which every seat has an unencumbered view of the pitch. Beneath the seats, the stands are crammed with restaurants and executive boxes, lounges and ligging facilities.

But the most striking thing about the ground is that, as it rises up from the surrounding back-to-back terraces and cobbled streets, it looks as if it is in the wrong place; like the space ship from Close Encounters has landed on the set of a 1960s kitchen sink drama starring Albert Finney.

And in a sense it is in the wrong place, or at least an unprecedented place. Until Jack Walker came along, small towns like Blackburn did not have teams or facilities like this. Glasgow, London and Manchester did, but not Blackburn.

'What's happened here is remarkable, truly remarkable,' Gennoe said. 'I remember when we had to sell Kevin Stonehouse to Huddersfield for £30,000 because we needed the money to stop the electricity being cut off. I remember the players used to be paid in advance, then one week, the chairman told us he was going to pay us in arrears: not having to fork out the wages for a week meant he could pay off a debt and keep the club from going under.

'I remember at the end of one season he came into the dressing-room and said, "The door's open lads, if any of you want away I'll not stop you. But for them that's staying. I have to tell you there'll not be a pay rise for two years." And now, suddenly, we're not playing at it any more. We're up there with the big boys.'

The speed of the change Walker's money wrought has had a profound effect not just on the players at Ewood Park (among whom it will be at least two years before they stop having rises), but on the whole town. Quite unexpectedly this small, deprived backwater in east Lancashire has something of national significance in its midst. And the locals love it.

'There's no doubt that Rovers' success has put a spring in the step of the folk in this town,' said Malcolm Doherty, the Labour leader of Blackburn Council, and a season ticket holder for 25 years. 'Lots of older people say not only it's the best team they've ever seen, but that it's the best time they can remember in this town. They just thought it would never happen.'

Away from Ewood Park, Blackburn remains poor. Only one member of the well-remunerated playing staff has a house in the borough, for instance; most live in the Lancashire hill villages roundabout. Kenny Dalglish commutes from the baronial pile in Southport he bought when at Liverpool. Ten per cent of the population are unemployed, much of the housing stock is in dire need of regeneration, walking around the town centre, there is no sign of conspicuous wealth, and plenty of conspicuous poverty.

Yet if Government ministers need convincing what the feel-good factor can do to a place, they should visit Blackburn. The economic knock-ons of Rovers' success have been significant. Five years ago, the administrative staff at the club was two, now there are more than 30 local people engaged in full-time jobs; many more find part-time work on match days.

Pubs and shops near the ground have benefited enormously from the fact that 30,000 happy people pass their doors once a fortnight, instead of 10,000 depressed folk. Seamus O'Donnell's, a pub opposite the Jack Walker Stand, opened a new extension the night of the Palace game. It was packed, and the 10 barmaids had difficulty coping with the celebratory thirst. Taxi firms have seen endless new business since the conference and entertaining facilities in the ground became available for hire.

'There's a function down there most every night,' said one cabbie, a Rovers mascot jiggling in his rear windscreen. 'Folk get pissed and need a ride home. Sometimes as far as Burnley, ha ha ha.'

And there are less tangible, longer term benefits. 'One of the things we do when we try to impress people how go-ahead this town is, is take them to the ground,' Malcolm Doherty said. 'We had teams from Tredegar and Caernarvon councils up here recently to see how we're spending the money we got from the Government's City Challenge scheme. So we took them for lunch at Ewood, it's something we're proud of. We're not the only ones. Businesses take clients there to clinch deals. The businessmen I talk to say since Rovers emerged it has opened doors for them. They don't have to explain where Blackburn is any more. We've always known what a great place this is. Now the country's waking up to it.'

Having gate-crashed the top of the League, propelled by Jack's wad, the club seem determined not to let things slip, to take advantage of their pre-eminence. Walker was fortunate that, though never rich, Rovers were never encumbered by debt. Thus his money could be lavished on the things that will keep them at the top. On a nationwide scouting system, for instance, or the most comprehensive community development programme in the Premiership. Run by Terry Gennoe, this includes an educational trip to the ground (measure the size of the pitch, map the seats in the grandstand) and a ticket discount scheme for schoolchildren. For every match, except those against Leeds, Liverpool, Newcastle and Manchester United, Gennoe distributes 2,500 tickets to local schools at £2 each, including transport from their school. Most matches, the shrill shriek of 'Shearer, Shearer' terrifies dogs all the way to Burnley. The benefit of all this youthful enthusiasm is not just one way.

'Five years ago if you went to a primary school playground in this area, you would have been lucky if half the kids were wearing Rovers tops,' Gennoe said. 'Most were wearing United or Liverpool. Now, it's 90 per cent Rovers. And these kids are our future. When the time comes when we're not top of the Premiership, they'll still be our fans, they'll still be here.'

The scheme has also taken the club into a potentially lucrative territory it previously ignored: the local Asian community, which accounts for about a fifth of the Blackburn population.

'Going to football was not part of Asian culture,' Gennoe said. 'It's up to us to make it part; it's up to us to draw them across. We've done that by targeting Asian schools. Now you're beginning to see the community leaders bending a bit and seeing football as a wholesome, family thing. You'll see a lot more Asian faces in this ground. It'll take time, but it will happen.'

Indeed, one thing the club has to be careful about, in its ambitious dash for the big time, is not to detach itself from the community from which it sprung. Blackburn does not have the metropolitan catchment area to sustain premium pricing of tickets: for the Palace match only nine of the 16 executive boxes were occupied, for instance. You cannot foresee many people from the Bolton Road stepping out of their front doors to sit in the £1,900 a season Premier Club seats, even if they do come with pre-match dining facilities in the restaurant overlooking the ground. As one local said: 'It's a dear do that Jack Walker Stand.'

At present, however, there remains an oddly intimate feel about Ewood. Before the game against Palace, Radio Rovers – the club was the first to set up its own station – was broadcasting birthday wishes.

'And it's happy birthday to Sandra,' said one of the two DJs.

'Is that Sandra in the club shop?' said his colleague.

'It is that.'

You get the sense, standing in the refreshment bars before the game, that this is the place Blackburn comes to gather, that everybody knows each other. Last year, after the match between the two teams, a Manchester United fan I know was attacked by a gang of young Rovers supporters outside the ground, one of whom hit him over the back of the head with a bottle.

He fell and, just as he was anticipating a kicking, half a dozen older Blackburn fans ran across the road and intervened. The thing that struck him almost as forcefully as the bottle was that they clearly knew all his attackers: 'Stop that, Steven, we'll have none of that here,' shouted one man, to disperse the group. And 'right, Lee, I know your dad and I'm telephoning him when I get home.' They then apologised to the victim, and offered to escort him back to his car. You would have to be of diehard claret-and-blue persuasion to begrudge supporters like that their moment of glory. They have waited long enough.

'Sometimes I sit in my seat in the Walkersteel Stand, and look round this ground,' Malcolm Doherty said. 'And I wonder if I'm going to wake up and find it's all been a dream.'

Independent, 29 April 1995

United's Gruelling Schedule
Patrick Barclay

Was there ever a time when footballing fortune was a simple matter, decided by bodies in prime condition and uncluttered minds; a time when each match, truly, could be taken as it came? If there was, let's pine for it.

Look at Manchester United's schedule. Today they visit Blackburn for the first of two matches in six days (the other is at home to Newcastle) whose significance to the Premiership needs no emphasis. Yet either the groundsman nor anyone else at Ewood Park should be offended if I state that the playing field is hardly level.

While Blackburn, knocked out of Europe last month by Trelleborg, are reasonably fit and ready, United have some players requiring surgery and all except Peter Schmeichel in need of rest, especially so because of the wonderfully draining nature of their Champions League encounter with Barcelona at Old Trafford; factors Alex Ferguson will have to weigh in making today's selection.

As if this were not enough before the visit to the Nou Camp, United must put out a side at Newcastle in the Coca-Cola Cup on Wednesday. Of course it will not be Ferguson's strongest, but the idea of their being punished was always ludicrous. They are merely trying to spread an impossible workload. It is not in the interests of spectators, let alone players, that domestic competition be distorted and the Premier League, belatedly to be reduced to 20 clubs at the end of this season, ought to take note of UEFA's renewed threat to impose a limit of 18 throughout the continent.

The question is one of adjustment. There is no longer any point in discussing the merits of a pan-European league system. It is here, to stay and to expand, because this is how the game can best be marketed through television. The United-Barcelona match was shown in dozens of countries, including the United States, and the entertainment was so stirring, the atmosphere so triumphant over the medium's restrictions, that one scarcely noticed 3,000 seats were empty.

This was mainly a consequence of the height of the advertising boards chosen by UEFA, though live coverage on a mainstream channel is bound to have an effect. I was put in mind of a warning by Silvio Berlusconi (before the Milan empire-builder switched some of his energies from football to politics) that admission charges might eventually have to be reduced, in some cases even waived, to ensure the necessary backdrop: people.

Not every night can be as Old Trafford experienced. This was a distillation of why England, in exile, missed Europe. It mattered to the fans, it mattered to the players and it mattered to the managers who, after technique and tenacity had fought an honourable 2–2 draw, had reason to believe both teams would qualify for the knockout stages.

Who was the more relieved? No doubt Ferguson, because, unlike Johan Cruyff, he has never won the European Cup and the prospect of a setback had, quite literally, kept him awake at night.

The United manager may be many things. A dilettante is not one of them. His preparations left no stone unturned. Some stones he turned over several times. Last Sunday he watched three full recordings of Barcelona matches (against IFK Gothenburg, Atlético Madrid and Espanol). On Monday he watched their European Cup final defeat by Milan; just to be sure he had their weaknesses correctly assessed, he watched it over again. On Tuesday he arrived home at midnight after representing the club at a function and played a tape of Newcastle-Athletic Bilbao before going to bed.

But Barcelona would not leave his mind. At 4am, after fitful dozing, he returned to the tyrant screen to study Gothenberg-Barcelona again. And a few hours later, on the morning of the match, he was at the training ground when a telephone call confirmed that Ryan Giggs, with whom he had planned to terrorise Ronald Koeman, was not fit.

Ferguson's other big decision had been to drop Steve Bruce in order that the more mobile Paul Parker could patrol Romario. Circumstances conspired reprovingly: Parker gave a goal away and Bruce, in his 21st and final minute as substitute, made the intervention of the night to deny Romario a winner. But the bits which went wrong for United largely reflected the difference in class between top-level Premier League football, which has been so exciting this season as to beguile the unwary, and, well, Barcelona. Ferguson would have loved to have done to the Catalans what Milan did in Athens. But Nicky Butt is not Marcel Desailly, and that is that.

The United manager could nevertheless take pride in the general thrust of a display that went straight for Barcelona's vulnerable flanks. Long before the inept Luis was withdrawn at half time, Cruyff had taken the award for dodgiest selection.

He was typically generous afterwards. Asked to develop the contrast-in-styles theme by identifying United's most impressive aspect, he referred to the speed with which they moved the ball forward but added: 'The trouble for them was getting hold of it.' A fair reflection, familiar to those who saw England's match with Romania.

The essence of the contest lay in Koeman and Paul Ince: one the laid-back sophisticate, devastating when he stepped into midfield, the other a relentless chaser and instigator of causes. Ince was responsible for the equaliser – the Adrenal Gland of God goal – that allows United to risk defeat in the Nou Camp.

Their most likely quarter-final opponents, to hazard premature speculation, are Paris Saint-Germain. The chances of Milan lying in wait will be enhanced if UEFA this week reduce the Italians' unjustly harsh two-point penalty for comparatively trivial crowd misbehaviour involving the Salzburg goalkeeper (as Celtic fans will recall, Austrians are world-class at making mountains out of molehills).

Strange, isn't it, this curse on European champions of the Nineties. Milan, having walked off the pitch at Marseille, were banned for a year. Red Star Belgrade fell foul of the United Nations. Barcelona were knocked out at home by CSKA Moscow. Marseille were stripped of their title. Now Milan are in trouble again. Perhaps United ought to concentrate on the League.

Observer, 23 October 1994

Ferry Across the Mersey

Ian Ridley

The bookshelves in the living room of the Everton chairman Peter Johnson's custom-built mansion on Merseyside are heavy with reading material symbolic of his and the club's position. There are novels entitled *Tycoon* and *Only The Best*, and, as if trying to double the chances, two copies of *Goodison Glory*, whose author is at present not being troubled for an addendum but is believed instead to be compiling a compendium of the Everton jokes that are now doing the rounds.

Then he enters, whistling that tune 'Three Cheers for the Red, White and Blue' more familiar to football fans in the version, lyrically minimalist but suitably stirring when sung by 35,000 that goes: 'Ever-ton, Ever-ton. Ever-ton'. It is late afternoon, so Peter Johnson is not yet whistling in the dark.

Everton's situation, anchored to the seabed of the Premiership, is not quite what Johnson envisaged when he jumped ship from Tranmere Rovers and crossed the Mersey bearing treasure. He was buying one of the great clubs of English football, founder members of its League; now the great is a weight and they are foundering members. The club's first 'owner-occupier', as he describes himself, has presided over the worst start in the club's 106-year league history.

Daily he reads about his multi-million pound misfits; that his manager Mike Walker is about to be sacked; that he is the one panic-buying players, the wrong players at that. And that is the more constructive material. Does he not look wistfully back the mile down the hill from his home to Prenton Park? 'I'd never dream of saying I wish I had never got involved. I'm enjoying it,' he insists. 'But it's a lot harder than I thought it would be.'

Peter Johnson grew up a Tranmere fan but became a Liverpool follower 30 years ago when a then rare opportunity to acquire a season ticket arose. He subsequently saw 23 years of unmatched success as his personal fortune was also growing with his Park Foods company. Never was he tempted, though, to seek a place on the Anfield board: 'I'm not very good in a supporting role. I like to build a team around me.'

Tranmere came to him to help them survive and instead they prospered. 'Dispirited', though, by their limited potential, he cast his eyes towards Goodison and after 15 months of wrangling he wrested control. 'I could see an organisational opportunity, a chance to use the skills I had learned in my work,' he says.

'The cynics on Merseyside will say, "How can he have any sentiment when he has supported Tranmere Rovers, Liverpool and Everton?" but I am as committed to Everton now as much as I ever was to the other two. I didn't put £10m into the club not to be committed. Anyway, I would only ever be interested in a Merseyside club.

'I believe Everton are where they are today because of those wasted 15 months. Lost time . . . lost time . . . lost time,' he pines. 'It has made the work so much harder. It is hard enough running a football club, especially one with such expectation.'

When he finally got to Goodison, he was alarmed by the club's condition. 'I saw Everton seemingly going nowhere before anyone else did but even I was surprised by the way it had all stagnated because nothing I had ever been involved in had stagnated. There was a lack of leadership. There was a board there with no clout and no money.'

Polite and reasonable, he is certainly a toff for the Toffeemen but you sense his firmness. The German Shepherd dog Max on the patio looks fearsome but is actually affable; you suspect it is the other way round with its owner.

Johnson is fond of the word impact as both noun and verb and, in his language, is clearly a hands-on operator. 'You have got to remember chairmen now are putting their money in. Chairmen in the old days didn't do that to such a degree.' It was he, indeed, who finalised the £2.2m for Vinny Samways and also did the deal with his Rangers counterpart David Murray for Duncan Ferguson and Ian Durrant, loans which are costing Everton some £150,000 a month, it was revealed last week.

They were, however, completed only at Walker's behest, he insists. 'Any chairman who takes it upon himself to buy players must be stark staring mad. There is no way a manager can cope with a chairman's players. You have to be careful that you don't impact on the manager's judgement. At the end of the day he will either keep his job or lose it on the success of a team. You can't foist a player on him.'

A successful football club these days, he says – and those who wonder how he would know have to recall his Tranmere experience – is about a blend of teams within the club from players, supporters, coaching staff, commercial department and administration. 'I don't think Everton have got the blend yet,' he understates. 'Although we say that boardroom battles shouldn't impact on the players, they always take the manager's eye off the ball and he is under a certain amount of pressure and it's not a comfortable ship.

'You can't just chuck money at a club. Sunderland tried that 30 or 40 years ago and it didn't work. It's a case of finding the right manager, having the money available and that man to have the backing of the chairman to provide a blend.'

The relationship of chairman and manager is the most important in the club, he says. How is his with Walker? 'Very good. He will come here for dinner and we will talk for four or five hours. The guy needs all the support he can get. I feel sorry for him because the media will not let him rest. It's not for the press to decide our new manager or to decide when he's going.'

It is always a sign of difficult times when the press is cited and in Johnson's, and of late Walker's, retaliation lies their surprise at the attention that has been turned on them; at the sheer size of the club they have taken on. 'Yes, that is true. It is a very much bigger club than even I thought. My postbag is amazing. I have even had letters from a warship off Bosnia. It's this intensity that takes you aback. I think Mike's been surprised too. Coming out of the backwoods of East Anglia doesn't really prepare you but he'll cope. He's very articulate and capable.'

From all his utterings, it would appear that Johnson is behind Walker – though Brian Clough used to say that he would prefer his chairman where he could see him – but realism can never be far away. Johnson admits, for example, that before his takeover, when consulted about the shortlist headed by Walker to succeed Howard Kendall, he wanted to add another name.

'At the last, it is down to the chairman to make sure he has the right staff and that's all one can say,' Johnson admits. 'It is very unfair to set time limits or expose them to the media.' He adds, apparently talking of Everton's sad start: 'It can't continue.'

Though time would seem to be on Everton's side, it is equally true that they have been losing touch and that one bad defeat and a few days can change much. Perhaps the bookshelves will give guidance for a swift solution. Near the double dose of *Goodison Glory* stands singularly *The 24-Hour Business Plan*.

Independent on Sunday, 23 October 1994

The Liverpool Boot Room
Ivan Ponting and Steve Hale

Few people took much notice at the time; the talk was all of Shankly's resignation and Paisley's promotion. But on the day in 1974 when 25-year-old Roy Evans was elevated from the poignantly plentiful ranks of footballers who would never quite make the top grade to become Liverpool's reserve-team coach, club chairman Sir John Smith made a startling prediction. He announced: 'We have not made an appointment for the present, but for the future. One day Roy Evans will be our manager.'

Those who pondered on that incongruously portentous proclamation, and they could not have been many, might have been excused for dismissing Sir John's words as wishful thinking, or even as well-meaning but fanciful encouragement for a youngster embarking on a demanding new career. But the Reds' chairman was not a man given to flights of fancy; he had meant what he said and, some 20 years on, his bold prophecy proved to be correct. In the wake of the Souness debacle, on 31 January 1994, Roy Evans became manager of Liverpool FC.

It was a welcome return to Boot Room rule. That cherished symbol of all that was best about the club might have perished physically, but everything it stood for was preserved in the person of the new boss. Roy had lived for Liverpool from the fateful mid-1950s afternoon when he had left his home in Bootle with his older brother Malcolm, boarded a number-68 bus to Stanley Park and walked into Anfield to watch his first big-time football match. He was seven then, just old enough to begin a lifelong love affair with the Reds.

In the years that followed he stood on the Kop week in and week out, relishing the exploits of Bill Shankly's first great side, packed with heroes like Roger Hunt, Ian St John and Ron Yeats. As he grew up, Roy enjoyed heartening success as a player, emerging as a skilful, if rather one-paced left-back. He played for England Boys and did well, moving his manager, that splendid judge of character Tom Saunders – himself destined to become a key member of the Anfield Boot Room brigade as youth development officer in the 1970s and 1980s – to describe him as having a heart the size of a lion's. And, glory of glories, Roy became a professional with Liverpool.

All too soon, though, that momentum evaporated. Although he reached the fringe of the senior squad, and made 11 first-team appearances in the early 1970s, it became apparent that he was never going to hold down a regular place. It seemed he faced an unappetising choice between lingering at Anfield as an eternal reserve and playing out his career at a lower level.

But those who had guided his professional progress since boyhood, the likes of Bill Shankly and Bob Paisley, had seen something special in the make-up of the unassuming but unwaveringly enthusiastic Merseysider. They had watched him with his peers and with younger players and had recognised the makings of a successful coach. Ronnie Moran had just stepped up to help with the first team and someone was needed to take over the reserves; Paisley identified Roy as that someone and offered him the job.

Now came an agonising decision for the young man. He had always dreamed of playing for his beloved Liverpool and, at 25, he was understandably reluctant to admit that he was not good enough. He informed his manager that he wanted to play, not coach, but Bob was persistent, spelling out the stark truth about his footballing capabilities and repeating the same offer three or four times. In the end, after protracted soul-searching and much encouragement from such as Joe Fagan, Ronnie Moran and Tommy Smith, Evans took the clear-headed option of remaining with the Reds in a new and potentially fulfilling capacity.

Of course, it was something of a gamble, but any doubts about Roy's capabilities were quick to disappear. Though possessing no official coaching qualifications, he was blessed with a lively mind and proved adept at communicating with the youngsters in his charge; and while he was the most amiable of men, he could exhibit steel at need, finding no problem in instilling discipline as well as soccer expertise. The upshot was that Liverpool reserves won the Central League in each of Roy's first three seasons at the helm, going on to enjoy almost non-stop success before he moved up to help Ronnie Moran with the seniors when Joe Fagan became manager in 1983.

Ronnie, who played an enormous personal part in Roy's Boot Room education, sums up his regard for his one-time protégé, now his boss, in one succinct sentence: 'He was always the right sort of lad, we never had the slightest doubt about him.'

Though his merits as psychologist, diplomat and father confessor have undoubtedly proved valuable to countless household names over numerous campaigns, Roy himself describes his input in characteristically modest terms: 'If the players were on cloud nine, then we (the coaches) made sure we weren't. If they were a bit down, then we would be chipper. That way we maintained the right balance.'

He believes that the Boot Room's sense of continuity helped, too. He stressed every manager's need for loyalty and solidity from their staff, adding significantly: 'But these men have not got to be subservient. They have to state their case. No club needs yes-men, they can't afford them.'

A further illuminating insight into the rise of Evans the Coach comes from David Johnson, who came under his aegis during the England centre-forward's periodic sojourns in the 'stiffs'. David recalls: 'Roy always had a lovely manner about him. You could go to him and talk about anything, and when he spoke you listened. Obviously he was marvellous with the youngsters, but he also did a lot for older players. They might be swearing and annoyed at being dropped from the first team but, almost invariably, Roy could calm them down with a few quiet words.

'He had the ability to harness people's understandable frustration for the good of the club, beguiling the best out of them. Certainly he helped to keep me ticking over on occasions. I was tremendously impressed by his man-management skills, and also by his knowledge of football. He could get people to play the right way, the way Liverpool expected. Overall, Roy did a great job.'

Having switched his area of operation from Central League to First Division, Roy continued to make a favourable impression and the conviction grew among close observers that he was top management material. His name was thrust forward in 1985, and again in 1991, but first Kenny Dalglish and then Graeme Souness received the call.

When Souness brought in Phil Boersma as his right-hand man, it seemed that Evans' influence had decreased hugely, perhaps terminally. But that all changed in May 1993 when Roy was made number-two to a chastened Souness, who had been expected to leave there and then, but survived thanks largely to the support of his friend, chairman David Moores. In fact, Graeme hung on for another eight harrowing months before stepping down and, at long last, Roy's hour had come.

In announcing the appointment of his club's 14th full-time manager, Moores described Evans as 'the last of the Shankly lads', an accurate and telling description. Having spent so much time in the Boot Room he had learned his trade from the best, and learned it thoroughly, knowing the club at every level.

It was an emotional moment for Roy, who told his inaugural press conference: 'Liverpool FC has been built on a sense of pride. I felt that pride when I first came to Anfield and it has lived with me throughout my time here. It's very much with me today as I am appointed manager.' He revealed that when offered the job, it took him all of two seconds to think about it before accepting it. He recognised that restoring the Reds to their rightful position at the top constituted a massive responsibility, but there had been not the slightest possibility of shrinking from it.

The football world was united in its affection for the engaging Evans, who accepted a contract that runs until midway through 1996. But one question seemed to be on everybody's lips – was he tough enough for such a formidable task? Those who knew him well insisted that there would not be a problem. Though he was renowned for the gentle touch, for lending a sympathetic ear to egos bruised by the high-level ranting of Ronnie Moran, there was no questioning his inner strength.

Early evidence that Roy could take tough decisions came with the axing of highly priced defenders Mark Wright and Julian Dicks after their poor showing in a friendly against First Division Bolton

Wanderers during his first pre-season preparation as boss. Openly and firmly, he explained his reasons – Wright's attitude and Dicks' lack of fitness – and made it devastatingly clear that any player who took liberties did so at his peril.

Yet here was a man who enjoyed sharing the occasional beer with the footballers in his charge, who was ready to enjoy a joke with them and who acted, in every way, like a civilised human being. Neither pushy in enforcing his authority, nor a pushover for those who might confront it, Roy offered a striking contrast to his two most recent predecessors. There was none of the obsessive privacy of Dalglish or the driven intensity of Souness; in their place was a more accessible personality, a figure to whom the fan in the street could relate with ease.

Exemplifying his reasonable approach, Roy wasted little time in introducing weekly players' meetings, at which all ideas could be pooled. Instead of fearing so-called player-power, he sought to harness it, feeling it foolish not to tap such a rich pool of experience.

One of the most senior Reds, Ian Rush, voiced the general opinion of his team-mates when he said: 'Roy knows the players and gets on with them, as well as knowing how to get the best out of them. He is a nice guy, but as a manager, you can't be nice all the time. I'm sure that, like Bob Paisley, he'll know where to cut the tape.'

All splendidly positive stuff but, that said, Roy still has to produce results, and although Anfield expectations are not as high as in recent decades, he neither expects nor desires a lengthy 'honeymoon'. The early indications were that he wouldn't need one, the Reds beginning 1994/95 with a thrilling sequence of victories, projecting a sense of purpose and team spirit that had been absent for too long. Roy had plenty to prove; for instance, his acumen in the transfer market had yet to be tested thoroughly, though the purchase of classy centre-backs Phil Babb and John Scales augurs well. But, to the undisguised joy of supporters driven to distraction by Souness, prospects were healthier than at any time since the club's last Championship success back in 1990.

And two things were certain. First, after working for 30 years to earn his chance in the top job, the new boss would not be relinquishing it lightly. Second, though football has changed and the world has moved on, Liverpool under Roy Evans will adhere to the timeless principles of Shanklyism. What could be more reassuring?

The Boot Room, An Anfield Legend, 1994

Forest First and Foremost
Kenneth Clarke

Most of my friends at school were Derby County fans and by rights I should have been a Derby fan too. As a child, I lived on the Derbyshire side of the Derby/Notts border, with Derby 10 miles away in one direction and Nottingham 10 miles away in the other.

In those early postwar seasons, Derby County were in the big time, a leading First Division side, one of the handful of clubs everyone knew and talked about. And even though they were in the Third Division (South), Notts County, too, had some star names.

So it was that, at the start of the 1947–48 season, Derby broke the transfer record by signing Billy Steel from Morton for £15,000. Notts County promptly capped it by bringing England's reigning centre-forward, Tommy Lawton, from Chelsea for £20,000, to play alongside the young Jackie Sewell.

Forest, amid all this, were down near the bottom of the Second Division. Yet I always supported Forest first and Notts County second. My father wasn't interested in football at all, but my grandfather used to take me in by bus, Forest one week, County the next. I think it was the name 'Forest' that made them my first team. They were also, as I say, in a higher division – just – though early in my spectating career, in 1948–49, Forest were relegated to Division III (South), which meant my first Nottingham derby.

The question of loyalty is perfectly easy. If Forest are playing County, I'll support Forest. If County are playing anyone else, I support County. Over the years I've probably grown less partisan, which is just as well because I don't just watch football in Nottingham. In any given year, I'd also like to see Leicester, Derby, Mansfield maybe, as well as some of the London clubs – though since becoming Chancellor I seem to have less time than in any other job I've done. In 1993–94, I saw just 10 matches – the lowest number since I was in short trousers. Among them were both the Nottingham derbies.

I had never believed for one moment the cliché that Forest were 'too good to go down' in 1993, but I was extremely relieved when we proved ourselves good enough to go back up again.

It's not that I can't cope with lower division football, mind you. If I'm doing weekend speeches or visits, I like to check what games are on nearby. A few years ago, I was up in the North West and managed to get in the first half of Stockport v Hartlepool, thanks to Labour MP, Peter Snape, who was then a director at Edgeley Park. And, of course, I'm fairly used to watching the lower division stuff down the years, both at County and Forest. There was a time when both were in the old First Division, but for decades Nottingham was like Bristol, one of those towns that most people saw as Second or Third division when it came to soccer, incapable of getting clubs in the top flight.

I was at the game we won to get promoted to the First Division in 1957, a 4–0 win at Bramall Lane. That was our first taste of the top division, but even then I never imagined that we would go on to be one of the really big names in English football. Yet thanks to Brian Clough, that is exactly what we did. Clough has to be, quite simply, the best club manager since the war. He took two very ordinary Midlands clubs, first Derby and then Forest, and turned them into world beaters. To turn Nottingham Forest into a club that won the First Division championship and then the European Cup was a genuinely remarkable achievement. He would develop a side, take it to the limit of its potential, then break it up, bring in new blood and get even better.

He turned average players into good players. He took players other managers had found hard to control and made them tick. Like Bertie Auld, who went on to a great career with Celtic. And he took Viv Anderson, gangly and ungainly and not naturally skilful, and made him a great player. And look what happened to Des Walker after he left Forest. Lost without Brian.

The other amazing thing about Brian was the way he managed his own son, Nigel. Most people will find it hard to imagine how a father can manage a son or how a son can be managed by a father, but he did it. And Nigel is a nice, uncomplicated man who just thrived on being managed by Brian. I'm not saying he was perfect, though. I thought it was a dreadful mistake to let Lee Chapman go. He may have looked our least skilful forward, but as soon as he'd gone, it was obvious that we lacked someone the other forwards could play off and come on to score goals.

As an outspoken Labour supporter, Brian's politics are pretty well removed from mine, so whenever we met, we tended to talk about football – not that either of us shirks a good debate. During the kerfuffle over Michael Heseltine's pit closures, Brian led a march past my surgery, which is a short walk from Forest's ground. At the time, Forest were heading for relegation and I threatened to lead a counter-march past the ground.

Being so well known, I get the occasional cat-call thrown my way, but it is generally in good humour. I do, however, sit in the directors' box now, not out of status consciousness, but more because I can better guarantee that people won't come up and lobby me about something or other. When I go to a football match, I like to lose myself in it. I forget about politics and everything else besides. I like to get involved.

I always go to the Cup final. Until a couple of years ago, I always went on the underground but my recognition factor has become a problem. We got absolutely jam-packed into a tube train and, although it wasn't nasty, it was a bit of a pain having a 20-minute journey with fans singing about you. Some of the songs were pretty good but it was a bit tedious nonetheless.

Yet I have never felt intimidated by crowds and I don't actually believe soccer violence was ever as bad as non-football followers sometimes imagined. I do not deny it was a problem and potentially still is, but the way some people talked, you'd visualise Saturday afternoon guaranteeing scenes of mayhem and bloodshed. I do remember occasions – particularly when I was living in Birmingham and going to St Andrews and Villa Park a lot – when violence was a real issue and one to which my children and I were occasionally too close for comfort. But, equally, you could go season on end without seeing a single incident to alarm you.

I was never involved in any discussions within Government about what to do about violence in the game. Mrs Thatcher ensured that Ministers who actually went to football had no say at all in developing the policies. I think she found it difficult to understand why anyone would want to go to a football match at all.

I wasn't keen on the ID scheme, which made us very unpopular, and I thought we handled the alcohol problem in a peculiar way, too. At one point, magistrates would grant a licence to some bars within the ground, but not those from where the pitch could be seen. This meant that any spectators could buy a drink – unless they were in the executive boxes. Executive boxes have never struck me as the best places from which to watch football, but nor do they seem to me to be centres of violence either.

It was clear, given the attention devoted to football safety and the public concerns, that something had to be done, but I think some of the things we did were unconvincing. When I first started going to football – back in the 1940s, as I say – the crowds were enormous. Even at Third Division County, you could get well over 30,000. It was so packed that if you arrived at all late, you'd be lifted down to the front with all the other small boys. Indeed, my first memory of football is of leaving the ground, very slowly, in the middle of a huge human mass shuffling its way out. Had there been lots of pushing or shoving, fighting or larking about, there would have been deaths every week. But behaviour was different, standards very different, and it didn't happen.

I never imagined that ID cards alone, or all-seater stadia alone, would deal with the problem. If people want to misbehave, they can misbehave in seats just as well as on the terraces. I remember the experience of Highfield Road, another ground I know well. When Coventry went all-seater, the hooligans started to hurl the seats about and they went back to terracing.

I was very pleased, at the 1992 election, that all the parties had agreed that the two lower divisions would not be forced to meet the demands of the Taylor Report. I will concede to Lord Justice Taylor that we are now having built splendid stadia that might not otherwise have been built. But I do not think they have made one jot of difference to crowd safety. The report has also cost clubs huge sums of money and several of them have only just survived.

I don't believe violence has ebbed because of the various reports and legislation. I think it is more that gang violence, and football's role in it, went out of fashion. That is not to decry the special role the police have played in keeping rival supporters apart or the effect of closed circuit TV inside the grounds.

We have always been fairly lucky at Forest. The fans have always had a good record. I'm sure that was partly because the team played good clean football, too. In 20 years, we didn't have a player sent off. The only real trouble, at the height of hooliganism, was with visiting fans. I remember the police being totally unprepared for this. They resisted segregation because they thought it meant putting all the trouble-makers together. They resisted CCTV because they were worried it could not be used as evidence. And they resisted fencing because it stopped them getting in to arrest people. It took about two seasons for them to sort it out and they now have an excellent arrangement.

I'm one of the lucky ones who represents a seat which is home to my club. The suggestion that some MPs go to football matches because they think there are votes in it is aired in the introduction to this book. Such MPs are wasting their time. It's the kind of nonsense you might hear from people who don't know what they're talking about. But voters aren't stupid. Why should they imagine that just because an MP shares an interest – or pretends to – that he or she is any good as an MP? If there are MPs who go to a match just to be seen, but who don't actually enjoy it, I strongly advise them to give it up.

For my part, as I say, I get very engrossed in the game. I get worked up. My idea of relaxing is not to do nothing. It is to get involved in something. It has to be intense, whether it's watching football or cricket – or bird-watching for that matter.

I get much more involved in club football than internationals. The worst game I ever saw was probably the World Cup qualifier, in 1993, between England and San Marino at Wembley. It was a total farce. Six-nil, ten blokes standing around the area just trying to stand in the way. I can't get switched on to internationals in the way I can with League and Cup football. If I was running a club, I would be club before country every time. I wouldn't release my players to play some silly friendly, or take on San Marino and risk a broken leg.

The game has changed out of all recognition and in many ways for the better. Money is a bit of a problem and I didn't like the way the Premiership was started to stop money being shared at all levels of the game, but you can't have too many hang-ups about the game's commercialisation. It is a business.

I like the competitiveness of sport. I like the speed. When I played as a schoolboy, you had a big leather ball, big boots, great big shin pads. On wet days it was sometimes difficult to kick the ball from one end of the mudbath into the other. The game today is horrendously fast. The top players are athletes. Their technical skills are genuinely impressive. Sometimes it is too fast, too furious, and the skills don't match. But when it's good, there is nothing like it.

When it's really good, you realise why Jack Dunnett, former Labour MP and former chairman of Notts County, became the first person to leave politics to spend more time with his football.

Football and the Commons People, 1995

The Toon Army
Harry Pearson

In the window of the print shop at the foot of Dog Leap Stairs there was a photo of the Tyne Bridge under construction. I stopped and looked at it whenever I'd been to the Crown Posada. The first steel spars are just edging out across the river; down below, parked practically next to the Guild Hall, you can see a submarine. I was looking at the two erectors standing nonchalantly on one of the outstretched girders, chatting as if they'd just met on a pavement somewhere in town, while six inches to either side of them there was nothing but fresh air and a hundred-foot drop into the river. And in those days you wouldn't have wanted to drop into the Tyne from any height. Now it's clean enough to rank as one of the finest salmon rivers in England; then it was an open sewer. Originally it was said that a Geordie was someone who'd been born within smell of the Tyne. By the early sixties that included an area from Dumfries to Filey. My father remembers coming up to Newcastle from Middlesbrough for a meeting at some offices down on the quayside. 'How do I get to the river?' he asked a porter at Central Station.

'Go in the Gents', flush yourself down the toilet and you'll be there in thirty seconds,' the porter replied helpfully.

I walked up Northumberland Street. By the time I got to the statue of 'Wor Jackie' the Centurion Bitter and pre-match nerves had started to nudge me into George Clarts mode: 'Jackie Milburn,' I prattled uncontrollably, 'Wor Jackie. The First World Wor indeed! Raven-haired, eagle-eyed, swift, swallow, chicken-in-a-basket. The magpie who popped up like a jackdaw-in-a-box to head home the winner that set the Black and Whites on the road to Wembley once more. Robledo, he was another star! Not a Geordie, but a Jorge. He came from Chile. And, my word, it was chilly on the afternoon he made himself part of United's great Cup-fighting tradition. And why were they always fighting cups, you might well ask. I'll tell you. Because this was in the days before television. People had to make their own entertainment. Cup-fighting, rug-wrestling and pummelling plates were but three of the pastimes that found popularity among the tough-as-teak, cobble-close families that eked out an existence in the sooty streets of the Toon.'

In St James's the mood was even more hysterical. It was the kind of wild and wanton hilarity which at a children's party would have all the mothers shaking their heads and saying, 'There'll be tears before bedtime.'

'Whack your lass with a Christmas tree. Ay-oh, ay-oh,' the fans chanted. 'Keegan. Keegan. Keegan. Gets the ball, scores a goal. Andy, Andy Cole. Toon Army. Toon Army.' Shredded paper fluttered through the air, black and white flags were unfurled, arms waved, a brass band played. 'Oh me lads you should've seen us gannin' . . .'

A crop-headed youth of such vast proportions that any Norwegians present must have been tempted to harpoon him and take him home for supper came into the Gallowgate eating a pie. It was one of those special football pies with asbestos-grey pastry that cracks to release the odour of a 1,000-year-old tomb. They're called football pies because they're made out of old casies. They even use the laces. 'Who ate all the pies?' the crowd howled. 'Who ate all the pies? You fat bastard. You fat bastard. You ate all the pies.'

The blubbery boy responded to this by shoving half the pie in his gob and then laughing. I rather wished he'd done things the other way round. I was picking gristle out of my ears for weeks afterwards. 'He's fat. He's round. He sprays his pie around. Big fat bastard. Big fat bastard,' the crowd celebrated.

The Gallowgate was the last standing area left at St James's. Opposite was the newly completed Leazes Stand, built on what had once been the popular end of the ground. Catherine's aunt recalled going in there just after the war with her father, brother and uncle. They'd been warned to stick together, but within five minutes were tens of yards apart, bobbing about as randomly as bottles in a choppy sea, the crowd surging back and forth across the terracing. At least she didn't end up down the front. The front of the Leazes End was notorious. A combination of heavy pre-match drinking and the impossibility of reaching the lavatories through the crush meant that standing there was like being at the bottom of a waterfall, albeit one that would never feature in a Timotei commercial. Ah, the good old days, eh? Earthy Chaucerian fun and the rapid spread of contagious diseases.

I'd been looking forward to seeing Peter Beardsley play ever since he'd been transferred back to Newcastle. Of the triumvirate of great players, Waddle, Beardsley and Gascoigne, who'd risen at St James's in the 1980s, Peter Beardsley was the one I most enjoyed watching.

There was a mischievous neatness about him – part Jack Russell, part Jack Buchanan. He passed sharply and decisively, and he had a way of dummying over the ball with a wiggle of his right knee that put me in mind of a club comic imitating Elvis. The thing I liked best about Beardsley, though, was that when he ran with the ball you caught a glimpse on his face of the joy of the thing; a reminder of those same moments when, as a kid, you went round a defender, or ran on to a pass, and all there seemed to be in front of you were acres of grass, and as the adrenalin kicked into your system you got that bio-chemically ignorant childhood feeling that you could go charging on with that ball at your feet for ever and ever and never run out of breath. Then some thunder-thighed numbskull would lumber up and give you a dead leg.

In Peter Beardsley's case the thunder-thighed numbskull was Neil Ruddock. In a friendly match at Anfield five days before Ruddock had fractured Bearsley's cheekbone with his elbow. The injury put Beardsley out for the first month of the season. Now he was said to be considering suing Ruddock for damages. Perhaps the supporters who'd brought tickets expecting to see him should have taken similar steps.

The game kicked off. Somehow the expectation had drained all the life out of it. The previous season Newcastle had seemed able to generate a destructive tempo of passing and movement at will, overwhelming opponents with a continuous flow of swift, jabbing attacks. Today they had all the rhythm of a one-legged tap dancer. Spurs sat back and waited for a break. Compared to the pre-match activity it was dull stuff. The William Tell Overture followed by a stylophone recital.

Not that I noticed much of it. By now my attention was focused on a little man with glasses and a ginger moustache who had come in to E Section with two friends ten minutes before kick off. I had never seen them in E Section before. I suppose they were only there because the Twats Section was shut. For the next half an hour these three men put on such a concentrated display of idiocy I began to suspect they were being employed by the Northumbria Tourist Board as part of a Viz Comic Heritage Trail. The little man was the ringleader. He was in his mid-twenties. The ironed creases down the front of his jeans suggested he still lived at home with his mother. He was certainly deeply frustrated. 'Get your tits out for the lads!' he bellowed at the raffle girls, his face turning puce and the veins on his neck bulging. Nobody except his mates joined in. 'What's the matter with these miserable cunts?' he shouted. 'They're worse than fucking Makems. We hate Cockneys and we hate Cockneys . . . (If any Londoners out there were thinking of inviting him round for dinner, I'd save the cassoulet and the tiramisu for somebody else if I were you.) When one of his friends dropped some matches and bent over to retrieve them the little man jumped on him and simulated anal intercourse. 'Soft southern rent boy,' he ranted at an injured Spurs player, 'You're just a soft southern rent boy.'

Then the little man made a mistake. 'Scotty!' he roared at Kevin Scott, the Newcastle centre-half. 'You're a fucking poof.'

'Scotty's all right by me,' a voice behind me growled. Everyone turned to look, including the little man. The speaker was in his late thirties, with deep-set eyes and a head and neck as solid as a butcher's block. His voice was a high-powered whisper. It sounded like a steam hose. His face was pale.

'You what?' the little man yelled. He was standing on his toes, staring up the terrace. He was about twelve feet below the other bloke.

'I said,' the other bloke repeated in exactly the same slow hissing tone, 'Scotty's all right by me.'

The little man's face flushed. He looked round at his mates, but for the first time all afternoon they seemed to be taking an interest in the game. 'He's playing like a fucking lass, man!' he screamed, saliva spraying everywhere. He was turning purple now, but whatever the other man was thinking he remained if anything paler than when the row had started. It was as if the blood was draining away from him and into the little man, swelling and colouring him like a bruise.

'He's all right by me,' he said again. I noticed that his lips, thin to begin with, had disappeared altogether. I always regard this as a bad sign. My rule is: no lips, no argument. Think of the great white shark. Would you get in dispute with it? I think not. The little man must have had the same rule because he tried a more placatory bellow, 'All I'm saying is, mate . . .'

Unhappily we never got to hear the rest because at this point Sheringham rather rudely interrupted the discussion by putting Spurs in front. They never looked likely to surrender that lead. Newcastle, for all their desperate effort, seemed incapable of worrying the Tottenham defence. Lee Clark, outstanding the previous season, was as anonymous as Salman Rushdie; Cole hardly had a touch, and the back four, Kevin Scott included, looked flimsy. Only goalkeeper Pavel Srnicek came out of the match with much credit. Signed by Keegan's predecessor, Ossie Ardiles, Srnicek had struggled during his first season. A wafer-thin man, he had stopped shots well, but reacted to crosses with a vampiric panic. He seemed to have conquered that phobia, though he still hadn't ditched his ridiculous haircut. He sported the short-front-and-sides-long-back style favoured by so many Eastern Europeans. It was a throwback to the first days of the Czech pro-democracy movement, when the crowds in Wenceslas Square could clearly be heard chanting: 'We want freedom. We want democracy. We want Chris Waddle's old barber.'

For Ossie Ardiles Spurs' win represented some sort of revenge at least. The Tottenham manager had been sacked by Newcastle in a manner that followed football's usual shabby pattern. 'Ossie's job is as safe as houses,' United director Douglas Hall had told the press on the Friday. The following Monday Ardiles was fired. Just as well Douglas Hall isn't a builder, really.

As we filed out I noticed the little man in front of me. He'd been surprisingly subdued after his clash with the butcher's block bloke. Now he'd spotted a small boy with his father and was leaning over talking to him in a liddle-biddy-baby voice, saying: 'Is it your first game at Newcastle? Who's your favourite player? Robert Lee? Aye, he's a canny footballer . . .'

Luckily for the child the little man stopped talking at this point because I heaved up all over him. It would be all too easy to dismiss the little man's behaviour as simply the product of abysmal ignorance, woeful insensitivity, and arrested mental development. But what the hell, eh?

As I trotted down the stairs of the Gallowgate I could hear the fans in front of me comforting one another.

'Well, I hope Sunderland lost anyway.'

'Against the run of play.'

'One-nil.'

'A goal in injury time.'

'From a penalty.'

'Aye, disputed.'

The Far Corner, 1994

Winning Ways at Highbury
Joe Lovejoy

Arsenal's stirring progress, against all the odds, to a second successive Cup-Winners' Cup final had Englishmen proud to be English, which has not always been the way of it lately, but will have been viewed with mixed feelings up at The Belfry, where it was a case of 'Do as I say, not as they do'.

David Seaman's goalkeeping heroics in the shoot-out against Sampdoria coincided with a mustering of Terry Venables's England fledglings in the Midlands for their latest master class in contemporary tactics. And, while it would be curmudgeonly to deny Arsenal one iota of the credit they deserve, it is fair to say that the reformist cause was scarcely advanced by a performance assembled from the traditional British virtues of physical strength, mental fortitude and the long ball, all applied in good, old-fashioned 4–4–2.

It was not without irony that, on the very day Venables was preaching the progressive gospel to impressionable young minds, Arsenal should overcome Italian sophisticates, and Blackburn Rovers take a stranglehold on the championship playing the sort of game that has hardly changed since 1966 and all that.

Certainly the siege Gunners' attritional power play bore no resemblance to the Total Football which saw Ajax bewitch and bewilder Bayern Munich in the Champions' Cup the previous night. It is the flexibility of the Dutchmen, who often seem to be playing with five forwards, that Venables is keen to develop in his England charges.

The objective, of course, is an entirely laudable one, but the struggle is mostly uphill at a time when the old ways remain firmly entrenched at club level. Why change, chorus the Luddites. Mighty Milan have just reached another European Cup final playing 4–4–2. Those of radical, as well as romantic, disposition will be rooting for an Ajax win.

Venables will continue to fight the good fight, but it may be a losing battle unless help is forthcoming from the clubs. He needs someone, a Manchester United or a Newcastle, to provide the sort of enlightened lead Milan gave Italian football when they lifted the dead hand of *catenaccio* and scrapped the sweeper system in favour of zonal defence. Serie A followed suit *en masse*.

It is beguiling, but doubtless naive, to think that the Premier

League might react the same way if there was a similar innovation in England as revolutionary as the five-man midfield David Pleat popularised with Tottenham nearly a decade ago.

David Platt, whose bulldog Britishness makes John Bull look like a fifth columnist, insists it is coming. England's captain greeted the press on arrival in Genoa and, during a lengthy discourse on everything from Gazza's fitness to the recession, volunteered the opinion that English clubs were embracing a more Continental approach.

Really? Italian television must be showing a lot of Nottingham Forest. With the honourable exception of Frank Clark's passing team, nobody springs readily to mind. Blackburn are long ball, Manchester United knock it earlier *sans* Cantona – even Liverpool and Tottenham are not averse to what is euphemistically called the 'direct' game.

Arsenal are direct to the point of rudeness. Give them a Christmas tree and they would probably impale George Graham on it. Not for them split strikers and the studious shepherding of possession. They get the ball forward early, from anywhere, with a target man (Hartson) to win it and an eager predator (Wright) to translate the assists into goals.

It is not always attractive to watch, and the Londoners are not everybody's cup of Rosie Lee, but minimalist simplicity has served them well throughout the most successful era in the club's history, and has given them a better-than-even chance of retaining the Cup-Winners' Cup, which would be another unprecedented achievement.

After coming from behind to see off Sampdoria away, they will be favourites to overcome Real Zaragoza, who made hard work of defending their 3–0 first-leg lead against Chelsea. The Spaniards will be technically superior, but Arsenal are used to that. It was the case last season, against Paris St-Germain and Parma, and again against Auxerre and Sampdoria, but indefatigable spirit has triumphed over adversity time and again.

The return leg in Genoa was a major test for an ageing team whose decline in the League had them flirting with relegation. A 3–2 win from the home game was a paper-thin advantage, given that 1–0 or 2–1 would have been enough for Sampdoria, courtesy of their away goals.

Platt had revealed that the Italians were confident. He, and they, expected to prevail. Not for the first time, Arsenal had been underestimated. Fatally. They were up for it. You could tell that from a macho war-dance of a warm-up that would have left many teams knackered before they started.

The older players (which means the majority) were smiling before the start, a picture of self-assurance. Perhaps Merson and company had read the English-language welcome in the match programme, which announced that Eddie Firmani, once of Charlton Athletic, had been 'the undisputed favourite of the Sampdoria fans, called the Cold Turkey'.

The smiles soon vanished, the confidence punctured after only 14 minutes, when Arsenal were hoist by their offside petard, looking vainly for a flag as Mancini ran through a square defence to score with a deft chip. It took Arsenal more than three quarters of an hour to come up with the equaliser, Wright profiting from Hartson's transference of a corner to attain the unique distinction of scoring in every round.

One-one was good enough. With Schwarz and Keown bossing the midfield, Sampdoria were in trouble. Instead of passing the ball short and finessing their way through, they were playing Arsenal at their own game, lofting hit-and-hope stuff which was meat and drink to Bould and Adams.

When the Italians kept it short and slick, it was Arsenal's turn to struggle, and a tie which swung more ways than an ambiguous archbishop seemed to be settled by two late goals from a 19-year-old substitute, Claudio Bellucci, who made it 3–1 with just four minutes left.

Instead, a winning position was thrown away at the death by Walter Zenga, once Italy's goalkeeper but now regarded as Sampdoria's weakest link. The World Cup veteran failed to organise an adequate defensive wall, then positioned himself poorly for Schwarz's last-minute free kick, which beat him at his left-hand post.

Extra time was notable chiefly for a couple of heroic, last-ditch tackles by Dixon, then Seaman compounded Zenga's embarrassment by saving three penalties out of five. England's No 1 could remember no more satisfying a contribution in a 16-year professional career.

Seaman's heroics evoked memories of a shoot-out at the same ground, five years ago, when one of Highbury's favourite sons, David O'Leary, scored the penalty which took the Republic of Ireland through to the quarter-finals of Italia '90. For others, the drama of the ersatz finish called to mind the 1980 Cup-Winners' Cup final, when tiebreak failures by Rix and Brady condemned Terry Neill's Arsenal to defeat against Valencia.

Fifteen years on, they will hope to settle it in normal time in Paris on May 10. Adams, who threatened to burst the net with his kick on

Thursday, spoke for everyone involved when he said: 'Settling a big game on penalties is not a nice experience, not something you can enjoy.' He sympathised with all the players who missed, but was 'absolutely gutted' for Bould, whose second booking of the tournament had put him out of the final.

Arsenal will miss him. The tall, flinty centre-back had an excellent match in Genoa, and his likely replacement, Andy Linighan, is less reliable, more prone to expensive errors.

Expensive errors of a different sort have left another vacancy to be filled. Reaching the final has done Stewart Houston's cause a power of good, but the caretaker manager probably needs to win it to have a decent chance of holding off more fancied contenders, such as Bruce Rioch and Ray Harford.

A European trophy – albeit one they already hold – would be a major fillip for the club and their supporters at the end of a troubled season, and might help to persuade Adams, who needs more than Mycil to cure his itchy feet, to stay put. Keeping the captain who personifies the Arsenal spirit is high on the list of priorities, according to the director who controls the purse strings, David Dein.

At the top, presumably, is the managerial position. Houston has made a good impression so far, and kept his head on Thursday when the pressure was on, but it is said that some senior players would prefer a high-profile appointment.

Be that as it may, they were happy enough, in every sense, on the champagne flight home in the early hours of Friday morning. Why the 3am return when, with no Saturday match, they could have lingered longer? They had to be back for Adams's testimonial golf day. If there was any justice, Seaman would have won it 3 and 2.

Sunday Times, 23 April 1995

Hi-tech Huddersfield
Simon Inglis

You may recall the scene from JB Priestley's *Good Companions:* 'Something very queer is happening in that narrow thoroughfare . . . called Manchester Road.'

Bruddersford had scraped a 0–0 draw against Bolton, and Jess

Oakroyd's mate Jim was moaning on about United's £2,000 centre-forward who 'were like a great lass on t'job'.

'To say that these men paid their shillings to watch 22 hirelings kick a ball is merely to say that a violin is wood and catgut,' wrote Priestley. 'For a shilling the Bruddersford United AFC offered you Conflict and Art.'

Manchester Road was, of course, Leeds Road and Bruddersford an amalgam of Priestley's native Bradford and Herbert Chapman's successful Huddersfield of the 1920s.

Now, 66 years on, something very queer is happening again in West Yorkshire. For Leeds Road read the brand new Alfred McAlpine Stadium. For Huddersfield Corporation read Kirklees Metropolitan Council. For one shilling terrace entrance read a £7.50 seat. And for Conflict and Art, how about Harmony and Architecture?

On Saturday Huddersfield's extraordinary stadium, whose banana-shaped roof trusses are now proudly advertised on buses all over town, opened in front of a 13,500 all-ticket crowd. Huddersfield lost 1–0 to Wycombe, but then the home team usually does falter when new grounds are inaugurated, and Town made up for it with a 3–0 win over Scunthorpe in their second game on Tuesday.

There have been the usual teething problems: dressing rooms too hot, a PA system too loud for the neighbours and too muffled for VIPs. Fire alarms go off unprovoked but the builders remain on the job, making progress before the next match, Huddersfield versus Barrow on Sunday.

Huddersfield versus Barrow? No mistake, for here, in the town where the Northern Union was formed in 1895, association football and rugby league have become formal bed-fellows – the first time both codes have combined to share and own a new, purpose-built stadium. The football club has a 40 per cent stake, as does Kirklees council. The rugby club holds the remaining 20 per cent.

Next year the stadium will host rugby league's centenary celebrations and one match in the World Cup.

Behind this admirable entente is an unlikely pairing, a sort of trans-Pennine Blair-Prescott dream ticket. Paul Fletcher, 43, the former Burnley striker and lately Town's chief executive, provides the flair. George Binns, 60 years man and boy in Huddersfield, club official since 1969, provides the grit.

'When I first met George four years ago I thought he was a bit of a pain, a typically dour Yorkshireman,' says Fletcher. 'Since then we've had our heads in the clouds and our feet on the ground.'

'Paul's learning,' Binns will admit dryly, though patently he too is bowled over by the stadium's popularity. Fletcher's commercial team – which includes Tony Stephens, advisor to David Platt and Alan Shearer – has raised an astonishing £7 million in sponsorship, and all 26 private boxes were snapped up for both football and rugby at a time when Town were facing relegation and Fartown, as the rugby league club are popularly known, were in administration. As someone remarked at the opening: 'Paul could sell ice-cream to the eskimos.'

'Paul and I have never fallen out, though,' said Binns. 'We've just had arguments. But the stadium's not finished. There's a lot of work to do yet.'

In fact, two stands were just about ready for Saturday, a third holding 4,100 should be finished by October. Opening in November is a 32-bay floodlit golf-driving range, while long-term plans include a rugby league museum and perhaps a hotel, cinema, bowling alley or even rock-concert stage behind the north end, which remains undeveloped behind 14 cricket sight-screens.

If nothing else, as Saturday's game demonstrated, the screens will deter crowds tempted to gather for a free view from Kilner Bank, whose dense woods rise steeply behind one stand. Here is the Alpine in McAlpine.

The builders like the place so much they have agreed to pay £2 million over 10 years in exchange for a consultancy deal and what are being called, American-style, the stadium's 'naming rights'.

This represents another coup for Fletcher, who recalls: 'When I was an apprentice at Bolton we used to sweep all the paper under the wooden stands, so we could get off home quick. Then, at Burnley, Bob Lord sold players to build a First Division stadium for a team heading for the Fourth. That's my background, so I understand the balance which has to be made.'

Apparently he does. A meat pie at the new stadium costs a reasonable £1, while sponsorship from the brewers Courage and caterers Gardner Merchant – suppliers to Buckingham Palace and Ascot – should guarantee beer and smoked salmon sandwiches all round. The former Prime Minister Harold Wilson, a Town devotee of old, would surely approve, as did old timers entering the stadium on Saturday through lovingly restored, pre-First World War turnstiles, brought over from Leeds Road.

Some things never change, however advanced the surroundings.

Watching Bruddersford, wrote Priestley, 'turned you into a member of a new community . . . you have escaped from the clanking machinery of this lesser life' into something 'altogether more splendid'.

Why else build a new stadium if it is not altogether more splendid?

Guardian, 26 August 1994

Knighton in White Armour
Stephen Brenkley

For as long as football is played, Michael Knighton will be the man who failed to take over Manchester United. He was pronounced then to have reached too far. You should hear him now.

'We will be buying the best players in the world in 10 years. We will be in the Premiership and we will be in the European Cup, competing with the very best. We will be a match for anybody, anybody, anywhere and we shall also have the finest soccer academy in the world right here. People will flock to this stadium.'

He could not have been accused of understatement had he been referring to Manchester United and Old Trafford, but he was not. Knighton was talking about Carlisle United and Brunton Park. If he smiled as he spoke, it was not because the assertion was ridiculous but because he found the prospect mouthwatering.

He will deliver much the same address to anybody who cares to listen and doubtless does so many times a day. The improbability of the task he has set himself as chairman, chief executive and absolute controller of fortunes of the Third Division club must occur to him quite as often, but Knighton pretends not to notice. He rejects any suggestion that he expects too much and might have been wiser to restrict his forecast to survival, a mid-table Second Division spot and an occasional cup run, and still risk charges of galloping over-ambition. He feels he is not, definitely not, reaching too far and the enthusiastic eyes twinkled winningly as he said so.

The way that Knighton, a former football apprentice, school teacher and property developer, intends to convert Carlisle from carthorse to thoroughbred is almost as revolutionary as the grand scheme itself. He is determined to make the club a self-financing, profitable operation. This seems as bizarre a proposition as Carlisle United's being conquerors of Europe, but not to Knighton.

'For far too long, football has not been run as a commercial enterprise capable of standing on its own two feet,' he said. 'I'm not a fairy godfather who is going to throw millions at this club because, for one thing, I haven't got millions. But it's not necessary. On a proper business footing with all the fringe activities around the club, with merchandising and sponsorship and the right direction, this place will be successful. Attendances will grow but while fans really can't expect to get something for nothing they are almost immaterial financially.'

He is slightly scathing about the contributions of rich men like Jacks Hayward and Walker because, while he admires their passion, he believes they have missed the point by treating football clubs as a private charity. Nor does he think that it would be ideal for there to be 92 such benefactors.

He said he chose Carlisle because of the challenge, the 18.2 acres of ground around Brunton Park, and the Cumbrian location which represented untapped potential. Not to mention the Lake District. Since he took over the club 26 months ago, forming an off-the-shelf company called Knighton Holdings to do so, he estimates some £2m has been spent. A plush restaurant has been opened at the back of a stand, executive boxes have been installed, the building of one new stand is under way, there are plans for two sports centres. The stadium, for two sports centres. The stadium, it is planned, will eventually seat 28,000 although Carlisle's record attendance in 66 years of league football is 27,500.

The whole will become somewhat immodestly called Carlisle Amphitheatre, which will house, among other things, the Euro International Soccer Academy. It will cost at least £10m. There will also be the trifling matter of building the team to ensure that they spend the maximum of three years he has permitted in each of the divisions on the way up.

The chairman frankly admits that he cannot do all this alone. Outside investors are welcome and he promises, in an almost matter of fact fashion, that if they leave the running of the establishment to him they will have a 15 per cent annual return.

Michael Knighton, 43, arrived at Carlisle after he finally severed connections with Manchester United. He was a director there for two years after his attempted takeover bid of the club was aborted amid boardroom recriminations, High Court injunctions and suggestions that he did not have the necessary funds in place to secure the deal.

He received a drubbing in the press (and claims to bear some of the scars still) and remains insistent that he was blameless for the way the affair transpired. He became a victim of circumstances, he claims, and says that his contribution to the restoration of United's fortunes, in every sense, was significant; maybe not as big as Alex Ferguson's, but fairly vital. As a non-executive director, he helped with ideas and off-the-field acumen.

The enduring image of his time at Old Trafford, however, is of his on-the-field flair, captured on his first August afternoon there when the new chairman ran on to the pitch in football strip and did ball juggling tricks. The picture of him heading the ball, head and shoulders perfectly balanced, is still recycled, as recently as last Thursday, in Carlisle's evening paper, *The News & Star* (not to mention on this page today).

'I don't regret that, not one bit,' he said, looking at the photograph again, though he might just regret the weight he has put on since, for a ball-juggling Knighton now would not cut quite so dapper a figure. 'It appeared on every back page. It made everybody happy – for 64 hours or so I was a hero.'

After 26 months, it is fair to say, he is still a hero in Carlisle and its environs. When he completed this takeover, the team were 92nd in the league and avoided relegation to the Vauxhall Conference only because Aldershot folded. Now they are second in the Third Division, playing attractive football, breaking away from the pack – together with Bury – and, perhaps most unlikely of all, have seen gates rise from 1,800 to yesterday's 6,155. More than 2,000 even attended a relatively meaningless Auto Windscreens Shield match last Thursday night.

The club secretary, Jim Thoburn, said the chairman was the most recognised man in Cumbria. The club's director of coaching, Mick Wadsworth, joshed about his inability to keep a diary and had some fun at Knighton's expense regarding his footballing knowledge (as coaches do about chairmen), but concluded: 'He's a bloody good bloke.'

Wadsworth is fundamental to Knighton's plans. It is the chairman's intention that his director of coaching – so called because he coaches while Knighton manages the club and negotiates all contracts – will take the team up the divisions, and into

Europe. He will mould and change the side when necessary, and Knighton believes he is the man for the job.

'I selected him very carefully,' said Knighton. 'It was a long process but he met all my criteria. I didn't want someone who had played at the very top level, I wanted somebody who had wide respect as a coach, who could pass on knowledge and was capable of communicating with young players. He met all of them.'

Wadsworth's league playing career amounted to 28 appearances for Scunthorpe but he coached Barnsley to two FA Youth Cup semi-finals, went on to coach England's youth and under-21 sides, and taught at a Barnsley school. It was, it seems, Wadsworth or nobody.

There was a brief period when results were not going well, the crowd were on his back, the sort of time when professional football people start dusting off the cv. Knighton merely told Wadsworth to look up a Kipling poem called 'The Thousandth Man'.

It says: 'One man in a thousand, Solomon says, Will stick more close than a brother,' and produces the pay-off 'but the Thousandth Man will stand by your side To the gallows – and after!' It is the vote of confidence you would, as it were, die for.

Knighton is so brimming with enthusiasm for the cause – and appears to have imbued the Carlisle backroom staff with similar zest – that you want to believe he can go all the way. When greeted with a hint of scepticism, with the suggestion that he might be more cautious, he invoked not the words of Kipling but those of Oscar Hammerstein II in 'Happy Talk', from *South Pacific*, about having a dream and making it come true.

If the suspicion that he is talking too good a game will never entirely disappear – not until the European Cup resides in the Carlisle Amphitheatre trophy room – there is no doubting either Knighton's lovely, disarming, boyish passion for football or his awareness of its place in the scheme of things.

'I love this simple game of ours and want no more than that people might say he contributed a little bit to the greatest game in the world,' he said. 'But I don't lose sight of the fact that football's a bowl of trivia.' After Kipling and Hammerstein, that was an echo of Bogart in *Casablanca* concluding that the problems of three people did not amount to a hill of beans.

He barely believed it either, and bowl of trivia or not, it does not stop Michael Knighton licking his lips.

Independent on Sunday, 23 October 1994

Rangers – Seven in a Row
Henry Winter

Many new foreign talents have graced British fields this season. Jürgen Klinsmann has won friends and greatly influenced matters at Tottenham Hotspur. Philippe Albert contributed immensely to Newcastle United's early-season verve before cruel injury intervened. But, without doubt, the most significant import this season has been Brian Laudrup, whose delicate skills have illuminated the drab landscape of Scottish football.

The Dane's all-round excellence and ability to humiliate defenders allowed Rangers to celebrate a seventh successive Premier League title in style yesterday. Ibrox, a sea of blue banners and bluer chants, lauded Laudrup's every touch during a highly open, hugely entertaining 3–1 victory over Hibernian.

When he jogged over for corner-kicks, thousands bowed before him. It was an extraordinary sight. Laudrup's reputation is such that even Hibernian's supporters joined in. His elevation as Scotland's player of the year is surely a formality.

The King of the Wing, as the T-shirts term him, inspires total devotion. Even for the uncommitted, such semi-deification is simple to comprehend. A talent misused by Fiorentina and under-valued by AC Milan has been cleverly employed by Walter Smith, Rangers' astute manager.

'When I talked to the gaffer at the start of the season,' the multi-lingual Laudrup said yesterday, 'he told me I had a free role in the team. That's how I play in the national team, that's how I can show my skills. In Italy, I was made to play in the wrong positions, and I wasn't able to perform as well.'

Problem solved. Not only does Laudrup supply the unpredictable, a quality that has bemused full-backs all season, but, unlike many wingers, he scores regularly (13 to date) and works diligently for the cause, chasing back when moves break down. When a Tina Turner lookalike ran on at the end to mime the Rangers anthem *Simply The Best*, it could have been sung solely for Laudrup.

His success has attracted the attention of larger clubs, notably Barcelona, where his brother, Michael, once starred. But Nou Camp will not be dancing to the tune of another Laudrup just yet. 'While it is always a pleasure and an honour to get an offer from a club like that, what I told them is that I'm very happy in Scotland,' Laudrup said earlier in the day. 'I like being at Rangers. I want to be part of the new era here. I want to stay for the next two years of my contract. Then we'll see what happens.'

Laudrup's performances reflect not only his innate gift but also the poor state of Scottish football, a game sorely in need of an overhaul from grassroots to elite. The issue has become so urgent, the dearth of home-grown talent so embarrassing, that the *Daily Record* and BBC Scotland have combined to hold forums on this pressing matter.

Rangers embody the predicament. They steamroll through the Highlands and Lowlands but, on reaching Europe, suffer immediate anxieties, as they found against AEK Athens earlier this season. Rangers' greatest strength – their reservoir of fine foreign talents like Laudrup, Mark Hateley, Trevor Steven and Alexei Mikhailichenko, who all finished at a canter yesterday – represents their major weakness when the Champions League comes around, due to UEFA's foreigner restrictions.

Smith plans a substantial summer spending spree. New signings are more likely to arrive by air than road. 'We have to go for more foreign players than is ideal because there are few Scottish players around who would raise standards high enough to compete regularly in the Champions League,' Smith asserted on Friday amid rumours that Holland's Dennis Bergkamp and Jesper Blomqvist, Manchester United's Swedish nemesis, were on their way.

Smith's frank appraisal is a sad reflection on the Scottish game. It also acknowledges the pending problems Rangers can expect in Europe. Again.

But do Rangers diehards care? Probably not excessively, because their oft-stated priority is rooted in parochialism. After seven championships on the spin, they are three short of eclipsing the Scottish record established by great rivals Celtic under Jock Stein from 1966–74. Smith, who has secured nine trophies since replacing Graeme Souness for years ago, stressed afterwards how important the Celtic mark was for Ibrox.

So Scotland's premier club are caught in a quandary: foreign internationals will bring them closer to Stein's record but, possibly, no closer to European Cup success. What Rangers require is to unearth a young Scottish playmaker in the mould of Gary McAllister and other tartan talents.

Youngsters are on the way up, but it was the older generation who orchestrated yesterday's tumult-inducing triumph. Celtic's surprise defeat at Aberdeen had removed Rangers' only rival to the tittle but they wanted to celebrate with a victory. Having taken the lead through Gordon Durie, who headed home after Hateley and Laudrup linked beautifully, Rangers failed to turn dominance into further goals until late on.

Laudrup weaved his way time after time down the right flank, making Graeme Mitchell's life a misery, but his constant service foundered on Jim Leighton's excellence in Hibernian's goal.

Hibernian, chasing a UEFA Cup slot, drew level with a magnificent goal against the run of play, Michael O'Neill driving the ball from 30 yards past Billy Thomson after 39 minutes.

Hibernian threatened occasionally on the break after that but it was predominantly Rangers to the fore. Ibrox, which on cacophonous occasions like this sounds like four ghetto-blasters at full volume directed inwards, began to become nervous until a furious final five minutes.

Ian Durrant played a marvellous one-two with Charlie Miller before slipping the ball wide of Leighton. Then came the best move of a hugely open, entertaining afternoon. Thomson lobbed the ball out to Laudrup, who drew its sting with a deft flick of his right boot. He then embarked on an extraordinary odyssey, leaving Hibernian players in his wake, before poking the ball out to Mikhailichenko, who darted in to drive Rangers' third past the unfortunate Leighton.

Simply the best. But Laudrup knows Europe, where Rangers should really be testing their mettle, represents a more searching test of their credentials.

Daily Telegraph, 17 April 1995

Why Scotland Means the World to Me
Gordon Brown

On the night of 18 June 1982, along with thousands of other Scots football supporters, I was in Seville. Scotland was playing Brazil. I stood on the terrace behind the Brazilian goal and watched as David Narey drove the ball into the top right corner of the net. It was joy, pure joy, for the Scottish team, for the thousands of us there on the terraces and tens of thousands more at home.

In the searing heat of a Spanish summer, Scotland – synonymous with its football team, of course – was doing well against the world's best. For just one moment Scotland was on top of the world. Out there in the heat, could the team that trained in the rain, under the grey skies of home, now go on and do the impossible?

Whatever the feelings of that moment, it couldn't and it didn't. Brazil went on to score four and I still remember the anger I felt for weeks about a comment made on TV by Jimmy Hill back in London. In his view our brush with greatness was merely a 'toepoke' – as if Narey's shot were an accident.

Both before and since I've followed our national team. I've travelled far for Scotland – the team has helped to open up the world for me. In 1990, I was one of the Tartan Army that went to Italy, for an all too brief visit to the World Cup. In Genoa, as the Italians prepared for a Scottish invasion, I saw Scotland beat Sweden 2–1 – two great Scottish goals followed by the almost inevitable soft goal thrown away by our defence – and the Italian police were prepared for trouble. There was none. The nearest thing to it came from the Swedish supporters, who drank a lot and then generally fell asleep.

Denied my chance to go to America in 1994, I am already planning my visit to France for the next World Cup finals in 1998. I have followed Scotland's World Cup ambitions ever since I was a schoolboy. I was one of thousands of teenagers who stayed off school when Scotland had to beat Italy to qualify for the 1966 finals in England – and failed to do so. As schoolboys, we were serious about Scotland. According to local legend, the headmaster in the adjoining school belted the boys in the morning for playing truant in the afternoon. He punished them in advance because he knew he could rely on them – to support Scotland.

You start young, and you can't give up supporting Scotland. You can't walk out simply because they are playing badly. You'll be there, irrespective of standards, performance, bad luck and the usual – mainly defensive and goalkeeping – errors that come from nowhere to snatch defeat from the jaws of victory for Scotland yet again. Once disappointed before, twice we turn up, and as optimists. Scotland's like that.

My passion for football started a long time before I ever got to see the national team play. I grew up in Fife, part of which I now represent at Westminster. My earlier football memories are of Stark's Park, the Kirkcaldy home of Raith Rovers. Indeed, my introduction to market forces was a season spent attempting to sell programmes outside the ground.

It was my father – a Church of Scotland minister but a keen follower of our national game – who first took me along to football matches, and together we travelled around Fife, seeing the local teams play. All my schooldays I turned to the sports pages long before I turned to news or politics. Those 1960s game were my first exposure to Cowdenbeath's unique style. The team is much loved and its home record in the 1993–94 season – a long run of bad luck when it failed to win at Central Park until it beat Arbroath 1–0 on 2 April – made it famous throughout Britain.

Such reputations are by definition temporary; in the Scottish League life goes on. A new season puts the old one firmly in the past: who knows what glories now await the 'Blue Brazils' of Cowdenbeath? Their ground is better than ever – cruel local humour about an all-seater stadium and a three-piece suite notwithstanding. As the local MP, I was delighted to receive an invitation to the official opening of the ground improvements, so can now conclusively deny this calumny.

It's sometimes said – enviously, and usually in England – that Scotland is so small that we all know each other: so it's hardly surprising that I've had the chance over the years to meet some of the managers of the national squad. I remember meeting Jock Stein during the seventies, by which time his reputation was secure, thanks to the efforts of Celtic's Lisbon Lions. I met Tommy Docherty years after his brief tenure in charge of the squad; I only wish that his results with the team had been as impressive as his subsequent charity fund-raising.

And I met Alex Ferguson, before his departure for Old Trafford, when he was still the toast of Scotland for his achievements with Aberdeen during the eighties. He struck me immediately as a man who had never lost touch with his roots in Govan, the working class area of Glasgow where my father was a minister in the thirties and forties. He gave the impression that no matter how high he climbed, his feet would remain firmly on the ground.

Andy Roxburgh was altogether different in his approach. I always suspected that, as a former primary school headmaster, he brought useful skills to the management of our more volatile international players. But perhaps his greatest achievement was to lower the expectations of the Scottish football-following public to a realistic level more in keeping with our small population and our real status in the footballing world.

Yet the fanaticism that has characterised Scotland's following – of which I can claim to have been a part for many years – of the national football team still demands some explanation. You need only to recollect the scenes of delirium among the Scottish fans when the team beat England 3–2 at Wembley in 1967 – when they tore up bits of turf to take home as a living memento – to realise that clearly there was a lot more at stake than the results of 22 men kicking a ball around.

They took a lot more turf after the 2–1 win in 1977. There's a pub in central Scotland that displays a lump of Wembley turf to commemorate victory over England. I wouldn't be at all surprised to hear that some of the hundreds who took a lump had, in the heat of the moment, eaten a bit. Some, I know, even jumped onto the crossbar and broke that up too. One – anonymous since he has failed to confess it in this book – is now a colleague, an MP and a respectable citizen. If you don't count Saturday afternoons.

It's often argued in Scotland that the problem with the team's following in the 1970s was that they were expecting the national squad to carry the burden of national pride, for a country that was denied its own parliament. And certainly, if English nationalism flowered on the playing fields of Eton, then Scottish nationalism has had one recurrent expression – on the pitch at Hampden. Which perhaps explains, in the context of the United Kingdom, why many Scots' pride in the team's performances has been enhanced periodically by the sheer joy of defeating the English at the game they regard as their own.

That's why 1967 was surely one of the greatest hours of the boys in blue. I was 16 then, but I still remember watching the humbling of England – on the very pitch on which they had been crowned only a year previously as the champions of the world – by the skills and audacity of 'Slim Jim' Baxter, one of my heroes. It was both a Home International and a European Championship qualifier. In Scotland, though, that day is still thought of as the real World Cup decider. I feel similarly about the 2–1 win at Hampden, in 1976, when Dalglish slid the winner through the legs of a disbelieving Clemence.

But such rare triumphs must be judged in an historical context in which disappointments and defeats at the hands of the English are legion. And I don't mean Flodden, Culloden and all that. There's that 9–3 defeat at Wembley in 1961. I will never forget listening on the radio, listening ever more incredulously as goal after goal went past Frank Haffey, the unfortunate goalie who said he'd have to emigrate. Nor would I dwell on our team's performance at Wembley in 1975: suffice it to say that England just slipped past us with a sneaky 5–1 win.

But as someone who was actually there at a lot of the games, I think that it's also fair to say that there were some other non-political reasons to account for the fans' fanaticism. In 1974, we managed not only to be the only team from Britain to qualify for the World Cup finals in West Germany, but we also managed to go out of the tournament without losing a single game. Players like Bremner, Jordan, Holton and Harvey were worthy of some fanaticism.

In 1978 – a national disaster for Scotland that many would compare with the Darien Scheme – part of the fanatical support generated by the team's qualification for the finals in Argentina must surely be explained by that extraordinary personality of the team's manager – the irrepressible Ally McLeod. Who else would have had the brass-neck to organise a Victory Party for thousands of the supporters at Hampden – before the team had even set foot on Argentine soil? In fact, come to think of it, perhaps he knew more about Scotland's relative strength than the rest of us. And even once the team had suffered the indignity and agony of the games against Peru and Iran – and Johnston's early, forced departure – we still had our moment of glory, when Archie Gemmill scored the goal of the tournament. For a few brief, flickering moments the impossible – Scotland beating Holland by the three clear goals needed to go through – seemed to be happening. But alas, once more it was not to be.

The 1980s have proved to be a harsh journey of self-discovery for the Scotland follower. What we've discovered is that we're really not World beaters and should therefore relish the chance to play among the world's best every four years. Yet, if our weakness at international level has sometimes been brutally exposed, Scottish football still has some great strengths. Wee boys still have kickabouts in the street, dreaming of glory. Old men in pubs will tell you what they have seen and what might have been. Middle-aged men like myself watch and hope.

Who knows? . . . Some day . . . And, if worst comes to worst, we still beat England sometimes.

Football and the Commons People, 1995

FC Barcelona and the Scottish Question
Simon Kuper

FC Barcelona's motto is 'More than a club', and next to *Barça*, Manchester United look like Rochdale. United do not have a weekly satirical BBC TV programme devoted to them, and nor do they run an art competition so prestigious that Salvador Dali once submitted an entry, nor boast the Pope as season-ticket holder no. 108,000. Even the *Barça* museum is the best attended in the city: more visitors than the Picasso Museum.

I arrived in Barcelona in October 1992, which was a good time for the city. The loudspeakers in the metro played genuine music, and every day shop signs in Spanish went down and were replaced by Catalan signs. The city had just staged an Olympic Games free of terrorists, drugs and boycotts, and was growing richer by the day, while that May, against Sampdoria at Wembley, *Barça* had won their first ever European Cup. A week after leaving Barcelona I returned to post-Black Wednesday in Britain, and noticed a different mood.

Fittingly, *Barça's* Nou Camp stadium is in the centre of town. One weekday morning I looked down from the fourth tier of the empty stadium, and felt that a side that dared face *Barça* here must regret it the moment they peered out of the tunnel. The stadium is a city in itself: it seats 120,000 people, or the entire population of Norwich, and is currently being enlarged. 'There comes a point when the people in the top tier need telescopes, and then you have to stop building,' lament the club.

In the catacombs of the Nou Camp that morning, 25 journalists were waiting by the changing-rooms for the squad to emerge after practice. These men and women have a hard life. Every day, they must wring quotes from *Barça* players who are trying to say nothing, and then improve the spoils. When half an hour had passed a senior quote-collector shrieked, '*Cruf!*', indicating that Johan Cruyff, the manager, had appeared, and that if caught quickly would surely reveal great secrets. A couple of hopefuls charged forward, and returned to derisive laughter. Eventually Michael Laudrup appeared, tastefully dressed for a man of his income. Denmark were playing Ireland that night, but Laudrup was still refusing to play for his country, so the journalists asked him about Möller-Nielsen. Naturally he answered in platitudes, which were eagerly noted. Then a club official announced that Cruyff would not be seeing the press that day. So who was going to fill the papers?

FC Barcelona are the biggest club in any country, in any sport, in the world. Why is this? There is a reason for everything.

I was granted an interview with Nicolau Casaus, First Vice President of *Barça*. I was told he had no English, but while waiting outside his room I heard him repeat several times, in an American accent, the word 'Siddown!' He seemed to be practising. When I came in he spoke Spanish, and had a big cigar in his mouth. I remarked on the club's motto, and asked whether it referred to FC Barcelona's status as a political item in Spain. Casaus denied *Barça* any political significance. He said that people of different parties and religions supported the club. Why, then, that motto? 'Barcelonism is a great passion,' he answered vaguely.

Club directors – at Rangers, at Celtic, at Barcelona – always prefer to say that their club is just a club. Nor do players tend to worry about their employers' political status. But what players and directors think is beside the point, because a club is what it means to its fans. *Barça* have fans everywhere – they have a fan club in Tianjin, China – but they belong to Barcelona, and to Catalonia, the region of which Barcelona is the capital.

The Catalans feel Catalan first and Spanish second, and to prove it they have long fought wars and made revolts against Madrid. Until recently they always lost. This century, for instance, in the civil war of the 1930s, Catalonia held out longest against General Franco, but then suffered under his yoke until he died in 1975. Now Catalonia has its own regional government, the *Generalitat*. But the five million Catalans want more: a state of their own, perhaps. 'Catalonia is the most powerful nation without a state in Europe,' Jordi Torrebadella, a young Barcelona economist and *Barça* fan, told me. 'You can't compare us to Scotland, because we're far more powerful within our state than Scotland is in the UK. We subsidise the rest of Spain, whereas Scotland is subsidised by England.' Or as Cruyff learned when he came to play for *Barça* in 1973: 'We earn it, and in Madrid they eat it up.'

I asked Professor Lluís Flaquer, a Catalan sociologist, if he could recommend me any books on *Barça*, but he could only come up with one, and it was 20 years old. I asked why academics had neglected the club. 'There are some subjects,' said Flaquer, 'which are considered too sacred to write about, and there are also subjects that are thought too profane'. I took it he was going to call football profane, but he concluded: '*Barça* are still too sacred.'

Barça are a hundred times more famous than Catalonia itself, and are the main source of Catalan pride. When Franco ruled Spain, they were the only source. Why, I asked a Catalan woman bored by football, do you care about *Barça* beating Real Madrid? She replied: 'Franco destroyed our autonomy and forbade our language, and he supported Real Madrid.' It was said that *El Caudillo* could recite Real line-ups going back decades, and when Real visited Barcelona during his reign there were always banned Catalan flags in the Nou Camp. *Barça*'s fans went home from these matches as exhausted as the players. 'You couldn't shout "Franco, you murderer!" on the streets,' explained Flaquer, 'so people shouted at Real Madrid players instead. It's a psychological phenomenon: if you can't shout at your father, you shout at someone else.' Only at the Nou Camp did Catalonia still exist, and the only Catalan symbol Franco never dared touch was *Barça*.

It is natural that when a region is silenced it turns to football. Yet Franco is long dead and *Barça* remain the symbol of Catalonia. 'When I go to the Nou Camp, I feel as though I am suddenly back in the days of Franco,' one woman told me. In 1992, when Barcelona introduced a new strip design that included a thin white stripe on the famous red and blue, there was an uproar: white was the colour of Real. 'I brought in the stripe,' Josep Lluís Núñez, the club President, argued paradoxically, 'because I don't want to be known as the president who introduced shirt advertising here.' (To preserve the sanctity of their colours, Barcelona refuse to wear advertising.) Even today, Catalans confuse Real with rule from Madrid, and find it confusing that a few cabinet ministers now support *Barça*. They take bias from Madrid for granted, and the Nou Camp often subjects referees to a hail of cushions. Cruyff and Núñez like to speak of political refereeing. After all, José Plaza, ancient boss of Spanish referees, is a self-confessed Real fan.

The passion persists, which becomes even harder to explain when you know that a great many citizens of Barcelona – fans of the club – are not even Catalans. So many, that some say there is no such thing as a Catalan working class: the lower classes in Barcelona are migrants from the rest of Spain. The typical migrant arrived in the 1960s, when the Catalan boom began. He jumped off the train, took a room where he could, found a job, and then made a choice: either to support *Barça*, or Español.

Now *Barça* are one of the best teams in the world, and from 1991 to 1993 they won the Spanish championship three times in a row. The man who has tamed Núñez is the Dutchman Johan Cruyff. Cruyff played for Barcelona in the 1970s, and returned to manage the club in 1988. By now Barcelona is his adopted home, and he can often be seen whizzing through the city on his motorbike. His wife, Danny, likes Barcelona because although the stress is as bad as in Amsterdam, the weather is better. Their son, Jordi, named for the patron saint of Catalonia, is in the *Barça* squad, and Chantal, their eldest daughter, has married one of the club's goalkeepers and is already a force in one of the *Barça* factions. The Cruyffs are as good as Catalan, except that Cruyff himself has failed to master the local language. Even his Spanish is suspect, and the weekly satirical TV programme on *Barça* portrays him constantly repeating his favourite phase, '*en el questo momento*'. It means, 'at this particular moment'.

On his first day at *Barça*, Cruyff told Núñez (in Spanish): 'The changing-room is for me and the players alone.' The president resisted in vain. For perhaps the first time, a *Barça* manager had defeated the board. 'Cruyff,' I was told by Pilar Calvo, of the daily *Sport*, which devotes most of its pages to the club, and which is owned by Joan Gaspart, another *Barça* Vice-President, 'has won because of his playing career. Venables was a nobody when he came to Barcelona. Menotti had a name, but he also had a personality more open to manipulation than Cruyff's.' Cruyff never compromises. He says, 'I am better off than the club, financially and in my private life', and he knows he can resign if he wants. Herrera, the last *Barça* manager to succeed, was another strong man who kept the directors out. (It upsets him that Cruyff alone has won the European Cup.)

Naturally, Cruyff's European Cup immediately became a political tool. All parties can still use *Barça* for their own ends, and they do whenever *Barça* win a trophy. When this happens, the players display it to the crowd at the Plaça Sant Jaume, a square with two political buildings: the *Generalitat*, and the Town Hall. At the celebrations, Jordi Pujol, President of the *Generalitat*, a sharp-featured character in a suit, always shouts from his balcony: '*Visca Barça, visca el Cataluña!*' Which, the nuances no doubt lost in translation, means, '*Barça* wins, Catalonia wins!' The crowd always cheers. But the city's Mayor in 1992, Pasqual Madragall, *socio* no. 107,024, was a Socialist, and thus opposed to separatism. So when the European Cup arrived, and Pujol had had his shout, Madragall told the crowd: '*Barça* is no longer "more than a club", and it has become the best club in Europe.'

And he was right. Cruyff has changed *Barça*. No longer are the fans happy as long as their team beats Real. Now they demand proper success. And by changing the club, the Dutchman has changed Catalonia. When *Barça* were ailing, this hurt Catalonia in the way that the Royal Divorces hurt Britain. The symbol of the nation was tarnished. Now that the club are doing well, the political impact is immediate. The city is suddenly confident. In 1992, after the Wembley victory and the Olympics, Madragall officially proposed that Spain become a federal state with two capitals, Madrid and Barcelona. 'So winning the European Cup helps Madragall make this proposal?' I asked Torrebadella, and he replied, 'Absolutely.'

It is rare for Barcelona to make a concrete proposal to Madrid. For a decade now, the Catalans have argued among themselves over whether they should seek independence from Spain. Pujol himself is unsure. He may call himself a Nationalist, but he has never called for secession, though he hints at it a lot. The debate goes on endlessly, but what is at issue became most clear during the Olympics of 1992. (How did Barcelona get the Olympics?

Juan Samaranch, head of the International Olympic Committee, is *socio* no. 7,965.)

From the first, Pujol tried to make it clear that the Games were being held in Catalonia and not in Spain. The Catalan crowds at the opening ceremony gave an extra cheer to teams from newly independent nations like Lithuania or Croatia, and politicians in Madrid panicked. The Spanish Olympic football team dreaded Barcelona. The full Spanish team never play there – for Catalans, *Barça* is the national side – and the fixtures for the Olympic team were arranged so that they could play in Valencia as long as they kept winning. But came the final, against Poland, and the Olympic eleven had to move to the Nou Camp. A Catalan demonstration was feared, or an empty stadium. Instead, *Sport*'s daily rival, *El Mundo Deportivo*, could describe the crowd as '95,000 spectators . . . with Spanish flags'. Spain won 2–1, and later that night fans were heard chanting, '*Pujol nos engaña/ Cataluña es España* – 'Pujol is deceiving us/Catalonia is Spain'. It appeared that Catalans do not despise Spaniards after all, or at least not if they win gold.

(On the other hand, Catalan TV made time during the Games to show in full *Barça*'s pre-season friendlies against northern Dutch provincial sides.)

When it comes to it, few Scots want to leave the Union, and few Catalans do either. They have done well enough as part of Spain. 'Most people here would say, "We don't need a state, but on the other hand we're more than just a region",' Torrebadella told me. 'It's more a matter of symbols.' The Catalans do not want a state of their own, but they do want something vaguer than that, symbols to prove that they are a separate people. During the Games, many foreign observers read the Catalan flags that draped Barcelona as a demand for independence, but in fact the flags themselves satisfied people: all Catalans want is the symbols of a nation. When Pujol stands on the balcony and shouts, '*Visca Barça, visca el Cataluña*', he is doing nothing more than restating Catalan symbols. People like to hear him say it. It makes them feel good.

And that is why *Barça* are the biggest club in the world, why they have 110,000 *socios*. They are the symbol that this nation needs in lieu of a state. 'And,' one Catalan told me, 'some people watch *Barça* because they like football.'

Football Against the Enemy, 1994

Every team dreams of an FA Cup final appearance, even non-League sides, although their more realistic hopes are a third round tie against the likes of Manchester United. Hitchin were no exception. Having reached the second round of the Cup, they faced Wycombe Wanderers at home. But their dreams of a lucrative third round tie were short-lived. Hitchin lost 5–0. Their misery was then compounded when Wycombe drew West Ham in the third round.

HITCHIN – WHERE CUP DREAMS BEGIN

Trevor Haylett

When Andy Melvin says he has dreamed the ultimate FA Cup dream for his non-League side, a visit to Manchester United in the third round, not everyone is prepared to dismiss it as the fantasy all managers are disposed to at this time of year. Among the folk who follow Hitchin Town are those who have come to believe that what he says may well come true.

Melvin is not your typical football manager, nor is he a typical 33-year-old. He not only runs the Hitchin side, he also owns the club, one of the oldest in the country and one which owes its health and prosperity today to his money and his enterprise. Then, during the week, he doubles as an employer to some of the members of the Diadora Premier League side who on Saturday go out to confront Wycombe Wanderers in the Cup's second round.

The FA Cup and Hitchin are old friends, going way back to 1871 when the Canaries and 14 others paid £25 to be the first entrants of the competition. Since then the Cup has become famous the world over as a touchstone for sporting romanticism and giant-killing heroics while Hitchin's reputation has struggled to spread further than their own corner of Hertfordshire.

They are the club the Cup forgot, but who prefer to regard themselves as slow starters in the competition they helped to launch 123 years ago. That first tournament saw them reach the second round (a hollow boast because in those days teams involved in a draw both progressed to the next stage), an achievement they were unable to match for another 102 years.

In only one subsequent season have they travelled as far. When they defeated Hereford in last week's thrilling first-round replay at their Top Field ground it was the first time the club, which has existed for 129 years, had seen off League opposition.

A gentle reminder at the start of the season from his chairman Terry Barratt – it has to be gentle when the manager is also the owner – persuaded Melvin to try and improve what has been a pretty depressing record.

The rewards have been immediate. Not only do Wycombe, high-flying in the Second Division, pay a visit on Saturday but the *Match of the Day* cameras will be there as well. Ian Scott, a key midfield performer, will not be there, however. This afternoon his own match of the day will be played out to the sound of wedding bells in Norfolk and Melvin was forced to concede defeat last night, having concocted an elaborate plan involving sponsors, a helicopter ride and the assistance of a vicar and a bride-to-be to get the player to the ground on time.

It will be a success for Hitchin just to run their visitors close and they are well prepared for a tense finish. At Tiptree in the second qualifying round they were 3–1 down with a minute remaining yet managed to scramble a draw. At Cambridge City in the following round they trailed 3–2 with 20 seconds left and forced a replay. Last week they were 2–1 behind at half-time before hitting Hereford with three goals in a magnificent second-half revival.

'The Manchester United dream came before the first qualifying round at Newmarket. To be honest it was more like a nightmare at the end. I can't remember what the result was though it might be significant that I woke up not in celebration but in a cold sweat.'

The chance to cash in by switching home advantage has been considered and rejected. Not so long ago Hitchin would have been unable to say no. Cash crises are a fact of life in football but in 1991 the Canaries were in grave danger of going under. Debts totalled nearly £100,000 and as treasurer it was down to Roy Izzard to find a saviour for a club he had followed with passion since he was small. He hardly expected one to emerge on his own doorstep.

'Although Andy Melvin was running our reserve side I didn't really know anything about him or his background when I was tipped off that he had just sold a business and might be able to help. It probably sounds daft coming from a 39-year-old but I look on him as my hero. He has so much confidence you can't help but believe in what he says. Without his money, time and financial expertise Hitchin would probably not be here today and he has done it all without drawing a penny from the club.'

Although Melvin had secured a controlling interest he was happy to leave day-to-day control in the hands of others as he began to investigate ways to raise funds to accelerate Hitchin's ambition of League football. He had no part in the decision two years ago to dispense with the first-team manager even though it was to pitch him deeper into the club. 'It might sound strange that the owner was not consulted and that I had to be asked to take over the first team but that's the way I wanted it to run.

'At first I thought I would only be running the side on a temporary basis but it has gone well and I enjoy the thrill of winning.' He is unusual as a manager working at this level in that he did not reach a high standard as a player.

'We clinched the Diadora First Division title in my first season, the first championship we had won in 58 years, and even though our league results have not been too clever this season we are making progress.'

Independent, 3 December 1994

The Dutch side Ajax were undoubtedly the European side of the year. Not only were they the first ever side to go an entire season undefeated in the Dutch league but they also went on to win the European Cup, beating AC Milan 1–0.

Ajax of Amsterdam
Joe Lovejoy

Another week of what might have been for English football, another example of the technical superiority of the Dutch. While Manchester United were signing off with a flourish from the European Cup, Ajax were cruising into the quarter-finals with another impressive win.

An easy group? Hardly. They played, and beat, the holders, Milan, twice.

After the World Cup debacle, the Football Association finally recognised that the game in England needed updating if it was not to sink ever deeper into the second division. Hiring Terry Venables to treat the malaise at international level was a first step. Eradicating the symptoms is the next.

While the FA cast about in search of inspiration, or rather the 'technical director' they regard as a panacea, the perfect role model stares at them across the North Sea. Less than 30 years ago, Dutch football was part-time, their international team an easy touch. A generation on, they have left England, among others, far behind, both in achievement and in style of play.

How? A visit to Amsterdam, to see Ajax toy with AEK Athens, offered the chance to seek out, and learn some of the answers from, the architect of Total Football, Rinus Michels.

After an innovative and successful coaching career with Ajax, Barcelona, Holland and Cologne, Michels is universally regarded as one of the grand masters of the world game, the respect in which he is held at home reflected in his appointment in 1985 as technical director to the Dutch Football Federation, with special responsibility for the development of new talent.

Even in retirement, at 66, the doyen has no time to tend the tulips. He is in constant demand for lectures, and arrived for our lunch date straight from one of his regular meetings with the national coach, Dick Advocaat, who wanted to pick his brains about this week's European championship tie against Luxembourg.

The credentials are impeccable. What, then, does Michels make of English football? Mr Ajax was quick to identify our Achilles' heel. Salvation lay not with the England team. There, Venables would have to use his organisational skills to make the best of a bad lot. Renewed and sustained prosperity was dependent upon radical improvements at schoolboy level.

Basic technique had to be ingrained by the age of 12, Michels said. After that, it was too late to create anything better than journeymen. He had shown Holland the way, and was happy to go over old ground in the cause of English enlightenment. 'The major change in our country started when I became coach of Ajax in 1965,' he said. 'When I joined them, Ajax were a semi-professional team, and at no level was Dutch football playing a role of any importance internationally.

'When I started, Ajax had only three training sessions a week, all in the evenings because the players were working during the day. Becoming fully professional and changing to daily sessions, under a good coach, made all the difference, because players with great potential, like Cruyff, Keizer and Suurbier, were already there, and they improved very quickly.

'Ajax started to be known internationally in the late 1960s. It took longer for the national team. When I became national coach in 1974, I was able to harmonise the two factions from Ajax and Feyenoord and, because we had very good players, the team performed very well. We had an attractive style, to do with pressing and dominating the midfield – a new development. To do that you need very good players, and you need to be mature tactically.'

In Michels's experience, tactical maturity was almost unknown in England. The English game's frenetic pace also militated against progressive football. 'There is nobody in the world who has the skills, or can develop the skills, for a whole team to play well at your speed.'

Persuading the public that a more studious approach was needed could be more problematical than educating the players. No English crowd is likely to sit back and take the long-term view while their team struggle to master a keep-ball style.

Michels nodded. 'That is your biggest problem. The clubs don't think they need another style because the crowds don't want it. To change things, you will have to start right at the bottom, and work on improving the development of your kids between six and 12.'

Nobody does it better than Ajax. Eight of the players used last Wednesday – including the scorer of both goals, Tariq Oulida – were products of a youth scheme which has boys playing under the club's tutelage from the age of seven. No problems here with UEFA's limitation on foreigners.

The Amsterdam production line is Michels's pride and joy. 'I started all that,' he said. 'We are a small country, and our youth structure has to be as near perfect as possible, so that good players aren't allowed to escape our notice. We have to perfect our scouting and coaching system, from the bottom to the top. It is still in development, nationally, but Ajax have perfected it.

'Once or twice a year, they have an open selection day for young boys from seven to 10. The kids come along – up to 2,000 of them – and obviously the club select the best on technical merit. They pick maybe 15 from each year, and those 15 will play against boys of the same age who are already playing for Ajax. The ones who are better, they keep.

'Every age group has its own coach, and at the top there is a youth director, independent of the senior regime. The club recognise the need for continuity in youth development. If the first-team coach is sacked, because results are not so good, the youth director stays.'

The man in question, Cornelius Adriaanse, is a teaching graduate, as well as an experienced coach, the dual qualification essential with the club sharing the academic schooling of the chosen few.

Michels explained: 'At seven, when it all starts, they have to go to normal school, and it is hard to get the boys more than twice a week. They come to the clubs on Wednesday afternoons, when there is no school, one evening, and then on Saturdays they play. Not for their school, for the club. There is practically no organised schools football in Holland.'

In England, the professionals say young boys with a natural aptitude for the game are ruined at primary-school age by the misguided direction of teachers with no football background. Tots of seven and eight are routinely encouraged to ape their adult heroes, and exhaust themselves playing kick-and-rush football on full-size pitches, with parents and teachers alike urging them to 'Get stuck in'.

Michels and his disciples fought long and hard to get Dutch boys away from the amateurs and under the wing of the professional clubs.

'The priority is to develop their abilities, not for them to win games. Of course everybody wants to win, but for kids it should never be the end that justifies the means. We lose against England at youth level because we are more interested in talent than winning. We are looking to develop skills, combined with the intelligence of the game. The basic craft of the game, and the feeling for it, was one of the secrets of street football. The kids develop the feeling for the game playing four against four, two against two, or whatever. They didn't need a coach or a grown-up to teach them. It was trial-and-error practice. They learned by instinct.

'That's what we missed for years in Holland, and in other countries they are still missing it. Between seven and 12 is the best time to develop skills and know-how, and to do that you have to play all kinds of games – smaller games, simplified games. Our equivalent of the Brazilians' beach football. People wonder how the Nigerians became so skilful, but in Nigeria they are still playing street football, or on wasteland, as we did a long time ago. Here we have to find another way, and the Dutch are doing that.'

Organised football, with boys beginning to settle into positions, starts at 11, Michels said. 'Before that, they play seven against seven on small pitches. From age 11 it becomes 11 against 11 in regional leagues. At that stage, they are still training with the club only twice a week but at B junior (14 to 16) level, it changes. Then they have the facilities to study at the club. There are teachers, as well as coaches, on hand. That way, the boys can be with the club four or five times a week.

'The important thing, if you have only two sessions a week with the younger ones, is to develop a common syllabus, like they have in the schools. A way of teaching that is generalised, and that everybody understands. In 1985, when I was technical director to the national federation, I started a development programme for Holland. It has taken nearly 10 years to get our message across to the whole country, even to the smallest clubs, but the framework is there now. The results, as always, are dependent on the quality of the coaching. If the coach is no good, then even the right programme will not produce the desired effect. For that reason, we put together courses specifically for youth coaches. To train them properly.'

The example was there, but it would not be an easy one for England to follow. 'First, you have the problem of the schools. Your schoolboy football is in the hands of teachers, and while there might be exceptions, in general the teachers have not attained the right level of the game.

'That's not going to be easy to resolve. Somehow, your FA must develop a process of youth football education and sell it to the schools, who have to be persuaded that this is the right path. If you want to improve your game in England, and compete successfully internationally, you need better players, with skill combined with cleverness. This is the way to find them.'

Simple enough, really. But if we can't convince Mr Chips, we've had ours.

Sunday Times, 11 December 1994

The Hardest Football Team in Britain
Tim Glynne-Jones

'So wee Ricky's gone up for a header and he's got caught on the side of the head. It's cracked the bone and gone right in at the temple, you know. He's out cold and one of the lads has got hold of him and he's slapping him round the face, saying, "Come on, Ricky, wake up. I've got a Mars Bar riding on this game".'

Senior Officer Willie McGurk, PTI at Barlinnie Prison, Glasgow, recounts this tale with a fond smirk. Wee Ricky was a hell of a player. A hell of a player.

'Anyway, this was when we only had kit for 11 men, so the subs had to stand there in their prison shirts.' McGurk laughs at the memory. 'Wee Ricky's laid out behind the goal and I've made a call to the infirmary to say we've got a serious injury and could they come out and pick him up. We've carried on with the game and when the lads from the infirmary arrive they find Ricky lying unconscious behind the goal. And he's stark bollock naked. The sub's had all his kit off him.'

Wee Ricky was a character. Got out on a Saturday, stabbed someone on the Friday. He brought a whole new meaning to man-to-man marking. But hey, you should have seen the bloke who nicked his shorts.

HM Prison Barlinnie stands in a bleak corner of Glasgow's East End, up by the motorway. On the walk up from Dennistoun, I'm expecting to find it more like *Scum* (Alan Clarke's terrifying vision of borstal life), than *Porridge* (the tale of Norman Stanley Fletcher's humorous stretch in Slade). More vicious fights with pool balls in socks than boxing matches in which both fighters go down with the first accurately landed punch.

The snow has receded into greying strands in the shadows of dark walls and scrubby bushes, leaving the pavements smeared with grit the colour of dog shit. This same grit (at least you hope it's the grit) forms the playing surface of Barlinnie's football pitch. And after a couple of sliding tackles, it forms the basis of each player's complexion.

I've come to visit the hardest football team in Britain. I've come tooled up with my preconceptions. And I've come without my boots.

Willie McGurk greets me at the main entrance and we walk past the halls to his gym. He is 42 and is in his 20th year at Barlinnie. He seems to know all the prisoners personally.

'Alright, big yin. What are ye dayin' back in here?'

He's taught them PE and confronted them through a riot shield. He is remarkably relaxed. He talks like Alex Ferguson but smiles more readily. '*Porridge*?' he grins. 'Aye, quite realistic actually.'

We walk past the famous Special Unit that held hard nuts Jimmy Boyle and Hugh Collins and countless other extreme dangers to society. The unit closed down in February.

McGurk has arranged for me to meet 20 of his footballers who are doing an SFA coaching course, D certificate, which qualifies them to coach kids up to 14 years of age. The group are in another gym converted from one of the work sheds. Next door is the textile shop, where inmates can earn on average £5.10 a week making prison shirts and baby seats. Nothing too complex, I'm told. 'There aren't many drug dealers who are good with a sewing machine.' Wrong kind of needlework.

In other sheds there's woodwork, metalwork, decorating. In each section McGurk is chastised for plundering the workforce for his coaching course. We pass the concrete works and enter the recreation rooms. There's snooker and pool and attractive pot plants. No menace. The prisoners are taking lunch. The balls are racked up neatly in the middle of the tables and the cues laid to the side. No sign of any socks. I look for traces of blood and brain on the baize but there are none. Strange.

In each of the five Victorian halls the cell doors are closed. A Senior Officer, more Barraclough than MacKay, says they're falling apart, possibly as a result of being thrown on the warders from the third storey during the riots of '87, when the prison service lost control of Barlinnie. Behind the battered doors the prisoners eat pre-packed lunches, after which the cutlery is counted carefully. The cells are stark, with no sanitation. It's slop out or clam up.

Barlinnie is the biggest prison in Scotland. Ever since 1882 it's been handling thieves, dealers, slashers, rapists and murderers. The towering walls have contained the very worst that humankind can offer. Category A prisoners who would stab as many warders as it takes to get a place in the relative comfort of the Special Unit. The grit on the football pitch has borne the training shoe prints of some seriously frightening characters.

Unlike other prisoners, Barlinnie can't turn anyone away. It's designed to hold 900 but the current population is 1,200. Which means they're sleeping two to a cell. And that's bad news if you're sharing with Bubbles.

Bubbles is one of the fittest looking prisoners in Barlinnie. He's also one of the most excitable. He looks a bit like De Niro in *Taxi Driver* (pre-haircut), with the smile of a man who brushes his teeth with Ralgex. Without sounding rude, he looks bloody terrifying. He obviously works out – when we enter the gym he's the only one not wearing a shirt. He's well-built and powerful and he drives every ounce of strength into the exercises. In pairs, they're having to control the ball with their chest and then head it to their partner. Bubbles, who is working near the gym wall, throws his head at the ball time after time, sending it flying towards his partner's face. I'm just waiting for the moment when his head goes clean through the wall.

But why 'Bubbles'? I'm just about to ask when he emits a piercing chimpanzee screech. He does this a lot, as well as a number of other jungle noises: parrots, gibbons, that sort of thing. And this is why you wouldn't want to share a cell with him. For some reason, I don't get to talk to Bubbles.

But I do talk to Grant, Paul and James, who all play for the first team. They represent the three different moods within the camp. Grant is keen to talk, a real enthusiast. Paul is more laid back; you can talk if you want, he's not bothered. James is more surly. When Willie McGurk asks him if he'll talk he just looks at me and shakes his head. But he comes back after a minute with an expression that says, 'come on, get on with it.' I ask him how he'd feel if he lost his place in the first team.

'I wouldn'ae be happy,' he understates. 'I might start fightin' wi somebody. It's that bad, so it is. Football's taken seriously in here.' His dark eyebrows furrow. A known thief, he was caught carrying a knife. He got 16 months. He gets out in two weeks. Then he'll revert from right-back to midfield.

Paul is 30. He doesn't look like a drug dealer but it's hard to tell under that moustache. He plays sweeper and he says he's clean, plays by the rules. Then he says, 'Now and again you get an outbreak of fucking violence.'

Grant could have been a contender. He played at Hampden Park three times as a junior, has two Junior Cup medals. He signed professional with Airdrie. Frank McAvennie and Mo Johnston are mates of his. But he got caught with an 'insignificant amount' of cannabis. That was his first stretch – seven years. He did it all in the gym. Then he got caught in possession of £100 worth of amphetamines. He's 38 but he's as fit as anybody in the prison and he looks like he's made of iron ore. Sport is everything to him. He's so keen to tell you that the words come too fast, his lips have to work overtime to spit them all out in machine-gun bursts that stop short of the end of the sentence. He plays upfront, scores goals 'all the time' and is known for his fiery temper.

During a bout of head tennis he is accused of cheating by almost everyone who comes up against him. Eyes glower, muscles flex. Fearing an outbreak of 'fucking violence', I try to disguise myself as a corner flag. But it blows over and the game goes on.

'In prison you've got to get rid of your frustrations,' says Grant. 'You can have a wee tussle but it never ends up in fisticuffs.'

According to Willie McGurk, Grant's intensity is fairly typical of the modern prisoner.

'Hyper, I would call it. If a prisoner wants something he will go and get it. I think that's part of the character that's caused the problem. They're very forward and a lot of times they don't have any respect for anybody. This is where PE in prison really scores, because it's probably the first time somebody has sat down and given them something that they like.'

This combination of single-mindedness and physical strength makes for a formidable football side. There's no need for a sports psychologist here. In the last four years they've played about 40 games and lost just two of them. This year, for the first time, McGurk is trying to enter the team in a local league. The trouble lies not so much in finding a league that is prepared to take them on as in finding one that meets his own requirements. With 90 per cent of Barlinnie's inmates coming from the Glasgow area (the first two taxi drivers I met had both been inside), the local leagues are littered with ex-cons – people on the outside who may want to get things smuggled inside.

Having found a suitable league, he then has to persuade that league's committee to take a team that can't play away games. It's tricky but if it doesn't come off it won't be the end of the world. The team already gets the opportunity to play against sides from the outside and that, says McGurk, is what matters most. Mixing with the community does them good.

Back in the gym they've just finished a passing exercise and are preparing to go out onto the grit for a match. The course has gone down well but there aren't many who reckon they'll be using their D certificate when they get out. Grant likes playing too much to coach others. James can't see himself getting into the right circles. But Tommy has discovered an aptitude for coaching since he's been inside and is planning to do a vocational course when he gets out.

Maybe they've been putting on a good show, but so far McGurk has been right. The atmosphere is definitely more *Porridge* than *Scum*. Every so often I've been trying to trip them up with one simple but effective question: Who's the Daddy? I'm not entirely sure what it means but I'm told it's guaranteed results. You have to ask it out of the corner of your mouth and pretend to be looking at something on the far wall as you say it.

'Who's the Daddy?'

'You wha'?'

'Who's the Daddy?'

Blank look. I try this on a few of them without success. So I try to coach it more subtly.

'How old are you?'

'27.'

'What are you in for?'

'Drugs.'

'What team do you support?'

'Celtic.'

'Who's the Daddy?'

'You wha'?'

'Who's the Daddy?'

Blank look.

'Who's the bleedin' Daddy?'

'Och!' The face unfurrows somewhat. 'You mean Jamie?' He points to a grey-haired, middle-aged man, heavily tattooed and struggling to control the ball with his weaker left foot. The face calls out and beckons him over. Jamie lumbers over, head bowed slightly. He speaks with a voice as gentle as Savlon. He could be someone's dad but he's not the Daddy at all. He's a qualified referee. The kind whose decisions are never questioned.

'I caught my wife with somebody and I lost my temper. I slapped both of them. I went a wee bit too far, but normally I'm not an aggressive person at all.'

And he's not. Out on the grit he tackles cleanly. They all do. The hardest team in Britain is also, it turns out, one of the cleanest. In most football teams an off-the-ball incident may earn you a few more months behind bars. They are, if you like, model professionals. They don't even make a break for the wall. The only ones who do that are the staff team, who like to wind up the security officers.

Grant, Jamie, Tommy and the lads pose for the big team photo, some of them appearing genuinely torn between looking at the camera and nicking it. Bubbles runs through his jungle repertoire and swings on the shoulders of his mates as they pose for more photos, thick as thieves. But before you can get too carried away with the heart-warming beauty of human nature, they're sent indoors to change and get locked up again. Total Sport's photographer gathers up his cameras and Willie McGurk offers a word to the wise that has Norman Stanley Fletcher written all over it.

'Keep an eye on your gear,' he warns the smudger, ''cos there's a strong criminal element in here, you know.'

FHM, May 1995

Chapter Six

Games of the Season

Jürgen Klinsmann's debut for Tottenham at Sheffield Wednesday back in August brought a remarkable 4–3 victory for his new club. It also brought him a winning goal and a sore head.

Klinsmann's Debut
David Lacey

When Jürgen Klinsmann, dazed after a collision of heads with Des Walker, fully regained his senses at Hillsborough he might have wondered momentarily where he was.

On being told that, shortly after scoring what turned out to be the winning goal for Tottenham, he had been borne away on a stretcher to a standing ovation from not merely an English but a Yorkshire crowd, he might have construed, like Blackadder, that this was just part of 'another bloody dream'.

Furthermore, had he been informed in 1990, after helping West Germany win the World Cup, that he would eventually play alongside a Romanian in a British team managed by an Argentinian he would doubtless have complimented the hypothesiser's imagination.

As much, at the time, would have gone for Gary Lineker, Terry Venables and Paul Gascoigne, who could hardly have suspected then that they were destined respectively for Japan, England and limbo. For

Tottenham, Saturday's events at Hillsborough confirmed for good an all the end of the era of Links, Venners and Gazza, and its aftermath.

Spurs still have to live with the epilogue, a six-point penalty in the Premiership and a season's banishment from the FA Cup for financial misdemeanours, but if the team continue as they have started they will quickly play their way back into the hearts and minds of the English game. Community service is usually a good way of shaking off a sleazy past.

In fact the club came closer to being relegated than their supporters knew. And Klinsmann's admiration for English football might not have extended to the prospect of winter evenings at Barnsley.

At ease with cameras, microphones and notebooks, careful to say plenty without saying too much, Klinsmann is another Lineker. 'The chaps accepted me immediately,' he explained, through a fat lip, after Saturday's game. 'They saw a guy come in who's very simple, like them.' Well quite, we all knew what he meant.

It took him 82 minutes to demonstrate that at 30 he is still capable of achieving what was second nature to him at 25. As one of Anderton's deceptive, drifting crosses floated into the Sheffield Wednesday goalmouth he took one pace forward, two steps back and so completely fooled Walker that he appeared to score with a free header. It was nothing of the kind: Klinsmann put a lot of thought into his first English goal.

Much thinking, too, had gone into Tottenham's first German joke which involved Klinsmann and Sheringham each taking a studied dive as part of the celebrations. Fortunately the referee had a sense of humour, otherwise the pair might have been booked for timewasting.

Klinsmann's goal completed a spectacular renaissance for the Tottenham attack without answering many of the lingering doubts about their defence. Ossie Ardiles played the German and Sheringham up front, with Barmby taking over the role in the hole previously occupied by Gascoigne and Samways. Dumitrescu played in his usual Romania position on the left, not fully fit but darkly hinting at skills to come.

Calderwood's presence in front of the back four was Tottenham's only serious acknowledgement of the need for midfields to defend occasionally. 'If we are going to play with five attackers then everyone has to work extremely hard,' Ardiles said. 'Dumitrescu and Nicky Barmby are not famous for their defending.'

Nor were Spurs' defenders last season, and when Sheffield

Wednesday began to match Tottenham's passing in the second half they needed only 20 minutes to wipe out the two-goal lead established by Sheringham, after Anderton's cross had evaded Petrescu, the opposition's obligatory Romanian, and Anderton, after he had accepted Sheringham's beautifully weighted return pass. Klinsmann, with a quick throw-in and a simple pass, had instigated both moves.

Muddled Tottenham defending, and a miscued shot by Sheridan, led to Petrescu bringing Wednesday back into the match, and before Bart-Williams could complete a neat exchange of passes with Bright, back charged Calderwood to thump the equaliser past his own goalkeeper. Then Sheringham back-headed Walker's long clearance on to Barmby, who had already established himself as an untouchable in the minds of Wednesday's defenders and now strode through unchallenged to restore Spurs' lead.

Klinsmann remained on the field long enough to see Hirst answer Tottenham's fourth goal with a stunning half-volley. His departure reduced Spurs, who had already used their substitutes, to 10 men and in the end their win was only preserved by Walker diving out to grab the ball from the feet of Bart-Williams.

Before long some canny counter-attacking side will punish the gaps left by White Hart Lane's latest surge of adventure. In fact Ardiles hinted that, despite being satisfied with his young central defenders, he was still in the market for a defender.

Ardiles has his Stuka. He is still several planks short of a stockade.

Guardian, 22 August 1994

Manchester United's 9–0 win over Ipswich at Old Trafford set a new record in the Premiership and also brought five goals for £7 million new boy Andy Cole.

Five-Goal Cole
William Johnson

In many ways it was relieving to see a Mark Hughes drive crash against the crossbar, a sparkling Paul Ince effort cleared off the line and several other goal-bound shots and headers blocked by Craig

Forrest, a hard-working Ipswich goalkeeper.

Had any of those missed opportunities found a way into the Ipswich net, Manchester United would have emerged from a remarkable Old Trafford afternoon with a perfect 10. And it is impossible to find fault with perfection.

A magnificent haul of nine was still good enough in the eyes of United's delighted manager Alex Ferguson to warrant the use of such superlatives. This was the club's biggest victory for over a century.

Tactically, in the context of a private duel for supremacy with Blackburn Rovers' Kenny Dalglish, Ferguson was correct in sending threatening messages to the rival camp, but the nagging feeling as this richly entertaining spectacle unfolded was that Ipswich were devaluing United's brilliance by refusing to offer even token resistance.

Relegated already in the eyes of many experts, Ipswich appeared to pin their hopes on frustrating United and on snatching a solitary goal like the one which brought them a shock victory at Liverpool in the first month of George Burley's short managerial reign.

That plan was scuppered inside 20 minutes as Andy Cole plundered the first of his five goals to supplement a well-taken opener by Roy Keane. Two behind against a team who had surrendered only three home league goals all season convinced Ipswich's experienced line-up that there was no way back, and what followed was probably the most lamentable display ever seen in the Premiership.

As United surged to what looked likely to be double figures, the Ipswich supporters began chanting 'we want one' with gallows humour that summed up their team's plight.

All credit, though, to Cole for sensing the opportunity to get even with those who have questioned his worthiness to wear the £7 million label of Britain's most expensive footballer.

The striker was whacked on the ankle by David Linighan in scoring his second goal eight minutes before the interval after another spectacular Hughes volley had rocked the bar, but he vigorously contested Ferguson's suggestion that he should not come out for the second half with the points already secure.

'I sensed a hat-trick was there for the taking and I was determined to get one,' he said, not believing that he would go on to amass his biggest haul in what has been an explosive career.

Most of a captivated crowd of 43,804 – by one click of the turnstiles the biggest gate in the country this season – were unsure that the hat-trick had been completed eight minutes into the second half. The scoreboard operator decided that Denis Irwin's cross had been bundled across the line by the man who left Newcastle in dramatic circumstances in January, but the consensus at the time was that Frank Yallop had inadvertently diverted the ball over his own line.

Cole was insistent that it was his goal, and television pictures indicated that he will keep it when any commission meets to adjudicate.

There was no doubt about his next strike, United's seventh, which wiped out a deficit on Blackburn in terms of goal difference and may ultimately decide the destiny of the title. Cole showed typical penalty box alertness to score on the rebound after Brian McClair's initial shot had been well saved by Forrest.

By then the indefatigable Hughes had scored two goals, which were scant reward for his contribution to the slaughter – a precise angled drive and an opportunist header after Ryan Giggs's intention of adding a solo spectacular had been thwarted.

The eighth goal would have created an outcry in any well-balanced contest, but there was no more than a collective shrug of the shoulders from Ipswich after Paul Ince's chip from a quick free-kick was allowed to stand as Forrest was being cautioned by the referee for handball outside the penalty area.

Fittingly Cole rounded off the rout with the type of goal which helped him to forge his formidable reputation. Facing the wrong way when Gary Pallister's downward header arrived at his feet on the six-yard line, he swivelled like a ballet dancer to deliver the coup de grâce.

Daily Telegraph, 6 March 1995

It was a sensational turnaround. In the fifth round of the FA Cup, Southampton led Tottenham 2–0 at the Dell. Then Spurs brought on Ronny Rosenthal and by the end of the evening they had won 6–2.

Ronny Inspires The Spurs
Clive White

Ronny Rosenthal, who developed the role of the substitute into a fine art during his time at Anfield, can surely never have made a more dramatic impact upon a game than he did in last night's FA Cup fifth-round replay for Tottenham.

Coming on just before half-time, with his side trailing by two goals, he hit two in two minutes in the second half, and then the decisive third from 25 yards in extra time, to take Tottenham into a quarter-final tie away against his former club, Liverpool. The fourth and fifth goals by Teddy Sheringham and Nick Barmby did Southampton an injustice. A sixth by Darren Anderton added insult to injury.

The competition rules nowadays, whereby drawn replays are brought to a swift conclusion by means of penalties, might have been designed with Southampton in mind. The Saints have finished all square in nine of their last 12 matches, and while it has been to the detriment of their League standing, it has helped advance them in this competition.

Alan Ball's team began as if they meant to leave nothing to chance, least of all the vagaries of a penalty shoot-out, going ahead after only five minutes. In an effort to diffuse the threat of Matt Le Tissier, outstanding – as is his wont – in the first game, Gerry Francis deployed a five-man defence in which Stuart Nethercott, in the absence of the injured Gica Popescu, was detailed to man-mark the elusive Channel Islander.

However, the tactic only succeeded in confusing Tottenham. And when Jim Magilton spread the ball wide to Jason Dodd, his cute pass inside found Neil Shipperley with so much freedom that Ossie Ardiles might have been back in charge of team talks. Shipperley had no more to do than sidefoot in his second goal since his £1.25m signing from Chelsea.

Apart from the misunderstanding the change caused in a Spurs defence also devoid of Sol Campbell, it drained their resources in midfield, where Magilton established himself as a prime mover. Worst of all, perhaps, it did not seem to dampen the performance of Le Tissier, who was soon heading down another chance at the far post for Shipperley, but the youngster, turning on his heel, drove just wide from three yards.

It seemed only a matter of time before Southampton added a second goal, and that time seemed to have arrived after 33 minutes when Ian Walker, under pressure from Ken Monkou, could only push a cross from Le Tissier out to the feet of Dodd. But with his opponents tottering before him, the full-back lashed his shot against the base of a post.

No matter. Six minutes later Dean Austin, in vain pursuit of Neil Heaney, tripped the Southampton player and, as at White Hart Lane, it earned a penalty for Le Tissier, who converted in not dissimilar fashion.

Just before half-time, and not a moment too soon, Nethercott was withdrawn – although anyone in defence would have done – in favour of Rosenthal. It proved to be a decision by Francis as patently right as his earlier one was wrong.

Other than an early miss by Jürgen Klinsmann, an anonymous figure, there was no inkling of the storm to come. Then, in the 56th minute, Sheringham back-heeled the ball to Barmby and before one knew it – and certainly before Grobbelaar did – Rosenthal had steered the cross over the goalkeeper's flailing arm. The equaliser was a real bolt from the blue, Rosenthal cutting inside to hammer a 20-yard left-footer past a bemused Grobbelaar. And then how things changed.

Independent, 2 March 1995

With the score level after 119 minutes Arsenal and Real Zaragoza looked to be heading for a penalty shoot-out until Zaragoza's Nayim spotted David Seaman off his line. And with a long hopeful whack upfield, Nayim won the European Cup-Winners' Cup for the Spaniards.

Nayim's Thunderbolt
Patrick Barclay

On the way home from Paris, where Arsenal's grit had been confounded by a stroke of genius, Terry Venables was asked where Nayim's goal stood among all the thousands he had seen. He paused, savoured a question that had obviously been on his mind, and replied: 'In the top . . . one.'

Yes indeed. I was beginning to wonder if my eyes, misty in gratitude at having been in the Parc des Princes to witness one of the great moments in football, had deceived me. It was reassuring to hear that England's coach, unlike those of his compatriots whose accounts referred to a 'freak' or, even more ludicrously, the perceived misjudgement of David Seaman, retained the capacity to appreciate virtuosity of the very highest order.

If you cannot do that, there is not point in following football. Yet so many quarters damned Nayim's goal with praise fainter than Pelé received a quarter of a century ago for *missing* one of comparable character and proportion. Tabloids gave us grotesque soap opera – Seaman, the hero of Genoa, was turned almost to villain – and even a broadsheet or two mildly reproved a goalkeeper who deserved nothing but congratulations for yet another faultless display.

I mean faultless. What on earth was Seaman supposed to do when Nayim took possession in a wide position at least 50 yards from goal: stay on his line, offering space into which a devil of a cross might be delivered? He could not discern, as Nayim did, that Juan Esnaider was flirting with the offside flag.

The rest was sheer inspiration, and execution so masterly that as soon as the ball was struck one could sense its destiny. As Venables said: 'Seaman wasn't that far out. If it had just been a lob, he would probably have got back, but Nayim really whacked it, put a whip on it. That's what beat Seaman.'

Venables, who brought Nayim to Tottenham from Barcelona in 1988, recalled that he would attempt such shots in training and, occasionally, matches. 'He and Gazza were always trying to outdo each other at that sort of thing.' A volleyed goal against Liverpool was perhaps the most memorable. Until now. While the Real Zaragoza players celebrated on the pitch in Paris, Nayim had looked up to where the television commentators sat and given Venables the thumbs-up. His old boss, grinning, had shrugged. How Arsenal must have wished Venables had not, in one of his last acts before being ousted from White Hart Lane by Alan Sugar, sold Nayim back to Spain, where he is guaranteed a place in footballing lore.

Esnaider, turning and so beautifully lashing Zaragoza in front, surely fancied his goal-of-the-season chances but didn't even get goal of the match. The richly gifted young Argentine will not have minded that it fell to Nayim to bring justice to the Cup-Winners' Cup final only seconds away from the nerve-racking hazards of a penalty shoot-out against Seaman, the bane of Sampdoria. Zaragoza deserved to win. Though Arsenal's teamwork was exemplary, as ever in Europe, and their tactics well prepared by Stewart Houston, they were given a lesson in technique for which, this time, there was a price.

It seemed for 119 minutes that the holders' luck would never run out. Just as in the home matches with Brondby and Sampdoria, they were favoured by a penalty decision against their opponents late in normal time; Miguel Pardeza, the Zaragoza captain and creative mainspring, fell in vain. But there was no shame in Arsenal's losing. Football won.

The task Arsenal now face is one for the boardroom, where the era of George Graham must be laid finally to rest and a new manager, or more likely chief coach on the Continental model, appointed. Houston's trial period, which ends with the match at Chelsea today and a tour of China, has been inconclusive. Even if Arsenal had won in Paris, they would have lost too often in the Premiership for Houston to be cast as a messiah. Yet a losing team was what he took over. Results have actually improved.

You can see that he is endeavouring to produce more of a passing game, and he talks sense about rebuilding the team with midfield the priority. The board's readiness to spend big and, more important, widen pay differentials will make it easier to recruit quality. The very shortness of Houston's spell as caretaker, however, lends weight to the theory that someone else will be in charge next season.

To the names of Bruce Rioch, Ray Harford and Ray Wilkins has been added that of Bobby Robson, who comes with the virtue of such seniority that Houston might serve under him. Despite Robson's happiness in Portugal, where his Porto secured the championship last weekend, he fancies the idea of one last crack at the English title, as he told *The Observer* last week, and Highbury would be an irresistible challenge.

Observer, 14 May 1995

It was the climax of the season as leaders Blackburn travelled to Anfield and Manchester United went to West Ham for the title deciders. The scenario was complicated, but the only certainty was that United had to win if they were to have any chance of being champions again. Even though Blackburn lost 2–1, United could manage only a 1–1 draw and the title went to Blackburn.

Liverpool 2, Blackburn Rovers 1
Henry Winter

At the cacophanous conclusion of this truly tense piece of sporting theatre, both sets of supporters joined in a delirious, hugely cheeky rendition of *Always Look On The Bright Side Of Life*, the song seemingly under copyright to the dethroned champions, Manchester United.

All corners of Anfield were united. This was a day for 'You'll Never Walk Alone' and 'You'll never beat Jack Walker', everyone present revelling in the perfect result for Anfield: a deserved triumph for Liverpool and a deserved title for Blackburn Rovers, who secured their first championship in 81 years by a point from United. It was a good gamble to have the real trophy here while the replica went to Upton Park.

What a finale to the season. How refreshing after a year of negatives that England's premier trophy should go to a friendly, family-orientated club unblemished by scandal or spoiled by their Lottery winners' wealth. What a finale to the match. Blackburn's emotional rollercoaster ride of recent weeks was encapsulated by last-minute see-sawing.

When Jamie Redknapp curled in a wonderful winner for Liverpool suddenly, cruelly, Rovers looked in danger of losing the race they had largely dominated since late November. Then, seconds later, came news of the final whistle at West Ham, where United had failed to achieve the victory they required. Cue euphoria.

All Anfield danced with joy. It could have been Kenny Dalglish's testimonial yesterday. Rovers' Scottish manager, his face unlined by the passing years, remains revered at this famous old ground.

The Kop certainly welcomed King Kenny back in style, successfully willing him to join Herbert Chapman and Brian Clough as the only managers to win championships with two clubs.

It could have been Ewood. Blue-and-white scarves proclaiming allegiance to Dalglish's present employers were held aloft by the host hordes; Rovers' 3,000 fans, touched by the reception, repaid the compliment by waving a large Liverpool flag.

Bonhomie pervaded. All combined in chanting 'Dalglish', their voices savouring the second syllable, as if scared of parting. When Dalglish's team were announced, each name was cheered to the top of the Kop's high-tech rafters. A Martian, let alone a Mancunian, would have needed counselling.

The surreal soon passed. Liverpool remain too proud a club, too ambitious for the future to stand on ceremony and simply usher Blackburn towards the podium they themselves have graced so often. The large banner stating '18 times' (Liverpool's title tally) pointed out to the visitors that reputations are made over decades, not overnight.

Only time will tell whether a Dalglish dynasty will develop at Ewood but the portents promise much. Walker, happily signing autographs if not cheques for Scally Wags, loves his hometown club so deeply that it is hard to imagine the fairytale turning grim.

After a lifetime spent in steel, an emotional Walker sought only silverware yesterday. As tenderly as a father nursing his first-born, Walker carried the trophy into the main stand, pausing only momentarily under that distinguished sign: 'This is Anfield'.

Maybe, one day, they will utter 'This is Ewood' with equal reverence. Such a day remains for the future. Plenty needs to be done, particularly if a club riding on Walker's millions are to cultivate their own players or prosper in Europe against more sophisticated opposition than Trelleborgs.

Encouragingly, yesterday's line-up would meet UEFA's awkward foreign regulation. New signings will doubtless arrive before the new season. A new dawn in English football has truly arisen.

Along with Dalglish and Walker, the man who has shed most sunlight on Ewood fittingly scored Rovers' goal. Alan Shearer's 21st-minute strike was Blackburn at their bulldozing best. In classic, counter-attacking style, Henning Berg swept the ball to Shearer, who deftly transferred play out to Stuart Ripley. Back came the cross for Shearer, perfectly positioned, to drive the ball low to David James's right, so equalling Andy Cole's Premiership record of 34 set last season.

Those who expected a depleted Liverpool to retreat to their deckchairs were soon surprised; instead Roy Evans's men came climbing out of the trenches. Languid in recent outings, here they played some delightful stuff, mainly via the darting feet of Redknapp and Steve McManaman, who profited immensely by swapping flanks to escape Graeme Le Saux.

As red-shirted youngsters piled the pressure on Rovers and their expectant, nerve-racked supporters, news filtered through that United had fallen behind. But, in seconds, tension consumed Blackburn's entourage again. These were dark moments but, heroically, the likes of Tim Flowers, Colin Hendry, Le Saux and David Batty, steadied a ship tossed on red waves.

Flowers tipped a Michael Thomas shot over; Hendry and Le Saux tackled hard, desperately repelling everything directed their way; while in front of them, Batty, nimble and disciplined, kept disrupting opposition moves. Rovers are a fine team, but within Dalglish's much-loved collective they are also a side of fine individuals.

Worryingly, the big red machine had built up an irrepressible steam. Tim Sherwood cleared off the line from Nigel Clough but, after 64 minutes, Evans's side finally equalised through John Barnes's driven finish.

Liverpool, justly furious at being denied a penalty when Batty took Robbie Fowler's legs, tore back into attack and achieved victory when Redknapp curled that splendid free-kick past Flowers. Of more import was a final whistle 200 miles to the south. Rovers, deservedly, were champions. A party that was 81 years in the planning began in earnest.

Judging by the intensity of the celebrations in Blackburn last night, there will be more than a few headaches this morning. Who cares?

Daily Telegraph, 15 May 1995

West Ham United 1, Manchester United 1
Paul Hayward

A lone French flag fluttered at Manchester United's end and it served as a symbol of surrender and loss. No Eric Cantona and no third championship. United are no longer the brightest of football's northern lights.

It was a cruel, haunting way to be felled. United received the unlikeliest of favours from their ancient foes up at Anfield but were unable to unravel West Ham in the bear pit of Upton Park.

Alex Ferguson's decision to leave Mark Hughes on the bench for the first half and play Andy Cole, who missed two late chances, alone in attack will provide one final debating point in a season of trouble and tumult.

The balance of power in the English game has shifted and the challenge to United is clear. Blackburn are now the pre-eminent force in league football and United will need all personnel to be present and correct next year if they are to regain their hegemony. Kung-fu, stamping and contractual disputes of the sort that kept Andrei Kanchelskis out of the side for so long will have to be left behind.

'Fate's like that,' said Ferguson after a 1–1 scoreline had sealed United's fall. 'It was a fantastic performance. You get your money's worth when you're watching us, all right. It's more disappointing because Liverpool won. But we couldn't have done any more.'

The white-knuckle climax of Super Sunday was everything the TV executives had promised. It began with United going a goal behind, escalated with an equaliser from Brian McClair and ended with a succession of spirited but fruitless incursions by a team skirting the edges of a miracle.

The single point that separates Ferguson's side from Rovers this morning equates to millions of pounds in revenue and enough prestige to keep the town of Blackburn bobbing along on euphoria for a whole summer.

At the denouement of the Blackburn-Manchester soap, United left Coronation Street to do battle with the Eastenders of West Ham in a match they must have been dreading.

Any team with a pair of hammers in their logo are unlikely to yield easily to their guests (expecting West Ham to surrender was about as promising as asking Michael Schumacher if you could borrow his car for the weekend). This was a smash and grab exercise, and it failed. Ferguson, who has restored United to the glories of old, will not need tactical tuition from the grandstand but he is certain to face justifiable scrutiny for leaving Hughes on the bench for the first 45 minutes.

When United's most formidable warhorse rumbled on after the break United possessed far more potency in attack and may even have seized the day had Cole not exhibited such fretfulness in front of goal.

Ferguson was right to gush pride. United have finished with just four fewer points than last season – when they set a record haul of 92 – and lost only two more matches than they did in that rampantly successful campaign.

But with Cantona and Kanchelskis missing for large chunks of the year, Giggs only intermittently effective and the youngsters requiring time to mature, United laboured to produce the technical brilliance and *joie de vivre* of the previous two seasons.

The first half here encapsulated United's dilemma. In the early stages of this febrile encounter they looked ordinary, one of the herd, just another team in the crash-bang-wallop realm of the Premiership. The might of Sharp electronics (United's sponsors) was giving way to the snort and shunt of Dagenham Motors (West Ham's backers) as United appeared drained of all hope or confidence.

That soon changed. With the arrival of Hughes new hunger spread through United's ranks. They pushed and prodded at West Ham's flanks and drove a red wedge into the heart of the home team's defence. In the traffic of goalmouth scrambles, one outstretched boot, one clever flick could have dragged Kenny Dalglish's new model army off their podium and completed a magnificently improbable treble of titles.

It has been a season of cracks in the normally solid edifice of Old

Trafford. There was Cantona's Bruce Lee impersonation at Selhurst Park and Kanchelskis's dance of anger towards the end of the campaign. There was the intemperate stamp from Roy Keane and mounting criticism about the rapaciousness of United's commercial division.

In the 4–0 defeat at Barcelona, we observed some of the deficiencies which afflict even the best of British teams and learnt how far United must climb to reconquer the peaks of European competition.

Standards and expectations are dizzyingly high at Old Trafford. With the team usurped at the vanishing point of a relentlessly eventful season, it is easy to forget that one more prime engagement awaits them. On Saturday at Wembley, United will be warm favourites to defeat Everton in the FA Cup and so add another gilded entry on the scroll of recent honours.

There is no reason to believe that Jack Walker will mount his charger and ride off into a Lancashire sunset. United must rise again, with Cantona, Kanchelskis and Keane obeying team orders. The game begins anew.

Daily Telegraph, 15 May 1995

Everton had been battling against relegation all season and nobody gave them much chance against Double hopefuls Manchester United. In the event, Everton won 1–0 and United ended up with nothing.

FA Cup Final
Ian Ridley

How fickle football's fortunes, how long an English season. Everton, who began the season with the worst start in their history, ended it by winning the FA Cup for the fifth time with a performance of resolve and persistence at Wembley yesterday. Manchester United, defenders of the Double, thus saw their towering twin achievements slip away under the twin towers.

They threw their all at Everton in a frenzied final flurry, including their giant goalkeeper, Peter Schmeichel, as they desperately sought to negate Paul Rideout's first-half goal, but it was another goalkeeper who was the most significant figure. This Neville Southall, astonishingly keeping out all United's best efforts, was the very Neville Southall who seemed to be waning along with his team when they were bottom of the Premiership just eight months ago.

Ryan Giggs, barely recovered from a hamstring injury and needing persuasion from his manager, Alex Ferguson, to be substitute, injected belated moments of incision, but this was more a game of broadsword than stiletto; mostly absorbing but rarely uplifting, however enduringly pulsating its atmosphere.

The gaze was inevitably attracted to the seats behind the substitutes where Eric Cantona sat wearing – in a rare occurrence – a club suit. Who can say that United, who had lost their League title in a similarly scrambled endgame seven days earlier, have not been properly punished? A place in the UEFA Cup, which their defeat denies Newcastle United, is cold comfort.

Everton's victory was a testimony to their turnaround under Joe Royle's management – all spirit and determination. Initially, when confronted by United's five-man midfield expected to support the spearhead of Mark Hughes, their dogs of war were muzzled, notably by Paul Ince and Roy Keane, themselves dogged. Everton's black and blue socks seemed appropriate. Without Duncan Ferguson, whose recent operation on a double hernia restricted him to a late appearance, they were denied an outlet for the pressure, tireless and selfless though Graham Stuart's running was.

Lee Sharpe's header over the bar from Nicky Butt's cross, Anders Limpar's low shot saved by Schmeichel at his near post, then Sharpe's volley – although hurried and stubbed straight at Southall – promised much, but the contest for physical control threatened to undermine the spectacle, and was not helped by the leniency of the referee, Gerald Ashby.

If not X-rated, this Cup final was at that point PG for the watching princes, William and Harry, although the presence of a Royle, a Fergie and a domestic spat should have made them feel at home.

Fortunately, the players' self-discipline and the arrival of a goal concentrated minds. When Ince lost the ball in midfield, Everton suddenly advanced with four attackers to United's two defenders. Limpar played the ball wide to Matthew Jackson on his right, who stepped inside Gary Pallister and crossed low for Stuart, whose shot rebounded from the bar for Rideout to head his 16th goal of the season.

Now Everton seized control, with Limpar's penetrative darts and passes hurting a United who were struggling along with their captain, Steve Bruce, who had tweaked a hamstring. Limpar again robbed Ince and sent in Stuart, but Schmeichel gathered his low shot. There was also the expected potency in the air from Andy Hinchcliffe's inswinging corner kicks, Gary Ablett heading one such just over the bar.

The interval helped United the more, giving them opportunity to regroup and reorganise faced with the loss of Bruce. Giggs immediately became a factor, his low cross from the left reaching Butt at the far post. It was but rehearsal for Southall, who smartly smothered at his feet.

Ferguson, replacing the hobbling Rideout, troubled United by rounding Pallister and forcing Gary Neville – now playing as central defender following Bruce's departure, with Keane having moved to right-back – to clear the cut-back for a corner, but it was an isolated retort from Everton.

Another low cross by Giggs that eluded the excellent David Unsworth as Brian McClair challenged and appealed for handball, was missed by Sharpe. Then Giggs, found with a neat chip by Ince, got past Jackson to the byline and crossed for McClair to loop a header on to the bar, the rebound being scrambled clear.

Paul Scholes now replaced Sharpe and to him fell the best chance of an equaliser; indeed, two chances. Giggs, cutting in from the left, threaded through a pass into his path as he emerged in space on the right. Southall clawed down his shot, then blocked his stab at the rebound.

Scholes sought to make amends by supplying a cross for Pallister, but there was a nonchalance to Southall's diving catch. This was his and Everton's day. Whenever his defence, so ably marshalled by the captain, Dave Watson, was breached, his positioning was intuitive, and it was no surprise when the ball stuck to his hand when he had seemed to get too far under a long ball forward. United – and some sympathy for them – were spent; Joe Royle's torment with Oldham at their hands in last year's semi-final was ended.

Everton were left to contemplate their reversal of fortune, and United theirs in their unlucky 13th final. Change is the only permanent thing in life as well as being football's lifeblood and continuing source of hope. The last can become the first.

Independent on Sunday, 21 May 1995

The First Division play-off between Bolton Wanderers and Reading looked to be heading for a Reading victory. Two goals up after just 11 minutes they then missed a penalty. But Bolton fought back, winning 4–3 in extra time.

Buccaneering Bolton
Henry Winter

So this is why a marvellous sport continues to intoxicate the senses. Two hours of the finest, most tense entertainment imaginable culminated in Bolton Wanderers being back among England's leading lights; a dramatic way for the domestic season to conclude.

What a tale to be passed down the generations. Of how Bolton, their defence initially dishevelled, fell behind to a delightfully intentioned Reading side in this absorbing First Division play-off final. Of how the buccaneers from Burnden Park passed their way back into contention before breaching poor Reading's defences twice again in extra time. Of how Bolton's players cavorted before their dancing followers. Of how their revered president, Nat Lofthouse, held the play-off trophy aloft, the epochs bridged.

But amid all the merriment doubts proliferated, most notably concerning the movements of Bruce Rioch and Alan Stubbs, the manager and captain so essential to Bolton's renaissance. Rioch's success in guiding his neat-passing team of many talents into the Premiership has rightly earned him a coterie of admirers.

His future resides among the elite, but possibly in charge of another club. Arsenal, ambitious and close to his Hertfordshire-based family, may tempt him yet. Stubbs, too, could decide his chances of England recognition improve in more glamorous surroundings. Bolton's board face an awkward summer.

What a calamity the departure of Rioch and Stubbs would prove for Burnden, a defeat snatched from the heartland of victory. For yesterday, Bolton resembled a club united, inspired by a famous past embodied by Lofthouse, and fired by the thought of future visits from Manchester United and Blackburn Rovers.

Here, too, was a club gracious in celebration, a feeling of generosity never more evident than when Jason McAteer broke away from the lap of honour to console Reading's heartbroken players, one by one, although Shaka Hislop, the Royals' heroic goalkeeper, was inconsolable.

McAteer claimed the central role in the afternoon's drama. Already booked as Bolton succumbed to fine early strikes from Lee Nogan and Adrian Williams, the tireless Irishman should have been dismissed for a 35th-minute tackle from behind on Michael Gilkes. Peter Foakes, acting contrary to FIFA edicts, deemed a penalty sufficient punishment.

The fates turned Lancashire's way. Keith Branagan saved Stuart Lovell's spot kick, a daunting 3–0 scoreline was averted, and Bolton set about retrieving the game. Rioch, so disappointed by Coca-Cola Cup defeat to Liverpool, clearly had strong words with his men at half-time, determined to avoid a Wembley repeat. Their spirit stirred, Bolton ran and passed their way upfield.

Alan Thompson, now deployed inside to escape Andy Bernal, found room to express his young talent. Prompted by Thompson's constant surges, space opened and Reading's impressive unity weakened. Gradually Hislop's goal came into range. After 75 minutes, the hugely promising Hislop was beaten from an exceptional passage of play. Stubbs swept forward as few English defenders can, the momentum he precipitated carried on by Mixu Paatelainen. And then on to John McGinlay, whose cross arrowed to the far post, where Owen Coyle rose above Jeff Hopkins to head home.

The force was with Bolton. Moments after directing a lob wide, Fabian De Freitas, the rangy Dutch substitute, equalised following a flowing move again begun by Stubbs and accelerated by Thompson. De Freitas's finish, dipping to deceive Hislop, dragged the game into extra time.

An extension to such epic entertainment was a privilege few expected when Reading, purposeful and full of passing, had taken the lead through Nogan's excellent run and shot, his fourth-minute opener soon followed by Williams's near-post flick-in of Simon Osborn's free-kick.

But Bolton are forged from a special mettle. Extra time saw them at their best, held steady by Stubbs and muscled forward by McAteer. After 105 minutes, the young Irishman, seemingly immune to exhaustion, powered down the left, past Dariusz Wdowczyk and Hopkins, before back-heeling the ball to Coyle. On this move went, gaining in pace and magnificence, as Coyle crossed long, McGinlay headed back and Paatelainen nodded over Hislop.

Bolton's joy ascended to the skies. Their end of Wembley, initially quiet and undermanned, was now a sea of banners and scarves. De Freitas delighted them further with a near-post strike, which proved crucial when Jimmy Quinn thumped in a 120th-minute effort for Reading.

Quinn and Mick Gooding, joint managers of a pleasing Reading side who finished above Bolton, deserve immense credit, not least for reminding a wide audience of the quality of football that can be created from small resources. But Bolton's resourcefulness seized the attention yesterday.

Daily Telegraph, 30 May 1995

Chapter Seven

The Business of Football

Introduction

Never has the gulf between the rich and poor clubs been so wide. Perhaps more than any other season, 1994/95 demonstrated that only half a dozen clubs can now compete at the top end of the transfer market, with moneybags Manchester United and Jack Walker's Blackburn leading the way. Even a millionaire chairman is no longer enough. Clubs today need a multi-millionaire man – or woman – at the helm. When it came to talking money, the name Manchester United was never too far from any discussions. With their astutely organised merchandising arm and full-up signs at Old Trafford, United have led the way in making money. Some of their practices, however, came in for criticism. Even Labour leader Tony Blair decided he had an opinion.

What a Waste of Money
Kevin Baldwin

As you make your way towards the ground, you will find your path blocked by more hawkers than you would encounter in a North African marketplace – though the ones here are less prepared to haggle. ('What d'yer mean, yer'll gimme a couple o' quid for it? Are yer takin' the . . .?')

The most obvious are the clothing sellers. Their wares are usually cheaper than those to be found in the club shop, principally because they have no overheads. Literally, when it rains, the stock either gets soaked or is covered in plastic sheeting so you can't see it.

However, there may be other reasons for the low prices. The clothing could be old and carry slogans or pictures which are now downright embarrassing. (You may recall the earlier warning about buying a scarf featuring the name of the current manager, since there is always the danger that he may soon leave or be fired. Some of the goods on sale outside grounds may bear the name of a manager or player who has already gone.) Alternatively, the stock could be faulty, which means that you may end up displaying your allegiance to Blackpoo or Dork City.

For these reasons, you should beware of items which are pre-wrapped; this could be intended to protect the seller rather than the merchandise. Watch out too for articles being taken from the bottom of a pile or the back of the stall – the old fruit seller's ploy. But the most extraordinary technique used to stop fans from seeing what they are buying would have to be that of the man seen outside Anfield brandishing a clutch of bare five-foot poles and calling out, 'Get yer flags 'ere!' Customers were expected to hand over their money before moving over to his mate, who stood a short distance away, and collecting the flag to tie on to the pole.

It is almost certain that the merchandise will not be officially licensed. (Note: when the sellers shout, 'Genuine scarves!', this simply means that, yes, these are scarves and not lawn-mowers or china figurines that they are selling.) There is a possibility that this is surplus stock acquired at a knock-down price, but you cannot escape the feeling that it is equally likely to be stock that was surplus to the storage capacity at the rear of a large transportation vehicle.

If you are an away supporter, it may not be possible to buy a scarf or hat from one of these unofficial traders. If there is a strong rivalry between the home club and yours, even the traders may not want to be seen displaying your colours – and they know that away fans would be loath to be seen buying them in any case. ('Look, there's one, let's get 'im!') As a rule, though, most scarf sellers will have one or two for away fans. Whether they have scarves for every club in the country seems doubtful; it seems more likely that there is a loose arrangement between traders at different venues to move stock around until it is sold. Certainly, there is one scarf in particular which I swear I have seen on sale outside eight or nine different grounds in the south-east.

Occasionally, a trader will offer a selection of foreign merchandise for sale. This is generally of limited appeal and bought only by fans who wish to suggest that they are well-travelled or well-informed about European football. However, there is sometimes a greater demand for such items. In the weeks following Manchester United's early exit from the European Cup in 1993, Galatasaray scarves suddenly became popular at grounds all over England, I wonder why.

You will probably find a number of unofficial T-shirts being sold – usually by a fat bloke. Either he is the brother of one of the dodgy burger sellers further up the road, gaining some experience on the street before he enrols for Del Smith's Catering College himself, or he has been recruited specifically for his size. The idea is that by wearing one of the T-shirts, he is able to give the prospective purchasers a practical demonstration of the tensile strength of the stitching. The trouble is that the slogan on the shirt is stretched and distorted so much that it is unreadable.

The shirts may not be the most hard-wearing on the market, but as their appeal is usually topical, this does not really matter. In some cases, it is made clear that the garment has a limited life, e.g. the Nottingham Forest T-shirts proclaiming, 'On loan to the First Division' or 'Limited edition – one season only'. Many shirts actually have the season's fixture list printed on the back, like the tour dates of a rock band. This is quite useful, except that if you are a Crystal Palace fan, the list will doubtless be headed by the words 'Eagles On Tour', which means that from a distance, you will look like a sad old rocker. (As for 'Wombles On Tour' . . .)

Some T-shirts may refer to specific events. For over a year after Tottenham defeated Arsenal 3–1 in the 1991 FA Cup semi-final, examples commemorating the win were on sale outside Spurs' ground. And it took only a couple of days for Manchester United's aforementioned elimination by Galatasaray to be marked by shirts with 'Europe – United-Free Zone' on the front and 'Turk Of The Town' on the back.

The event that prompts the printing does not have to be a football match. Soon after Terry Waite was released in Beirut, there were T-shirts bearing his picture and the caption: 'Have Manchester United won the League yet?'

Current ads and catchphrases are other favourites. 'United Colours of Sheffield' shirts have been spotted outside Bramall Lane, while 'Stavros Says Up The Arse' did a roaring trade outside Highbury a few years ago. Current favourites in the team may be celebrated, usually with a picture nicked from a newspaper or magazine.

But, of course, shirts that focus on long-standing rivalries between clubs are always going to be steady, long-term sellers for the traders. Fortunately, ones which display naked hatred and aggression (e.g. 'These colours don't run') are on the decline and have been largely replaced by humour. In some cases, it seems that unscrupulous entrepreneurs have taken a leaf out of the Government's book and are selling materials to both sides. I have seen almost identical shirts on sale near Anfield and Old Trafford, the only difference being that in one design, the Liver bird was, um, going to the bathroom on the Red Devil's head – while in the other, the Devil was sticking his trident up the Liver bird's backside.

This Supporting Life, 1994

How Our Soccer Idols Are Betraying Britain

Tony Blair

Last week something happened which not only caused grieving in the Blair household, but which was also symbolic of a wider sadness.

The cause of my misery was the devastating news, delivered to me just as I was preparing for a meeting with a diplomatic dignitary, that Andy Cole was leaving Newcastle United. Like my colleague Jack Cunningham and tens of thousands of others, I am a Newcastle fan. Though never tempted to have Cole's picture tattooed on my leg as one supporter did, I was a great admirer of his goal-scoring skills and his elegance.

So when the news came that he was, without warning, being transferred to another club for a record-breaking £7 million I was first shocked, then puzzled. Shocked that he was going. Puzzled that, good though he is, lottery-type money could be spent on a single player.

He is now earning in a week sums that fans at both Newcastle and

Manchester United can only dream of. In football terms, he may be worth it. But as a reflection of our society's priorities, Andy's transfer fee was as devastating as any hat-trick he scored.

I wish Andy Cole well in his career. I'm sure he will go on to more and greater things with the blessing of one of my children who is a Manchester United fan. Indeed, my children couldn't care two hoots if I go home and say I've met Jacques Delors or John Major. But when I told them I'd met United boss Alex Ferguson and he'd invited us to see United v Forest and meet the players, they finally realised there was a point to their dad's new job after all.

And now Alex does this to me . . .

Not that I'll be the only parent with cause to be unhappy with Manchester United of late. For in another example of the sport's growing obsession with money-making, this club, like many others, has just changed its strip . . . again. Less than a month after thousands of youngsters pulled on their favourite club jersey at Christmas, the men who run the club ordered the Red Devils to trot out in blue at Southampton. Loyalty doesn't seem to be enough any more; rather it is exploited to make us pay more. Which brings me to my fear that the values that make soccer the people's game are being eroded.

Tonight I have a rare treat when I speak to the Football Writers' Association at a dinner in honour of Sir Stanley Matthews's 80th birthday.

How much would Sir Stan have been worth in today's money? £10 million? £15 million? £20 million? When he went back to Stoke from Blackpool in 1961 for just £2,500, the average gate rose by 25,000. Could Andy Cole put 25,000 on a crowd? Could Shearer or Le Tissier or even Romario?

Sir Stan graced three Cup finals including probably the most memorable in history, in 1953. And he was never booked, let alone sent off. He never pushed past children waiting for autographs, for he knew they were the future of the game he loved. He served club and country well: a marvellous ambassador for Britain.

Football is a game that millions in Britain follow. It has a unique place in our culture and one that we must treasure.

And yet, I worry. I worry that the game in which one individual is deemed to be worth £7 million and whose club must raise the money with ever more lucrative and exclusive TV deals, merchandising and expensive seats, is a game which may lose touch with its roots.

I worry that fans are taken for granted. I worry that the TV deals are ignoring the smaller clubs that becomes ever more voracious in its quest for success. I worry too that the dividing line between marketing and exploitation may have been crossed amid the plethora of ever-changing strips.

I wonder how clubs can justify charging more for away fans than for home fans in identical seats. I wonder how clubs, all too commonly, can deny concessionary prices to travelling children while granting them to home fans.

Given the extraordinary publicity the game has attracted, it is hard not to worry, too, that some of the allegations of illegal backhanders may be true. I hope not, for those at the top of the game have the greatest responsibility to show it at its best.

When Sir Stanley speaks tonight, people will remember the values he embodies – fair play, the role of the individual within a team or community, honesty and romance.

I feel unease about what is happening in British sport. And I believe that much of what is wrong stems from over-emphasis on the individual – the get rich quick, something for nothing philosophy of recent times and the erosion of values like service to the community and wider responsibility that people in the public eye have for those we follow and idolise.

When do we ever hear players express shame at being sent off? Why do managers take for granted the swearing all too easily lip-read by children watching on television? I wince at players who cheat and foul, who abuse referees and who only think about winning and the money it will bring; at some people at the top of our national game who think nothing of loyalty to club and community.

Sport is not just about gold medals, glory, fame, wealth and winning European Cups. It is about kids playing in the park, dreaming they might one day pull on their Newcastle strip in a European Cup final. It is about learning through mind and body the values that help make a complete and rounded individual working within a strong community.

A nation that neglects sport at grass roots because it is obsessed with the commercial gains from sport at the top is a nation set for sporting and social decline.

I will not overstate the case. I merely say that when I heard Andy Cole had gone, I don't think the sadness was caused by news of his departure alone.

Mail on Sunday, 15 January 1995

Money-Bags United
Paul Wilson

Manchester shopper beware; there are two superstores centrally located within the city whose business it is to prise large amounts of money from the parents of small children. Shamelessly cashing in on youthful adulation for heroes and favourites regularly seen on television and video, these shops knock out an endless variety of well-made but expensive licensed products, anything from pens and toothbrushes at a few pounds each to bronze statuettes (for the serious fan) costing several hundred times more.

Yet despite the fact that the Disney store and the Warner Brothers emporium are both American owned, with the considerable profits ultimately leaving the country, no one bats an eyelid. Mickey Mouse wouldn't endorse anything cynical or exploitative. But when Manchester United muscle in on the same market, a famous British concern harnessing the appeal of their own powerful iconography, Bambi cries foul.

What the Labour party leader specifically objected to was United's new third strip, which happened to be a poor illustration of his sub-text, the commercialisation of football. The vilification subsequently heaped on United's merchandising department – their head, Edward Freedman, was labelled 'Mr Greedy' in the *Daily Express* last week – was not only out of proportion but suggestive that the whole country is as confused as Mr Blair about the ethics of football clubs making money off the pitch.

A few facts. United have had three strips for some time, like several other Premiership clubs. They change each one every two years, and the new blue number is simply a replacement for the even more hideous green-and-yellow halves. The basic shirt costs £37 (children's £28), and if you want a name, number and all the other paraphernalia it is available at extra cost. As it is at Chelsea or

Newcastle. When the new shirts went on sale this week, United's two stores shifted around a thousand on the first day, almost all in adult sizes. In the last three years, since Freedman's arrival from Spurs, United's turnover from merchandising has gone up from £2 million to £14 million. This figure represents more than a third of the club's total turnover, and is growing, so that it is not difficult to envisage a time when merchandising makes as much money for the club as footballing activities.

Perhaps the most surprising aspect of this success story is that it took United so long to wake up to their own potential. Five years ago, Spurs were further along the secondary income road than anyone else in the country, even if not everything their merchandising department touched turned to gold. But when United finally realised that millions were slipping through their fingers, Martin Edwards made a shrewd move in tempting Freedman north. Remember Tottenham's baggy shorts in the 1991 FA Cup Final? That entire strip was down to the 52-year-old former retailer. There was, if you recall, almost universal disapproval at the time, but within months the whole of the League were running about in fashionably retro bags, and still are.

Look at any part of United's slick merchandising operation now, and one thing is immediately clear. The club are not playing at it. The first-team stars modelling leisurewear in the brochures project the product, not bored expressions or studied indifference. The new megastore behind the Stretford End is impressive not so much for its size as its attention to detail. Want to see what a teenage United fanatic's bedroom might look like, complete with branded duvet and wallpaper? Here's a full-size mock-up. There's a junior-school-age version next door.

You don't have to come to Manchester for this, there are licensed outlets for United goods as far apart as Belfast and Plymouth, but perhaps the most significant innovation of Freedman's is the *United* magazine, a sales tool capable of reaching a much wider market. 'There was a lot of opposition at first, but Liverpool and Arsenal have since copied us,' Freedman said. 'The magazine wouldn't sell if it was just a sales brochure. I don't think anyone is giving us credit for what a good product it is, but it does vastly extend our range of customers. We recently conducted a survey, and 83 per cent of those who responded said they only visited the ground once a season. People are looking for ways to express their loyalty to United, and we service that demand.'

Loyalty is where the depiction of United as just another name on the high street falls down. Marks & Spencer's shoppers are free to look round C & A if they choose, but United's customers are not going to go anywhere else. 'So what should we do?' asked Freedman. 'Ignore them? Go back to just selling scarves and bobble hats in a supporters' shop which only opens on Saturdays? United's fame and name are saleable all over the world, we are still only scratching the surface. People always complained that British clubs were behind the times, saying we should market ourselves like the Americans, but now we are doing that it seems that's wrong as well.'

Which brings us back to the question of what people do want from a football club. Manchester United do not really need to defend themselves, just point to their burgeoning support around the world and a profit line which speaks for itself. Given that few object to commercial and merchandising departments *per se*, United can hardly be blamed because they do it better than anyone else and make a lot of money on the way. It hardly takes a degree in Thatcherite economics to recognise that if no one wanted United's new shirt, the club would lose revenue and probably not repeat the exercise again.

No club actually needs three strips, and undeniably something has been lost, something cheapened, on the journey from football to fashion, but this cannot be laid at United's door alone. Many a traditional fan would applaud Jack Walker, who likes the Blackburn Rovers shirt exactly as it is and wants to see his side wear it as often as possible, although in this, as in other areas, Ewood is the exception. Walker would not be able to turn back football's clock had he not made a gargantuan profit elsewhere.

Talking of gargantuan profits, the significant development at United is surely the conviction of all concerned that Andy Cole's £350,000-a-year wage will be dwarfed by endorsements and other spin-offs. Cole and his cohorts at the top of the Premiership earning scale could be about to take British team sports into the stratospheric salary bracket long accepted in America. Politicians might do better to worry about that prospect instead of supposedly hard-pressed parents forking out for a third shirt for their doubtless spoiled offspring. Thanks to America, parents already know how to deal with that. Just say no.

Observer, 22 January 1995

Designer Shirts

Clive White

When the Labour leader, Tony Blair, tore a strip off Manchester United and their lucrative replica kit business recently there must have been many who wished he had gone a step further and put the boot into the club for its flagrant disregard for tradition, too. Commercial exploitation in the shape of their strip is one thing, but what on earth has blue and white got to do with the Red Devils?

It was an open invitation to ridicule which, thankfully, was not passed up. 'They're trying to look like us,' Tony Gale, of United's Premiership rivals, Blackburn Rovers, said. Others, even more cuttingly, reckoned it was a desperate attempt to pretend they were still in the European Cup – by aping their conquerors, IFK Gothenburg.

Of course the blue and white strip is no more an impostor than the green and yellow it replaced (despite Umbro's insistence that the latter were the club's colours in its earliest days) or, come to that, even the all-black reserve number currently in use at Old Trafford. It seems there is no end these days to the technicolour dream coats in which clubs will adorn their teams on the pretence of being unable to wear their first-choice kit. So much for showing your colours.

When I was a boy, and an avid United supporter, the merest deviation from the regular red, white and black was something to be abhorred. I remember well the feeling of being short-changed when they turned out at the start of one season in the usual red and white shirts but with all-white socks. There was nothing wrong with all-white socks. On the contrary, they had a certain cachet – Real Madrid wore them – but they were not as distinctive as a black stocking topped with red and white. And, crucially, it just wasn't United.

In those days of innocence, when shirt sponsorship was in its infancy, clubs rarely had cause not to wear their full colours. And if they did have to change, every effort was made to retain them in some form, usually in a reverse format. Indeed, for me there was a novelty value in, just occasionally, seeing United in all white fringed with red; shades of my second favourite club, Real.

Some of the reverse kits were extremely attractive. I remember the appeal of Aston Villa's in the 1957 FA Cup final against United: sky blue shirts with a thin claret stripe. Nowadays their change strip is black, green and red, hardly traditional.

Respect for tradition, of course, disappeared long ago. The advent in the Sixties of Don Revie's image-conscious Leeds, replete with sock tabs and 'Smiley' badges, along with the ill-conceived revamp of England's kit by Admiral, heralded the relaunch of an industry which has rocketed in value to something like £80m a year today in England alone.

It is a seasonal fashion business and if the English regard it as a commercial rip-off they should spare a thought for the poor Dutch parent: Ajax change their strip every season instead of every two as is the case in England. If that seems excessive, it is because first and second choice kits change alternately (other than when there is a new sponsor and they change again) and because some clubs, such as United, Spurs and Celtic, have three kits.

Many clubs may occasionally play in a third but do not market it, even though the demand is there. When Arsenal played in an emergency third kit recently 'the phones didn't stop ringing the next day from fans who wanted it,' John Hazell, the club's commercial manager, said. 'It's not our policy to produce the third kit for commercial resale. We're aware families are under enough financial pressure without that. I must say, though, I've been here five years and I could count on my fingers the number of complaints I've received about changing kits. Yet I've got files and files of letters from kids suggesting new ones.'

Since the sales of shirts in children's sizes, according to the manufacturers, are outstripped by those for adults there does not seem to be much of a case to answer on the commercial side even if Umbro, which has been at the forefront of this shirt revolution, did display a certain cynicism in introducing the third United kit immediately after Christmas.

Umbro, which numbers England, Brazil, Manchester United and Ajax among its clients, claims to be a company run by football fans, and to honour tradition. 'We were the people who put England back in a proper white shirt with navy shorts after the Admiral days of funny blue,' Peter Draper, the marketing director, said. 'We were the people who put Brazil back in a proper gold and green and the right kind of blue shorts. We understand this view which says "don't mess". Sadly, rather like putting in seats where there was terracing, sometimes you've got to. You have to move on.'

Unfortunately the 'messing' is not restricted to just change strips. They are nibbling away like moths at the very fabric of tradition. Take Liverpool for example. From a distance, unadulterated red and white. A closer inspection reveals that the shirt sleeves and collar are edged with green. Since when was green an integral part of the Reds?

It is, however, an integral part of Adidas, the makers, which subtly slipped in the green to reflect its own corporate identity.

One could be excused for wondering these days what exactly are the club colours of some teams. They can change more readily than a chameleon, often quite needlessly. Last Saturday's FA Cup tie between Tottenham and Southampton was a case in point. No clash of colours there between Spurs' white shirts and navy blue shorts and the red and white striped shirts and black shorts of Southampton. But what did the Saints turn out in? Turquoise and royal blue.

Philip Don, the referee on that occasion, explained that contrary to popular belief both teams can wear the same coloured shorts. 'It's just the predominant colour in the shirts and, obviously, the socks which must not clash,' he said. 'Unfortunately it's not up to the League what colour a club chooses to play in away from home.'

What chance tradition, though, when the ruling body itself ceases to pay it any due, preferring instead to pay homage to its own sponsors? If ever there was change for change's sake it was the switching from black to green for referees – of which most disapprove – when the FA Premier League signed a sponsorship deal with Umbro.

Generally, though, it is the change strip which is most widely open to abuse, the manufacturers experimenting wildly, and often coming up with some truly hideous mutations. Most people have their favourite abomination, including the players. In fact particularly the players, who have to wear them and are rarely consulted as to their preference.

As if finishing bottom of their group in the 1986 Mexico World Cup finals was not humiliating enough, Scotland's players had to be seen doing so in an unflattering outfit which consisted of a thick blue band around the area of their genitals. 'It didn't do those fellas with big backsides much of a favour,' recalled Gordon Strachan, the recently retired Leeds and Scotland midfielder. 'Some of the strips are a mess; they don't even look like a football kit.

'Do you remember that awful Coventry one? In a chocolate brown with black and white curvy stripes down it. Then there was one at Dundee with a broad white band down the front flanked in blue. They looked like 11 penguins running around. The one thing about strips these days, I must admit, is that they're being used as a fashion accessory and not just as a strip, so I suppose you could say they're serving two purposes for the price of one.'

Umbro, the perpetrators of that little Scotland number, claimed that those shorts were a best seller. 'It was absolutely pasted in the Scottish media but the Jocks bought it in their thousands,' Draper said. 'It was very popular beachwear.' Strictly for beach bums.

Having a sponsor's name emblazoned across the chest, of course, does not exactly help appearance. Designer clothes may be all the vogue nowadays but Auto Windscreens or Walker Crisps do not have quite the same ring as, say, Giorgio Armani. It can hardly have done much for the self-esteem of Brighton's players a few seasons back when, as if turning out in a white and pink patterned check was not bad enough, they had to do so with the word NOBO written on their chest in large capital letters. Mind you, their supermarket carrier bag look (blue and white stripes on shirts and shorts, *à la* Tesco's) was hardly an improvement. And the FA rules on clothing are supposed to prohibit 'anything regarded as distasteful'.

One wonders just what comes over some designers and how on earth they manage to impose their ideas upon clubs. What, for instance, was Umbro's pitch when selling Chelsea their second kit? 'We have got this nice grey look for you.'

'It's just a case of sitting down with a pen and colouring pad and thinking what can I do to make it interesting and different,' Barry Griffin, the UK sales manager of the Japanese company Asics, said. 'The current United strip has got the names of 101 United players past and present woven into it. I mean who would have thought of that? Certainly not the club.'

'If you think some of the designs of manufacturers leave something to be desired you should see what high fashion experts came up with a while back when people such as Jesper Curran were asked to design a football shirt,' Draper said. 'You've never seen such a joke in all your life.'

It has not all been in the worst possible taste, however. The return to the old-fashioned style of baggy shorts and shirts has been well received. The pacesetters Blackburn are the trendsetters in that respect, and yet remain very traditional. The Italians may still prefer their shorts like knickers, according to Griffin, whose Asics are Blackburn's kit suppliers, but the likes of Gale welcome the loose-fit look. 'You can't see the little bulges around your midriff,' he explained.

Some Arsenal fans are convinced their team look slow and cumbersome in their new Nike kit, with its hooped red and white socks; others say it is because they *are* slow and cumbersome. A few seasons ago Crystal Palace, at the behest of Ian Wright and Mark Bright, opted for the Brazilian kit as their second choice, though it has to be said nothing much appears to have rubbed off. Likewise some years ago Newcastle tried a variation on Brazil's colours in order to make Mirandinha feel at home. He went back to Brazil.

Some designers might glean a few ideas from Desmond Morris's book *The Soccer Tribe* in which he sees a definite advantage in wearing certain colours. 'There is a strong chance that, if the body is clad in vividly bold and contrasting colours, like a giant stinging insect, it will be more threatening than if it is adorned in baby blue or some soft pastel shade,' he wrote. 'Given this thought, it might seem logical to expect a predominance of reds, yellows and oranges among the Tribal Colours, instead of the reds, blues and whites.'

Nike says it sends its designers on what the company calls 'inspirational tours' where they talk to everyone from the chairman to the tea lady before fixing upon a design. 'A lot of people have lucky colours. For example, Arsenal have always been lucky in yellow,' Jim Pearson, of Nike, said. 'It took a lot of persuasion for them to change to blue and teal as their second kit. Personally, I think talent comes into it somewhere down the line, or lack thereof.'

Though British goalkeepers are generally more flamboyant in their dress sense these days none has gone as far yet as the peacock-like Mexican Jorge Campos. His multi-coloured jerseys, replicated throughout Mexico, are probably more designed to dazzle his bank manager than opposing forwards.

Peter Shilton once tried a white polo neck jersey in an attempt to make himself appear even larger in goal, but he quickly discarded it once opposing teams started taking it as a sign of surrender. Conversely, Everton's Neville Southall has opted for black in the belief that it enables him to blend in with the crowd behind the goal and thereby take strikers by surprise. For a while last season, and in the early part of this, he certainly seemed invisible at times.

To those of my generation even the material the modern kit is made of does not look particularly inviting. Surely these synthetics are not as cool as good old cotton. 'A load of nonsense,' Draper said. 'Cotton just holds the sweat. The modern man-made fibres move the moisture from the inside to the outside of the garment and allows it to move away normally. It's also more robust when it comes to retaining shape and size.

'It's a part injury-preventive, too. That's why athletes are using Lycras. Nothing sillier than Linford Christie moving down the running track three years ago, but no decent athlete would be seen without it now. On that basis, potentially, it's not a long way off footballers wearing the same because it is a performance garment.'

Football fans in ballet tights. I'd like to see the manufacturers try to market that one for public consumption.

Independent, 23 February 1995

In January Manchester United smashed the British transfer record with a £7 million deal that brought Newcastle's Andy Cole to Old Trafford. It took everyone by surprise. This was the inside story.

Cole for Sale: The Inside Story
Bob Cass

The British football transfer record was triggered by a fit of frustration. A day that began with Manchester United manager Alex Ferguson scrambling to sign Nottingham Forest striker Stan Collymore ended with him snatching Andy Cole. Unbelievably, the £7 million deal was done because one manager answered the telephone and another did not.

Ferguson put three calls into Forest manager Frank Clark but could not make contact. After the third he received a message from Clark's assistant Alan Hill that the Forest chief had left the ground feeling unwell and would contact him next week.

Ferguson was in a fix. Knowing Clark's reluctance to talk about selling his star forward, he felt – wrongly as it turned out – that he was being messed about. Back at his desk at Old Trafford, Ferguson, frustrated by the lack of activity, had a flash of inspiration. He recalled a light-hearted conversation with Newcastle manager Kevin Keegan at the start of the season.

'Let me know if you feel like selling Andy Cole,' Ferguson had said. He got little encouragement. But now, he thought, it was worth a second try. Ferguson's fingers went to his personal organiser. He called up Keegan's number and dialled. It was the prelude to a chain of events which were to rewrite the record books and bring turmoil to Tyneside.

The conversation went like this:

'Kevin? Alex Ferguson here. Look, this is probably a daft question but I'm asking it anyway – what's my chances of getting Andy Cole?'

Ferguson waited for the rebuff. Nothing. The silence spoke volumes.

The Newcastle manager countered with an inquiry about the availability of Northern Irish teenager Keith Gillespie and in the following minutes the seeds of the most unlikely deal in football were sown.

'It was a shot in the dark,' said the United manager. 'I was after Collymore. If I had been able to speak to Frank Clark I might have been able to sign him. But it's amazing how things can turn out in this game.'

An initial offer of £5.5m was rejected and the fee was eventually settled at £6m plus the £1m-rated Gillespie. Keegan asked for time to consider. By Sunday night the Newcastle manager had decided to recommend the deal to his chairman Sir John Hall.

Sir John was told on Monday morning and agreed. Later that day, Ferguson's phone rang again. It was Keegan. United had got their man.

As United set off for their third round FA Cup visit to Sheffield United on Monday night, neither Cole nor Gillespie had been informed. Ferguson told Gillespie before the match that he had agreed to allow him to move to Newcastle and that Kevin Keegan would be at the game to discuss personal terms.

Cole, meanwhile, was at home in Gosforth, unaware of what was going on. It was an evening his Cheshire-based agent Paul Stretford will never forget for, by coincidence, Collymore is another of his clients. For weeks, Stretford had been gearing himself towards the Forest player going to Old Trafford.

'I would have put money on it. Everything pointed in that direction,' he said.

Stretford was about to leave his Wilmslow office when he took a call from Keegan. 'He told me he had received a bid which he thought was good for the club. It included a player coming from Manchester United and he thought the deal was the right thing for Newcastle and Andy Cole. That was the first mention of his name and I was thunderstruck. I was stunned into silence long enough for Kevin to ask if I was still on the line.'

Stretford rang Cole and made the pretence of going to see him regarding some commercial business.

'I told him not to go out. I got into my car and drove to Newcastle,' he said. 'The first he knew that Newcastle had agreed to sell him was when I told him just as the second half was kicking off at Bramall Lane. He couldn't believe it. Moving from Newcastle was the last thing on his mind. He hadn't long signed a four-year contract. He hadn't been scoring but he was working hard and enjoying his football. But once he had got over the fact that Newcastle were committed to selling him it wasn't a big leap from there because it was Manchester United. If it had been any other club I don't think he would have gone.'

Cole and Stretford travelled to Manchester the following day. The player met Ferguson and managing director Martin Edwards and thrashed out a five-and-a-half-year contract worth £3 million.

Keegan defended his sale of Cole to rain-soaked supporters at the club's Durham training ground on Wednesday. He did it to such effect that those who had come to criticise burst into applause.

Keegan is aware he has taken the biggest gamble of his career as a manager. By Thursday, he was talked out about Cole. 'Look,' he said. 'I've done it and it's over with. I will be judged on my decision. Now please allow me to get on with the rest of my life.'

Mail on Sunday, 15 January 1995

Joao Havelange

Alex Fynn and Lynton Guest

'I am never arrogant,' said Fifa's president Dr Joao Havelange. Yet as the 49th congress of Fifa took place in the plush surroundings of the Sheraton Hotel, Chicago, Havelange's high-handedness had led some delegates to wonder whether it wasn't time for the 78-year-old president to be stepping down. Rumours of a challenge to Havelange had been boosted when he banned Pelé from the World Cup draw in Las Vegas in December 1993 because Pelé had questioned the commercial practices of Havelange's son-in-law, Ricardo Texeira, who is president of the Brazilian Football Federation. This upset the head of the World Cup organising committee, Alan Rothenberg, who said Pelé had 'lit the fires' for soccer in the USA and was 'the single most important person in bringing the World Cup to the USA'. Havelange's autocratic style of presidency was never better illustrated. 'If you have children,' he said, 'and one of them misbehaves, you give them a smack. That's what happened with Pelé, but now it's all forgotten.'

Three possible contenders for Havelange's position emerged: Lenart Johansson, president of Uefa; Antonio Matarrese, president of the Italian federation, and Sepp Blatter, Fifa's general secretary (and the organisation's chief career bureaucrat). In the end, Johansson and Matarrese could not draw support from South America, Africa or Asia, where Havelange's backing remained solid, while Blatter, as part of the secretariat, would have had to have been party to a palace revolution to dethrone his boss, an unlikely occurrence given Havelange's power base.

Havelange appeared offended by the possibility of a challenge, though he later said his objection was to 'certain manoeuvrings' which had taken place on behalf of Blatter. Having seen off the threat, Havelange sat back as the chastised Blatter felt compelled to deliver an eulogy in Chicago, paying homage to a man 'who made Fifa into a business of worldwide standing'.

Since coming to power in 1974 Havelange has taken Fifa far away from the old-world, gentlemen's club atmosphere which existed under his predecessors. Fifa is now a worldwide enterprise, and its central institution, the World Cup, is the only rival to the Olympic Games in the mega-event stakes. The award of the World Cup to the USA, a country with no real football tradition, was a gamble, if only because it was the first time the hosting of the World Cup had been offered to a country outside Latin America or Europe. The USA was the watershed in Havelange's global ambitions and thus assumed greater importance than any previous World Cup.

Havelange's objective to take football to every corner of the globe was conducted through close links with many multi-national companies like Coca-Cola. These companies underwrote Fifa's expansion in the years after Havelange gained power through the creation of sponsored tournaments based on age-levels and programmes encompassing coaching, administration, refereeing and sports medicine, all designed to raise standards in the new football-playing countries. The World Cup was the centre-piece of the strategy, with an increase in the number of teams taking part in the final tournament (since Spain 1982 there have been 24 teams, to be further increased to 32 in France 1998).

One reason why some of the largest multi-nationals were happy to back Havelange was the president's adroit handling of inflammable political, ethnic and religious issues. There have been no boycotts of the World Cup. Under Havelange's Machiavellian guidance, both China and Taiwan agreed to participate, North and South Korea to operate in the same Asian Division and Israel and the Arab states played in the World Cup at the height of their mutual loathing by the simple expedient of moving Israel into the European Division (this also meant Israel had virtually no chance of qualifying for the finals, thus preventing a potentially explosive encounter).

These diplomatic coups encouraged multi-nationals to believe they could open up new markets with Fifa. This fitted perfectly with Havelange's aim of taking the new age-based tournaments to countries which had little chance of staging the World Cup in order to enhance football's status in those countries. Hence the assault on China, which hosted the World Under-16 Championship in 1985.

Within Fifa, there has never been any real debate about the direction Havelange has taken. The decision to take the World Cup to the USA was defensible, but Fifa's desire to alter the game, if necessary, for American consumption (four quarters, larger goals, etc) was several steps too far. Eventually, Fifa drew back from some of the more extreme wheezes but nevertheless they approached USA '94 with two underlying principles. Italia '90 had, it was commonly agreed, been a disaster as a spectacle and the American public was used to exciting sport, with a definite winner and loser at every turn. Sepp Blatter revealed Fifa's thinking when he said the organisation must improve 'the quality of the game in order that this World Cup (USA '94) is a success'.

In defence of Havelange, it must be said that football all over the world has had to accommodate new commercial thinking. Fifa seems to have made a better fist of it than many other sports bodies. The FA had been consistently outmanoeuvred by television while UEFA had created a hybrid competition in the Champions League and has managed to gain control of the commercial aspects of its competitions only by selling out to an unholy alliance of big clubs, television networks and international sponsors. Fifa has never done that with the World Cup. The sponsors have come in on Fifa's terms and Fifa is the senior partner. There is no title sponsorship (although expediency has seen Fifa go down the route for its less glamorous, age-based competitions, with the under-17s competing for the JVC Cup and the under-20s the Coca-Cola Cup), which safeguards the integrity of the event, thereby enabling a high premium to be charged for exclusive category rights to World Cup logos, symbols and nomenclature as well as ticket and hospitality benefits. The authority of the World Cup is demonstrated by the fact that skilled marketing practitioners like Coca-Cola, McDonald's and General Motors are prepared to pay upwards of £10m in 1994 so that they can build their advertising and promotional programmes around their involvement.

None of this can justify the amazing commemorative brochure, entitled *90 Years of Fifa*, published to coincide with the ninetieth anniversary of the organisation in May 1994 – just in time to circulate to delegates before the Chicago election. Under the guise of presenting the history of Fifa, the brochure turned out to be a hagiography to the president, and is worthy of a Roman emperor. Subtitled *20 Years of Presidency*, the brochure features 25 pictures of Havelange, one of Sir Stanley Rous and none of Pelé or any other great player. Where Havelange is not alone, he is the centre of the action, seen receiving or being greeted by the great and good. Even the picture of Sir Stanley Rous cannot escape the treatment. Rous is seen congratulating Havelange after Havelange ousted him from the Fifa presidency. The text is even worse: 'It is thanks to Dr Joao Havelange that football has taken on an unprecedented universal dimension . . . (he) is imbued with imagination, resolve and flair. In spite of his many triumphs he has never lost sight of fundamental issues or recoiled from the enormous responsibility resting on his shoulders . . . He is in every sense the "world's leading footballer".'

The estimated economic impact of the circus on the USA was a cool $4 billion, worth a direct profit of more than $20m to the US organisers. Fifa had ensured the financial windfall by changing its stadia specifications in 1988. The USA was spared the enormous expense borne by the Italians in upgrading stadia ($300–500m against $45m). While agreeing it would be wrong to impose costs which a host country found unrealistic, stadia expert Simon Inglis saw a more practical purpose behind Fifa's attitude. 'Fifa will do anything possible to put the World Cup in the place they want it. If I were a cynic I would say that Fifa knew that the States couldn't or were unwilling to fulfil the requirements and they decided very conveniently to forget it.' The Americans were allowed to use facilities which would not have passed the UK's stringent requirements laid down in the Safety At Sports Grounds Act. There were wooden stairways, too many seats per row and fences. 'When you looked at the Rose Bowl and Stanford and compared them with even a basic stadium in Europe,' Simon Inglis concluded, 'it was clear they were way below those standards. If they deem the Rose Bowl safe then, quite frankly, you could stage the World Cup in Poland.'

The main cause of concern to fans was the ticketing arrangements. In Fifa's desire to get money up front, travel agents were hand-picked and they paid a 20 per cent premium which was passed on to the customer. This meant travelling fans had to buy package deals if they wanted a guaranteed ticket. Fifa's over-generous allocations to its own delegates were frequently returned and competed with vast numbers of black-market tickets from touts. Right up to kick-off (even for the Italy-Ireland match) $30 tickets were available from official sales booths, while just around the corner, fans, unaware of the existence of the open booths, were paying touts up to five times face value for the same tickets.

The blatant commercial nature of the tournament was apparent inside the stadia where food, drink and merchandise were all sold at vastly inflated prices. Alan Rothenberg gave the game away when he bemoaned Germany's exit, wailing that Bulgaria 'won't sell many T-shirts'.

The legacy the World Cup should bequeath to the USA is a domestic league. It is an equally wide-spread belief that the plans for one, as currently constituted, will fail. These plans were put forward by the head of the World Cup organising committee. Alan Rothenberg, a 55-year-old lawyer from Los Angeles, won a bitter power struggle within the US Soccer Federation (USSF). His company, Major League Soccer (MLS), subsequently won the right to set up the US Professional League with Fifa support. By the end of the World Cup, Rothenberg's league had awarded only seven out of the proposed 12 franchises. There is a TV contract with ABC and ESPN in the offing but it is doubtful whether anything other than a championship game will make it onto the network. So desperate is Fifa for the US league to succeed that it has indicated that it may grant Rothenberg special dispensation to change the rules of the game. Currently, the inter-regional leagues, which are a level below the intended MLS, are being used as a hot-house to run a number of experiments in different divisions. Goals have been expanded, shoot-outs awarded after every seventh foul (giving a player a free run on goal from the centre circle), kick-ins have replaced throw-ins and a stock-clock introduced to determine 60 minutes of actual playing time.

Just as controversially, there will be no individual franchises in the MLS as with other major US sports. Every club and all the players will be owned by the MLS ('crazy', according to Rodney Marsh), with the draft system operating from a central pool. Imagine an ageing foreign star being told: 'Sorry, but the roll of the dice means you're going to Baltimore instead of Orlando.'

Whatever happens, the new league can only succeed if it wins over national TV, and that is unlikely. Paradoxically, the success of the US team has worked against the league. The US stars now either want to play in Europe or in other, better paid sports. Tony Meola, for instance, accepted an offer to become a place-kicker in gridiron. So the new league will have few, if any, of the players the American public has come to know and spectator sport in the USA cannot exist with no stars.

Rothenberg must know all this. Why, then, has he persisted?

Perhaps it is merely window-dressing so that Havelange can claim to have achieved his objective. Then, later, the league will quietly die with minimum embarrassment.

Tony Soave, co-owner of the Wheels, the semi-pro team in Detroit, warned Fifa not to demand too much too soon. 'They're creating an image, a lot of smoke without the barbecue. You have to build soccer from the ground up.'

There is another way, one which has not been considered by FIFA, so wedded is it to the concept of national leagues. Recent experience shows that professional football matches need to be 'events' to attract sufficient interest and generate enough money to keep the game going at all levels. The event-like theory has been decisively vindicated by what happened in the USA. The US public and television will support sport when it is presented as a big event and when it is of the highest quality. They simply will not be interested in a third-rate league.

While a league grows organically Fifa should plan to hold big-event soccer tournaments in the USA on a regular basis to keep the pot boiling. An annual world club tournament, for instance, could draw large crowds and television coverage, while an all-embracing pan-American international competition might keep the national team in the public mind. The collective brains at USSF ought to be able to think of a dozen 'event-like' ideas to keep football on TV while a league develops. But perhaps USA '94 has shown that football has been finally divorced from its marriage to leagues. The USA could herald a new dawn, not just for soccer in the USA but also for Fifa. It might also prove a fitting end to the presidency of Joao Havelange.

He is now 78. Where will Fifa go when Joao decides it's time to join the great sponsor in the sky? Of those gathered for the succession, Sepp Blatter is best employed as an administrator, while Lenart Johansson is an amiable, if slightly more gifted, version of Bert Millichip. One candidate for the succession stands head and shoulders above all the others. A world figure, incorruptible, known to have the best interests of the game at heart. He is no stranger to the commercial side of football, yet he is loved throughout the world. He used to play a bit, too. His name is Edson Arantes do Nascmento, also known as Pelé, a man you really could call the world's leading footballer.

Out Of Time, 1994

A League of their Own

Alex Spillius

As the taxi burped up the hill towards St James's Park, home of Newcastle United, the driver chatted amiably about a friend recently released from prison. He had done a few years for GBH ('Nothing too bad, he just tapped the fella like') and freedom promised reacquaintance with his heroes in black and white stripes. This was easier said than done. Admission to St James's these days is restricted to 34,000 season ticket holders and there is a waiting list of 10,000. It would be simpler acquiring a ticket for Glyndebourne than Newcastle versus Coventry. The permanently excluded must beg or borrow from the permanently endowed, and if the cabbie's friend ever gets lucky he is in for a few surprises.

The Gallowgate terracing, where generations stood and swayed and burst their lungs for the lads, has been replaced by civil rows of seating which stretch round four-fifths of the ground. The centre of worship will be entirely enclosed when the final corner is finished, complete with English football's first rooftop restaurant accessible by exterior sky-lift, offering an ascending view of the docks and glorious Tyne Bridge. Inside the main stand the dingy concourses have given way to uniformly blue-carpeted, pastel-papered corridors yielding to this suite and that lounge of drinkers and diners. Chablis and salmon *en croûte*; blazers and bottle blondes; football has never been like this. Three thousand meals are served on match days. Three thousand meals! Not long ago they would have been glad to shift that number of meat pies and Bovril. It is all part of what the club's chairman Sir John Hall – a former north-eastern businessman of the year, chairman of the Millennium Commission and founder of the Metro Centre, Europe's largest shopping mall – calls 'added value'.

Five years ago, as Sir John contemplated a rescue bid for a club stifled by debt, English football was paralysed by the shaming memory of the Heysel and Hillsborough disasters. The Government's enforcement of the Taylor Report's recommendation for all-seated stadia threatened bankruptcy for many clubs. Yet two weeks ago the final FA Carling Premiership matches of the season were watched in comfortable, airy, occasionally exalted, refurbished arenas. Attendance is up, turnovers are up (anything from 30 per cent to 100 per cent over three years), the quality of the spectacle has improved, while players are costing more and earning more Armani suits than they know what to do with. In some respects football has never had it so good. Forget the bungs, the kung fu, the tales of lager-top and cocaine frenzies, the match-fixing allegations, the post-training session spliffs; the real lesson of the past nine months is that mammon has made the team for good. Money has always talked in football, but now it shouts and is generally obeyed.

Sir John Hall's is one of the loudest voices: 'The Premier League – the Premier League, *not* the Football Association – will take English football into the 21st century,' he asserts. 'They [the Premier chairmen] have got the money, they've got the power and they've got the will.' The future of the game rests in the hands of men with more money or more ambition, or both, than the sport has ever known.

Football chairmen are not the sort of people one would refer to simply as 'chair'. These are big men in a man's world. Traditionally chairmen and directors were butchers and builders, arch committee men, unpaid and happy to donate a few grand when required but even happier to enjoy the networking, trips abroad and cigar-smogged banter that boardroom life brought.

The modern chairman is more an entrepreneur and a hands-on sort. Property development is still a likely background, only on a grander scale. He may well have streamlined his board of directors, relying on a couple of rusty lieutenants to run things while he holidays in Marbella or the West Indies. His Rolls or top-of-the-range Mercedes testifies to a career which as often as not has culminated in a lucrative sell-out. With money in the bank, he has diverted his attention to the sport that has obsessed him since youth.

The former steel tycoon Jack Walker has gone furthest towards emulating the inspirational patronage lavished by the Italian magnates Berlusconi and Agnelli on AC Milan and Juventus respectively, or the millions with which the Scottish businessman David Murray has turned Glasgow Rangers into seemingly perennial champions.

Since British Steel bought him out for £330 million in 1990, Walker has spent £54 million on a new stadium and players for Blackburn Rovers, more than double the borough council's budget for 1993–94. Walker, who has only ever submitted to one interview, is by repute an old-fashioned hirer and firer of a boss. But when the team that Jack built won its first league championship for 81 years, he was instantly reduced to tears. As a Jersey resident Walker, 64, is forbidden from UK directorships and consequently holds the nominal post of vice-president at the club, though his influence is paramount. Walker has also had a dramatic influence on players' wages and transfer fees generally; when Blackburn paid £5 million last year for Chris Sutton, a 21-year-old with no international experience, the rest of football gasped. At some stage every big club chairman, feeling something of a pauper to the prince of Blackburn, has had to apologise: 'I'm no Jack Walker . . .'

Ambitious men like Walker fall just short of making up a team of 11: Sir Jack Hayward, who made his fortune with various developments in Grand Bahama, has put £20 million into Wolverhampton Wanderers; Sir John Hall has invested £14 million in Newcastle United; Lionel Pickering (free newspapers), £15 million in Derby County; David Sullivan (*Sunday Sport* publisher), £10 million in Birmingham City; Peter Johnson (Christmas hampers), £10 million in Everton; Alan Sugar (Amstrad), £10 million in Tottenham; Francis Lee (bog rolls and race horses), has led a consortium investing £8.6 million in the club he played for in his prime, Manchester City; while Matthew Harding, a 41-year-old reinsurance broker personally worth £140 million, has deposited £7.5 million into Chelsea and bought the freehold of the club's Stamford Bridge stadium for £16 million, though he is only chairman-in-waiting to Ken Bates. Most of these men are supporters of the teams they have benefited; in many cases their club was desperate before they intervened. But just as great, perhaps, is their need of abstractions that a lifetime in business rarely provides; fame and gratitude. Self-interest and sporting compulsion fuse uniquely. Football immediately delivers them to the back pages, where many discover a latent gift for public relations, and presents an opportunity to be associated with glory that the manufacture of hampers or PCs could never bring.

Sullivan and Sugar are two who seemed to discover football late in life. As Terry Venables, the England manager and former chief executive of Tottenham, puts it in his autobiography: 'I remain fairly sceptical of Sugar's claim to be a lifelong Spurs fan. Anyone who comes out with a remark like "Double? What Double? Is that something from the 1950s?" can scarcely be described as a Tottenham devotee.' (The double in question being the rare feat Tottenham achieved in 1960–61 of winning the League and FA Cup in the same season.)

Venables and Sugar later had a seismic falling out, but even Venables acknowledges in his book his adversary's tenacity, which, combined with sound business methods, has turned Tottenham around from debts of £11 million. Sugar's style, however, can be on the curt side. After the traumatic takeover in 1991 was finally negotiated by telephone with the outgoing chairman Irving Scholar in his Monte Carlo apartment, Scholar's representative in London suggested Sugar pay his air fare to convey the documents to Scholar swiftly. Sugar responded: 'You can fuck off.'

Three years later, at a party aboard a yacht moored off the glittering principality, Sugar met the solicitor of the German *über*-striker Jürgen Klinsmann, commencing a transfer that at a stroke earned years of goodwill from Tottenham supporters – even if Klinsmann did depart early – and proved Sugar may already be cannier about players than the northern director once accused of wanting to buy Salford Van Hire because he thought he was a Dutch international. According to Peter Johnson, the Everton chairman: 'Alan may have been a late convert but I think he's got the white-knuckle job now, he's as keen and committed as anybody.'

Johnson himself has transferred his own white knuckles from Liverpool, where he held a season ticket for 18 years, to Tranmere Rovers, where he was chairman for seven, and now to Everton. 'I would only have got involved with a Merseyside club,' he says, with the strong pride of the region. Johnson's slightly flushed, boyish features don't hide a regard for the good life; he breaks into humour with ease. He would rather debate the merits of a particular referee than football politics, though his blitheness masks the tenacity he showed in the grinding takeover of Everton. I asked whether it was worth spending 10 per cent of a personal fortune of around £100 million (built up from his hamper company Park Foods) on a football club. 'I'm very proud of it, it gives one a very warm feeling – it's a beautiful stadium. I'm not going to need the £10 million back, same way as I'm sure Jack's not going to need his £50 million back. There's no pockets in shrouds you know.'

Money alone cannot buy success in football, but money wisely spent can do so quickly. The chief tasks facing a chairman are to employ a talented, ambitious manager (of whom there are surprisingly few) and stay out of team affairs. Mention of the 'r' word – relegation – drains a chairman's face of pleasantry. The divisions below the Premier League represent a black hole which wipes £2 million off the balance sheet immediately and from which promotion opportunities are limited. The upper reaches of football's greasy pole have never offered such riches. The five-year, £304 million contract agreed with Sky TV and the BBC, worth at least £1 million a year to each Premier club, exceeded all expectation, as did the phenomenal sales of replica shirts, the most unlikely fashion item since polyester bell-bottoms. Winning the championship will have been worth £4.5 million to Blackburn. A decent run in one of the European competitions is worth £3–4 million in gate receipts and TV and commercial revenue.

The modern chairman is no simple philantrophist. An examination of clubs' annual reports suggests some chairmen and executives are not doing too badly out of their clubs. Martin Edwards, the publicity-shy Manchester United CEO in the exceptional position of having inherited his place at the table and profited from a stock market flotation, was paid a £214,000 salary in 1994 and recently sold shares worth £1.25 million owned by his Children's Trust, leaving him with a 26.3 per cent holding worth £21 million.

David Dein of Arsenal earns a more modest £110,219 per annum as an executive vice-chairman and owns or 'speaks for' shares worth £8 million – not bad after an initial investment of £300,000 in 1983. Among recent arrivals Alan Sugar received emoluments of £50,000 as chairman of Tottenham Hotspur Plc, compared to £20,835 the previous year. Sir John Hall and his family have invested £14 million in Newcastle United in four years, chiefly through the parent company Cameron Hall Developments, but Sir John has so far personally lent £2.58 million and last year received £94,606 in interest charged at 10 per cent. He told me: 'We will pump-prime the business as a family but we will not subsidise it. Our family money is in there but must be repaid some time because the business must stand on its own feet.'

Of others, Lionel Pickering's money has only been loaned to Derby, while David Sullivan is likely to want his money back if not profit from Birmingham City. As only Walker and Hayward are simple benefactors, and old enough to seek no other fortunes, there is some concern that other investors might make a premature evacuation.

To meet Sir John Hall is to come face to face with ambition. The unbending zeal of this stern, occasionally Gradgrind-ish but courteous 62-year-old leaves you questioning what on earth you have done with a much shorter life, and I walked away from St James's half-wondering if I shouldn't give up journalism and build a museum. 'When we came to the club it was like a holiday camp, run by the blazer brigades. There was no business strategy at all,' proclaims Sir John, as we discuss the business of football across his boardroom table. 'I'm saying to myself: "How can I run this as a business?" And it's really no different. I operate for profit and that's what we're here for.' He resoundingly affirmed this occurred three years ago, when, as Newcastle toyed with relegation, to what is now the Second Division, under manager Ossie Ardiles, he ran some projections through a computer and concluded the club would not survive if demoted. Ardiles was promptly sacked.

'I'm not so much bothered about the FA Cup or the Coca-Cola Cup, I would want to win the Premier League season after season after season, because I'm then in Europe and the TV exposure and the financial rewards are unbelievable,' declares Sir John. I have rarely seen someone's eyes widen so. Although he describes his tenure at Newcastle as 'enterprise with responsibility, capitalism with a social conscience', like other chairmen, self-made men who have subverted the social hierarchy, Sir John is not keen on the term 'traditional working-class fan'. 'You are living in Victorian days,' he tells me.

Nonetheless, some of the Tyneside tribe are beginning to feel priced out of his vision, and there runs an argument, expounded not least a few months ago by Tony Blair, that football's élite is neglecting the traditional supporters' loyalty by the rapacious marketing of souvenirs and spin-offs. Sharp modern business practices supposedly disregard the fact that supporters are not mere customers who can switch their allegiance from club to club as a shopper can from Safeway to Tesco. They might have their ashes scattered on their field of dreams but not by the frozen meat section.

The argument is a little spacious. Manchester United, derided as Merchandise United, last year made £14 million from brand name products, 180 per cent up on the previous year, with 1,500 product lines ranging from ladies' knickers to children's slippers. Arsenal and Newcastle are next, though way behind, with projected merchandise earnings of around £4 million this year. The marketing may be frantic and the products tacky and overpriced, but no one is obliged to buy the stuff and the money, executives affirm, goes into the team or facilities, while ticket prices are generally lower than Italy or Spain.

Americanisation is another criticism never far from purists' lips, and the Arsenal vice-chairman David Dein has a particular case to answer here. Being married to a US citizen led to many trips across the Atlantic to sunny, family afternoons at American football: 'That was my call to arms in a way, to see if we could adapt any of those concepts to English soccer, which was living in the dark ages,' he says, eyes glinting with satisfaction at his perspicacity. Arsenal fashioned the first model, all-seated, consumer-friendly stadium, complete with museum, and the first supermarket-size souvenir shop.

While the other power brokers are rich and influential more by manner than appearance, the handsome, hirsute Dein has more flamboyance on his side and would look just as comfortable in Annabel's as the Arsenal boardroom. Though he has been known to knock a year or two off his 51, Dein is, along with Sir John, the most forward-looking of football's honchos, though more of a diehard fan.

He began business life as a tropical fruit importer in Shepherd's Bush market, later moving into commodity broking and on to the Arsenal board at 39, juvenile by football's standards. His caginess with information leads one to suspect he employed the trader's negotiating talents to full effect as he took up the top clubs' cause, later becoming a prime mover behind the Premier League.

It was Dein who suggested players' shirts should bear their names and last year he installed two 'jumbotrons' – giant screens – at Arsenal's Highbury stadium, showing instant replays of dramatic – though not controversial – incidents. 'What we want is to give the fan the sort of experience they have at home, where they see a replay of a goal half a dozen times,' says Dein. 'If that is moving with the times and people enjoy it, I think that's the way to go.'

Another direction in which the top clubs may be heading is towards a European League. Peter Johnson's eyes become distinctly dreamy at the prospect, though he wouldn't want it to exclude Everton's domestic participation. 'Nowadays it's as easy to get to Juventus [in Turin] as it is to get to Southampton. In some ways it would take away the hooligan problem – like in American football, where distances are so great they don't have away fans. So if Juventus or Inter Milan came here for a league match you would have it full of 40,000 Evertonians. It would be quite exciting,' he mused.

The game's power brokers can now either develop English Football Plc responsibly, and prosperously, dividing the spoils a little more evenly, ensuring its health from the bottom up, or become utterly preoccupied by the bottom line. They could go the way of the American sports that have so influenced them, where television and team owners call all the shots, players strike over millions and the lower classes who supply their ranks can't afford to witness live events. The TV contract negotiations in two years' time, when it is already rumoured Sky will bid £500 million for another five years, will determine much. Enlightened self-interest is the sport's best bet.

The chairmen agree an élite within the élite is quickly forming, although the greater surprise is it has happened later rather than sooner. As in many continental leagues, only a few clubs can afford to buy top performers and keep them in the wages to which they are accustomed. Only a major outside investment will give a mediocre, moderately off club a serious prospect of silverware or a place in Europe. The big city clubs have always enjoyed the lion's share of triumph, but now the possibility of a Norwich or Southampton nipping in for a trophy seems very remote.

The season of 1994–95 should go down as the season fantasy died, when followers of all but a handful of clubs had to relinquish the quaint belief that their heroes could be kings or even princes no matter the odds. I discussed this with Rob Shepherd, football correspondent for *Today* and a fan of West Ham. 'I know it might sound daft as we don't win much,' said Shepherd, 'but this was the first season ever I actually thought West Ham had no chance of winning the championship. I couldn't even dream about it.'

Sky TV tediously trumpeted its initial coverage of the Premier League in August 1992 with the slogan: 'It's a whole new ball game.' It was hard to see any difference for the first year or so, apart from the referees' green shirts. Same old game, it seemed. But not now.

Observer Life, 28 May 1995

Chapter Eight

The Press

Gary Lineker joined the BBC during the season, exchanging his football boots for a microphone to line up with the fresh-faced Alan Hansen and the Radio 5 team.

GARY LINEKER
Michael Parkinson

I had this fab idea. Instead of interviewing Gary Lineker face to face why not do the job on the golf course? I could see the headline: 'A Round With Gary Lineker. But why interview Lineker in the first place? His cuttings file would sink a fair-sized cargo ship and he is no longer playing the game.

Well, for one thing there is the new career outside football to talk about. He has just completed his first 100 days as a BBC TV pundit and – more significantly and taxingly – as host of a live weekend sports programme on Radio 5 live. There was also talk he wasn't up to the job, that he would be too bland, and his voice too boring. How does he think he has done so far? More to the point, are his bosses at the BBC happy?

Also, I wanted to talk to him to be reminded that the game of football is still capable of producing men in the tradition of Finney and Charlton; real and proper heroes who proved that being a good sport, a modest man and a well-behaved member of society was not incompatible with becoming a great player and a stern competitor.

In other words I am sick of the ugly side of football, of the in-your-face skinhead, foul-mouthed, yobbish, violent aspect of the game. I need the antidote and what better than a round of golf with the man who was never booked in his entire career and who has been called: 'The Queen Mother of football' (*An Evening With Gary Lineker*), 'The nicest man on earth' (Spurs fanzine), and 'One of nature's Boy Scouts' (Hunter Davies).

If honest to Mr Lineker I have to say he cringes at the mention of these descriptions and much prefers the assessment made by Joe Kinnear, the feisty manager of Wimbledon. After Lineker had said that he preferred to watch Teletext than Wimbledon play, Mr Kinnear was asked his opinion of the former captain of England. 'He is,' said Mr Kinnear, 'an arsehole.'

We came together on the first tee of Woburn's Duke's Course, a piece of golfing terrain nearly 7,000 yards long snaking through a forest of trees in glorious countryside near Milton Keynes. Since 1985 it has been the home of the British Masters and has sorted out many a great player.

The first hole is a 514-yard par five. As we surveyed what we had to do the sun was shining, a light breeze trembled the very tips of the slender pine trees and there were yellow flowers on the gorse. During Mr Lineker's practice swing I positioned myself behind and slightly to his right. It was as if I was fielding at gully. Had I been positioned at old-fashioned deep point I would certainly have been in with a chance at catching his tee-shot which remarkably flew at right angles from his club into the forest.

'Mmmm,' said Mr Lineker, which is not what I would have come out with had I been in his position. During our round I was to marvel at his iron control and limitless patience. It wasn't until much later in the game that he snapped, which is more than can be said for your correspondent. After much hacking in the pines Mr Lineker finally hit his ball out of bounds and settled for a blob.

The second hole is a 384-yard par four. Again we were both unconvincing off the tee and I began to see a problem emerging. I am a left-hander with a slice, he is a right-hander with a tendency to hit the ball left to right. That being the case our natural game was designed to take us to different parts of a golf course. Normally this wouldn't matter. However it is difficult to conduct an interview when both parties are in dense undergrowth on opposite sides of the fairway. When we did finally meet we were sharing a bunker. This was neither the time nor the place to discuss the state of the modern game or Mr Lineker's views on the influence of French philosophers on the career of Eric Cantona.

'We're crazy. We came on the course without warming up and expect to play well. It's silly,' said Mr Lineker. I didn't tell him that I hated practice and that my idea of warming up was a double egg, sausage, bacon and fried bread breakfast which I had managed to scoff that morning. I did the decent thing and sympathised.

I told him that when I once complained about playing badly, the golf pro I was with said: 'It's your own fault. You walk on to a course without preparing yourself. You never see a pro do that.' I said something sarcastic like that was because pros had nothing else to do. He said: 'Let me ask you a question: when you do a show on television do you rehearse?' I said we did. 'That's exactly what we do,' he said.

Mr Lineker managed a wan smile at my homespun wisdom. At the time he was knee-deep in sand looking at an impossible shot on to a sloping green and thinking he would settle for a double bogey. Could it be I am losing my sense of timing?

The third hole on the Duke's course is one of the most photogenic in British golf. It is a 134-yard par three across a valley to a green far below. The hole is surrounded by trees and rhododendrons. It was here that Gary Lineker showed his mettle. He hit a high, soft nine-iron to within 15 feet but left the ball above the pin. When the sun shines and the greens are running this is a bit like putting down a glacier. He nicked the cup with his first putt and holed from six feet coming back for a par.

We can now talk golf. He played first as a teenager but gave it up when he became a professional footballer. He started playing again when he went to Japan. He hasn't got a handicap but thinks 20 or 22 might be fair at present and hopes to get down to single figures. No reason why he shouldn't. He's got a slow, rhythmic swing, a calm temperament and a self-belief that comes with being a top-class professional athlete.

His problem will be finding the space in what has become a full-time occupation with the media. In addition to radio and television he also writes a column for *The Observer*. It is typical of the man, and the wise counsel offered by his agent Jon Holmes, that

Lineker chose to grind out his own thoughts for a broadsheet rather than take the easier, ghost-written and more lucrative option offered by the tabloids.

When we recommenced our round we played quietly and without much incident until the eighth hole when there was a most remarkable occurrence. Gary Lineker hit his drive into the trees. He called that he had located his ball and the next sound I heard was a ball hitting timber followed by quiet. More scuffling in the undergrowth and then terrible clatter as a ball seemed to strike four or five trees before silence descended once more.

As I waited on the fairway, my ears as sensitive as tuning forks to any indication of what might be happening to my opponent, there came the crack of ball on tree followed this time by an anguished cry of 'Shit!'. It is the moment Gary Lineker lost his claim to sainthood. It was so unexpected I'm thinking of sponsoring a commemorative plaque on a tree at the spot where it happened.

I only mention the incident because it does Gary Lineker a disservice to portray him as a sickeningly perfect goody-goody with a halo and whipped cream for blood. Any athlete who gets to the top has to be tough, mentally and physically. Lineker's self-control and patience are part of his physical toughness just as his ability to learn quickly using a mind which is not befuddled by either booze or fame is an indication of his mental strength.

One of Lineker's new bosses, Bob Shennan, who is BBC Radio's Head of Sport says: 'He's single-minded, intelligent, works hard, takes nothing for granted and, most important of all, wants to succeed. Our only worry was the voice. It sounded flat and monotonous. We sent him for voice training. He knows what he has to do and is improving all the time.

'But most of all he's a star. He has a quality people like. He improves the ratings because he attracts kids who normally only listen to radio if it's playing music. He's close to becoming the finished article,' he said.

In BBC execspeak this can be taken as meaning that Auntie is very much taken with Gary Lineker, and the feeling is mutual. Lineker is heading off down the media super highway on yet another episode in an extraordinary career. Will it end there? Will being a witness to events be as fulfilling as becoming a shaper of the future? He would love to help decide the direction his sport takes in years to come and thinks it sad that soccer tends to ignore its great names.

As we approached the final hole on a day when we had been soundly beaten by the course, he said: 'Sometimes I hate this game and sometimes I love it. Today I think I hate it.' Then he knocked in a 15-footer for a par and changed his mind.

As I walked off the course a man who must have thought I was Mr Lineker's minder or, alternatively, possessed a kindly face, asked me if I could get him the star's autograph. I said he should make a direct approach as Mr Lineker was not renowned for assaulting autograph hunters. 'Where's he off to?' the man said. 'He's going up to Leicester,' I answered. 'Why?' the man asked. 'He's going to be given the Freedom of the City in order that he might graze his sheep near the town hall,' I said.

'Quite right, too,' said the man as if it was the only sensible thing to be done for the likes of Gary Lineker. Which it is.

Daily Telegraph, 22 April 1995

ALAN HANSEN
Jon Henderson

Interviewing Alan Hansen in a public place may not be a good idea. As it turns out the foyer restaurant of the London hotel is populated almost exclusively by air crews from the Far East and foreign businessmen, and the only interruption comes right at the end. 'Who was that?' asks a Saddam Hussein lookalike sitting alone on the next table.

At least it is a question that is not difficult to answer. 'What's he like?' would have been much harder.

Very self-contained is the former Liverpool defender, now in his fortieth year, whose punditry will help draw millions when the BBC begin their live FA Cup coverage this afternoon. Open and cordial, but self-contained. His porcelain-pale face, with the scar diving down the forehead, is either deadpan or wears a smile, but the second expression seems to say 'keep your distance' just as firmly as the first. You feel he probably intimidated opponents even before going on to the pitch, treating them in the tunnel to a look as bleak as a Scottish hillside in mid-February.

Hansen's detachment is unsurprising given his abundant natural gifts, which make reliance on others superfluous. As well as having an aptitude for a number of games – his golf handicap was two at 16 (it's now four) and he was outstanding at squash and volleyball – he is academically above average, one of the few professional footballers of modern times able to conjugate *amo* and decline *mensa*. Latin is one of four 'Highers', the Scottish equivalent of A levels, he obtained at his comprehensive school: English, history and maths the others.

'I was going to study history at Aberdeen University,' he says, 'but then something at the back of my head said that, because I was proficient at two or three sports, why not become a PE teacher.' Here Hansen encountered a rare failure. 'The college I applied to had a rule they would take only one from each school and five guys applied from mine. I missed out.'

In fact it was only a failure of sorts, because it meant Hansen, rather than striving to qualify as a teacher, became a professional footballer, signed by Partick Thistle at the age of 18. Four years later he moved south to join Liverpool and start one of the most successful associations in the history of British club football. Between 1979 and 1990 Hansen collected eight English League championship medals, a total equalled only by another Liverpool player, Phil Neal, between 1976 and 1986.

Hansen says his playing career can be divided into two, the years when he came forward as a defender and those when he hardly crossed the halfway line. It is typical of his self-assurance that he can say he was 'exceptional going forward' without feeling the need to leaven the remark with a note of modesty, although he does concede that defensively he was inconsistent.

'The last time I was getting forward was 1984–85,' he says. 'At Liverpool we played a system where you pushed up and held the line, which meant a lot of recovery, a lot of chasing back. I think a combination of getting forward and chasing back was what changed me. It was easier not getting forward so much. Towards the end Ronnie Moran used to say, "Go and sit in your armchair".'

Those who look to denigrate Hansen's playing career point to his gaining only 26 international caps. 'The one thing that might annoy me,' he says, 'is that people say I never played well for Scotland, which is rubbish. It's also rubbish that I never played as well for Scotland as I did for Liverpool.'

He recalls that the Scotland manager Jock Stein called him his most important player before the 1982 World Cup and that he played well in Scotland's three matches in that tournament. 'After that I won fewer than 10 caps, which is incredible really,' says Hansen.

When he stopped playing in 1991 he knew only that football management was out of the question. 'That last year I played I was really feeling it and I thought if I'm struggling as a player, the pressure as a manager will be 10 times worse. But I didn't have a clue what I was going to do.'

Such an intrepid departure by a married man with two school-age children is further evidence of Hansen's belief in himself, as was his telephone call to BSkyB when fellow Scot Andy Gray left the satellite station to become assistant manager at Aston Villa. 'I phoned Sky up and said, "Andy's gone, is there a place for me?" I went down there and they gave me a six-month trial doing Italian football.' But the BBC had also become interested after hearing him on Radio 2 and it was they who signed him up, offering him the four-year contract that currently binds him to them.

One knows what he means when he says, 'I was a professional footballer, I don't think I'm a professional broadcaster,' but in many ways his impact on his new career has been as striking as on his old one. He would be near the top of most people's poll of pundits – 'I never liked pundits before I became one,' he says – and, despite feeling himself an amateur, his approach has never been less than wholehearted.

'When I started I thought there's got to be a certain way I'm going to do this,' he says, 'and I decided I was going to say exactly what I saw, although I never like criticising individuals as such.'

His trenchant fault-finding earned him a mild rebuke in these pages recently when Trevor Brooking remarked on Hansen's tendency to regard goals almost unfailingly as defensive errors. Hansen offers a token defence, before making what amounts to an admission of guilt.

'I'd rather be talking about brilliance than errors, but defending is about organisation and being in position. I go along with the Liverpool way of thinking, that any goal is a bad goal and you've got to make the opposition do something special to get one.'

Having established himself in television you might expect Hansen to have settled for a long-term association with the medium. But he feels no need to make a commitment that would threaten his independence. 'I'll decide when my four years with the BBC are up. They might not want me, I might not want them. The way I look at it is that there's no way I'll achieve working for TV what I did playing for Liverpool.

'There's a lot more to *Match of the Day* than turning up and talking for three minutes. I really enjoy doing it, but, as far as I'm concerned, football was my life. The memories that I've got from football can bring a smile to my face.'

The interview over, Hansen offers his hand and leaves. I am struck by the warmth of Saddam's enquiry and almost accept the drink he offers even though I have a pressing appointment.

Observer, 8 January 1995

When Radio 5 Live began broadcasting last year there was much debate about whether it was a news station or a sports station. That debate may remain unresolved, but there is no question that its sports programming has achieved success beyond expectation. Alan Green is one of its most popular commentators.

Radio 5 Live
Henry Winter

It seems strange to report that there was actually a moment yesterday when Alan Green, BBC Radio 5 Live's hugely popular, outspoken commentator, could not talk. But then he was at the dentist.

Even then it is difficult to imagine a mouthful of metal deterring this JFK of the airwaves, this affable purveyor of high-speed patter both lyrical and honest. 'Diabolical,' you can hear that familiar, cadence-filled Irish voice insisting. 'It's simply not good enough,' as the hygienist fails to top up the mouthwash quickly.

Green is the radio star made by television. The Sky contract proved an enormous boon for 5 Live as, in a stroke, the cheapest access people had to (increased amounts of) live football came via those magical numbers of 693 and 909 (rumoured to be Green's lowest and highest words per minute). With outstanding broadcasters like Green and Mike Ingham, 5 Live's success was ensured.

The pair, who next week share the high-profile Wembley assignments of England and the Coca-Cola Cup final, could not be more different: for Green, every incident is either black or white while Ingham can see the shades in between. Comparisons, though, are invidious: like contrasting the Beatles with Bach. Both Green and Ingham, in their own inimitable ways, weave irresistible webs on the airwaves.

Green, the babbling brook from Belfast, lets his emotions run free. Yet the view of him as cocky Irish urchin obscures a complex character, who joined the BBC by the notoriously demanding news trainee scheme. 'There were 7,500 applications for eight jobs. I got one of them – I was a high flyer,' said the man whose main ambition in broadcasting was to edit the *Nine O'Clock News*. 'Still is – but it won't happen now.' Fame claimed him.

'I think now I am viewed as the voice of BBC football because I say things that fans would say if they had a microphone. I am a glorified punter with access to a microphone.' It is easy to comprehend why many within the BBC see him as an obvious replacement for David Mellor, who seems to have lost the *Six-O-Six* plot.

Green's obsessive outpourings of opinions rankle leading managers, like Kenny Dalglish and Alex Ferguson. The fall-out with Ferguson is both substantial and sad, given their shared passion for the game. A clear-the-air meeting in June '92 failed to end the rift and, this season. Green aggravated Dalglish.

'Before the Newcastle Cup replay at Blackburn, Kenny had just come back from his operation and I saw him in the reception area. We go back many years so I said: "How's your health, Kenny".' He replied: "Oh, I'm fine – better than your commentary. You'll never be forgiven for what you said at the Trelleborgs match; you said my team was a waste of money."

'I said: "Kenny, you know I always say what I think and I have never thought or said your team was a waste of money". Kenny then walks off and a steward pulls me by the coat; a woman, of course, so I couldn't turn round and clock her. The following morning I wrote Kenny a long letter, saying that I will always say on the radio what my genuine feelings are. I haven't heard back from him.'

The adrenalin-charged, categoric manner in which Green expresses his opinions undoubtedly upsets managers. Green, though hugely sensitive with an ego that needs intelligent handling, insists he simply tells it like it is.

Yet his post bag regularly accuses him of bias. 'Mainly towards Manchester United,' he laughs. 'I wrote back to one letter accusing me of being a United fan, saying "Alex Ferguson would kill himself laughing at the very suggestion.' I certainly stir emotions.'

His popularity is undoubted: in a famous press box moment one young fan stretched out an autograph book past three greats, Jimmy Armfield, Frank McLintock and George Best, to seek Greeny's scrawl.

Green is part journalist, part showman. He loves working with summarisers who fuel banter. 'Mark Lawrenson is fearless. We were trying to get through Crystal Palace and Liverpool, which was over when Liverpool scored, and were going off on tangents. Mike [Ingham] brought a statistic into the commentary which Mark made some comment about. Mike said: "Oh you must have a *Rothmans* [*Football Yearbook*] tucked down your trousers" and Mark says "No, I'm just excited to see you."

'Bobby Gould won't mind me telling this story, but Bobby's pronunciations are awful; he's Mr Malaprop. In Bruges, Bobby memorably referred to their sweeper Okon as Hongkong. I thought, I mustn't look at him because I'll corpse. For the second leg, I said to Bobby I'm going to give out the team and you can give the names as they sound to you. So if I say Okon and you say Hongkong, people will know we are referring to the same guy.'

What of the future? Heavyweight forces in BBC television would like him to pep up the place. 'But I'm probably too forthright for them. Sky could certainly never take me on. They couldn't risk me slaughtering a match they are paying a fortune for.'

A restless soul, who treats the final whistle as a starting gun to return home to domestic bliss in Macclesfield, much rankles him. 'I bitterly resent people thinking that because the profile is big, I automatically earn big money. I don't. I'm earning pathetic money in broadcasting terms. I resent it because I don't feel inferior to anyone commentating nowadays.'

He gives stick but can he take it? 'If it's right yes I can. If it's unfair I'll go for the jugular. There are people at Radio Sport who are intimidated by me, but they shouldn't be because actually I'm a little kitten.'

Daily Telegraph, 25 March 1995

Perhaps the most controversial of all Radio 5 Live programmes was David Mellor's Six-O-Six *show on a Saturday evening. Not everyone appreciated Mellor's diet of Conservatism and Chelsea.*

DON'T LISTEN WITH MELLOR

Peter Corrigan

We must not complain when politicians favour us with their opinions on sport. It means, at the very least, that some more vital and vulnerable part of the nation's business is receiving temporary relief from their attentions and, who knows, we may even reach the day when one of their shafts will carry enough wisdom to illuminate the darkness through which sport often gropes.

Since few of them are capable of playing anything other than their own trumpet, however, this is a faint hope. There is far more likelihood that when they speak out in tones calculated to attract gasps of admiration they do no more than compound confusions, reinforce resentments or embarrass all concerned. Into this last category was fired an outburst by David Mellor last week when he aimed at Belgium every insult he could muster on behalf of his fellow Chelsea supporters.

This is not the first time he has used Chelsea to make a stand. Like many an astute MP, he has found that an affiliation to a football team adds a 'one-of-the-boys' earthiness to the public image. On this occasion, to be fair, there was justification for complaints by the innocent Chelsea supporters caught up in the ruthless anti-hooligan measures employed by the Belgian police at the European Cup-Winners' Cup quarter-final in Bruges 10 days ago. But Mellor went so far over the top in his rage that, if he is an example of the peace-loving Chelsea faction, the Belgian cops will have taken it as confirmation that they acted wisely.

To call one of our European partners a 'ramshackle' country, question their right to be in the competition and say that Bruges had 'a silly little football ground with a pitch that Farmer Brown wouldn't let his cows loose on' may be straying off the subject a little. In any case, no farmer would allow his cows out with Chelsea fans about.

Mellor's attack would have been more acceptable had he made

it in his guise as a sports broadcaster. Since he was de-Cabineted, the former Heritage Minister has become a flourishing media-man and among his offerings is the Saturday evening sports phone-in *Six-O-Six*, on Radio 5. I happen to think that phone-ins are the last refuge of an idea-less station so I am not a sound witness as to his proficiency but I will say that listening to it in my car on a Saturday, I'm invariably surprised that I arrive home much earlier than it feels.

As a sports pundit, of course, Mellor joins that all-seeing, all-knowing and all-ignorable fraternity of which I am proud to be a fellow member. Had his comments been made from our ranks they could have been dismissed as the normal lunatic ramblings. But they were on a BBC2 programme called *Westminster On-Line* and Mellor was in his other role of temporarily grounded political highflier. As such, his words carry weight, particularly as he criticised his own government for not speaking out against the high-handed approach taken by the Belgian police.

The government would not have been so daft. After the criticism of the pussyfooted way the English hooligans were handled by the Irish police in Dublin two weeks earlier, they could hardly have made the exact opposite allegation about the Bruges constabulary. As for his sneer at Belgium's footballing credentials, has Mellor compared their recent international record with England's? The jibe about Bruges looks to have had the same amount of consideration. Is he not aware that many of our greatest cup-ties have been played in silly little grounds with cow-patch pitches?

He even went so far as to say that the Heysel Stadium tragedy 10 years ago was partly caused 'because the thing was badly policed and the ground was unsafe'. I trust the Liverpool fans whose rampage caused the fatal crush have found it as easy to salve their consciences.

'Mounted police,' said Mellor, returning to Bruges, 'behaved quite outrageously towards perfectly respectable supporters.'

If it wasn't for the prompt action of mounted police at Stamford Bridge recently, those perfect respectable supporters might have been outraged in the comfort of their own stadium. Perhaps the Belgians took note of that incident. Perhaps they, too, remembered Heysel. Perhaps they took note of Dublin and of the reports in British newspapers that thousands of ticketless Chelsea fans were going to Bruges looking for trouble.

An over-reaction under those circumstances should not have been a great shock. There are many Continental cities still bearing the bruises of British hooliganism over the past 20 years who wish that they had over-reacted at the time. Our complaints appear to be like blaming the demise of the Light Brigade on the Russian cannons rather than on the blundering fools who sent them in their direction.

If we can't or won't differentiate between our good and bad fans we can hardly expect other countries to do so. Their priority is the protection of their streets and their citizens and until we can guarantee that the supporters we send over are well behaved we are going to be unwelcome *en bloc*. We will not be wanted until the government find a way to keep troublemakers from travelling.

If we have exclusion orders why can't we have inclusion orders? Mellor's undoubted energies would be better directed towards that aim than slamming the countries we insist on invading and the Chelsea victims ought to reflect that their experience was more the fault of under-motivated British politicians than over-zealous Belgian police.

Independent on Sunday, 12 March 1995

The BBC's David Davies took the unusual step of leaving broadcasting to become public relations supremo at the Football Association. Was this a case of the poacher turned gamekeeper?

David Davies – The Spin Doctor

Martin Thorpe

David Davies could be forgiven for thinking it was something personal. He became the FA's public relations supremo 12 months ago and what follows? The most scandal-ridden year in soccer history. If he thought that leaving a 21-year career of television reporting would mean fewer appearances on the box, he was wrong.

Venables, Tottenham, bungs, match-fixing allegations, drugs and alcohol, Cantona: turn on the news and the odds are on that Davies's face will be there, explaining to the media for the umpteenth time that the FA is not a police force and that due processes need to be gone through before punishments are handed down.

But does he ever wish he never took the job, given what has happened, given the persistent phone calls and persistent questions from the very persistent media? 'No,' he says. 'I relish the challenge. My wife says that I laugh less now. But I hope that's not true. Despite all the serious matters I like to think I can smile a bit.'

The 46-year-old Davies was, however, not hired by the FA for his smile. One suspects Davies was brought in mainly to dust down the FA's image of doddery old men fishing little balls out of velvet bags and lead them into the multi-media world of 24-hour-a-day news.

'I wouldn't have left journalism for any other job. I saw this as an opportunity you get once in your life. I am a football fan first and foremost and there was clearly a job to be done here. The FA has had to come to terms with the fact that arguably no other public organisation generates so many column inches, even before this year, and for the first time they recognised that they had to get their message across.'

He has impressive credentials to be called a fan at heart. He was bitten by the football bug as an eight-year-old watching Manchester United fans come into the family grocers' shop near Euston station on their way to the 1957 FA Cup final and that turned him into the original United fan who does not come from Manchester. He saw United's last game before Munich, at Arsenal, was at all England's 1966 World Cup games and his TV work brought him close friendships with Shankly and Busby.

All this, plus a degree in politics and a time spent working in the lobby at Westminster, gives him ample qualifications for his current job. Though where a TV reporter takes care of how he says something, Davies is now more careful of exactly what he says. He regularly punctuates his sentences with pauses for thought. He will start a sentence, stop, then start again with a fresh phrase.

He has learned a lot of the politician's art, too. He begins answers with statements such as: let me talk about that; let me tell you this; let me answer that in this way. He knows how to answer awkward questions: ask him if the FA's problem image is hindered by Kelly's stone face, Sir Bert's age and the fusty old Cup draw and he talks about the Cup draw.

Ask him if the FA's image has been bad in the past and he insists: 'I'm not interested in the past other than the lessons that can be learned,' and he follows up with the Tony Blair broad sweep: 'Our responsibility is to take the game into the 21st century and to make sure that it goes into the 21st century ready for what the 21st century will bring.'

This is not to say that Davies is a shallow man, a dodger of questions. He speaks with passion on the sport he loves and is determined to see the FA dragged into the next century.

'The FA has the opportunity and responsibility for the future of the game, full stop. If I didn't believe the FA had the wherewithal to change and take the game successfully into the 21st century then I would be wasting my time.

'Those changes in structure are on the way, and they were before the present problems. It is disheartening that we have to go through those but, if there has been wrongdoing in the game, it must be cleared up.'

But how does he answer charges that the FA does nothing? 'I know that, when we stand up and say we don't believe that corruption is rife in the game, and to suggest that is an insult to thousands of professional players, you are in danger of appearing complacent. And if there was anything more we could do I would want us to do it. But I believe we are doing everything we can.'

He is so passionate about his new job that one night, as he drove home along the motorway, something was said on Alan Green's Radio 5 phone-in and chat show which so annoyed him he pulled off and phoned in. 'We're not always on the phone as soon as someone says something we disagree with,' he stresses, 'but what I won't have is someone saying certain things that in my view they knew to be slightly unfair. I am aware of certain phone numbers at Broadcasting House and I expressed a point of view. The FA has allowed itself to be aunt sallies but we're not going to be aunt sallies any more.'

Guardian, 18 March 1995

The retirement of Manchester Evening News *journalist David Meek after covering his beloved United for 37 years brought this tribute from Frank Keating.*

David Meek, Mr United
Frank Keating

The three concluding peeps of the referee's whistle at Wembley this afternoon will be the signal to dam up a free-flowing spate of words that has been gushing for 37 years. At last, David Meek will write 'ends all' on his final line of copy – and mean it.

Meek was 65 on Tuesday. He had known, as soon as Manchester United won their FA Cup semi-final, that the editor of the *Manchester Evening News* would ask him to postpone his retirement party for a week. Because, simply, it would not feel like a United final if Meek was not there to report it.

His first was in 1958, that poignant match when young Meek was the paper's stopgap for old Tom Jackson, one of the eight journalists killed with half of Matt Busby's 'Babe's' in the slush of a Munich runway less than three months earlier.

Since when, Meek has seen over 2,000 of United's first-team matches – missing only four – and written 4,000 words each week, every month of every year except for his six-week summer holiday: with a few books on the side, call it well over seven million words.

A gush of words but no flannel. Meek's style has always been poised and punctilious, even donnish. He has never punctuated his stuff with phoney intimacy. He has been inquiring and literate, never purple-prosed – although, always, red was the colour.

To miss only four matches in 37 seasons was beyond the call of duty. There was flu, twice; a broken ankle (trying to tackle Stuart Pearson in a friendly); and his daughter's wedding day.

Mind you, young Meek should have known that longevity went with the territory. Jackson had covered United for the MEN for exactly a quarter of a century when he died.

Before him, H P Renshaw retired in 1933 after doing the job since 1890, when the club were still called Newton Heath and played on the corner of Church Lane and Northampton Road and the players changed at the Three Crowns pub on Oldham Road; United did not open up at Old Trafford until 1910. In turn, Meek's replacement will be Stuart Mathieson, a young man who has learnt the ropes as a freelance for the MEN.

Meek knew all about fidelity. His journalist father reported York City matches for 45 years in the *Yorkshire Evening Press* – 'and ended up on the board as vice-chairman, although I can't quite see such distinction coming my way at United,' laughs his son.

Young Meek trained on the *Yorkshire Post*. After a year's scholarship in Australia, sponsored by the English Speaking Union, he joined the MEN as a political correspondent and leader writer – taking over from a callow Harry Evans, later editor of *The Times*.

Aware of Meek's affection for the game, with the paper stricken by the Munich crash, the grand old MEN editor Tom Henry asked his leader writer to fill in the breach 'till the end of the season'. It would not, said Henry (adding an extra guinea to his salary), stunt the young man's wider political ambitions, for Henry himself had moved into the editor's chair via the sports desk.

There was another 21-shilling increase at Christmas 1958 and a note from Henry saying: 'Matt Busby tells me you are doing a good job.'

Meek recalls: 'The guinea rise was fine but as a journalist I was none too sure about the plaudit from Mr Busby. It made me realise what a delicately balanced job it was: steering the line between the interests of readers and truthful reporting, and the interests of the paper, which properly included United in its sales strategies, and of the football club itself.' He had wanted to be a political writer and, well, now he was.

Fourteen Christmases later, after the board, with (now) Sir Matt as kingmaker, secretly decided to sack Frank O'Farrell as manager, Meek coincidentally that same day wrote a strong piece demanding a stay of the rumoured execution headlined Be Fair To Frank.

'Busby thought I was stirring it up mischievously, and I was sent a letter saying I was no longer welcome to travel on the team coach. The ban has never been rescinded and, professionally, was the best thing that could have happened to me because it reminded me I was a journalist first and not a "fellow traveller" depending on Sir Matt telling my editor I was "doing a good job".'

His editor by then was the late Brian Redhead, and complacently basking United knew for sure they were being watched with wary, sometimes suspicious, rigour as well as with, sure, warm affection.

So what is Meek's all-time Manchester United XI? He begins confidently, 'Schmeichel in goal, good as the Greggs and Stepneys were, goalkeeping needs utter dominance now.' At right-back? Pause. He cannot think of one. 'We have always been short of top-drawer right-backs. I'll sleep on that one. But left-back has to be Tony Dunne, hasn't it? Centre-backs will be dear Bill Foulkes, and Nobby Stiles alongside him to give me more scope in midfield, which will be Paddy Crerand and the "older" Bobby Charlton – which will allow me a forward line of . . . well, of course, Denis [Law] is a must, and so is George [Best].

'Which leaves us with David Herd at centre-forward and . . . er . . . if George plays on the left wing (because he could play anywhere), Kanchelskis would be my outside-right. What a team, eh?' I give him one sub. Long think, then 'Ryan Giggs'.

Early next morning the telephone rings. No, still no rightback, 'but I'm mad, I forgot "Magic Man" Eric, didn't I? Why didn't you notice I'd not chosen Cantona, the picker of locks, the visionary. He has to be my No. 9, and Herd goes to the subs' bench.'

Meek, the ambitious young political writer, has no regrets that football sidetracked him. 'As well as the great game itself, the politics of United has always intrigued me. And for all the millions of words, there has always been something fresh and different about United.' Like kung-fu kicks at Crystal Palace? 'As I watched Cantona launch himself, my immediate reaction was "Crikey, what a story!" I was not as outraged as some. On a scale of badness it was not the end of life as we know it. I'm convinced if he'd walked over, tight-lipped and British-style, and just bloodied the fellow's nose with a straight left jab, everyone would have understood and applauded him.'

Meek's most memorable moment was the 1968 European Cup victory against Benfica – 'a night heavy with poignancy; Sir Matt, Charlton and Bill Foulkes had seen their team destroyed only 10 years earlier; that day touched me deeply'.

Five years earlier, the seeds of that victory, he reckons, were sown with the FA Cup win over Leicester City by Noel Cantwell's team – 'I loved Noel, and he talked so well about the game'. United's best Wembley goal? 'Norman Whiteside's in extra-time against Everton in 1985, snipping in from the right and bending it past the keeper.'

The best player in red he ever saw? 'It has to be George. The man was incredible, and not only for his dribbles and goals, he was the best tackler ever. He'd chase back, slide in, get his foot round the ball and then stand up and be balanced and ready to go all in one movement like an ice skater rising up from a crouch but still going at full lick. People say he wasted his career. Nonsense, he was hunted down by defenders for 11 full seasons, starting at 17. He paid his dues to the game all right.'

Now, for the first time since Busby left the manager's office, Meek is content that the game of musical chairs is over. In Alex Ferguson, 'United have at last got the man who combined the better qualities of his predecessors: the decency and application of O'Farrell, the scholarliness of Sexton, the fun and humour (to a degree) of Docherty, and the media awareness and approachability of Atkinson.'

Meek is not going to put down his pen and walk into Saturday's sunset, however red it might be. He hopes still to write about the game – 'more measured stuff perhaps; an evening paper, of necessity, is a bit of a sausage machine churning out words, words, and more words'.

He will still watch United's home games. 'It's in the blood, and my blood's red – but, you bet, I'll be happy not having to go, like this season, to Chelsea on Boxing Day and Southampton on New Year's Eve.' Which thought triggers a wide smile of contentment.

Guardian, 20 May 1995

A selection of non-fiction from Headline

THE DRACULA SYNDROME	Richard Monaco & William Burt	£5.99	☐
DEADLY JEALOUSY	Martin Fido	£5.99	☐
WHITE COLLAR KILLERS	Frank Jones	£4.99	☐
THE MURDER YEARBOOK 1994	Brian Lane	£5.99	☐
THE PLAYFAIR CRICKET ANNUAL	Bill Findall	£3.99	☐
ROD STEWART	Stafford Hildred & Tim Ewbank	£5.99	☐
THE JACK THE RIPPER A–Z	Paul Begg, Martin Fido & Keith Skinner	£7.99	☐
THE *DAILY EXPRESS* HOW TO WIN ON THE HORSES	Danny Hall	£4.99	☐
COUPLE SEXUAL AWARENESS	Barry & Emily McCarthy	£5.99	☐
GRAPEVINE; THE COMPLETE WINEBUYERS HANDBOOK	Anthony Rose & Tim Atkins	£5.99	☐
ROBERT LOUIS STEVENSON; DREAMS OF EXILE	Ian Bell	£7.99	☐

All Headline books are available at your local bookshop or newsagent, or can be ordered direct from the publisher. Just tick the titles you want and fill in the form below. Prices and availability subject to change without notice.

Headline Book Publishing, Cash Sales Department, Bookpoint, 39 Milton Park, Abingdon, OXON, OX14 4TD, UK. If you have a credit card you may order by telephone – 01235 400400.

Please enclose a cheque or postal order made payable to Bookpoint Ltd to the value of the cover price and allow the following for postage and packing:

UK & BFPO: £1.00 for the first book, 50p for the second book and 30p for each additional book ordered up to a maximum charge of £3.00.
OVERSEAS & EIRE: £2.00 for the first book, £1.00 for the second book and 50p for each additional book.

Name ....

Address ....

....

....

If you would prefer to pay by credit card, please complete:
Please debit my Visa/Access/Diner's Card/American Express (delete as applicable) card no:

Signature .... Expiry Date ....